Microsoft® Visual Basic® 2008 Express Programming for the Absolute Beginner

Jerry Lee Ford, Jr.

Course Technology PTR
A part of Cengage Learning

COURSE TECHNOLOGY
CENGAGE Learning™

Australia • Brazil • Japan • Korea • Mexico • Singapore • Spain • United Kingdom • United States

COURSE TECHNOLOGY
CENGAGE Learning

Microsoft® Visual Basic® 2008 Express Programming for the Absolute Beginner: Jerry Lee Ford, Jr.

Publisher and General Manager, Course Technology PTR: Stacy L. Hiquet

Associate Director of Marketing: Sarah Panella

Manager of Editorial Services: Heather Talbot

Marketing Manager: Mark Hughes

Acquisitions Editor: Mitzi Koontz

Project Editor: Jenny Davidson

Technical Reviewer: Keith Davenport

PTR Editorial Services Coordinator: Jen Blaney

Interior Layout Tech: Value Chain

Cover Designer: Mike Tanamachi

Indexer: Kevin Broccoli

Proofreader: Sara Gullion

Microsoft and Visual Basic are registered trademarks of Microsoft Corporation in the United States and/or other countries.

All other trademarks are the property of their respective owners.

Library of Congress Control Number: 2009921545

ISBN-13: 978-1-59863-900-1
ISBN-10: 1-59863-900-5

Course Technology, a part of Cengage Learning
20 Channel Center Street
Boston, MA 02210
USA

Cengage Learning is a leading provider of customized learning solutions with office locations around the globe, including Singapore, the United Kingdom, Australia, Mexico, Brazil, and Japan. Locate your local office at: **international.cengage.com/region**

Cengage Learning products are represented in Canada by Nelson Education, Ltd.

For your lifelong learning solutions, visit **courseptr.com**

Visit our corporate website at **cengage.com**

Printed in Canada
1 2 3 4 5 6 7 11 10 09

To my mother and father for always being there, and to my wonderful children, Alexander, William, and Molly, and my beautiful wife, Mary.

ACKNOWLEDGMENTS

This book represents the combined efforts of many individuals to whom I owe many thanks. For starters, there is Mitzi Koontz, for helping me get this book started and for her support as acquisitions editor. I also owe an extra debt of gratitude to Jenny Davidson, for serving as the book's project editor and for working hard to make sure that in the end everything came together like it was supposed to. I also need to thank Keith Davenport, who served as technical editor for this book. Finally, I'd like to thank everyone else at Course Technology PTR for all their contributions and hard work.

ABOUT THE AUTHOR

Jerry Lee Ford, Jr. is an author, educator, and an IT professional with over 20 years of experience in information technology, including roles as an automation analyst, technical manager, technical support analyst, automation engineer, and security analyst. He is the author of 31 books and co-author of two additional books. His published works include *Windows PowerShell 2.0 Programming for the Absolute Beginner, AJAX Programming for the Absolute Beginner, Scratch Programming for Teens, Microsoft WSH & VBScript Programming for the Absolute Beginner, DarkBASIC Programming for the Absolute Beginner,* and *Microsoft Windows XP Professional Administrator's Guide.* Jerry has a master's degree in business administration from Virginia Commonwealth University in Richmond, Virginia, and he has over five years of experience as an adjunct instructor teaching networking courses in information technology.

TABLE OF CONTENTS

5 STORING AND RETRIEVING DATA IN MEMORY 157

Introduction

elcome to *Microsoft Visual Basic 2008 Express Programming for the Absolute Beginner*. Visual Basic 2008 Express is the most recent incarnation of Visual Basic. Microsoft Visual Basic 2008 Express has been specifically designed to meet the needs of first-time programmers and computer hobbyists. It is designed to enable the development of applications that execute on computers that run Microsoft Windows.

Unlike other current versions of Visual Basic, Visual Basic 2008 Express is limited in scope. It provides access to a subset of Visual Basic functionality found in other versions of Visual Basic. For example, it cannot be used to develop software for smart device applications or to develop web-based applications.

Microsoft created Visual Basic 2008 Express with the individual user in mind, intending it to provide a lightweight programming experience targeted at first-time programmers. Microsoft's intention is to introduce Visual Basic programming to as many people as possible. That's why it makes Visual Basic 2008 Express available as a free download for anyone who wants it. Yet Visual Basic 2008 Express still packs plenty of punch, providing a powerful, yet easy to learn, programming language from which first-time programmers can quickly learn how to develop their own fully featured Windows applications.

Why Visual Basic 2008 Express?

Visual Basic 2008 Express makes for an excellent first programming language. It is one of a number of programming languages supported by the Microsoft .NET Framework. The .NET Framework provides everything that programmers need to test, debug, and run Windows applications. Other .NET-supported programming languages include Visual C++ and Visual C#. Of these languages, Visual Basic is the easiest to learn and use. It is certainly the most popular.

If you want to develop Windows applications, Visual Basic 2008 Express will suit your needs well. Once you have mastered the basics of programming using Visual Basic 2008 Express, you'll find yourself well prepared to upgrade to the full version of Visual Basic 2008, where you can then apply your programming skills to the development of Windows and web-based applications. In addition, you'll be able to apply what this book has taught you to the development of applications that support smart devices such as Smartphones, the Pocket PC, or PDAs (personal digital assistants).

WHO SHOULD READ THIS BOOK?

This book is designed to teach you how to develop Windows applications using Microsoft Visual Basic 2008 Express. Although a previous programming background is helpful, this book does not assume that you have any previous experience with Visual Basic or any other programming language. However, a good understanding of computers and Microsoft Windows operating systems is expected.

Whether you are an experienced programmer looking for a jump start on learning Visual Basic 2008 Express, or a first-timer looking for a friendly programming language and a book that will help you to begin your programming career, you will be happy with what this book has in store for you. You will find that this book's unique games-based teaching approach makes learning easier and a lot more fun.

WHAT YOU NEED TO BEGIN

This book was written using Microsoft Visual Basic 2008 Express for its examples. All of the figures and examples that you see as you read along will show Microsoft Visual Basic 2008 Express running on Windows Vista. Therefore, if you are using a different Windows operating system, or if you are using a different version of Visual Basic, such as Visual Basic 2005 Express, you may notice small differences in the way some things look. However, you should still be able to follow along with the examples shown in this book with little, if any, trouble.

If you don't already have Microsoft Visual Basic 2008 Express, you can download it from http:// www.microsoft.com/express/download/. Before you download it, you'll want to make sure that your computer has enough horsepower to run it. First off, your computer must run one of the following operating systems:

- Windows XP
- Windows Server 2003 Service Pack 2
- Windows Server 2008
- Windows Vista

In addition, you'll want to make sure that your computer meets the minimum hardware requirements specified in the following table. However, minimum requirements are just that. In order to really take advantage of Visual Basic 2008 Express, you'll be a lot better off if your computer meets the table's recommended requirements.

TABLE 1 MINIMUM REQUIREMENTS FOR RUNNING VISUAL BASIC 2008 EXPRESS		
Requirement	**Minimum**	**Recommended**
Processor	1.6 GHz	2.2 GHz
Memory	192 MB	384 MB
Hard Disk	5400 RPM hard disk	7200 RPM hard disk
Disk Space	1.3 GB free space	1.3 GB free space

*Note: On Windows Vista you'll need a 2.4 GHz processor and 768 MB of memory.

That's it. All you'll need is a copy of Visual Basic 2008 Express running on your computer and this book. You'll find that everything you need to write, test, and compile Visual Basic programs is provided as part of the Visual Basic 2008 Express package.

CONVENTIONS USED IN THIS BOOK

This book uses a number of conventions in order to make it easier for you to read and work with the information that is provided. These conventions are as follows:

 Different or better ways of doing things to help make you a better and more efficient programmer.

 Places where mistakes might be made and advice for avoiding them.

 Shortcuts and other techniques to help make your work easier.

In The Real World

As you read through this book, I'll outline real-world situations where the information and programming techniques you are learning can be applied.

Challenges

I will end each chapter with a series of suggestions that you can follow up on to enhance and improve the chapter's game project and to continue to advance your Visual Basic programming skills.

An Introduction to Visual Basic 2008 Express

The driving force behind Microsoft's development of Visual Basic 2008 Express is an effort to attract a new generation of programmers to Windows. Microsoft has put a great deal of time and effort into creating the best possible development environment for Windows applications. In this chapter, you will begin your Visual Basic programming journey by learning some necessary background information. You will then get the chance to jump right in and get your feet wet by developing your first Visual Basic application. Through the development of this application, you will learn the basic steps involved in creating a Windows application as well as get a preview of just what makes Visual Basic the most popular programming language ever developed.

Specifically, you will learn:

- What Visual Basic 2008 Express is and what it can do
- What .NET is and how it works with Visual Basic 2008 Express
- About the many new improvements and features added to Visual Basic 2008 Express
- What Visual Studio is and how Visual Basic fits into it
- The five basic steps involved in developing a Visual Basic application

PROJECT PREVIEW: THE JOKE MACHINE

In this chapter, as in all the chapters to follow, you will learn how to create a computer game using Visual Basic. Game projects provide a fun and engaging learning experience while you learn about Visual Basic .NET 2008 Express.

In this first chapter, you will learn how to create the Joke Machine game. The Joke Machine game begins like most other Windows applications, displaying a window that controls the game's execution. Compared to most Windows applications, the Joke Machine game is relatively simple, consisting of just two buttons, a label, and a text box. However, the development of this game will demonstrate powerful programming techniques that make up the foundation of any Windows application.

When first started, the Joke Machine will appear on your desktop, as shown in Figure 1.1.

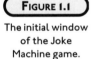

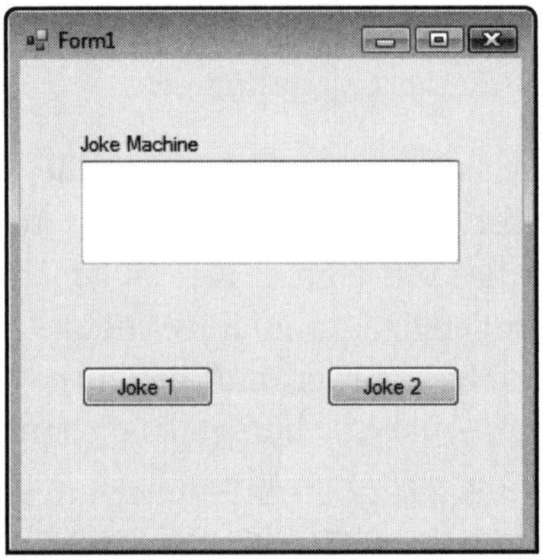

FIGURE 1.1

The initial window of the Joke Machine game.

FIGURE 1.2

Viewing the first joke told by the Joke Machine game.

Figure 1.3 shows the joke that appears when the Joke Machine's second button is clicked.

FIGURE 1.3

Viewing the
second joke told
by the Joke
Machine game.

A FEW OPENING WORDS

Learning a new computer programming language is a challenging experience. But it can also be very enjoyable and fulfilling. In this chapter, we'll start your Visual Basic programming journey by going over background information that you'll need in order to advance to later chapters. This will include a brief overview of what Visual Basic 2008 Express is and what it can do. It will also include a high-level explanation of what .NET is and how it interacts with Visual Basic 2008 Express.

In this chapter, you will also learn how to create your first Visual Basic application. You may find it a little intimidating to begin putting together a Visual Basic application before you have had a chance to learn a little more about the language. This is to be expected. But don't worry about it. Just follow along and perform the steps that I'll lay out exactly as shown and you'll be able to get the application working. You'll find that as a result of writing your first program and stepping through the application development process, you'll develop a better understanding of just what Visual Basic and .NET are and will be better prepared to understand the chapters that lay ahead of you. The most important thing for you to do as you go through this chapter is to try to focus on the big picture and not to get too caught up in the details.

A QUICK OVERVIEW OF VISUAL BASIC

Visual Basic is *visual* because of the process that programmers go through to create the part of the application that users see, also known as the GUI (*graphical user interface*). Visual Basic is Basic because it was created based on the BASIC (*Beginners All-Purpose Symbolic Instruction Code*) programming language.

Visual Basic is a programming language that is used to develop Windows applications. Once you have written a Visual Basic application and compiled it into executable code, the application can run on its own. It doesn't require anything else to execute except for the Windows operating system.

 DEFINITION *Compiling* is the process of translating the code statements that make up a computer application into a format that can be executed by the computer operating system.

Right from its initial release by Microsoft, Visual Basic earned a reputation for being very easy to learn while simultaneously delivering development capabilities previously only made available by more complex programming languages. As a result, it quickly became the most popular programming language in the world. Today, you'll find that Visual Basic is taught in colleges all over the world. It is also used by companies internationally to create Windows applications that drive mission-critical business processes.

There are a number of reasons why Visual Basic is so popular. Three of the most important reasons include its support of the following:

- Drag-and-drop GUI design
- Rapid application development
- Object-oriented programming

GUI Development

One of the first things that you will come to appreciate about Visual Basic as you work your way through this book is the ease with which it enables you to create a really slick looking GUI. When you first begin working on a Windows application, Visual Basic automatically creates a new blank window for you. It also provides you with a collection of Windows components, such as buttons, check boxes, and text boxes, that you can then add to the window by clicking on and dragging them over to the window and placing them where you want them.

 DEFINITION A *GUI (graphical user interface)* is the part of the application that the user sees and can interact with using the mouse.

Rapid Application Development

Visual Basic is a RAD (*rapid application development*) Windows application tool. RAD allows you to quickly create a mockup of your application so that you can show users what the application will look like even though it lacks the underlying code that actually makes it work. This allows users to provide early feedback and helps programmers to deliver a final product that meets user expectations.

 **DEFINITION** RAD (*rapid application development*) is a process whereby programmers quickly create a mockup of an application's GUI for initial review by the users for whom the application is intended in order to demonstrate how the application will ultimately look and operate.

Object-Oriented Programming

Visual Basic is also an object-oriented programming (OOP) language. OOP refers to the coding part of creating a Visual Basic application as opposed to the development of its GUI. From an OOP perspective, everything in a Visual Basic application is treated like an object. Objects store information about themselves and provide access to this information. Objects also provide the ability to perform tasks and react to events. For example, in Visual Basic, a button is an object. Any information about a button is stored alongside the button, such as its size, color, and what actions the button initiates if it gets clicks. As you will learn in Chapter 9, "Getting Comfortable with Object-Oriented Programming," OOP supports code sharing and reuse and can greatly simplify program development.

DEFINITION OOP (*object-oriented programming*) is a methodology that combines the storage of information along with predefined program code that can be used to interact with the object and its information.

INTRODUCING VISUAL BASIC 2008 EXPRESS

Visual Basic 2008 Express is a special version of Visual Basic that Microsoft created especially to attract first-time programmers. It provides a simplified and streamlined introduction to Windows application development. It supports Microsoft's .NET Framework and like every other version of Visual Basic, it is relatively easy to get started with and can be used to create world-class desktop applications.

If you have not done so yet, now would be a good time to pause and install Visual Basic 2008 Express. The first time that you start it up, you'll see the screen shown in Figure 1.4.

HINT During installation, you will be prompted to install Microsoft SQL Server 2008 Express Edition, allowing you to build small database applications. You will not need to install this software to perform any of the exercises demonstrated in this book.

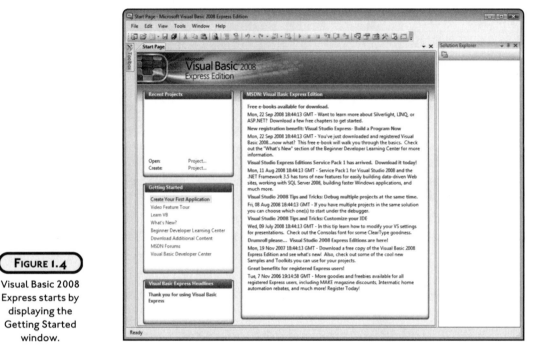

FIGURE 1.4

Visual Basic 2008 Express starts by displaying the Getting Started window.

As you can see, Visual Basic 2008 Express has a standard Windows menu and a default toolbar at the top of its IDE (*Integrated Development Environment*). Prominently displayed in the middle of the IDE is the Start Page window. This window is divided into four sections. The Recent Projects pane lists Visual Basic projects that you have recently worked on and contains links that when clicked let you open and create new Visual Basic projects. The Getting Started pane provides access to help information, Visual Basic articles, and various other Visual basic resources. The Visual Basic Express Headlines pane displays links to recent Visual Basic news made available online. The MSDN: Visual Basic Express Edition pane displays links to different headlines, news releases, and resources available on the Microsoft Developer Network. Of course, for all this content to be made available, your computer must have a working Internet connection.

DEFINITION An IDE (*integrated development environment*) is a workspace (the collection of menus, toolbars, and Windows) provided by Visual Basic with which you create new Visual Basic applications.

What Can Visual Basic 2008 Express Do?

Visual Basic 2008 Express has been designed by Microsoft to support the development of Windows applications. It is awfully good at creating Windows applications that run on the Windows desktop. For example, using Visual Basic 2008 Express, you can create applications that:

- Create Windows games
- Create Windows desktop applications
- Generate reports and text files
- Work with graphics
- Interact with the Windows file system
- Access local databases

To help make application development as easy as possible, Microsoft lets you download and use templates, also known as Start Kits, with Visual Basic 2008 Express. Templates are used to create a particular type of Windows application. Visual Basic Express makes it easy for you to locate and download new starter kits. Just click on File > New Project and double-click on the Search Online Templates icon. This displays a Search window that allows you to perform an online keyword search for new templates, which you can then download. Once downloaded, double-click on the starter-kit install package and follow the instructions provided to add it to Visual Basic 2008 Express.

DEFINITION A *template* is a collection of base files, program code, property settings, and tasks that assists you in creating a particular type of Windows application.

What Can't Visual Basic 2008 Express Do?

Unlike other versions of Visual Basic, Visual Basic 2008 Express is limited to the development of Windows applications. Therefore, it cannot be used to create any of the following types of applications, whose development is supported by the full version of Visual Basic 2008:

- Web applications
- Web services
- Windows services
- Windows Dynamic Link Libraries (DLLs)
- PDA applications
- Mobile device applications (cell phones, pagers, and so on)

It is important to remember that Microsoft's reason for creating Visual Basic 2008 Express was to provide first-time programmers and computer hobbyists with everything needed to learn how to create Windows programs. Once you have mastered this, you'll be ready to move on to these other programming platforms.

IN THE REAL WORD

Microsoft packages Visual Basic as a standalone product that it calls a Standard Edition. This version of Visual Basic generally sells for around $100 and will support the development of different types of Visual Basic applications other than just Windows applications. The Standard Edition of Visual Basic is intended for the individual user. Companies that develop Visual Basic applications generally purchase Visual Basic as part of a package deal that Microsoft calls Visual Studio. When purchased this way, you get access not only to Visual Basic but also to the other languages and tools that make up Visual Studio.

HINT   Because the focus of this book is on Visual Basic 2008 Express, from this point on in the book I use the terms Visual Basic and Visual Basic 2008 Express to refer to Visual Basic 2008 Express, unless otherwise specifically stated.

WHAT'S NEW IN VISUAL BASIC 2008 EXPRESS

Visual Basic 2008 Express supports a large number of new features not found in Visual Basic 2005 Express. These features include things like new support for working with databases and a range of new language features and capabilities. Some of the more notable improvements to Visual Basic 2008 Express are outlined in the sections that follow, many of which will be demonstrated as you make your way through this book.

Support for Microsoft SQL Server Compact 3.5

One new feature that has been added to Visual Basic 2008 Express is the ability to access and process data using Microsoft SQL Server Compact 3.5. This single-user database can be used to create Windows applications that store and manage data locally on the computer where your application runs. Microsoft SQL Server Compact 3.5 supports databases up to 4 GB in size, supports a wide range of data types, and is used to store application data in a single database file. To facilitate interaction with the databases, Visual Basic 2008 Express now includes support for Language-Integrated Query (LINQ). LINQ provides data query capabilities allowing you to submit data queries and retrieve database data.

Coverage of Microsoft SQL Server Compact 3.5 and LINQ is outside the scope of this book. If you are interested, you can learn more about both of these topics by visiting http:// www.microsoft.com/sql/.

Multi-Targeting

Another new Visual Basic 2008 Express capability is the ability to specify the version of the .NET Framework that an application is designed to work with through a process referred to as multi-targeting. With multi-targeting, you can specify whether your Visual Basic 2008 Express application will work with .NET 2.0, 3.0, or 3.5. By default, all new applications created with Visual Basic 2008 Express are set to work with .NET. If you need to develop applications that must be run on computers running an earlier version of the .NET Framework, you can do so by specifying a particular version of .NET. When you select a particular version of .NET, Visual Basic Express 2008 automatically adjusts the list of controls displayed in its IDE, providing access only to those controls that are supported by the targeted version of .NET. More information about multi-targeting is provided later in this chapter.

More IntelliSense

IntelliSense is an application feature that assists in the formulation of code statements and keywords. To use IntelliSense, begin typing in a Visual Basic command and then press Ctrl+Space and Visual Basic Express will respond by displaying a list of options for completing your keyword or statements that make sense based on whatever you are currently doing.

In Visual Basic 2005 Express, IntelliSense assisted programmers in formulating keyword and code statements. Microsoft has significantly improved IntelliSense in Visual Basic 2008 Express, now calling it IntelliSense Everywhere. IntelliSense Everywhere now provides filtering support. By default it displays only the most commonly used set of possible matching options. However, it allows you to view every possible option with the click of the mouse.

IntelliSense Everywhere can also make lists transparent, so that you do not lose sight of the code statements that they might overlap. IntelliSense Everywhere also now provides access to code snippets, which assist you in formulating code statements by adding template statements to your applications that you can then modify to fit your particular situation.

You will learn more about IntelliSense Everywhere in Chapter 2, "Navigating the Visual Basic 2008 Express Development Environment."

Support for New WPF and WCF

Thanks to improvements made to .NET 3.0, Visual Basic 2008 Express supports a number of new components, as listed here:

- **Windows Presentation Foundation (WPF).** A new framework that supports the development of Windows applications that integrate audio, video, and graphics.
- **Windows Communication Foundation (WCF).** A new messaging system that facilitates the development of Windows applications that communicate with one another locally or across a network.
- **Windows CardSpace.** A new component that facilitates the secure storage and retrieval of the user's digital identity.
- **Windows Workflow Foundation (WF).** Supports the development of Windows applications using transaction-based workflows, allowing incomplete transactions to be rolled back.

You will learn how to use the WPF to develop Windows applications in Chapter 3 "Creating an Application Interface."

New Language Features

Visual Basic 2008 Express provides a number of new language features that extend Visual Basic's functionality and capabilities. These new features are made possible though Visual Basic 2008 Express's new support for .NET 3.0 and 3.5 and are only available when you develop applications that target these versions of .NET. These new language features are listed in Table 1.1.

TABLE 1.1	NEW VISUAL BASIC 2008 EXPRESS LANGUAGE FEATURES	
Feature	**Requires**	**Description**
Local Type interface	.NET 3.0	Allows you to declare a variable without specifying its data type. The variable's data type is determined the first time you assign data to it.
Queries	.NET 3.5	The use of LINQ expressions, as opposed to SQL query statements, to generate data requests from databases.
Object Initializers	.NET 3.0	Provides a shortcut for instantiating objects and assigns them properties in a single expression.
XML Integration	.NET 3.5	Provides the ability to incorporate XML data in your application using LINQ.
Anonymous Type	.NET 3.0	Provides the ability to instantiate compiler-defined objects without having to specify the object's data type.
Extension Methods	.NET 3.0	Provides the ability to add custom methods to existing data types, which you can then work with as if they were a native data type method.
Lambda Expressions	.NET 3.5	Unnamed inline functions that return a single value when executed.

You will learn more about a number of these language features as you make your way through this book.

Improved ClickOnce Deployment

ClickOnce deployment is a new feature that lets you create deployable Windows applications and now supports the distribution of the WPF Web Browser Application, which, since they execute within a web browser, require special deployment and security considerations. You can use it to distribute your application online or on CD/DVD. It allows you to specify whether your application, once installed, appears on the Start menu and lets you specify application prerequisites for your applications. When your application installer executes, it will automatically verify the presence of these prerequisites and if they are not found, it will download them from Microsoft.com or any site that you specify. You will learn how to work with ClickOnce Deployment in Chapter 3, "Creating an Application Interface."

Integrated Power Pack Controls

Like Visual Basic 2005 Express, Visual Basic 2008 Express supports the installation of power packs. A *power pack* is an add-in collection of controls, components, and tools that provide

Visual Basic with new capabilities and features. Visual Basic 2008 Express now includes Microsoft Visual Basic Power Pack 3.0, which provides it with the following enhancements.

- `PrintForm`. Facilitates the porting over of Visual Basic 6.0 applications to Visual Basic 2008 Express by supporting existing printing logic already within the application.
- `LineShape`. A graphical control that lets you draw lines on containers and forms when designing application layout as opposed to programmatically generating them using graphic objects, brushes, and pens.
- `OvalShape`. A graphical control that lets you draw oval shapes on containers and forms when designing application layout as opposed to programmatically generating them using graphic objects, brushes, and pens.
- `RectangleShape`. A graphical control that lets you draw rectangles on containers and forms when designing application layout as opposed to programmatically generating them using graphic objects, brushes, and pens.
- `DataRepeater`. Displays rows of data in a scrollable container on top of Windows forms.

You will learn how to work with the line and shape controls listed above in Chapter 10, "Integrating Graphics and Audio."

OTHER VISUAL STUDIO 2008 EXPRESS PROGRAMMING LANGUAGES

Visual Basic 2008 Express is just one member of a family of Visual Studio Express programming languages. A listing of other Visual Studio Express programming languages include:

- **Visual C# 2008 Express.** A Windows program development language that grew out of C, C++, and Java, which is also aimed at first-time and casual programmers, hobbyists, and students.
- **Visual C++ 2008 Express.** A Windows program development language aimed at more experienced programmers with a need for greater control.

Visual C# 2008 Express

Visual C# is a relatively new programming language that Microsoft created based on a combination of C, C++, and Java. Microsoft first introduced Visual C# with the initial release of Visual Studio. Though a little more difficult to learn than Visual Basic, C# provides former C, C++, and Java developers with a program development platform that is easy to learn and leverages their existing program development skills.

Visual C++ 2008 Express

Visual C++ is an updated version of Visual C++ that now allows the development of C++ applications to leverage the power of the .NET Framework. In addition, Visual C++ 2008 Express can be used to create applications that run independently of the .NET Framework. Visual C++ is the most difficult of the Express family of languages to learn and master. It provides greater program control and more horsepower than other Express languages. As a result, it is the preferred language of power-programmers.

THE MICROSOFT .NET FRAMEWORK

All of the various Visual Studio programming languages, whether Express or full-featured versions, are designed to work with the Microsoft .NET Framework. Microsoft created the .NET Framework to provide a multilanguage application development environment capable of supporting the creation of applications and services for Windows, the web, and mobile devices.

IN THE REAL WORLD

Thanks to the multilanguage development environment provided by the .NET Framework, applications created using Visual Studio .NET can involve multiple languages. For example, an application might include code written in both Visual Basic and another Visual Studio programming language such as C#. This allows companies to break application development projects into parts and to assign the various parts to programmers who are using different programming languages based on their particular areas of expertise or upon the strengths and weaknesses of a particular programming language.

The .NET Framework is at the core of the Windows application development environment. Therefore, a basic understanding of .NET is a critical part of any Visual Basic programmer's foundation.

 .NET is a Microsoft framework that has been designed from the ground up to support integrated desktop, local area network, and Internet-based applications.

Before .NET

Before the introduction of .NET, Microsoft created and encouraged the use of the COM (*Component Object Model*). Using COM, Windows programmers were able to gain access to numerous system resources. COM also represented Microsoft's first attempt at creating an OOP standard. COM provided programmers with the ability to create component libraries made up of code that could be reused by different languages, such as Visual Basic and C++.

Before the arrival of .NET, early versions of Visual Basic depended on Windows DLL (*dynamic link library*) files for much of their core functionality. Visual Basic automatically loaded DLL files onto your computer when you installed Visual Basic. Things would get complicated when programmers finished developing their applications and were ready to deploy them. In order for their applications to work, the programmers had to make sure that all the DLLs that their applications needed to run were also installed on each user's computer. To help make this task easier to manage, Microsoft gave Visual Basic the ability to create a deployment package that automatically collected all the DLLs required by a given application. Although this made things easier on the programmer, it also made for some very large deployment packages. In most cases, even the smallest Visual Basic deployment package would easily grow to be 30 to 40 MB in size.

Unfortunately, package deployment size was not the only DLL problem that programmers had to contend with. Problems sometimes occurred because deployment packages would replace DLL files already installed on a user's computer with older versions of DLL files. This often caused other applications on users' computers to break. This situation was so common and difficult to deal with that programmers referred to it as DLL Hell.

Microsoft's solution to DLL Hell is the .NET Framework. The .NET Framework is now responsible for providing Visual Studio programming languages with the functionality that they used to get from DLL files. Because DLL files are not needed to develop Windows applications, deployment packages are now a lot smaller. Now, instead of worrying about what version of DLL files users have installed on their computers, programmers need only to make sure that users have the appropriate version of the .NET Framework installed.

.NET Components

The .NET Framework is a collection of programming services that support application development and execution on Windows operating systems, the Internet, and mobile devices such as PDAs. The .NET Framework acts as an interface between the operating system and your applications. Figure 1.5 depicts the .NET Framework's role in the application development process. As you can see, it enables applications to be developed using any combination of .NET-supported programming languages. It is responsible for translating the code created using these programming languages into a format that can be executed on the intended execution platform, whether it is a PC, web server, or a Pocket PC device.

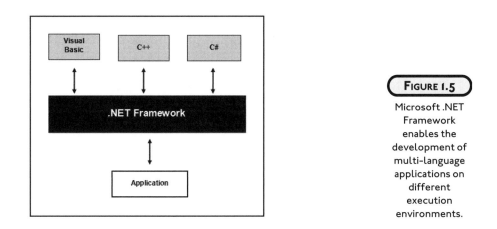

FIGURE 1.5

Microsoft .NET
Framework
enables the
development of
multi-language
applications on
different
execution
environments.

.NET 2.0

.NET Framework 2.0 was introduced in 2005. It is a requirement for Visual Basic 2005 Express and is still supported by Visual Basic 2008 Express. As Figure 1.5 shows, the .NET Framework is made up of two primary components. These are:

- .NET Framework class library
- CLR (*common language runtime*)

Together, these two components provide everything needed to support the execution of your Visual Basic applications. Their specific function is explained in the sections that follow.

The .NET Framework Class Library

The .NET class library is made up of an enormous amount of prewritten code that is available to any Visual Studio programming language. The class libraries are used to define objects within applications.

 DEFINITION A *class* is a collection of code representing a programming object, such as a form, a button, or a text box. When you create a new form or add a control to a form when building an application interface, you are instantiating new objects based on predefined classes stored in the .NET class library.

The .NET class library contains the code required to create forms, buttons, and other Visual Basic controls. For example, to create a new form within a Visual Basic application, you would call upon a predefined class that already had everything defined within it to create the new form. This saves you from having to write all the underlying low-level code yourself. If you then dragged and dropped a `Button` control onto the form, the .NET class library would automatically supply your application with all the underlying code, defining how the button looks and how your application can interact with it.

The CLR

The CLR provides the .NET Framework with a collection of services that facilitate application execution. These services include:

- Debugging
- Memory management
- Compiling
- Security
- Exception handling

In order for your Visual Basic applications to run, they must be compiled. When your Visual Basic applications are complied, the Visual Basic statements that make up your applications are translated into MSIL (*Microsoft Intermediate Language*). One of the jobs of the CRL is to convert MSIL code into binary code that the computer understands.

 DEFINITION *Compiling* is the process of converting the programming statements that make up a given application into a format that can be executed by the operating system.

Once converted to MSIL, it does not matter whether the original source code for the application was written in Visual Basic, C++, or any other programming language supported by Visual Studio. Because of this, you can mix and match multiple programming languages together to create a single application.

 HINT If you want to learn more about .NET, visit http://www.microsoft.com/net.

.NET 3.0 and 3.5

Since the release of .NET 2.0, the CLR has remained unchanged and the .NET class library has been enhanced and expanded. In .NET 3.0, Microsoft added the following previously discussed new framework components.

- Windows Presentation Foundation (WPF)
- Windows Communication Foundation (WCF)
- Windows CardSpace
- Windows Workflow Foundation (WF)

.NET 3.0 includes updates that support new features, including:

- Local Type interface
- Object Initializers
- Anonymous Type
- Extension Methods

In .NET 3.5, which accompanies Visual Basic 2008 Express, Microsoft has added support Language Integrated Query (LINQ). Figure 1.6 provides a depiction of how all the components of .NET fit together.

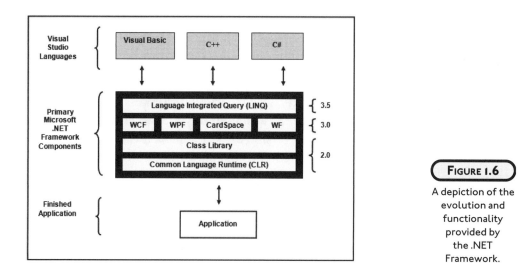

FIGURE 1.6

A depiction of the evolution and functionality provided by the .NET Framework.

.NET 3.5 includes updates that support new features that include:

- Queries
- XML Integration
- Lambda Expressions

Multi-targeting .NET Frameworks

All projects that you create in Visual Basic 2008 Express are automatically configured to work with .NET 3.5. Any Visual Basic applications that you migrate into Visual Basic 2008 Express from an earlier version of Visual Basic, such as Visual Basic 2005 Express, will automatically get converted to work with .NET 3.5. However, using multi-targeting, you can instruct Visual Basic 2008 Express to work with .NET 2.0, 3.0, or 3.5 by executing the following procedure.

1. Load your project into the Visual Basic 2008 Express IDE.
2. Right-click on the name of your project in the Solution Explorer window and click on Properties.
3. The Properties page for your application is displayed. Click on the Compile tab.
4. Click on the Advanced Compile Option button located at the bottom of the page.
5. The Advanced Compiler Settings window is displayed. Click on the Target framework drop-down list and select the version of .NET that you want your application to work with and then click on OK.

The primary benefit of using multi-targeting is to allow you to continue providing support for Visual Basic 2005 applications without introducing new .NET Framework dependencies. This way, if you still have a large number of customers running .NET 2.0, you can continue to update and support your applications without forcing your clients to upgrade their systems. If not for this new capability, upgrading your application to Visual Basic 2008 Express might result in preventing your applications from running on all your clients' systems.

Once you have completed this procedure, Visual Basic 2008 Express will automatically modify the list of controls and commands made available to you, presenting you only with those features compatible with the specified version of .NET. The next time you compile your application, Visual Basic 2008 Express will generate an application designed to run with whatever version of .NET you specified.

BACK TO THE JOKE MACHINE

Okay, let's turn the focus of this chapter back to the development of its main project, the Joke Machine game. Through the development of this game, you will learn the basic steps involved in developing a Windows application. As you go through the steps involved in creating your first Visual Basic application, try to focus on the overall process that is involved and don't get caught up in the details too much, which will be explained in later chapters.

Designing the Game

The Joke Machine game's design is very straightforward, involving basic, yet fundamental Windows programming techniques. The game begins by displaying its GUI. It then waits for the user to click on a button before displaying a joke. The game continues to run, allowing the user to click either of its buttons as many times as desired. Like other Windows applications, the game can be minimized or maximized and continues to run until the user clicks on the close button in the upper-right corner of the window.

The Joke Machine game is created in four steps, as outlined here:

1. Create a new Visual Basic project.
2. Create the GUI.
3. Modify form and control properties.
4. Add program code.

Each of these steps will be demonstrated in detail in the sections that follow.

Step 1: Creating a New Visual Basic Project

So let's get started.

1. Start up Visual Basic 2008 Express.
2. Next, create a new Visual Basic project by clicking on File and then selecting New Project. The New Project dialog appears, as shown in Figure 1.7.
3. Select the Windows Forms Application template.
4. Enter **JokeMachine** as the name of your application.
5. Click on OK.

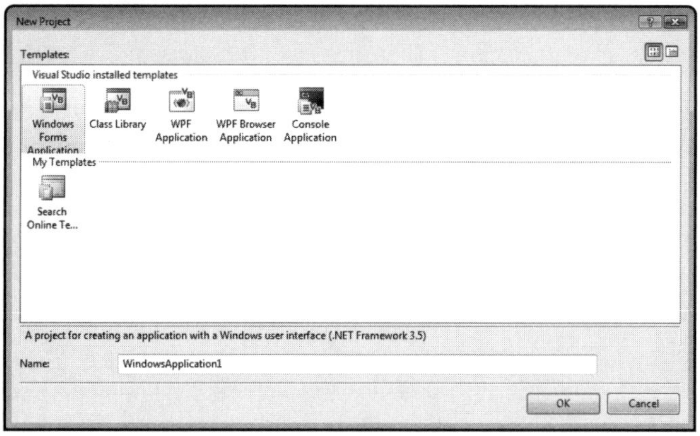

FIGURE 1.7

Select the Windows Forms Application template to create a new Windows application.

DEFINITION A Visual Basic *project* is a container that is used to store and manage the items that make up your Visual Basic application.

TRICK   On Microsoft Vista, Visual Basic stores your new applications, by default, in their own folder located in C:\Users*UserName*\Visual Studio 2008\Projects. However, if you want, you can configure Visual Basic to automatically store them elsewhere by clicking on the Tools menu and selecting the Options submenu. This will open the Options window. From here, you can click on Project and Solutions and set the default location where you'd like all your Visual Basic applications to be stored.

IN THE REAL WORLD

Visual Basic 2008 Express allows you to create the following types of applications:

- **Windows Application. A graphical Windows application that runs on the Windows desktop. Examples of this type of application include Microsoft Word, WinZip, and any Windows application that you interact with using a mouse.**

- **Windows Class Library. A custom-built class (.dll) that can be added to or referenced from within a Windows application. This type of application is one in which you define your own customized Windows controls for the purposes of adding them to other Windows applications that you'll develop.**

- **WPF Application. A new type of Windows application that supports a graphical user interface and desktop execution. WPF applications represent a new type of Windows application and are especially good at integrating sound, video, and graphics.**

- **Console Application. A text-based application typically run from the Windows Command Prompt. A console application is one in which the user interacts with the application by running it from the Windows Command Prompt and then typing in commands as directed by the application.**

The full version of Visual Basic is capable of creating many additional types of applications. Examples include web applications, applications for smart devices, and Windows services.

Visual Basic creates a new project for you. In the middle of the IDE, you will see a blank window as shown in Figure 1.8. Within Visual Basic, this window is referred to as a *form*. You will create the GUI for the Joke Machine by adding controls to this form. Note that by default, Visual Basic names the form Form1. As you'll see in the next chapter, you can change the name of forms to anything you want.

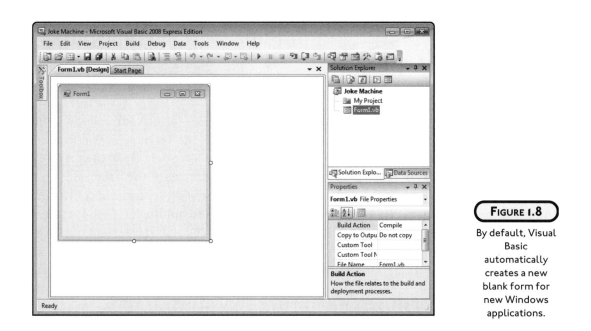

FIGURE I.8

By default, Visual Basic automatically creates a new blank form for new Windows applications.

At this point, you now have a fully functional, though not very interesting, Windows application. You can run your application by clicking on the Debug menu and selecting the Start Debugging option. You could also press the F5 key or click on the Start icon on the Standard Visual Basic toolbar. Once started, the application will begin running. The name of the application's form, Form1, is displayed in the title bar, and Minimize, Maximize, and Close buttons will appear in the upper-right corner of the application's window. Click on the Close button to stop your application and return to the Visual Basic IDE.

Step 2: Creating the User Interface

In order to create the interface for the Joke Machine game, you need to add controls, such as buttons and text boxes, to the form. Visual Basic makes controls available to you via the Toolbox window, which by default is displayed on the left-hand side of the IDE. To access it, click on its tab.

You can add controls to your form using a number of different techniques. For example, you can drag and drop a control from the Toolbox onto the form, or you can double-click on a control located in the Toolbox and Visual Basic will automatically place a copy of the control onto the form for you, which you can then move and resize.

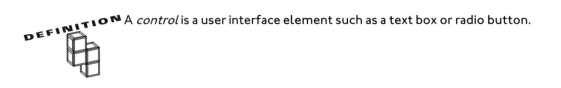

DEFINITION A *control* is a user interface element such as a text box or radio button.

The first control that you will add is the TextBox control. To do this, double-click on the TextBox control in the Visual Basic Toolbox. Visual Basic adds the Textbox control to the form assigning it a default name of TextBox1. Next, locate the Multiline property in the first column of the Properties window (located by default in the lower-right side of the IDE) and change its value to True. This will enable the display of multiple lines of text within the control. Using the mouse, move and resize the TextBox control by clicking and holding on to the small white squares that define its parameter, as shown in Figure 1.9.

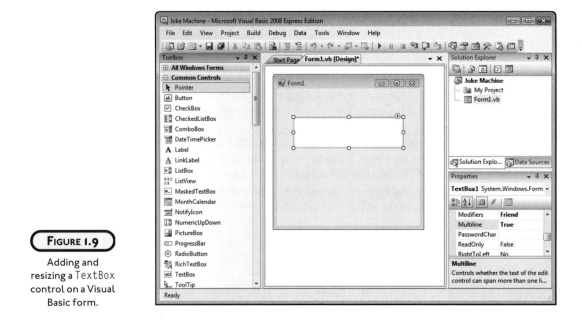

FIGURE 1.9

Adding and resizing a TextBox control on a Visual Basic form.

Now, let's add a descriptive label to the form just above the TextBox1 control. Start by double-clicking on the Label control located in the Toolbox. Using the mouse, move the control just above the upper-left corner of the TextBox1 control. Note that Visual Basic automatically assigned the label a default text string of Label1.

Now let's add the first Button control to the form by double-clicking on the Button control located in the Toolbox. Visual Basic adds the control to the form assigning it a default text string of Button1. Using the mouse, reposition the button beneath the TextBox1 control. Add a second button to the form and reposition it just to the right of the first button. Note that Visual Basic automatically assigned this control a default text display string of Button2. At this point, your game's interface should like the one shown in Figure 1.10.

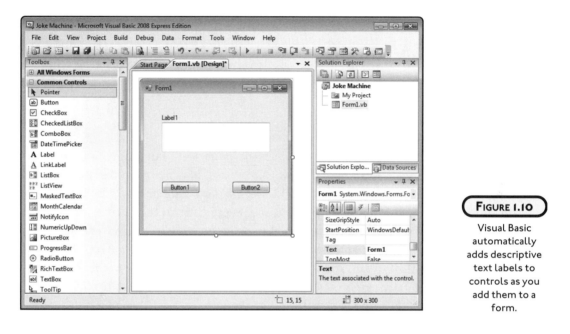

FIGURE 1.10

Visual Basic automatically adds descriptive text labels to controls as you add them to a form.

Now, let's pause for a moment and do a test run of your application by clicking on the Debug menu and then selecting Start Debugging. Within a moment, your new application will start. As you can see, it doesn't do much yet. If you click on its buttons, nothing happens. Once you are done looking at it, click on the Close button located in the upper-right corner of the game's dialog box to close the application and return to Visual Basic's design view.

Step 3: Customizing Control Properties

Now that all of the controls that are needed to build the application interface have been placed on the form, it is time to customize each of the controls to make them look and act like they should. This will be achieved by selecting each control in turn and editing selected properties associated with each individual control.

Let's begin with the Label1 control. This control needs to be modified so that it displays a text string of "Joke Machine." To do this, click on the Label1 control. Once you have done this, you will notice that the Properties window in the lower-right side of the IDE has changed and now displays properties associated with the Label1 control. The name of each property is displayed in the left-hand column and the value assigned to the property is shown in the right-hand column.

Scroll down and select the Text property. As you will see, a text string of Label1 is currently assigned to the Text property of the Label1 control. To replace this string, highlight the currently assigned value and type in the string "Joke Machine" in its place. Now, click back somewhere on Form1 and you'll see that Visual Basic has already updated the text displayed by the Label1 control.

Next, click on the first Button control (Button1) that you added to the Form1. It should be located just below the lower-left corner of the Textbox1 control. Change the text string stored in its Text property field to "Joke 1". Then click on the second Button control (Button2) and change its Text property to "Joke 2".

Step 4: Adding a Little Programming Logic

As I mentioned earlier in the chapter, Visual Basic is an OOP language. Controls like the Button control provide a good example of how OOP works. In order to make these buttons do something when the Joke Machine is run, you'll need to associate or attach some Visual Basic programming statements to them. As you will see, every control that you attach to a Visual Basic form is capable of storing program code alongside the control. You enter this code using the Visual Basic code editor. To enter code for a given object, such as a Button control, you simply double-click on the button. The IDE will automatically switch from the form designer, where you have just visually assembled the application's interface, to code view, where programming statements associated with selected controls are stored.

To make the Joke Machine work, all that is required is to add two programming statements. The first statement will be assigned to the Button1 control. To prepare to enter this statement, double-click on the Button1 control. The IDE will open the code designer window as shown in Figure 1.11.

 TRICK

Because the IDE has so many bells and whistles, it is impossible to display every available toolbar and window at the same time. Therefore, Microsoft makes some windows share the same space. If you look at the code editor window in Figure 1.10, you see that it is currently sharing space with the Form designer window and the Getting Started window. You can switch between these windows by clicking on their associated tabs.

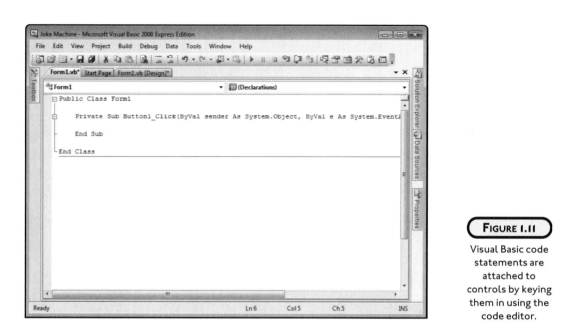

FIGURE 1.11

Visual Basic code statements are attached to controls by keying them in using the code editor.

TRICK
You may have noticed that the code editor window shown in Figure 1.10 takes up almost the entire display area of the IDE. I expanded it to make it easier to view and edit programming statements. One way to make more room for the code editor window is to close other windows in the IDE, such as the Toolbox, Solution Explorer, and Properties windows. The problem with this option is that you use these other windows so often that it is just too inconvenient to have to keep opening and closing them. Instead, I temporarily thumbtacked the Toolbox, Solution Explorer, and Properties windows to the side of the IDE. Look at the upper-right corners of the title bars for each of these three windows and you will see a thumbtack button. Clicking on the thumbtack button tells the IDE to shrink the display of the window down to a tab docked on the side of the IDE where the window is docked. As you can see in Figure 1.10, there is a tab on the far-left side of the IDE representing the Toolbox and two tabs on the far-right side of the IDE representing the Solution Explorer and Properties windows. When you are ready to view these windows again, just click on their tabs. When you do, the IDE will temporarily display them again. To make these windows remain open, click on the thumbtack button for each window again.

As you can see, Visual Basic has already generated some code for you. I'll explain what this code is in later chapters. For now, just enter the following statement, exactly as shown below. To make the statement that you are supposed to enter stand out, I have highlighted it in bold.

```
Private Sub Button1_Click(ByVal sender As System.Object, ByVal e As
System.EventArgs) Handles Button1.Click
    TextBox1.Text = "What is black and white and red all over?     " & _
    "A sunburned penguin!"
End Sub
```

Without getting into the technical details at this point of the book, the statement that you just entered assigns a string of text as the Text property value of the TextBox1 control. The text that you are assigning will display in the TextBox1 control when the Button1 control is clicked.

Next, return to the form designer view for Form1 by clicking on the tab labeled Form1.vb [Design]. Then double-click on the Button2 control. As you can see, you are now back in the code editor window, and a pair of new program statements have been added for you. Add the line of code shown below, in bold, inside the two new statements.

```
Private Sub Button2_Click(ByVal sender As System.Object, ByVal e As
System.EventArgs) Handles Button2.Click
    TextBox1.Text = "What ceases to exist when you say its name?" & _
    "Silence!"
End Sub
```

Just like with the previous statement, the code that you just added will execute when the Joke Machine is run and the Button2 control is clicked.

Testing the Execution of the Joke Machine Application

That's it. The Joke Machine game is complete and ready to run. Press F5 to run it. As long as you didn't make any typos when modifying control properties or entering program code, it should run exactly as shown at the beginning of this chapter. Otherwise, go back and correct your typos and try running your application again. Once everything is working correctly, click on File > Save All and then Save to save your new Visual Basic project.

SUMMARY

This chapter has covered a lot of ground for an introductory chapter. You learned about what Visual Basic 2008 Express is and what it is not. You learned about the history behind Visual Basic and how Visual Basic fits into Microsoft Visual Studio. On top of all this, you also learned the four basic steps involved in developing a Visual Basic application. You then put this information together and developed your first Visual Basic application, the Joke Machine.

Before you move on to the next chapter, take a few more minutes and see if you can improve on the Joke Machine game by implementing the following list of challenges.

CHALLENGES

1. Improve the Joke Machine by adding additional buttons along with additional jokes.
2. Currently, the Joke Machine game displays the text string of Form1 in the Windows title bar. Replace this text string with the phrase "Visual Basic Joke Machine". (Hint: Click on the form and modify the form's Text property.)
3. As it is currently written, the TextBox field on the Joke Machine window allows the user to enter text into it, when it should really just display the text of jokes. Prevent this behavior from occurring. (Hint: Click on the TextBox1 control and set the ReadOnly property to True.)

CHAPTER 2

NAVIGATING THE VISUAL BASIC 2008 EXPRESS DEVELOPMENT ENVIRONMENT

Now that you know what Visual Basic 2008 Express is and what it can and cannot be used for, it is time to get better acquainted with its IDE (integrated development environment) and to learn how to better work with all its pieces and parts. Mastery of the IDE is very important and will help you to work more efficiently and effectively. This chapter will review the most commonly used IDE windows and provide instruction on how to use them.

Specifically, you will learn:

- How to work with the IDE menu and standard toolbar
- The basics of working with the form designer and code editor
- About IntelliSense and how to use it to your advantage
- How to work with the Toolbox, Solution Explorer, and Properties windows

PROJECT PREVIEW: THE CLICK RACE GAME

In this chapter's game project, you will learn how to develop the Click Race game. The object of this game is for the player to use the mouse to click on a pair of buttons as many times as possible in a 30-second period. To make things more challenging, the game forces the player to alternate the clicking of each button. To play well, the player must be a fast clicker and be skilled at quickly and accurately moving the mouse.

The Click Race game starts up, as shown in Figure 2.1. The game buttons that the user must click to accumulate points are located at the bottom of the game window and are disabled (grayed out).

FIGURE 2.1

Starting the Click Race game.

To begin playing, the player must click on the Start Game button. When this happens, the game button located at the lower-left corner of the window is enabled, as demonstrated in Figure 2.2.

FIGURE 2.2

Players score points by clicking on the currently active game button.

The player scores a point by clicking on the button. Once clicked, the game button is disabled and the other game button is enabled. The final score remains visible after game play has ended, as demonstrated in Figure 2.3.

FIGURE 2.3

To score another point, the player must click on the second game button.

The Click Race game gives the player 30 seconds to accumulate as many points as possible. Game play stops at 30 seconds when both game buttons are disabled. The total number of points scored by the player is displayed, as demonstrated in Figure 2.4.

FIGURE 2.4

Game play ends at 30 seconds when both game buttons are disabled.

By the time you have created and run this game, you'll have learned how to exercise dynamic control over Windows controls by responding to events generated by the player. You will also have learned how to work with the Visual Basic Timer control.

GETTING COMFORTABLE MOVING AROUND THE VISUAL BASIC 2008 EXPRESS IDE

Visual Basic applications are created using Visual Basic's built-in IDE. The Visual Basic IDE provides tools such as a compiler, which translates application code into a finished executable program; a debugger, which assists in tracking down and fixing programs; and tools for managing projects.

The exact appearance of Visual Basic's IDE varies depending on the type of application you are building. Since this book is primarily focused on teaching you how to develop Windows desktop applications, it will begin by reviewing the IDE as it looks when developing applications based on windows forms. Then it will provide you with a look at the differences you will see when developing Windows Presentation Foundation (WPF) applications.

The Visual Basic 2008 Express IDE features a standard menu, numerous toolbars, and a number of different windows. Because Microsoft has crammed so much into the IDE, there is no way that all of the available toolbars and windows can be displayed at the same time. Instead, Microsoft has come up with a number of clever ways of allowing these resources to share the same space.

Figure 2.5 shows the how the Visual Basic 2008 Express IDE looks the first time you use it to open up a new Windows Forms Application project.

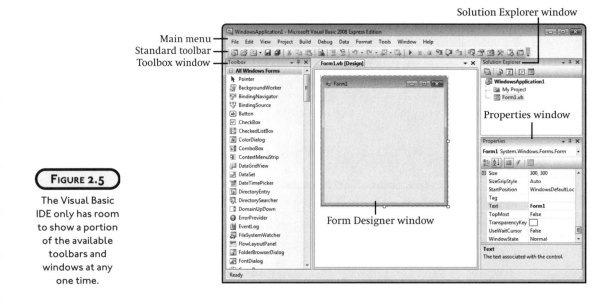

FIGURE 2.5

The Visual Basic IDE only has room to show a portion of the available toolbars and windows at any one time.

As Figure 2.5 shows, the default layout of the Visual Basic IDE features a number of different elements. Each of the key elements shown in Figure 2.5 will be covered in detail later in this chapter.

One nice feature of the IDE is AutoDock. AutoDock allows you to move windows around in the IDE by using your mouse to reposition them. As you move them near the edge of the IDE, an outline appears, showing where the IDE will automatically redock the window if you let it go. This makes it easy for you to reorganize the placement of windows within the IDE to suit your own personal preferences.

Be careful when repositioning windows within the IDE. There are so many windows available that it is all too easy to misplace them or even accidentally rearrange them.

From time to time, you will either accidentally or deliberately close a window within the IDE. Don't panic if you later discover you need it back. Instead, click on the View menu and select the appropriate window to display it again. The IDE provides so many different windows that it cannot show them all directly under the View menu. If you don't see the window that you are looking for listed there, select the Other Windows option and look for it in the submenu that appears.

Because the IDE is so packed full of features, Microsoft has had to employ a few organizational tricks to make everything fit. In some cases, two or more windows may share the same space in the IDE. Each tab identifies its associated windows. You can jump between windows by selecting the appropriate tab.

Another useful feature that you'll see a lot in the IDE is the presence of a thumbtack at the top of windows, such as the Solution Explorer and Properties windows. The thumbtack represents an autohide feature that allows you to shrink down a window to a tab that is connected to the edge of the IDE where the window is docked. This way you free up space in the IDE for other windows without having to close any windows, and you can later restore a docked window by clicking on its tab. For example, take a look at Figure 2.6. Here you will see that the Solution Explorer window has been docked as a tab on the right side of the IDE to provide additional room for the Properties window.

 TRICK   The IDE is highly customizable. Click on the Tools menu and then select the Customize option to configure which of the IDE's many toolbars are displayed. In addition, you can customize any number of IDE features, such as how the form designer looks and how the code editor behaves, by clicking on the Tools menu and selecting Options.

Docked Solution Explorer window

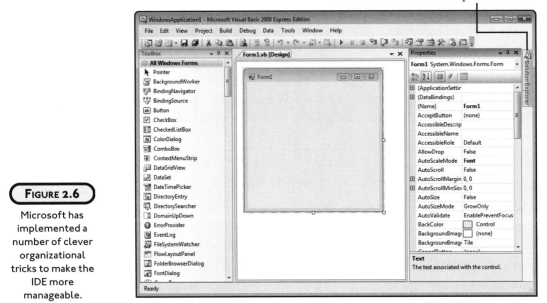

FIGURE 2.6

Microsoft has implemented a number of clever organizational tricks to make the IDE more manageable.

Navigating the IDE Menu

The Visual Basic 2008 Express IDE includes a comprehensive menu, which lists and organizes the various commands and options available to you as you work. Visual Basic's IDE is a dynamic tool. It automatically changes based on the particular task that is before it.

The following list identifies the IDE menus and summarizes the functionality that they provide:

- **File.** Menu options for opening and saving projects and solutions
- **Edit.** Text-editing options such as Undo, Copy, Cut, and Paste
- **View.** Switch between the form designer and code editor and access other windows such as the Toolbox, Solution Explorer, and Properties windows
- **Project.** Add new forms, controls, and components to a project
- **Build.** Build or compile a standalone version of your application
- **Debug.** Test the execution of an application or step through a program that has been stopped with an error or a breakpoint
- **Data.** Configure connections to data sources such as a local database
- **Tools.** Collection of different options, including the Options submenu where you can customize the IDE and various project settings

- **Windows.** Select and arrange open windows
- **Help.** Access to Visual Basic's integrated help system, including access to both local and online help topics

Working with Toolbars

As is the case with any Windows-based application, Visual Basic 2008 Express makes it easy to access certain commands using toolbars. By default, Visual Basic automatically displays its Standard toolbar, shown in Figure 2.7. The items displayed by toolbars may also change dynamically based on what you happen to be doing at the time.

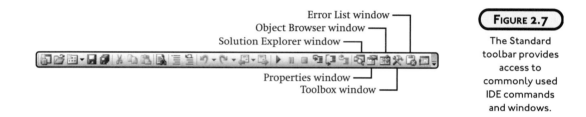

Error List window
Object Browser window
Solution Explorer window

Properties window
Toolbox window

FIGURE 2.7

The Standard toolbar provides access to commonly used IDE commands and windows.

The Visual Basic 2008 Express IDE includes more than a dozen toolbars, each of which provides single-click access to various commands. For some of the toolbars, you can configure whether or not they are displayed by clicking on the View menu and then selecting the Toolbars option. Optionally, you can configure the display of all the available toolbars by clicking on the Tools menu and selecting Customize.

TRICK You can also configure the display of toolbars by right-clicking on any visible toolbar and selecting the desired toolbar from the list that will appear.

Each icon on a toolbar performs a specific command or task. Visual Basic 2008 Express has too many toolbars to go over each of their icons in this book. You can find out about the specific function for each toolbar icon by placing your cursor over it, which results in its name being displayed as a ToolTip. However, you can get a pretty good feel for the purpose behind each toolbar based on its name.

Form Designer Basics

The form designer, shown in Figure 2.8, allows you to visually create GUIs (*graphical user interfaces*) using drag and drop. The form designer shares space within the IDE with the Getting Started window and the code editor window, which is what you'll use to enter your Visual Basic programming statements.

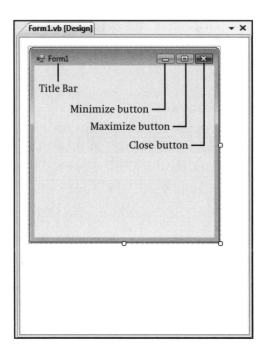

FIGURE 2.8

Visual Basic
automatically
creates a new form
containing basic
Windows
elements each
time you open up a
new Windows
Forms Application
project.

TRICK

Sometimes when you are working with the form designer, you may notice that there is an asterisk in the tab for the window just to the right of the form name. This asterisk indicates that you have made changes to the form that you have not saved yet. It is always a good idea to frequently save changes any time you modify your Visual Basic applications.

As you have already learned, Visual Basic 2008 Express lets you create graphical applications using either forms or WPF. An application can have more than one form. As you saw when you created the Joke Machine application in Chapter 1, "An Introduction to Visual Basic 2008 Express," an application window is created by adding controls to it. These controls are copied over from the Toolbox. Once added to your form, you can customize controls by changing their size or editing their associated properties. Once you have a prototype of your form set up to look like you want it to, you'll need to add code to the controls to make them behave and work like you want them to.

The form designer makes relocating and aligning controls easy. It provides visual indicators that show the location of each control relative to the location of other controls on the form, as demonstrated in Figure 2.9.

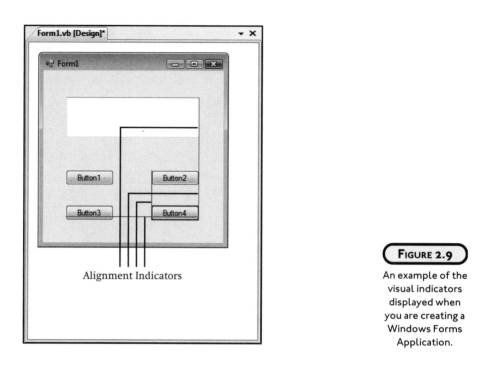

FIGURE 2.9

An example of the visual indicators displayed when you are creating a Windows Forms Application.

TRICK You can also use commands located on the Format menu to automatically align controls on a form. For example, if you had three buttons of varying sizes on a form and wanted them all to be the same size, you could select them all by holding down the Ctrl key as you click on each button, and then click on Format, Make Same Size, and the Height and Width commands.

Understanding the Code Editor

The code editor facilitates the storage and viewing of the programming code that drives your Visual Basic applications. The easiest way to access it when developing a Windows Form Application is to double-click on a form or one of the controls on the form. This automatically switches you from the form designer view to the code editor view, as shown in Figure 2.10. Best of all, it also automatically places your cursor at the right location to begin entering code for the resource that you double-clicked on.

TRICK You can configure a number of features that affect the way the code editor looks and acts by clicking on the Tools menu and selecting Options. When the Options window appears, expand the Text Editor Basic link and select the Editor option located on the left-hand side of the Options window and change any of the configuration settings that will be displayed on the right-hand side of the dialog.

Class Name drop-down list   Method Name drop-down list

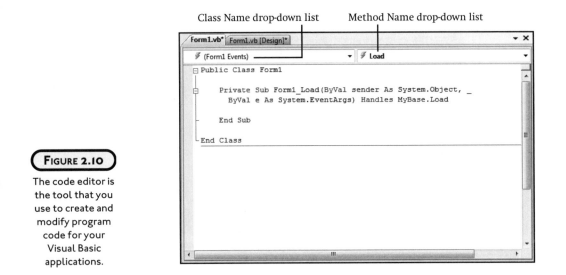

FIGURE 2.10

The code editor is the tool that you use to create and modify program code for your Visual Basic applications.

Program code associated with a form and any of the controls placed on that form is stored alongside the form. Therefore, if a Visual Basic application contains more than one form, the code associated with each form is stored and displayed separately.

TRICK   In addition to storing program code alongside a form, you can store the code in a separate module, which you can then use to refer back to a form and its controls.

At the top of the code editor are two drop-down lists. The first drop-down list is the Class Name list, from which you can select any of the controls located on the form. The second drop-down list is the Method Name list, which provides access to any event associated with the currently selected object. By using these two drop-down lists together, you can locate any code procedure. If you use these controls to look for a procedure that has not been created yet, the code editor will define a new procedure for that control and event on your behalf.

Visual Basic Assisted Code Development

One of the really nice things about Visual Basic is that it does so much work for you under the covers. For example, you don't have to figure out how to create a button or a text box. Visual Basic already makes them available to you as controls located in the Toolbox. Just as Visual Basic greatly simplifies form design, it helps streamline the code development process. For example, as you saw in Chapter 1 when you created the Joke Machine, Visual Basic automatically generates a lot of code for you. For example, create a new project and place a label, a textbox, and a button on the form. Then double-click on the form and you'll see that Visual Basic automatically generates the following code for you.

```
Public Class Form1

    Private Sub Form1_Load(ByVal sender As System.Object, _
        ByVal e As System.EventArgs) Handles MyBase.Load

    End Sub

End Class
```

 TRICK Actually, the format of the code statements that you will see when performing the above steps will vary slightly from the statements presented here. In order to make things fit onto the pages of this book, I will have to split up some programming statements into multiple pieces, using the continuation character (_).

As you can see, Visual Basic has already framed out the overall organization of the program statements that will make up the application. Now, using the Class Name and Method Name drop-down lists, select Button1 control and the click event. As soon as you do this, the code editor defines a new procedure for you, as shown here:

```
Public Class Form1

    Private Sub Form1_Load(ByVal sender As System.Object, _
        ByVal e As System.EventArgs) Handles MyBase.Load

    End Sub

    Private Sub Button1_Click(ByVal sender As Object, _
        ByVal e As System.EventArgs) Handles Button1.Click

    End Sub

End Class
```

Now all that you have to do is type in the Visual Basic code statements that you want to be executed as part of these procedures, as was demonstrated in the Joke Machine project. I'll talk more about the benefits and use of procedures later in Chapter 8, "Enhancing Code Structure and Organization."

Color Coding, Automatic Indentation, and Spacing

You may have noticed back in Chapter 1 when you were creating the Joke Machine game that the Visual Basic code editor did a number of things that made it easier for you to key in your Visual Basic code statements. For example, certain Visual Basic keywords were color coded to make them stand out. You will really learn to appreciate this feature as your applications grow in complexity and you end up writing more and more code. Color coding helps to make your code easier to read and work with by providing visual indicators that make your program code intuitively easier to follow along.

Another nice feature that you may not have noticed is the automatic indentation of code statements, as demonstrated in Figure 2.11. By indenting groups of related code statements, your code is visually organized into logical chunks and becomes easier to read and understand.

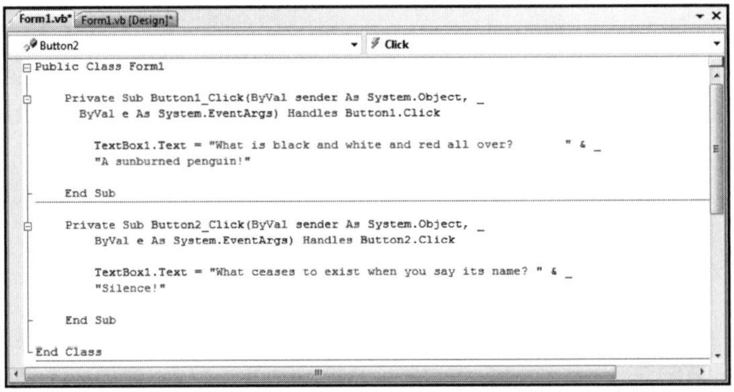

FIGURE 2.11

The Visual Basic code editor automatically color codes statements and indents them to make them easier to read.

Another really handy feature of the code editor is automatic spacing. For example, you might try to enter the following code statement, exactly as shown here:

```
TextBox1.Text="Hello"
```

As soon as you press the Enter key, the code editor changes the statement to look like the line of code shown here:

```
TextBox1.Text = "Hello"
```

The changes to the line of code are subtle, but very important. If you look closely, you'll notice that a blank space has been added just before and after the equals sign to make the code easier to read. This is just another way that the Visual Basic code editor works to help make your coding experience as easy as possible, allowing you to focus on the task at hand without having to worry about little organizational details.

IntelliSense Eveywhere

A really nice feature that is directly integrated into the code editor is IntelliSense. IntelliSense was first introduced with Visual Basic 5.0. IntelliSense can be so helpful that many times you'll be able to get what you need from it without having to turn to other resources for help.

Visual Basic 2008 Express has significantly expanded IntelliSense. Microsoft has improved IntelliSense so much that it decided to give it a new name: *IntelliSense Everywhere*. Among other enhancements, IntelliSense Everywhere kicks in quicker, requiring fewer keystrokes on your part.

IntelliSense Everywhere is responsible for displaying the pop-up boxes that you may have noticed when you were creating the Joke Machine back in Chapter 1. With IntelliSense Everywhere, the Visual Basic IDE keeps an eye on your program statements as you type them and displays windows showing all the possible options available to you as you enter your code.

To better understand IntelliSense Everywhere, let's look at a couple of examples. In the first example, shown in Figure 2.12, I created a form that contained a button and a text box. I then double-clicked on the button to open the code designer. I entered the word TextBox1 followed immediately by a period. In response, IntelliSense Everywhere kicked in and displayed a pop-up window showing all the possible coding options available to me. In this example, I clicked on Text, which represents the TextBox control's Text property, and IntelliSense Everywhere automatically appended the word to my code. All that remained for me to do was to finish writing the rest of the code statement as shown here:

```
TextBox1.Text = "Click on Me!"
```

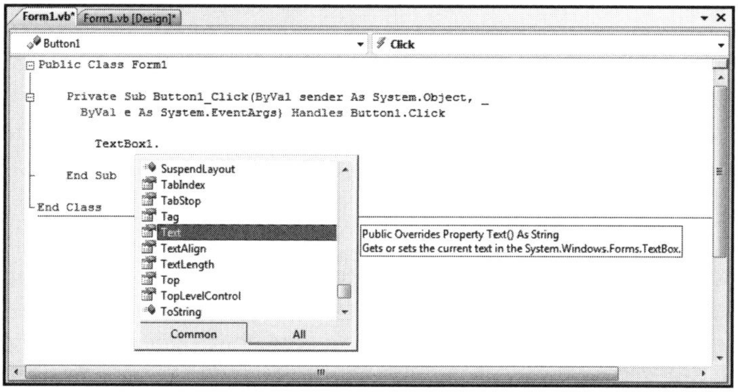

FIGURE 2.12

IntelliSense Everywhere provides dynamic assistance as you enter your code statements.

IntelliSense Everywhere can help in the formation of more complex programming statements as well. For example, with the next code statement, my intention was to gray out and prevent the user from being able to click on a Button control named Button1. I started the statement by keying in the name of the Button1 control followed by a period. In response, IntelliSense Everywhere displayed a pop-up window, as shown in Figure 2.13, showing all available options. I clicked on Enable and IntelliSense Everywhere then appended that word to the code.

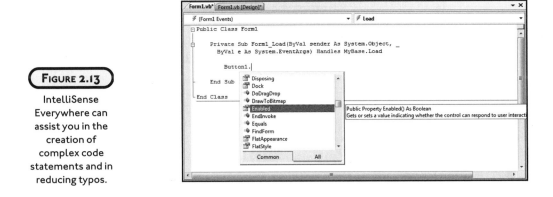

FIGURE 2.13

IntelliSense Everywhere can assist you in the creation of complex code statements and in reducing typos.

TRICK

As you may have already noticed, suggestions displayed by IntelliSense Everywhere appear in a small two-tabbed window. By default, the Common tab is selected, which means that the number of options you are presented with is filtered down to just the most commonly used ones. If you want to see every possible matching option, click on the All tab.

Next, I typed a space and pressed on the equals (=) key. Once again, IntelliSense jumped into action, displaying a pop-up window showing the two options that were available to me. (Also, just to the right of the pop-up dialog, a ToolTip was displayed, explaining what the Enabled method does.) I selected False and IntelliSense completed the code statement by appending the word False to the end of it.

TRICK

Another nice IntelliSense feature is the ability to use the Ctrl and Space keys together to tell the code editor to start it up. For example, suppose you created a form with a large number of controls and were having trouble remembering the name of a particular control for which you wanted to write some code. In this scenario, you could type the first letter or two of what you thought the control might be named and then press and hold down the Ctrl key while also pressing the Space key. When you do this, IntelliSense starts and displays the names of all available resources that begin with those letters, as demonstrated in Figure 2.14.

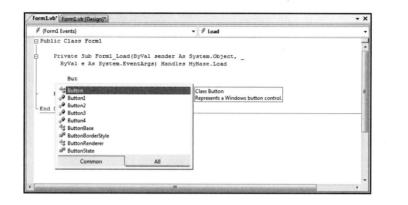

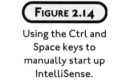

FIGURE 2.14

Using the Ctrl and Space keys to manually start up IntelliSense.

IntelliSense Everywhere now assists you in writing Visual Basic language keywords like If, Then, Dim, and End, and in using them to formulate code statements. For example, if you were to type the first letter or two or three letters of a Visual Basic keyword and then press Ctrl + Space, IntelliSense Everywhere would kick in, as demonstrated in Figure 2.15.

FIGURE 2.15

IntelliSense Everywhere also displays keyword syntax in ToolTips.

One additional new IntelliSense Everywhere feature that can be very helpful to new programmers is its support for code snippets. A *code snippet* is a template statement that you can add to your program code, which you can then modify as necessary to perform a particular task. Visual Basic 2008 Express comes equipped with hundreds of code snippets for you to choose from. To tell Visual Basic you want to work with a code snippet, all you have to do is right-click on the location in the code editor where you want to place a new statement. In response, a series of folders is displayed in which Visual Basic's snippets are organized, as shown in Figure 2.16.

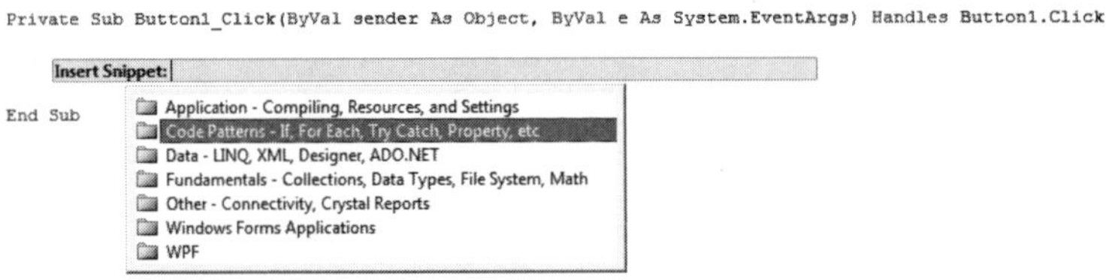

```
Private Sub Button1_Click(ByVal sender As Object, ByVal e As System.EventArgs) Handles Button1.Click
```

FIGURE 2.16

Snippets are organized into a series of seven high-level folders.

```
End Sub
```

Insert Snippet:
- Application - Compiling, Resources, and Settings
- Code Patterns - If, For Each, Try Catch, Property, etc
- Data - LINQ, XML, Designer, ADO.NET
- Fundamentals - Collections, Data Types, File System, Math
- Other - Connectivity, Crystal Reports
- Windows Forms Applications
- WPF

The next step in finding the snippets you need is to double-click on the appropriate high-level folder in order to drill down into it, as demonstrated in Figure 2.17.

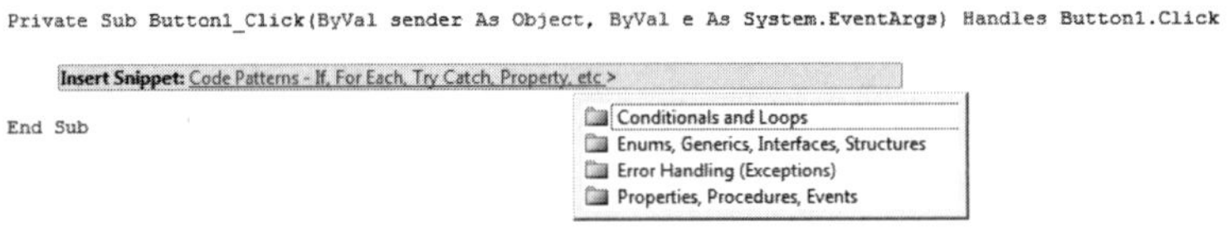

FIGURE 2.17

Snippets are further organized into different sub-categories.

```
Private Sub Button1_Click(ByVal sender As Object, ByVal e As System.EventArgs) Handles Button1.Click
```

Insert Snippet: Code Patterns - If, For Each, Try Catch, Property, etc >

```
End Sub
```

- Conditionals and Loops
- Enums, Generics, Interfaces, Structures
- Error Handling (Exceptions)
- Properties, Procedures, Events

By drilling down into the appropriate sub-folder, you will access individual code snippets, as demonstrated in Figure 2.18.

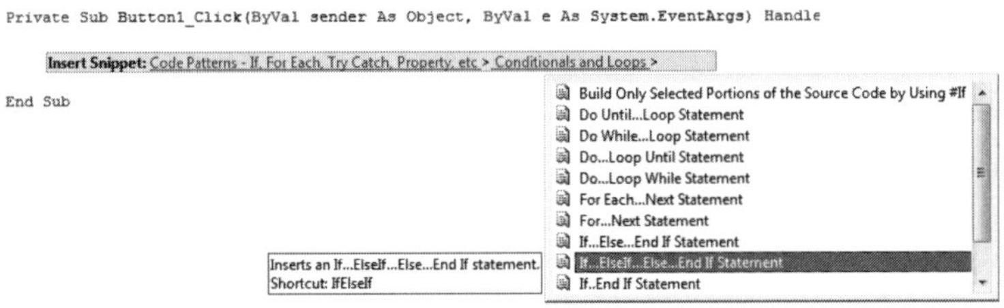

```
Private Sub Button1_Click(ByVal sender As Object, ByVal e As System.EventArgs) Handle
```

FIGURE 2.18

You can use any of over 200 code snippets to simplify the coding process.

```
End Sub
```

Insert Snippet: Code Patterns - If, For Each, Try Catch, Property, etc > Conditionals and Loops >

- Build Only Selected Portions of the Source Code by Using #If
- Do Until...Loop Statement
- Do While...Loop Statement
- Do...Loop Until Statement
- Do...Loop While Statement
- For Each...Next Statement
- For...Next Statement
- If...Else...End If Statement
- If...ElseIf...Else...End If Statement
- If...End If Statement

Inserts an If...ElseIf...Else...End If statement.
Shortcut: IfElseIf

Once you have gotten to a point where you can view individual code snippets, all you have to do is double-click on one to add it to your program code. Once added, you can fill in the highlighted areas in the template code, as demonstrated in Figure 2.19.

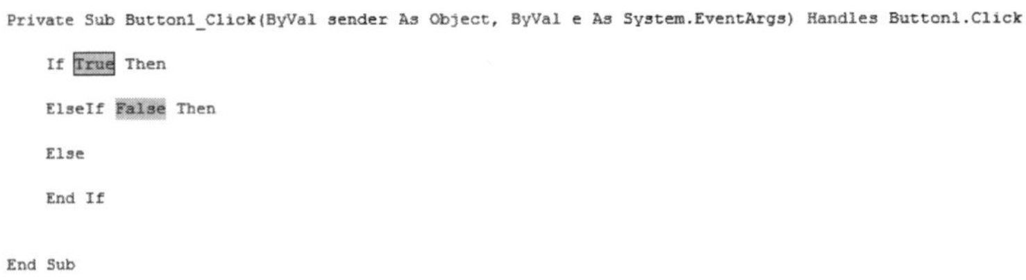

FIGURE 2.19

Snippets help to eliminate syntax errors by formulating code statements for you.

```
Private Sub Button1_Click(ByVal sender As Object, ByVal e As System.EventArgs) Handles Button1.Click
    If True Then

    ElseIf False Then

    Else

    End If

End Sub
```

What's in the Toolbox?

The Toolbox window, shown in Figure 2.20, contains all of the controls available to your Visual Basic applications. The controls displayed in the Toolbox vary based on what type of application you are creating and the version of .NET that the application is targeting. By dragging and dropping an icon from the Toolbox onto a Visual Basic form, you automatically add its functionality to your application. For example, in this book you will learn how to work with controls such as Label, Button, and TextBox.

FIGURE 2.20

The Toolbox window provides access to the controls with which you create windows.

The Label control allows you to place a string of text anywhere on a form. The Button control allows you to add as many buttons to your form as you need. You can then customize the appearance of each button and add code to it to make your application perform a specific task whenever the user clicks on it. The TextBox field collects text input directly from users. These are just a few of the dozens of controls that are available to you.

By default, the Toolbox window displays a list of controls with their names just to the right of each control. ToolBox controls are organized into groups, which you can expand or collapse by clicking on the plus or minus characters located just to the left of the group name.

TRICK   Because there are so many available controls in the Toolbox, you have to scroll down to view them all. Once you learn to identify each control by its graphic icon, you can modify the Toolbox window so that it only displays a list of icons. This enables you to view the available controls at one time with no scrolling. To set this up, right-click on the Toolbox window and select the List View option from the drop-down menu that appears. Also, if you forget what a given control icon represents, just place you cursor over it and its name is displayed as a ToolTip.

There isn't enough space in this book to cover every Visual Basic 2008 Express feature, such as all of the ToolBox controls. However, rest assured that as you work your way through this book, you'll learn how to work with a lot of other controls.

TRICK   Visual Basic provides access to more controls than are displayed by default in the Toolbox. You can view these additional controls and add them to the Toolbox as necessary by right-clicking on the Toolbox and selecting Choose Items. This opens the Choose Toolbox Items dialog box where you will find additional controls listed on three tabs. The first tab is .NET Framework Components. It stores controls that are designed to work with the .NET Framework. The second tab is listed as COM Components. The controls listed here are legacy controls for which .NET-equivalent controls have yet to be developed. The third tab provides access to additional controls that work with WPF applications. To add a control, select it and click on OK.

Working with Solution Explorer

Solution Explorer displays the projects and files that make up your Visual Basic applications. Solution Explorer organizes its contents in a hierarchical format, starting with the solution, followed by its member's projects, and then all the files that make up those projects, as demonstrated in Figure 2.21.

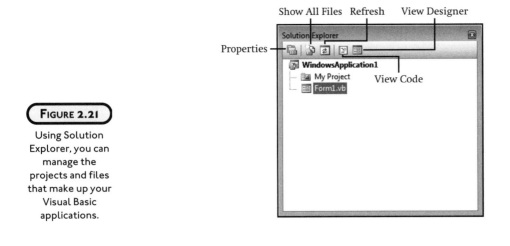

FIGURE 2.21

Using Solution Explorer, you can manage the projects and files that make up your Visual Basic applications.

You can also use the Solution Explorer to locate and open a file by double-clicking on it. If you select a file that is associated with both the form designer and code editor, you can select which tool you want to work with by clicking on the appropriate icon, as shown in Figure 2.21.

 **DEFINITION** A Visual Basic s*olution* is a container that stores all the projects that make up your Visual Basic applications. In the case of the Joke Machine game, the entire application consisted of a single project. More complex applications may be made up of more than one project.

Understanding How to Use the Properties Window

Properties are a key component in the development of any Visual Basic application. By specifying the values assigned to a form using the Properties window, you are able to specify its initial appearance and behavior. Later, in your program code, you can modify the value of many properties and dynamically change them as your application executes.

Every control that you can place on a form when creating your application's graphical interface also has its own collection of properties. By setting property values associated with a control, you can specify control text, size, color, location, and behavior.

You have already seen how to work with control properties back in Chapter 1 when you created the Joke Machine. All you have to do is select a control and its associated properties are automatically displayed in the Properties window, as demonstrated in Figure 2.22.

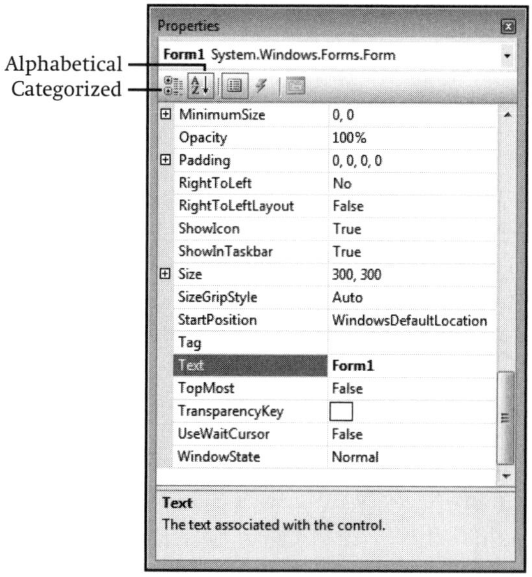

Alphabetical ─
Categorized ─

Properties	
Form1 System.Windows.Forms.Form	

⊞	MinimumSize	0, 0
	Opacity	100%
⊞	Padding	0, 0, 0, 0
	RightToLeft	No
	RightToLeftLayout	False
	ShowIcon	True
	ShowInTaskbar	True
⊞	Size	300, 300
	SizeGripStyle	Auto
	StartPosition	WindowsDefaultLocation
	Tag	
	Text	Form1
	TopMost	False
	TransparencyKey	
	UseWaitCursor	False
	WindowState	Normal

Text
The text associated with the control.

FIGURE 2.22

Examining the properties associated with a Form.

As you can see, the name of each property is shown in the left-hand column of the window, and any values assigned to those properties are shown in the right-hand column.

By default, the Visual Basic IDE organizes the display of properties by category. This assists you in finding the right properties to modify when you are not sure what the name of the property you are looking for is but you have a good idea as to what category it belongs. However, as you become more comfortable with Visual Basic programming, you may find that you prefer to have control properties listed alphabetically, so that you can quickly scroll down and locate the one that you know you are looking for. You can switch between category and sort view by clicking on either the Categorized or Alphabetic icons located at the top of the Properties window, as shown in Figure 2.22.

For most controls, all that you have to do to modify one of their associated properties is to type a new value for it in the Properties window. However, some properties have a finite number of available values. When this is the case, an iconic arrow is displayed when you select the properties. For example, as demonstrated in Figure 2.23, only two possible values are available for the Button control's Enabled property (True or False).

FIGURE 2.23

When only a finite number of values are available for a property, the Properties window displays them in a drop-down list for your selection.

For some properties, such as the Font property, you'll notice that when you select them, three ellipses are displayed in the value field. When you click on the ellipses, a dialog appears, from which you can select the appropriate value. For example, Figure 2.24 shows the dialog that appears when you want to modify the values associated with the Font property.

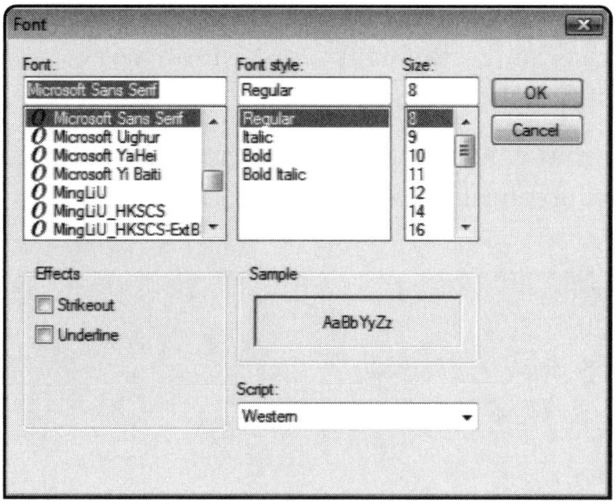

FIGURE 2.24

Sometimes you will be presented with an additional dialog from which you can select the values that you want to assign to a given property.

TRICK You can edit most, but not all, of the properties belonging to a given object at design time, which is when you are developing your application using the IDE. However, some properties are only available at run-time, which is not until your application has been finished, saved, and then executed. For example, the font type and size associated with a control is always available at design time, whereas the text entry for a control that holds user input, such as a TextBox control, won't be available until your application is running. You cannot, therefore, set properties only available at run-time from within the Properties window at design time.

The Component Tray

Most of the controls on the Toolbox work by copying an instance of the control onto a Visual Basic form. Once added to a form, you can modify the control and access its properties. However, some controls don't actually appear on your forms when you add them because they don't take a visual form that users can see and interact with. Perhaps the best example of this type of control is the Timer control.

A Timer control provides the ability to trigger activity at certain time intervals. For example, the Click Race game that you will learn how to create later in this chapter uses a Timer control to limit the amount of time that the player has to play the game. So if the Timer control does not appear on a form, how can you see that you have successfully added it to your application, and how do you access its properties at development time? The answer is by using a component tray located at the bottom of the form designer.

Any time that you add a control that cannot appear on a form, Visual Basic automatically displays it in a component tray, as demonstrated in Figure 2.25.

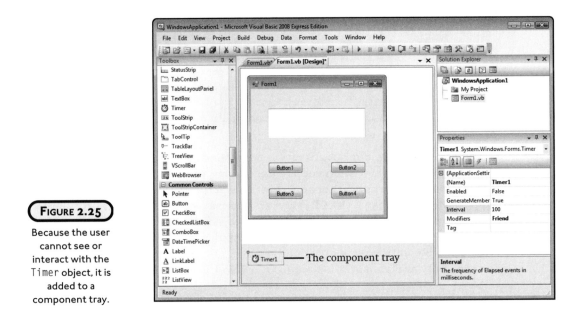

FIGURE 2.25

Because the user cannot see or interact with the Timer object, it is added to a component tray.

As you can see in Figure 2.25, the Timer control has been added to the form. You can now select it and set its Properties just like any other control that you can add to a Visual Basic form.

Other Windows

There are a number of other IDE windows available to you as you develop your Visual Basic applications. Some are very specialized, and you will only need to work with them at certain times. For example, the Error List window automatically appears if you attempt to run a program with an error in it within the IDE. Table 2.1 lists these other windows, which are discussed, where relevant, in later chapters.

TABLE 2.1 ADDITIONAL IDE WINDOWS	
Windows	**Description**
Database Explorer	Provides the ability to look for databases
Object Browser	Provides the ability to view objects and their members
Error List	Displays information about errors that occur when testing your applications
Immediate	Provides the ability to issue commands and test expressions while testing your applications
Task List	Displays tasks that Visual Basic identifies as needing to be done

IDE COMPONENTS SPECIFIC TO WPF APPLICATIONS

As previously explained, in addition to Windows Forms Applications, Visual Basic 2008 Express supports a second type of graphical application known as a Windows Presentation Foundation or a WPF application. WPF applications have graphical user interfaces and look and run like Windows Forms applications. However, they are created using a different collection of internal source libraries that leverage the power of DirectX to provide WPF applications with the ability to better integrate sound, video, and graphics.

Since WPF applications do not rely on Windows forms, their application interfaces are not created using the Forms Designer. Instead, WPF application GUIs are created using a new combined designer surface window with an integrated XAML editor. This new design reflects a new methodology in which interface design and application logic are kept separate.

As Figure 2.26 demonstrates, like Windows Forms Applications, new WPF applications begin with a blank window. You can change the size of the window using the slider control located in the upper-right corner of the designer surface window. Moving the slider up increases the windows size and moving the slider down reduces the size of the window. Below the designer surface is an XAML editor.

As Figure 2.27 demonstrates, you can build application interfaces by dragging and dropping controls from the Toolbox onto the application's window. When you do, graphical indicators are automatically displayed, assisting you in properly positioning interface controls. Note that in Figure 2.27 a TextBox control has been added, which is immediately reflected by the addition of a code statement in the XAML file.

 **DEFINITION**   XAML stands for Extensible Application Markup Language and is pronounced "zammel." XAML is an XML-based markup language that is used to define an application's graphical user interface.

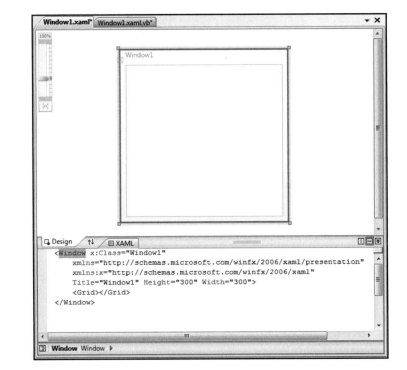

FIGURE 2.26

All WPF applications begin with a single window.

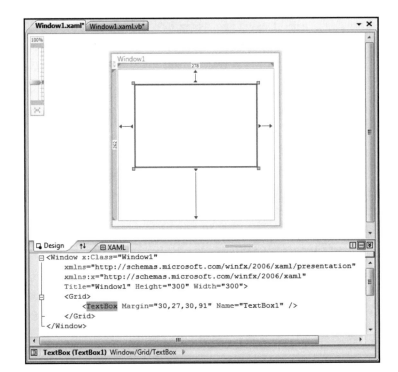

FIGURE 2.27

Changes made to the window are immediately reflected by changes to the XAML code shown beneath.

Figure 2.28 shows how the XAML file looks when a second Button control is added to the application.

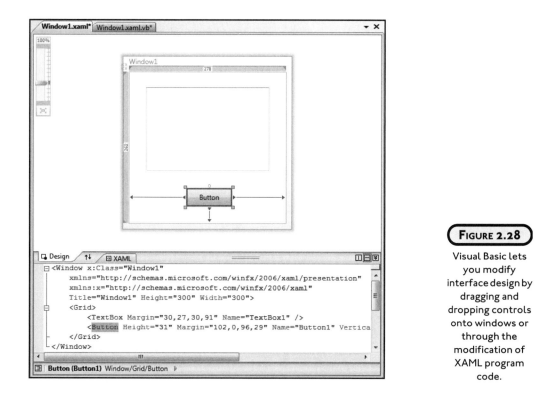

Again, you will see that a new XAML statement has been added to the application's XAML file. If you prefer, you can modify an application's interface by modifying a WPF application's XAML new code statements. By defining the instructions required to generate the application's interface within XAML, the application's interface can easily be modified and changed (by replacing its XAML file). In this manner, it is possible to separate the development of the interface from the underlying programming logic.

As you have probably realized, XAML is a complex markup language that takes time and practice to learn. A detailed examination of XAML is beyond the scope of this book. As such, all of the WPF examples that you see in this book will focus on the development of WPF applications created by dragging and dropping controls onto application windows.

BACK TO THE CLICK RACE GAME

In the Click Race game, which is created as a Windows Forms Application, the player is required to click on two buttons as many times as possible to score points in a 30-second period. However, in order to rack up points, the player must click on one button and then the other button before returning to click on the first button. Therefore, the game requires that the player be not only quick with the mouse button, but also quick and precise in moving the mouse around.

Designing the Game

The Click Race game is played on a single window. It is made up of a form and six controls shown in Table 2.2.

TABLE 2.2 FORM CONTROLS FOR THE CLICK RACE GAME	
Control	**Description**
TextBox1	Displays the number of valid mouse clicks
Label1	Descriptive label for the text box
Button1	One of two game buttons
Button2	One of two game buttons
Button3	Button used to start game play
Button4	Button used to close the game
Timer1	Timer control used to control the length of a game

Step 1: Creating a New Visual Basic Project

The first step in creating the Click Race game is to start Visual Basic and open a new Windows Forms Application project.

1. If you have not already done so, start up Visual Basic 2008 Express and then click on File and select New Project. The New Project dialog will appear.
2. Click on the Windows Form Application icon.
3. Next, type **Click Race** as the name of your new application in the Name field located at the bottom of the New Project window.
4. Click on OK to close the New Project dialog.

Visual Basic will now create a new project, including an initial form, in its IDE.

Step 2: Creating the User Interface

Now it is time to add the controls required to assemble the game's interface. The overall layout of the game's interface is shown in Figure 2.29.

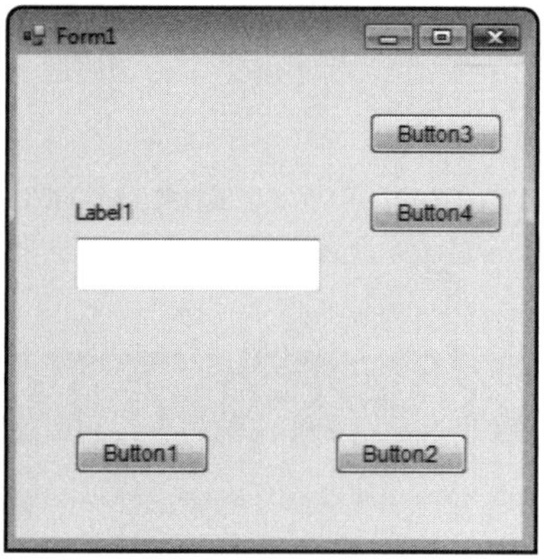

FIGURE 2.29

Completing the interface design for the Click Race game.

1. Let's begin by adding a TextBox to the form. By default, Visual Basic assigns the name Textbox1 to the control.
2. Then let's add a Label, which Visual Basic automatically names Label1, to the form.
3. Move and resize TextBox1 and Label1 to the approximate location shown in Figure 2.29.
4. Add the first button to the form and place it in the lower-left corner. Visual Basic assigns it the name Button1.
5. Add the second button to the lower-right corner. Visual Basic assigns it the name Button2.

TRAP It is important that you not get the buttons mixed up. You will need to know which button is which when it is time to begin adding code to the application.

6. Then add the third button to the upper-right corner of the form. Visual Basic assigns it the name Button3.
7. Next, add a fourth button just beneath it. Visual Basic assigns it the name Button4.
8. Finally, add a Timer control to your form, which Visual Basic names Timer1. Since the user doesn't interact directly with the timer, the Timer1 control is displayed in the component tray rather than on the main form.

The layout and design of your Visual Basic form is now complete and should look like the example shown in Figure 2.29, except that the Timer1 control is displayed in a component tray just below the form.

Step 3: Customizing Form and Control Properties

Before you start customizing the properties associated with the controls that you just added to the form, let's change one of the properties belonging to the form itself. Specifically, let's modify the form so that it displays the text string of Click Race Game in its title bar. To do this, click anywhere on the form, except on top of one of its controls, and then locate the Text property in the Properties window and replace the default value of Form1 with Click Race Game.

The first control to modify is the Textbox1 control. Table 2.3 lists all of the properties that you should modify and shows what their new values should be.

TABLE 2.3 PROPERTY CHANGES FOR THE TEXTBOX1 CONTROL	
Property	**Value**
BackColor	Info
ForeColor	HotTrack (on the System Tab)
ReadOnly	True
Font	Arial
Font	Regular
Font	Size 14
Size	132, 29

Once you have completed making the property changes for the TextBox1 control, let's work on the Label1 control by making the property changes shown in Table 2.4.

TABLE 2.4 PROPERTY CHANGES FOR THE LABEL1 CONTROL	
Property	**Value**
Font	Arial
Font	Bold
Font	Size 12
Text	Number of Clicks

Now, referring to Table 2.5, modify the properties associated with Button1, Button2, Button3, and Button4.

TABLE 2.5	PROPERTY CHANGES FOR THE BUTTON CONTROLS	
Button Name	**Property**	**Value**
Button1	Text	Click Me!
	Font	Arial
	Font	Regular
	Font	Size 9
Button2	Text	Click Me!
	Font	Arial
	Font	Regular
	Font	Size 9
Button3	Text	Start Game
	Font	Arial
	Font	Regular
	Font	Size 9
Button4	Text	Exit
	Font	Arial
	Font	Regular
	Font	Size 9

There is one last property modification that needs to be made. It is to the Timer1 control located in the component tray. By default, the Timer1 control's Interval property is set to 100 by Visual Basic at design time. Interval represents the amount of time in milliseconds that passes during each interval measured by the Timer control. It is a lot easier for people to think in terms of seconds than in terms of milliseconds. So let's change the value assigned to Interval1 to 1000 as shown in Table 2.6.

TABLE 2.6	PROPERTY CHANGES FOR THE TIMER1 CONTROL
Property	**Value**
Interval	1000

That's all the property modifications that are required for the Click Race game. Now it is time to give life to the application by adding the programming code that will make the game run.

Step 4: Adding a Little Programming Logic

Okay, it is time to start coding. If you double-click on Form1, Visual Basic starts things off for you by adding a number of lines of code, as shown next. Actually, what you'll see in the code editor window is slightly different from what you see here. Take a look at the end of the second line of code shown below. Notice that it ends with the underscore character. In Visual Basic, the underscore character is used as a continuation character. I added it where I did so that I could make the code statement a little easier to read by breaking it out into two lines. Other than this cosmetic change, everything else is exactly the same.

```
Public Class Form1

    Private Sub Form1_Load(ByVal sender As System.Object, _
        ByVal e As System.EventArgs) Handles MyBase.Load

    End Sub

End Class
```

Visual Basic 2008 Express is an OOP (object-oriented programming) language. In order to work with an object, you must define an instance of the object in your application. In the case of the above code, in the first statement, Visual Basic defines an object named Form1 on your behalf, which extracts everything it needs from the Visual Basic Class Library. All code for the Form1 object or any of the controls that you have added to the form is placed somewhere after the Public Class Form1 statement and before the closing End Class statement. These two statements define the beginning and end of the code affecting the Form1 object.

TRICK

In between the Public Class Form1 statement and the End Class statement are two more statements. These statements identify the beginning and end of the Form1_Load event procedure. Take a look at the first of these two statements and you will see that the first statement assigns the procedure the name Form1_Load. You can change the name of the procedure to anything that makes sense to you.

The Load keyword refers to the form's Load event. Events occur in Visual Basic whenever something happens. For example, when a form first appears or loads, the Load event for that form executes. Therefore, this procedure executes when the application starts (for example, when the form first loads). Don't worry if this explanation is a little difficult to grasp just yet. I shared it with you now just to try to give you a feel for what Visual Basic is doing. I'll go over procedures and events in much more detail in later chapters.

Now it is time to begin adding code to the Click Race game. Again, since you won't start learning how to formulate Visual Basic statements until Chapter 4, "Working with Menus and Toolbars," just follow along and make sure that you enter any Visual Basic statements exactly as I'll show you.

For starters, add the two statements shown below in bold exactly where shown. These statements define two variables that the application will use to keep track of how many times the player has clicked on the game's buttons and how long the game has been running.

```
Public Class Form1

    Dim intCounter As Integer = 0
    Dim intTimerCount As Integer = 0

    Private Sub Form1_Load(ByVal sender As System.Object, _
       ByVal e As System.EventArgs) Handles MyBase.Load

    End Sub

End Class
```

Next, add the two statements shown below in bold in the Form1_Load procedure. These statements execute as soon as the form loads and gray out the two buttons used to play the game.

```
Public Class Form1

    Dim intCounter As Integer = 0
    Dim intTimerCount As Integer = 0

    Private Sub Form1_Load(ByVal sender As System.Object, _
       ByVal e As System.EventArgs) Handles MyBase.Load

        Button1.Enabled = False
        Button2.Enabled = False

    End Sub

End Class
```

Now click on the Form1.vb [Design] tab to return to the designer view and then double-click on Button1. This switches you right back to the code editor, where you will see that Visual Basic has added a new procedure named Button1_Click. Add the four statements shown below in bold to this procedure exactly as shown. The first statement adds a value of 1 to the intCounter variable, which the game uses to track the total number of mouse clicks made by the player. The second statement displays the value of intCounter in the Textbox1 control so that the player will know that a click has been counted. The next two statements gray out or disable Button1 and enable Button2 (because the game forces the player to alternate the clicking of these two buttons).

```
Private Sub Button1_Click(ByVal sender As System.Object, _
    ByVal e As System.EventArgs) Handles Button1.Click

    intCounter = intCounter + 1
    TextBox1.Text = intCounter
    Button1.Enabled = False
    Button2.Enabled = True

End Sub
```

Now click on the Form1.vb [Design] tab to return to the designer view and then double-click on Button2. This switches you back to the code editor. You'll notice that Visual Basic has added a new procedure named Button2_Click. Add the four statements shown below in bold to this procedure. As you can see, these statements look almost exactly like the four statements that you added to the previous procedure, except that the last two statements switch the enabling and disabling of the two game buttons.

```
Private Sub Button2_Click(ByVal sender As System.Object, _
    ByVal e As System.EventArgs) Handles Button2.Click

    intCounter = intCounter + 1
    TextBox1.Text = intCounter
    Button1.Enabled = True
    Button2.Enabled = False

End Sub
```

Now it is time to add some code to the game's Start button (Button3). Start by clicking on the Form1.vb [Design] tab to return to the designer view and then double-click on Button3. This switches you back to the code editor. You'll notice that Visual Basic has added a new procedure named Button3_Click. Add the six statements exactly as shown below to this procedure. This procedure is used to start or restart the game at any time. The first two statements reset the values assigned to the game's two variables back to zero. The next statement clears out Textbox1. Two statements that follow enable Button1 and disable Button2. The last statement restarts the Timer1 control.

```
Private Sub Button3_Click(ByVal sender As System.Object, _
   ByVal e As System.EventArgs) Handles Button3.Click

    intCounter = 0
    intTimerCount = 0
    TextBox1.Text = ""
    Button1.Enabled = True
    Button2.Enabled = False
    Timer1.Enabled = True


End Sub
```

Now let's fix up the Exit button (Button4) so that it will close the Click Race game when the player clicks on it. Click on the Form1.vb [Design] tab to return to the designer view and then double-click on Button3. This switches you back to the code editor, where you'll see that Visual Basic has added a new procedure named Button4_Click. Add the following statement to it, shown in bold, exactly as shown next. This statement tells Visual Basic to exit the application.

```
Private Sub Button4_Click(ByVal sender As System.Object, _
   ByVal e As System.EventArgs) Handles Button4.Click


    Application.Exit


End Sub
```

Now all that is left to do is to add some code to the Timer1 control so that it will limit the player's turn to 30 seconds. Click on the Form1.vb [Design] tab to return to the designer view. Double-click on Timer1. Visual Basic automatically adds the Timer1_Tick procedure to your application. Add the five Visual Basic statements shown below in bold to this procedure. The first statement tells the Timer1 control to keep track of the number of seconds that it has run. Remember that you previously configured the Timer1 object's Interval property so that the Timer1 control would execute every second. The next four statements will execute as soon as the Timer1 control has run for 30 seconds, at which time the two game buttons will be disabled, thus ending the player's turn.

```
Private Sub Timer1_Tick(ByVal sender As System.Object, _
   ByVal e As System.EventArgs) Handles Timer1.Tick

    intTimerCount = intTimerCount + 1

    If intTimerCount = 30 Then
      Button1.Enabled = False
      Button2.Enabled = False
    End If

End Sub
```

Step 5: Testing the Execution of the Click Race Game

Okay, that's it. The Click Race game should be ready to go. Try running it by pressing the F5 key. If any errors occur, double-check the code statements that you added to make sure that you did not make any typos.

SUMMARY

This chapter provided detailed coverage of the most commonly used windows in the Visual Basic 2008 Express IDE. This included learning how to work with its menu and toolbars. You also learned how to work with the form designer and the code editor. In addition, you learned about IntelliSense and how to use it effectively. On top of all this, the chapter provided additional information on how to work with and take advantage of the Toolbox, Solution Explorer, and Properties windows.

Before you move on to Chapter 3, "Creating an Application Interface," take a few minutes to further improve the Click Race game by implementing the following challenges.

CHALLENGES

1. Spice up the Click Race game by redecorating it a bit. For example, play around with the background and foreground colors of the form and other controls to create a color scheme that is more to your personal liking.

2. If you place the cursor over one of the edges of the Click Race game's window, you can resize it, resulting in a less-than-attractive result. Prevent this behavior by locking the

dimensions of the window into place. (Hint: Click on the form and set the FormBorderStyle property equal to one of the "Fixed" border styles in the drop-down list that appears.)

3. As it is currently written, the Timer1 control keeps on ticking after the player's turn ends. This is OK because the Timer1 control is restarted as soon as the player clicks on Start again. However, allowing the Timer1 to keep running does waste CPU processing cycles. It would be more efficient if you had the Timer1 control disable itself at the end of the player's turn. (Hint: Add Timer1.Enabled = False as the last statement in the Timer1_Tick procedure.)

4. Make the game a little slicker by adding a Textbox that displays the amount of time that the player has left as the game progresses. (Hint: Add a TextBox to the form.) Make sure it is named TextBox2 and then modify the code associated with the Timer1 control as shown below in bold.

```
Private Sub Timer1_Tick(ByVal sender As System.Object, _
   ByVal e As System.EventArgs) Handles Timer1.Tick

       intTimerCount = intTimerCount + 1

       If intTimerCount = 30 Then
           Button1.Enabled = False
           Button2.Enabled = False
           Timer1.Enabled = False
       End If

       TextBox2.Text = intTimerCount

End Sub
```

CREATING AN APPLICATION INTERFACE

I n this chapter, you will learn how to spice up your Visual Basic application's graphical user interface. This will include learning how to create ToolTips, designing a status bar, and posting an icon representing your application in the System Tray located on the Windows taskbar. You will learn how to create WPF applications and see an example of how XMAL can be used to modify an application's interface without affecting its underlying programming code. In addition, you'll get the chance to put to practical use some of the tricks that you'll learn in this chapter's game project, the Speed Typing game.

Specifically, you will learn how to:

- Write text to a status bar and display additional information as ToolTips
- Assign an icon to your application and display that icon in the System Tray
- Use the `MessageBox.Show` method and the `InputBox` function to display messages and collect user input
- Control the tab order and specify the location where your application first appears on the user's desktop
- Specify the type of border used to frame your application windows and how to create splash screens
- Create WPF applications and provide them with different skins

Project Preview: The Speed Typing Game

In this chapter's game project, you will learn how to develop the Speed Typing game. The object of this game is to see how accurate and fast a typist the player is. The game begins by displaying a text string, which the player is then supposed to retype exactly as shown.

The player must type the string accurately. If an extra space is added between words or if a typo is made, the game calls a strike on the player. The game tests the player's typing skill using five different levels. The player gets 15 seconds to type in the text string associated with each level. To advance to the next level, the player must first successfully complete the current level. The player also gets a strike if the time runs out before the current text string is typed.

Each level is a little bit harder than the level that precedes it. The game ends when the player either successfully completes all five levels or when three strikes are accumulated. At the end of game play, the game ranks the player's skill level as beginner, intermediate, advanced, or expert. Figures 3.1 through 3.5 demonstrate the overall flow of the Speed Typing game.

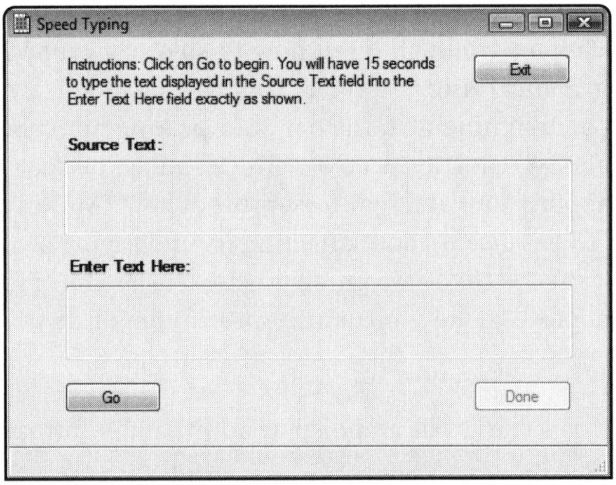

Figure 3.1

The Speed Typing game begins when the player clicks on the Go button.

Custom Icon

Status Bar

FIGURE 3.2

Players advance by typing in the required text string within the allotted amount of time.

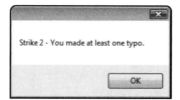

FIGURE 3.3

Players who fail to type the required text in time receive a strike.

FIGURE 3.4

Players who make a typo when keying in the required text string receive a strike.

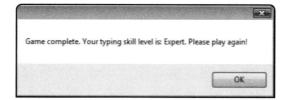

FIGURE 3.5

The player's typing skill level is analyzed and displayed at the end of game play.

By the time you have created and run this game, you'll have increased your understanding of Windows application interface design and will have had the opportunity to implement several of the graphical interface design techniques that are presented in this chapter.

PUTTING TOGETHER A GRAPHICAL USER INTERFACE

The first thing users typically see when they start up a Windows application is its graphical user interface. Today, most users have enough experience working with computers running Windows that they approach each new application with certain expectations. For starters, they expect application windows to be well organized and clearly presented. Users also expect other things, such as being able to tab between controls in a logical order and to see messages displayed in a status bar located at the bottom of windows.

The type of interface your applications have and the manner in which you assemble them varies based on application type. Windows Forms Applications are created by dragging and dropping interface controls onto forms. WPF applications can be created either by dragging and dropping controls onto forms or through the development of XAML statements that define interface design. Console applications, which run without user interaction, do not have graphical user interfaces. The rest of this chapter is devoted to demonstrating how to design and create each of these types of applications.

GUI DESIGN FOR WINDOWS FORMS APPLICATIONS

You have already seen a number of examples of how to create Windows Forms Applications and have learned the basic steps involved in adding controls and configuring their properties. Now it is time to spruce up things a bit more by learning how to control form borders and tab order, create ToolTips, add and control a status bar and an icon for your application in the System Tray, and take advantage of easily accessible built-in dialogs.

Specifying a Windows Starting Position

By default, Windows opens your Visual Basic application's windows at the location of its choice. Sometimes this is in the middle of your screen; sometimes it's not. However, if you want, you can exercise control over the screen position that Windows chooses. This is accomplished by setting the form's StartPosition property. The StartPosition property can be set to any of the values shown in Table 3.1.

Property	Description
	TABLE 3.1 VALUES SUPPORTED BY THE FORM STARTPOSITION PROPERTY
Manual	The form's Location property determines where the form is displayed, and the form's Size property specifies its bounds.
CenterScreen	The form is centered in the middle of the screen and the form's Size property specifies its bounds.
WindowsDefaultLocation	Displays the form at a location chosen by Windows but the form's Size property specifies its bounds.
WindowsDefaultBounds	Displays the form at a location chosen by Windows using bounds (size) also chosen by Windows.
CenterParent	The form is centered within the bounds of its specified parent, which could be the Windows desktop or another form in the application.

By specifying one of the values shown in Table 3.1 at design time, you can exercise various levels of control over where your form is initially displayed and in what size it will appear.

Specifying Windows Border Style

By default, Visual Basic allows users to resize a form's window border at run-time. However, this can result in some undesired consequences, as demonstrated in Figure 3.6. As you can see, once resized, the window shown in Figure 3.6 suddenly looks very unprofessional, with far too much empty space on the right-hand side of the window.

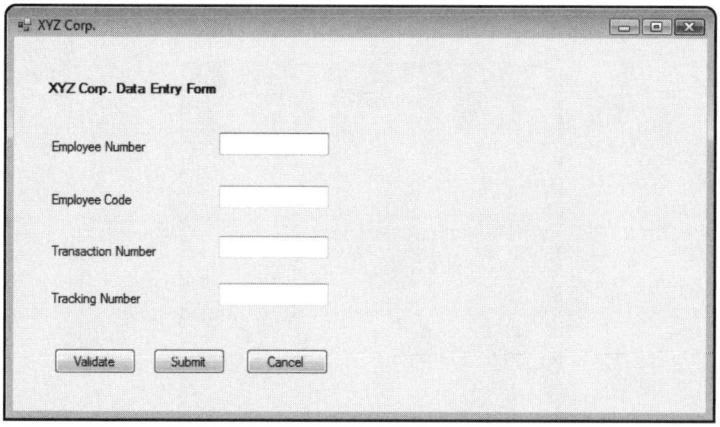

FIGURE 3.6

Unless you specify otherwise, Visual Basic will allow users to change the size of your application's window.

The easiest way to deal with this situation is to control the form's border style using the FormBorderStyle property. Table 3.2 outlines each of the available FormBorderStyle property values.

TABLE 3.2 AVAILABLE OPTIONS FOR THE FORMBORDERSTYLE PROPERTY	
Value	**Description**
None	Displays the form without a border
FixedSingle	Sets up a fixed single line form border
Fixed3D	Sets up a fixed three-dimensional form border
FixedDialog	Sets up a thick fixed form border
Sizable	Sets up a resizable border
FixedToolWindow	Sets up a tool window border that cannot be resized
SizableToolWindow	Sets up a tool window border that can be resized

 DEFINITION A *tool window* is one that does not appear in the Windows taskbar when the application is running.

Dynamically Altering Title Bar Messages

Unless you change a form's Text property, Visual Basic displays the name of the form in its title bar, as shown in Figure 3.7.

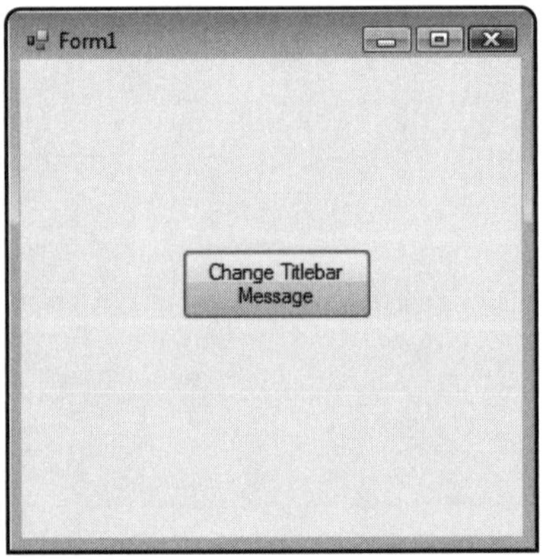

FIGURE 3.7

By default, Visual Basic displays a form's name in its title bar.

Typically, you will set the form's `Text` property to display any text string you wish using the Properties window. In addition, you can set it with code at run-time, as demonstrated here:

```
Private Sub Button1_Click(ByVal sender As System.Object, _
  ByVal e As System.EventArgs) Handles Button1.Click

        Me.Text = "Speed Typing Game"

End Sub
```

This code is associated with the click event belonging to the `Button1` control on the form. When the button is clicked, the code executes, updating the text string displayed in the title bar, as shown in Figure 3.8.

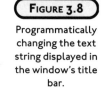

FIGURE 3.8

Programmatically changing the text string displayed in the window's title bar.

TRICK   Note the use of the keyword `Me` in the previous example. `Me` is a Visual Basic keyword that refers back to the parent object that is currently executing, which in the case of the previous example was `form1`.

By programmatically changing the text string displayed in the form's title bar using code, you create the ability to dynamically change its contents. However, you should exercise this capability very carefully. Most users don't look at the title bar, and even when they do, they don't go back and view it over and over again, so they'll miss any text changes that you have posted to it.

TRICK   If you plan to post dynamic text content, you should look at setting up a status bar on your form, as discussed later in this chapter.

Setting Up Control Tab Order and Focus

Users can interact with controls that appear on your Visual Basic applications by using their mouse to click on or select them. However, users can also use the keyboard Tab key. By repeatedly pressing the Tab key, focus is transferred from control to control. You can visually tell which control has focus by examining it. Controls such as buttons are highlighted when they receive focus, whereas controls such as textboxes display a blinking cursor.

 Focus is a term used to identify the currently selected control (the control that will receive any keyboard input).

The tab order between controls is based, by default, on the order in which you add the controls to the form. Each time you add a control to a form, it is assigned a tab index number. The first control added to the form is assigned an index number of 0, and each control that is added after that is assigned an index number that is incremented by 1. So by carefully adding controls to a form in the exact order in which you want them to be accessed via the Tab key, you can control the form's tab order. However, in most cases this option is too bothersome to try to implement. Instead, most programmers add controls in any order they want and then come back and specify the tab order.

 By default, each control's TabStop property is set to True. If you set this property to False, your application will not include the control in the tab order.

One way to modify tab order, after you have added all the controls to a form, is to set each control's TabIndex property. Specify 0 for the default control (the control that initially receives focus when the form loads) and 1 for the control that will be the next control in the tab order. However, a better way to specify tab order is to click on the View menu and select the Tab Order option. This tells the IDE to display numbers in the corner of each control representing each control's order within the tab index, as demonstrated in Figure 3.9.

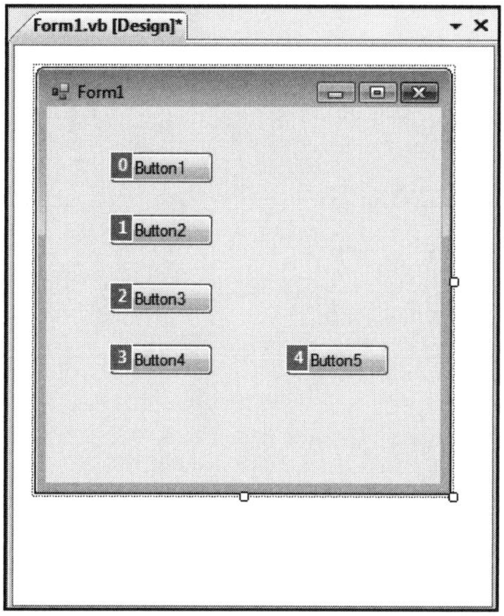

Form1.vb [Design]*   ▾ ✕

Form1   ▭ ▭ ✕

0 Button1

1 Button2

2 Button3

3 Button4   4 Button5

FIGURE 3.9

Modifying the
default tab order
of the controls
located on a Visual
Basic form.

To modify the tab order, just click on the control that should be first, followed by each remaining control in the order that you want them to be ordered. When done, click on the Tab Order option located on the View menu a second time to remove the tab order indicators.

Adding a Status Bar to Your Application

One feature that you may want to add to windows in your Visual Basic applications is a status bar. A status bar is a window control typically located at the bottom of a window where applications display all sorts of information as they run. Examples of information commonly displayed by status bars include the current date and time, help information, hints, error information, or the name of a currently open file.

TRICK   Although the IDE automatically places the status bar at the bottom of the form by default, you can move it to any edge of the form by setting the Dock property, which supports any of the following values: Right, Left, Top, Bottom, and Fill.

A status bar can display different types of data, including text and icons. Status bars can also be divided up into panels, enabling one status bar to display many different types of information, each in its own defined section of the status bar, as demonstrated in Figure 3.10.

In order to add a status bar to a window in a Visual Basic application, you must first add the StatusBar control to the Toolbox by right-clicking on the Toolbox, selecting Choose Items, and then scrolling down and selecting the StatusBar control before clicking on OK. You can then drag and drop an instance of the StatusBar control to the appropriate form. Once added, you can configure the StatusBar control by modifying any of the properties shown in Table 3.3.

TABLE 3.3   CONFIGURING PROPERTIES BELONGING TO THE STATUSBAR CONTROL

Property	Description
Text	A text string to be displayed in the status bar
SizingGrip	A visual indicator in the right-hand corner of the status bar indicating that it can be resized
Panels	Adds or removes panels from the status bar
ShowPanels	Determines whether the status bar displays panels

To get a better understanding of how to work with the StatusBar control, let's work on a couple of examples. First, let's create a status bar and write some text for it, as outlined here:

1. For starters, create a new Visual Basic application.
2. Add a Button control and a StatusBar control to your application's form.
3. Modify the button's Text property to Push me.
4. Select the StatusBar control and then modify its Text property to display the string Hello World!.

Now, press the F5 key to run your application, and you should see that Hello World! is displayed in the left-hand side of the status bar. Stop your application in order to return to design mode. Next, let's modify the application's status bar by organizing it into two panels and displaying separate pieces of information in each panel, as outlined here:

 TRAP You might want to set the StatusBar control's SizingGrip property to False if you plan on preventing users from being able to resize your application window. Otherwise, your users are going to get confused.

1. Select the StatusBar control and then set its ShowPanels property equal to True.
2. Next, select the Panels property and click on the ellipsis (...) button shown in its value field to open the StatusBarPanel Collection Editor window.
3. Click on the Add button to define the first panel. A panel named StatusBarPanel1 will be displayed in the Members pane.
4. Modify the StatusBarPanel1 object's Text property for the first panel to say Ready.
5. Modify the StatusBarPanel1 object's AutoSize property to equal Spring.
6. Click on the Add button again to define a second panel. By default, the panel will be named StatusBarPanel2.
7. Modify the StatusBarPanel2 object's Text property of the second panel to say Click on the button.
8. Modify the StatusBarPanel2 object's AutoSize property to equal Spring. At this point, the StatusBarPanel Collection Editor should look like the example shown in Figure 3.11.
9. Click on OK to close the StatusBarPanel Collection editor.

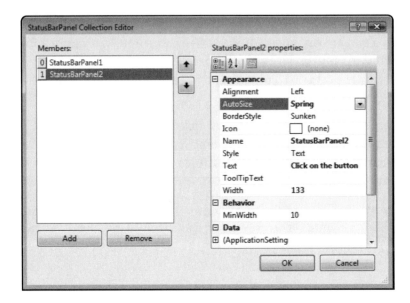

FIGURE 3.11

Using the
StatusBarPanel
Collection Editor,
you can organize a
status bar into any
number of panels.

TRICK
You can control the amount of space allocated to each status bar panel by specifying any of the following values for the AutoSize property.

- **None.** Does not display a border
- **Spring.** Shares space with other panels that have their AutoSize property set to Spring
- **Contents.** Sets panel width based on its current contents

Press F5 to run your application. Now your application's status bar displays two separate pieces of information, each in its own status bar panel. Or course, to make a status bar truly useful, most applications need to be able to dynamically change their contents as the application runs. For example, if you have defined a status bar named StatusBar1 that does not have any panels, you could add the following statement to the click event of the Button control. When clicked, the text Hello World! is displayed in the status bar.

```
Private Sub Button1_Click(ByVal sender As System.Object, _
     ByVal e As System.EventArgs) Handles Button1.Click

        StatusBar1.Text = "Hello World!"
End Sub
```

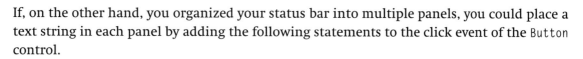

If, on the other hand, you organized your status bar into multiple panels, you could place a text string in each panel by adding the following statements to the click event of the Button control.

```
Private Sub Button1_Click(ByVal sender As System.Object, _
     ByVal e As System.EventArgs) Handles Button1.Click


        StatusBar1.Panels(0).Text = "Hello World!"
        StatusBar1.Panels(1).Text = "Today is " & Now()


End Sub
```

 TRICK Now retrieves the current date and time as set on the computer running your Visual Basic application.

As you can see in Figure 3.11, the StatusBar control organizes panels into a collection, assigning each panel in the collection an index. The first panel has an index of 0. The next panel has an index of 1, and so on. Each StatusBarPanel object in the collection is its own object and can display its own content. To write a text string to a particular panel, you must specify its index position within the collection. Figure 3.12 shows how the two-panel example from above looks after the user has clicked on the button.

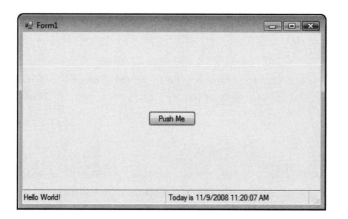

FIGURE 3.12

Status bars provide an effective tool for communicating information with users.

 TRICK If you want, you can set up your application so that it can respond when the user clicks on the status bar. This is achieved by adding whatever code you want to the Click or PanelClick events, depending on whether you have set up a simple or panel-based status bar.

```
Private Sub StatusBar1_PanelClick(ByVal sender As System.Object, _
        ByVal e As System.Windows.Forms.StatusBarPanelClickEventArgs) _
        Handles StatusBar1.PanelClick

        MessageBox.Show("Status bar has been clicked.")

End Sub
```

Posting a NotifyIcon in the System Tray

Using a `NotifyIcon` control, you can add or remove an icon representing your Visual Basic application in the System Tray, as demonstrated in Figure 3.13. By placing an icon in the System Tray, you provide the user with an alternative way of communicating with your Visual Basic applications. For example, you might want to place an icon in the System Tray in the event that an error occurs in your application when it is in a minimized state. Alternatively, you might make the icon blink in order to catch the user's attention. You can even set things up so that your application reappears when the user clicks or double-clicks on the icon.

| FIGURE 3.13 |

The Windows System Tray provides single- and double-click access to various Windows utilities, processes, and applications.

DEFINITION The *System Tray* is an area located on the far-right side of the Windows taskbar that displays icons representing active system processes, utilities, and applications.

`NotifyIcons` are implemented by adding a `NotifyIcon` control from the Toolbox onto your form. Actually, the `NotifyIcon` component will appear on the component tray, just below the IDE form designer. Once added, you can edit its properties, which include:

- **Icon.** Specifies the name and location of the icon to be displayed in the System Tray
- **Text.** Specifies text to be displayed as a ToolTip when the user moves the pointer over the icon
- **Visible.** Enables or disables the display of the icon in the System Tray

By default, the `Visible` property is set equal to `True` at design time, meaning that the application's `NotifyIcon` will be displayed as soon as your application begins to execute. You can programmatically enable the display of the `NotifyIcon` by executing the following statement where appropriate in your application code:

```
NotifyIcon1.Visible = True
```

Alternatively, you can disable the display of the `NotifyIcon` as demonstrated here:

```
NotifyIcon1.Visible = False
```

You can also set up your application to react to events, such as the `Click` and `DoubleClick` events for the `NotifyIcon`, as demonstrated here:

```
Private Sub NotifyIcon1_MouseDown(ByVal sender As System.Object, _
    ByVal e As System.Windows.Forms.MouseEventArgs) _
    Handles NotifyIcon1.MouseDown

    MessageBox.Show("The Notify Icon has been clicked.")

End Sub
```

Adding a Splash Screen to Your Application

One thing that you might want to do to spice up your application is to give it a *splash screen*. The IDE makes the creation and setup of a splash screen very straightforward. All that you have to do is create a new form and then tell the IDE to make it your application's splash screen.

 **DEFINITION** A *splash screen* is a window that appears briefly when an application first loads. Application developers use splash screens to display product information or to distract users while their application loads.

The following example demonstrates the steps involved in adding a splash screen to your Visual Basic applications.

1. Open a new Visual Basic Windows application project, and expand the default form to approximately twice its normal size to make it distinguishable from its splash screen. Place whatever controls you want on it.
2. Click on the Project menu and select the Add Windows Form option.

3. Select the Splash Screen and click on the Add button. A window named `SplashScreen1` is added to the project.

4. The IDE will display the `SplashScreen1` form. At this point you may add a `Label` control to the form and specify whatever text you want to have displayed. Optionally, you may add a `PictureBox` control to display a graphic. Visual Basic will automatically display text on the splash screen form representing your application's name, version, and copyright date. You do not need to modify this information. Visual Basic will supply this information for you.

5. Click on the Properties option located at the bottom on the Project menu. A new window will appear in the IDE.

6. Make sure that the Application tab is displayed, as shown in Figure 3.14.

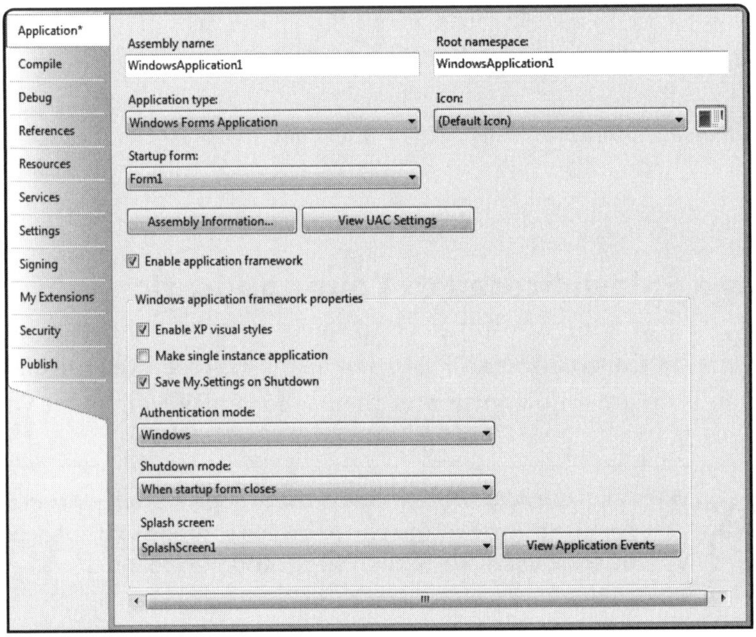

FIGURE 3.14

Configuring a
Visual Basic
application to
begin by displaying
a splash screen.

7. Using the Splash screen drop-down list at the bottom of the window, select `SplashScreen1` as your application's splash screen.

Now, close the Properties window and press F5 to run your application. Just before the main menu starts, you should briefly see your splash screen appear. After a moment, it will close and your application's main window will be displayed, as demonstrated in Figures 3.15 and 3.16.

FIGURE 3.15

A splash screen gives the application developer a chance to share additional information with the user before the application starts.

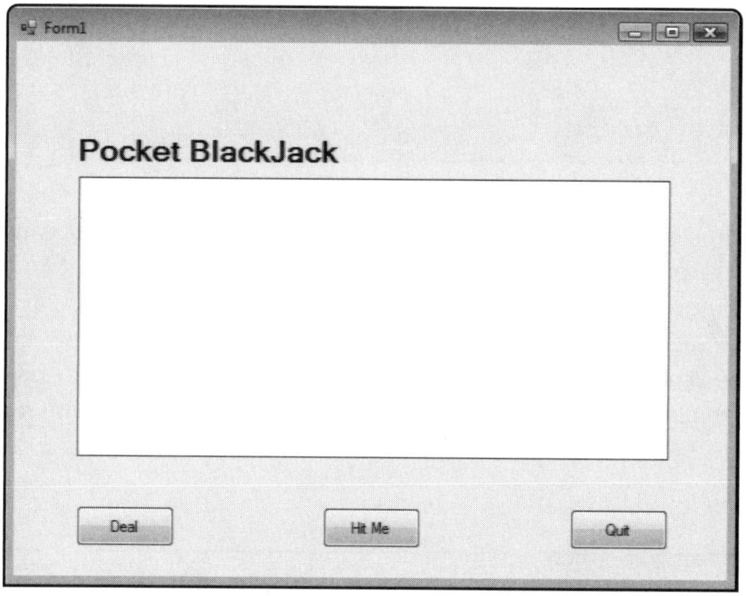

FIGURE 3.16

The application's main window appears as soon as the splash screen closes.

Leveraging the Convenience of Built-in Dialogs

In some applications, you may want to interact with and collect information from the user using more than one window. One way to accomplish this is to create additional forms and to call upon each form when needed. You've just seen one way to do this using a splash screen. You'll learn how to create and display your own custom windows in later chapters. Another option available to you is to take advantage of a couple of built-in options for displaying pop-up windows.

The MessageBox.Show Method

Sometimes all your application may need to do is ask the user a simple question. You can always add controls to a form to collect this information, or even create a new form especially for this purpose. Optionally, you may be able to collect the information you want using the MessageBox.Show method, which is made available through the .NET Framework. The MessageBox.Show method is used to display a pop-up window that contains a custom text message along with an icon and buttons.

Figure 3.17 provides an example of the kind of pop-up window the MessageBox.Show method is capable of producing. As you can see, it supports a number of different features.

Caption goes here

This is an example of the type of pop-up window that can be displayed using the MessageBox.Show method.

OK   Cancel

The MessageBox.Show method supports 21 different formats, meaning that you can pass it different information in different ways depending on what you want it to do. As a demonstration of this, look at Figure 3.18. As you can see, as soon as I typed MessageBox.Show(", IntelliSense kicked in and started offering its assistance in the formulation of the rest of the statement. Take note of the up and down arrows surrounding the 1 of 21 text at the beginning of the first line of text in the IntelliSense window. By clicking on these up and down arrows, you can scroll through and view each of the different variations of the MessageBox.Show method.

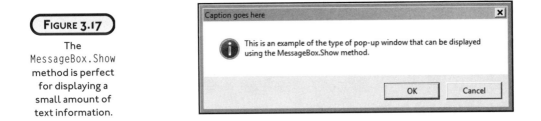

Regardless of which format of the MessageBox.Show methods you choose to use, they all require the same basic information in order to execute, as outlined in Table 3.4.

TABLE 3.4   PARAMETERS AVAILABLE TO THE MESSAGEBOX.SHOW() METHOD

Parameters	Description
Text	The text string to be displayed in the pop-up windows
Caption	The text string to be displayed in the pop-up window's title bar
Buttons	The button or group of buttons to be displayed in the pop-up window
Icon	The type of icon to be displayed in the pop-up window
DefaultButton	The button that will serve as the default button
Options	Display options that affect how the pop-up window and its text are displayed

The text and caption parameters are simply text strings. The Buttons parameter is used to specify any of six different sets of buttons, as shown in Table 3.5.

TABLE 3.5   BUTTONS AVAILABLE TO THE MESSAGEBOX.SHOW() METHOD

Button	Description
AbortRetryIgnore	Displays Abort, Retry, and Ignore buttons
OK	Displays an OK button
OKCancel	Displays an OK and a Cancel button
RetryCancel	Displays a Retry and a Cancel button
Yes/No	Display a Yes and a No button
YesNoCancel	Displays a Yes, a No, and a Cancel button

The MessageBox.Show method also allows you to display an icon to further help inform the user about the nature of the pop-up windows and the information it is trying to convey or collect. Table 3.6 identifies the various icons supported by MessageBox.Show.

TABLE 3.6 ICONS AVAILABLE TO THE MESSAGEBOX.SHOW() METHOD

Button	Description
Asterisk	Displays an Asterisk icon
Error	Displays an Error icon
Exclamation	Displays an Exclamation Mark icon
Hand	Displays a Hand icon
Information	Displays an Informational icon
None	Displays the pop-up window without displaying an icon
Question	Displays a Question Mark icon
Stop	Displays a Stop icon
Warning	Displays a Warning icon

You can also specify which button should be used as the default button. You specify which button to make the default button based on its position. Table 3.7 lists the available selections.

TABLE 3.7 DEFAULT BUTTON VALUE OPTIONS FOR THE MESSAGEBOX.SHOW() METHOD

Button	Description
Button1	Makes the first button the default
Button2	Makes the second button, if present, the default
Button3	Makes the third button, if present, the default

You can also specify any of the values listed in Table 3.8 for the Options parameter.

TABLE 3.8 OPTIONS VALUES FOR THE MESSAGEBOX.SHOW() METHOD

Button	Description
DefaultDesktopOnly	Displays the pop-up window on the active desktop
RightAlign	Displays the text in the pop-up windows as right aligned
RtlReading	Aligns text, icon and title bar right-to-left

To help make the `MessageBox.Show` method easier to understand, let's look at a few examples. In this first example, I'll create a pop-up window that asks the user a question, displaying Yes and No buttons and the Stop icon. I'll also make the Yes button the default button and right-align the message text (including the caption text).

```
Private Sub Button1_Click(ByVal sender As System.Object, _
     ByVal e As System.EventArgs) Handles Button1.Click

        MessageBox.Show("Click on Yes to continue or No to Stop.", _
          "MessageBox.Show Example 1", _
          MessageBoxButtons.YesNo, MessageBoxIcon.Stop, _
          MessageBoxDefaultButton.Button1, _
          MessageBoxOptions.RightAlign)

End Sub
```

When executed, this example generated the pop-up windows shown in Figure 3.19.

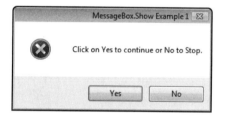

FIGURE 3.19

Prompting the user for permission to continue.

Next, let's look at an example where I'll only supply the first two parameters. As the following statements show, I only supplied the parameters for the Text and Caption.

```
Private Sub Button1_Click(ByVal sender As System.Object, _
     ByVal e As System.EventArgs) Handles Button1.Click

        MessageBox.Show("This is an informational message.", _
          "MessageBox.Show Example 2")

End Sub
```

When executed, this example generated the pop-up windows shown in Figure 3.20.

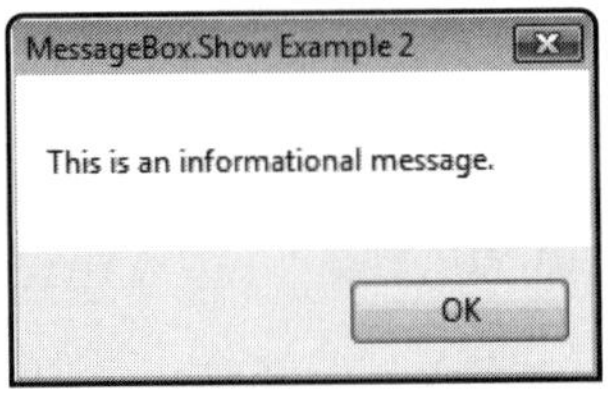

This is an informational message.

OK

FIGURE 3.20

Displaying a
simple
informational
message.

In addition to displaying informational messages for users, you can use the `MessageBox.Show` method to collect and analyze the user's response, as demonstrated in the following example.

```
Private Sub Button1_Click(ByVal sender As System.Object, _
      ByVal e As System.EventArgs) Handles Button1.Click

     Dim UserResponse As String
     UserResponse = MessageBox.Show("Please click on a button", _
       "MessageBox.Show example 3", _
       MessageBoxButtons.AbortRetryIgnore)
     MessageBox.Show("You clicked on " & UserResponse)

End Sub
```

In this example, the user is asked to click on one of the three buttons displayed by the pop-up window. A number representing the button that the user clicked is passed back and stored in a variable named `UserResponse`. A second `MessageBox.Show` method is then used to display the user's response, as shown in Figures 3.21 and 3.22.

DEFINITION A *variable* is a piece of memory where data is stored by your application as it runs.

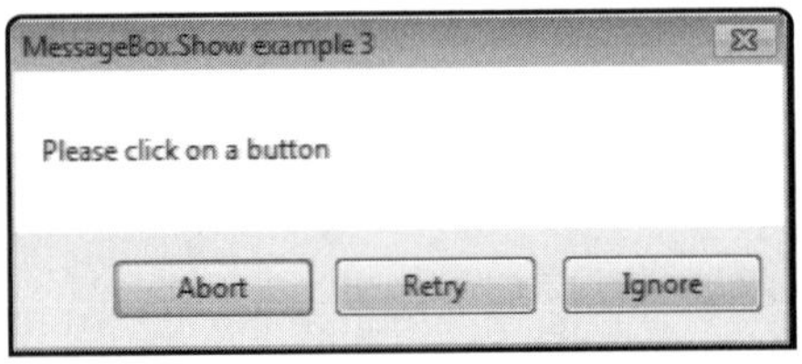

MessageBox.Show example 3

Please click on a button

Abort   Retry   Ignore

FIGURE 3.21

Prompting the
user to select
from three
options.

FIGURE 3.22

Viewing the results of the button selection made by the user.

As you can see in Figure 3.22, a numeric value was passed back representing the button that the user clicked on. Table 3.9 defines the range of values that may be returned by the MessageBox.Show method.

TABLE 3.9   RETURN VALUES ASSOCIATED WITH THE MESSAGEBOX.SHOW() METHOD

Button	Description
OK	1
Cancel	2
Abort	3
Retry	4
Ignore	5
Yes	6
No	7

TRICK   Visual Basic also supplies the MsgBox function as another tool for displaying information in a pop-up dialog. However, all of the functionality provided by the MsgBox function is already provided by the MessageBox.Show method.

The InputBox Function

Another option for interacting with the user and collecting user input is the Visual Basic InputBox function. The InputBox function provides the ability to collect text-based information from the user, as demonstrated in Figure 3.23.

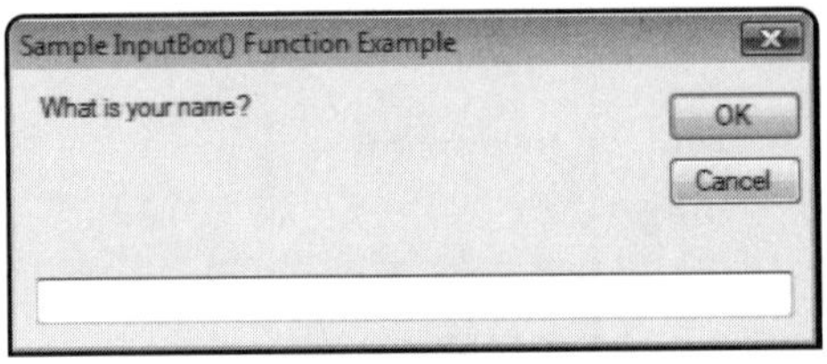

FIGURE 3.23

Examining the
composition of a
pop-up window
generated by an
InputBox
function.

The basic syntax of the InputBox function is shown here:

```
X = InputBox(TextMessage, Caption, DefaultResponse, Xpos, Ypos)
```

X is a variable used to hold the text string supplied by the user. TextMessage is a placeholder representing the text message you want to display in the pop-up window. The text message can be up to 1,024 characters long, depending on the length of the letters used. Caption is another placeholder representing the text string you want displayed in the pop-up window's title bar. XPos and YPos are used to optionally specify, in twips, the horizontal and vertical placement of the pop-up windows on the screen.

DEFINITION A *twip* is a unit of measurement approximating a value of 1/1,440th of an inch.

The following example shows the statements that were used to generate the example shown in Figure 3.23.

```
Private Sub Button1_Click(ByVal sender As System.Object, _
        ByVal e As System.EventArgs) Handles Button1.Click

    Dim UserResponse As String

    UserResponse = InputBox("What is your name?", _
        "Sample InputBox() Function Example")

End Sub
```

TRAP Once the user enters a response and clicks on the OK button, the text that was entered is assigned to the variable X. However, if the user clicks on the Cancel button without first entering text, an empty string ("") is returned.

WINDOWS FORMS VERSUS WPF APPLICATIONS

Given that Visual Basic 2008 Express supports two different types of graphical Windows applications, you are probably wondering which one is better. The answer is that it depends. Both Windows Forms and WPF have strengths and weaknesses that make them better suited to particular situations, though in many cases you can use them interchangeably with no significant differences.

Windows Forms represents the more mature technology, having been around for many years. WPF, in contrast, is new, having been made available through the instruction of .NET 3.0. Table 3.10 provides a high-level comparison of the advantages and disadvantages of both technologies.

TABLE 3.10   WINDOWS FORMS VERSUS WPF

Windows Forms	WPF
Advantages:	**Advantages:**
Provides access to the widest audience of users through its support of .NET 2.0	Supports numerous advanced features including: vector graphics, animation, 2D and 3D graphics, hardware acceleration, and skinning
Has a larger suite of controls making it better suited to RAD development	Routes graphics through DirectX (Direct3D), which offloads processing on to the computer's graphics processing unit, relieving some CPU load
Is supported by a host of third-party controls	
Disadvantages:	**Disadvantages:**
Lacks support for advanced graphics and hardware acceleration	Is still very new with limited third-party support for add-in controls
	XMAL extends the learning curve and requires additional graphics designer expertise to be able to reap full advantages of its capabilities
	Execution of WPF application is limited to Windows XP SP2, Vista, 2008, and 2003 SP1
	Does not support the full range of controls provided by Windows Forms (e.g., missing controls like `DataGrid` and `Timer`)
	Does not support RAD development as well as Windows Forms

Microsoft remains committed to supporting both Windows Forms and WPF, though you can expect WPF to evolve further over the years while Windows Forms will more or less remain in its current form. As it stands today, Windows Forms represents a great choice for any applications that do not require advanced graphic effects. WPF, on the other hand, is a good choice for any high-end graphic-oriented application.

Over time, as WPF matures and best practices and third-party support evolves, WPF will become a requirement for most advanced Visual Basic programmers to learn. Because of the book's focus on getting you up and running as quickly as possible with Visual Basic 2008 Express, it will use Windows Forms to support the development of the end of chapter game projects and will leave a detailed examination of WPF and its supporting XMAL language to other books that provide an advanced examination of Visual Basic programming.

To learn more about the differences between Windows Forms and WPF and Microsoft's ongoing support for both technologies, visit the Official Microsoft WPF and Windows Forms Site located at http://www.windowsclient.net/.

GUI DESIGN FOR WPF APPLICATIONS

Now let's take a look at how to create and design an interface for a WPF application. Excluding the development and implementation of its GUI, a WPF application is no different than a Windows Forms application. Like Windows Forms Applications, WPF application interfaces can be created by dragging and dropping controls onto them. However, one of the primary differences between WPF and Windows Forms is that WPF applications maintain a clear separation between an application's graphical front end, defined using XAML, and its underlying programming logic. As such, using a single program code base, you can easily create any number of skins, or custom interfaces, for your application.

Suppose you owned a small software development company that specialized in developing order entry systems for small businesses, promising to customize the look and feel of your application to suit each of your customer's individual tastes. Using Windows Forms, you would have to create and customize 10 copies of your application, one for each customer. If down the road, you later added an enhancement to your application, you would have to repeatedly make that same enhancement over and over again to the source code for each of the 10 customers in order to keep their application up to date. However, if you created the application using WPF instead of Windows Forms, you could use XMAL to create a unique interface design for each company while maintaining a single application with a single code base, applying each company's XAML code just before installing the application on your customer's systems.

To help make things clearer, let's create a new WPF application based on the above scenario. In this scenario, we'll assume that two people have been assigned to work on the application: you as the programmer and a graphic designer who will work on the layout of the application interface, creating a custom interface for each customer. Begin by starting Visual Basic 2008 Express and then clicking on File > New Project. When the New Project window appears, select WPF Application and then click on OK. Using drag and drop, add a Label, three Button controls, and a TextBox control to the default window, as shown in Figure 3.24.

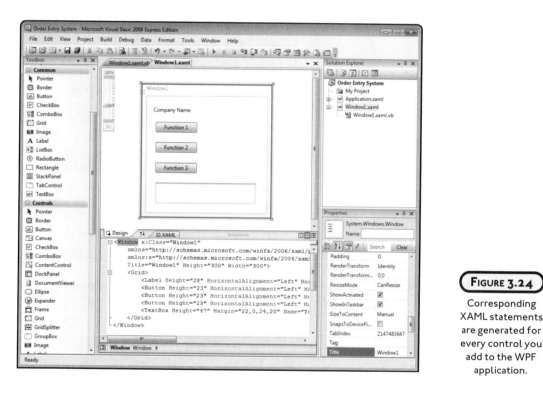

FIGURE 3.24

Corresponding XAML statements are generated for every control you add to the WPF application.

Take a look at the XAML editor located at the bottom of the screen and you will see that for each control you added, a corresponding XAML tag has been added. Now, using the Properties window, modify each of the application's controls, as shown in Figure 3.25. As you can see, as it now stands, the interface is generic in design but nonetheless functional.

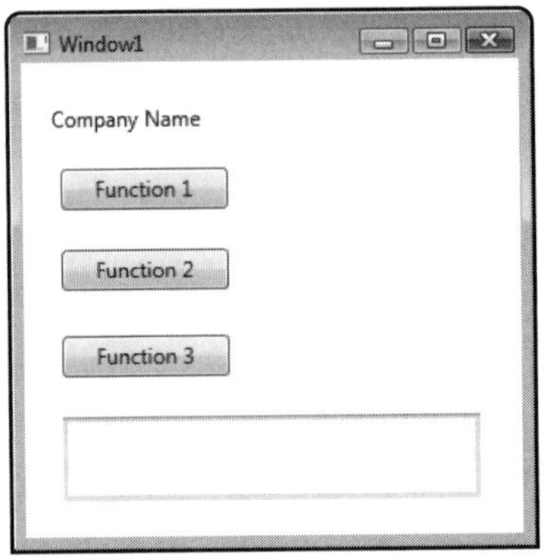

FIGURE 3.25

The initial
interface design is
functional but not
terribly intuitive.

If you prefer, you could have produced the exact same interface by copying and pasting the following XAML statements into the XAML editor.

TRICK
As demonstrated here, this means that while you, the programmer, are working on developing the internal design of the application's programming code, a graphics designer familiar with XAML would be off somewhere else designing the application GUI (provided you agree in advance on the number and type of interface controls that the application will consist of).

```
<Window x:Class="Window1"
  xmlns="http://schemas.microsoft.com/winfx/2006/xaml/presentation"
  xmlns:x="http://schemas.microsoft.com/winfx/2006/xaml"
  Title="Window1" Height="300" Width="300">
  <Grid>
    <Label Height="28" HorizontalAlignment="Left" Margin="12,18,0,0"
      Name="Label1" VerticalAlignment="Top" Width="120">Company Name
      </Label>
    <Button Height="23" HorizontalAlignment="Left" Margin="22,59,0,0"
      Name="Button1" VerticalAlignment="Top" Width="96">Function 1</Button>
    <Button Height="23" HorizontalAlignment="Left" Margin="22,104,0,0"
      Name="Button2" VerticalAlignment="Top" Width="96">Function 2</Button>
    <Button Height="23" HorizontalAlignment="Left" Margin="22,0,0,89"
      Name="Button3" VerticalAlignment="Bottom" Width="96">Function 3
      </Button>
    <TextBox Height="47" Margin="22,0,24,20" Name="TextBox1"
      VerticalAlignment="Bottom" BorderThickness="3" />
  </Grid>
</Window>
```

To really breathe life into the application, you would next have to go through the process of adding program code to the application window and the control you added to it. To do so, double-click on each of the applications three Button controls in succession and modify the source code for the application, as shown here:

```
Class Window1

    Private Sub Button1_Click(ByVal sender As System.Object, _
      ByVal e As System.Windows.RoutedEventArgs) Handles Button1.Click
        MessageBox.Show("Enter order number to create.")
        TextBox1.Text = ""
    End Sub

    Private Sub Button2_Click(ByVal sender As System.Object, _
      ByVal e As System.Windows.RoutedEventArgs) Handles Button2.Click
        MessageBox.Show("Enter order number to delete.")
        TextBox1.Text = ""
    End Sub

    Private Sub Button3_Click(ByVal sender As System.Object, _
      ByVal e As System.Windows.RoutedEventArgs) Handles Button3.Click
        TextBox1.Text = "Order Information: Bla Bla Bla"
    End Sub


End Class
```

As you can see, the first set of statements is for the first Button, the second set of statements is for the second Button, and the last set of statements shown in the program code are for the third Button. Take a moment to test the execution of this application by pressing the F5 key to start it and then click on each of the application's buttons to see how things work. When done, close the application and return back to the Visual Basic IDE.

At this point, you have a functional application with a generic interface. But to satisfy your customers, you need to modify the application's interface to suit their needs. To wrap up work on the application, you need to replace its XMAL with XMAL provided by your co-worker. For this simple example, let's assume that your co-worker has provided you with the following XMAL file:

```
<Window x:Class="Window1"
  xmlns="http://schemas.microsoft.com/winfx/2006/xaml/presentation"
  xmlns:x="http://schemas.microsoft.com/winfx/2006/xaml"
```

```
Title="ABC Order Management System" Height="300" Width="300">
<Grid>
  <Label Height="28" HorizontalAlignment="Left" Margin="12,18,0,0"
    Name="Label1" VerticalAlignment="Top" Width="120">ABC Inc.</Label>
  <Button Height="23" HorizontalAlignment="Left" Margin="22,59,0,0"
    Name="Button1" VerticalAlignment="Top" Width="96">Create Order
    </Button>
  <Button Height="23" HorizontalAlignment="Left" Margin="22,104,0,0"
    Name="Button2" VerticalAlignment="Top" Width="96">Delete order
    </Button>
  <Button Margin="0,59,24,0" Name="Button3" Height="23"
    HorizontalAlignment="Right" VerticalAlignment="Top" Width="96">
    Display Order</Button>
  <TextBox Height="82" Margin="22,0,24,20" Name="TextBox1"
    VerticalAlignment="Bottom" BorderThickness="3" />
</Grid>
</Window>
```

To set up and complete a working copy of the application for the first customer, all you have to do is copy and paste these statements over the application's existing XAML statements. Once done, you should test the application again, to make sure everything turned out as expected. Figure 3.26 provides a look at the application's new interface design. As you can see, the controls have been rearranged, resized, the label has been modified to display the company's name, and the name of the application is now displayed in the Window title bar.

FIGURE 3.26

By modifying the XAML statements used to define the application's interface, you are able to completely change its appearance.

The previous example did not make use of any advanced graphics controls, relying instead on typical ordinary interface controls like buttons, labels, and textboxes. A more professional example would probably have integrated different types of graphics, including the company's logo, thus justifying the need for your co-worker with design experience.

What this example demonstrates is that by default, the controls you use to develop WPF applications have the same look and feel as their Windows Forms counterparts. To really take advantage of WPF and its advanced interface design capabilities, you must learn a lot more about XAML and WPF than can be covered in this book.

CREATING CONSOLE APPLICATIONS USING TEXT-BASED INTERFACES

Not all applications need to interact with the user when they execute. Once started, some applications need only quietly run in the background where they perform their specified task. These types of applications are usually referred to as console applications. They run within a Windows Console window and the only type of output they can display in the console window is text. Console applications have all kinds of uses. For example, console applications can be created that perform mundane tasks like cleaning out obsolete log files on your computer. Console applications can also be used to perform a host of administrative tasks like executing systems commands that administer services, clear event logs, and set up network printer and drive connections.

Creating a console application is not much different from creating windows forms or WPF applications. You still have to provide the program code required to make the application do whatever you want it to; you just don't have to design a GUI for it. As a quick demonstration of how to create a console application, take a look at the steps outlined in the following example.

1. Open Visual Basic 2008 Express and then click on File > New Project. The New Project window appears.
2. Select the Console Application template, enter Hello World in the Name field, and then click on OK.
3. Instead of presenting you with a form or window with which to design a GUI, the code editor is displayed.
4. Add the following code statements to the code statements that were automatically generated for you, as demonstrated in Figure 3.27.

```
Console.WriteLine("Hello World!")
Console.Beep()
Console.ReadLine()
```

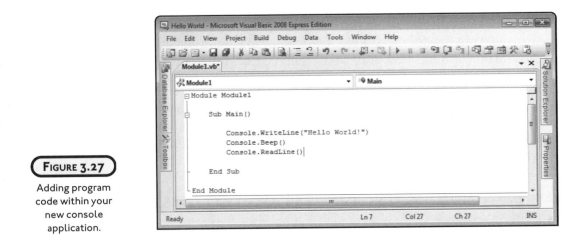

FIGURE 3.27

Adding program
code within your
new console
application.

5. Press F5 to run your console application. In a moment a Windows console should appear, as shown in Figure 3.28.

FIGURE 3.28

Running your
console
application.

6. Press the Enter key to terminate the application and close the console window.

The three statements that make up this application display a text string, play a beep sound, and then pause execution waiting for the user to press the Enter key, after which the application terminates and the console window is automatically closed. I added the third statement for the sole purpose of preventing the application from running so quickly that you might miss it. To see what I mean, delete the third statement and then execute the console application again.

ClickOnce Application Deployment

Up to this point in the book, you have executed all the Visual Basic applications that you have worked on within the Visual Basic IDE. This version of your application is sometimes referred to as the design or debug version. However, what you really want to do is create a standalone program that can be run by itself, outside of the IDE. This requires that you generate a run-time or release version of your application. Visual Basic 2008 Express makes it easy for you to create and deploy a standalone executable copy of your Visual Basic application through a feature called ClickOnce.

With ClickOnce, you can deploy your Visual Basic applications on CD-ROMs or DVDs. You can also make them available for download via websites. In addition to creating a distribution package for your application's source code, ClickOnce can also include any external files, images, video, etc, that your applications may require. You can even include a copy of .NET in your application's installer package.

When executed, installer packages using ClickOnce guide users through the process of installing your application, adding a shortcut for your application to the Programs menu. If your application has any prerequisites that the user's computer does not have, the installer will prompt the user for permission to download and install them from www.microsoft.com or any website you specify. On top of all this, once installed, your users will be able to uninstall your applications from the Windows Control Panel. Now that is cool!

To get a better understanding of how all this works, let's look at an example. The following procedure demonstrates how to use ClickOnce to create an installation CD for the Click Race game (which you created in Chapter 2).

 TRICK If you want, you may specify prerequisites for your application and configure it in a number of other ways by selecting its name in the Solution Explorer window and then clicking on the Properties button. This opens the application's properties sheet where you can select the Publish tab and then click on the Prerequisites button. From here, you specify which version of .NET needs to be installed, whether or not Microsoft Visual Basic Power Packs are needed, and so on. For each prerequisite that you select, you can then specify from where it can be downloaded in the event it is not already installed on the user's computer.

1. Begin by opening the Click Race application.
2. Rebuild the application by clicking on the Build > Build Click Race Game.
3. Click on Build > Publish Click Race Game. The Publish Wizard appears asking you to tell it where you want to publish your application.

4. Click on the Browse button and then specify the location on your computer where you would like to store a copy of the game's distribution package.

5. Click on the New Folder icon located in the upper-right corner of the window. If necessary, click on the New Folder icon located at the upper-right corner of the window to create a new subfolder. Click on the Open button to select the new subfolder.

6. Click on Finish. An installation program named setup.exe, along with additional installation files, is created in the location that you specified.

Your application is now ready for distribution. Use Windows Explorer to access the folder that contains your application's installation package. Open it and you will see contents similar to those shown in Figure 3.29.

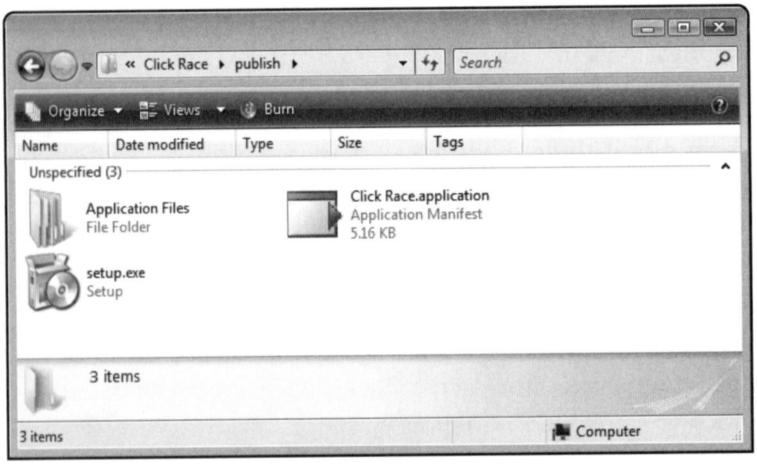

FIGURE 3.29

Reviewing the contents of your application's distribution package.

To install your application, double-click on the setup.exe file and follow the instructions that are provided. Once the install process has finished, the application should automatically start. In addition, a new application group and shortcut has been created, allowing the game to be accessed like any other Windows application. In addition, if you open the Control Panel's Uninstall a Program option, you will see that an entry has been added for your application, allowing it to be uninstalled at any time, just like any other Windows application. Once you have successfully tested the operation of your application's installation package, all that remains is for you to burn it to a CD or DVD for distribution to your family, friends, or customers.

BACK TO THE SPEED TYPING GAME

Now, let's return our attention to this chapter's game project. You will create the Speed Typing game by following the same set of steps that you have used to complete previous chapter projects. By the time you are done creating the Speed Typing game, you will have demonstrated your ability to implement many of the advanced design techniques that you learned about in this chapter.

Designing the Game

The Speed Typing game is played on a single window, comprised of one form and the 11 controls listed in Table 3.11.

TABLE 3.11	FORM CONTROLS FOR THE SPEED TYPING GAME	
Control Type	**Control Name**	**Description**
Label	lblInstructions	Displays the game's instructions
Label	lblSourceText	Identifies the Textbox field that displays the source text that the player is to copy
Label	lblEntryText	Identifies the Textbox field where the player is to type game input
Textbox	txtDisplay	Name of the Textbox control where the game's source text string will be displayed
Textbox	txtEntry	Name of the Textbox control where the player will type game input
Button	btnGo	Name of the Button control that the player will click on to start the game
Button	btnDone	Name of the Button control that the player will click on to tell the game to check the player's game input
Button	btnExit	Name of the Button control that the player will click on to end the game
Timer	tmrControl	Name of the Timer control that controls the length of game play
ToolTip	tipControl	Name of the ToolTip control that allows the game to display ToolTip messages
StatusBar	stbControl	Name of the StatusBar control used to display informational messages as the game runs

Step 1: Creating a New Visual Basic Project

The first step in developing the Speed Typing game is to start Visual Basic and open a new project using the following procedure:

1. If you have not already done so, start up Visual Basic 2008 Express and then click on File and select New Project. The New Project dialog will appear.
2. Select Windows Forms Application template.
3. Type **Speed Typing** as the name of your new application in the Name field located at the bottom of the New Project window.
4. Click on OK to close the New Project dialog.

Step 2: Creating the User Interface

Now, let's begin by adding all the controls required to put together the game's interface, which is shown in Figure 3.30.

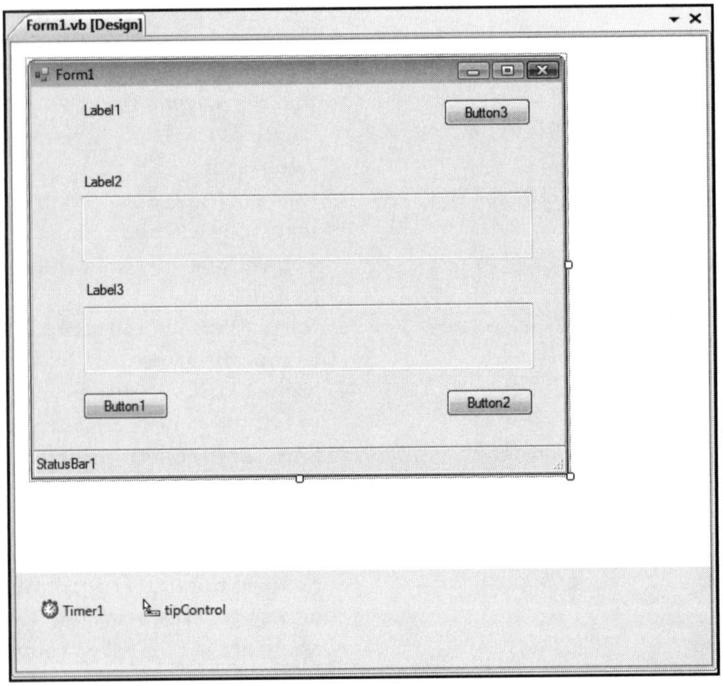

FIGURE 3.30

Completing the interface design for the Speed Typing game.

The following procedure outlines the steps involved in setting up the application's graphical user interface.

1. Add the Timer control to your form. By default it is assigned a name of Timer1 and is displayed in the component tray.
2. Add a TextBox to the form. Its default name is TextBox1. Expand and reposition it right in the middle of the form, as shown in Figure 3.30.
3. Add a second TextBox to the form. Its default name is TextBox2. Expand and reposition it under the previous TextBox control, as shown in Figure 3.30.
4. Add a Label control to the upper-left corner of the form. Its default name is Label1.
5. Add a second Label control to the form just above the first TextBox control. Its default name is Label2.
6. Add a third Label control to the form just above the second TextBox. Its default name is Label3.
7. Add a Button control to the lower-left corner of the form. Its default name is Button1.
8. Add a second Button control to the lower-right side of the form. Its default name is Button2.
9. Add a third Button control to the upper-right corner of the form. Its default name is Button3.
10. Add a StatusBar control to your form. Its default name is StatusBar1.

Step 3: Customizing Form and Control Properties

The next step in completing the Speed Typing game is to customize properties associated with the form and the controls that you have added to it. Once this is done, you'll be ready to begin adding the program statements that will make the controls perform their required tasks.

IN THE REAL WORLD

Going forward, I am going to start applying a naming convention to the controls and other programming elements within the chapter game projects. Naming conventions help to make program code easier to read and understand. Before I explain the naming convention that I plan to use, you need to know about a few rules that Visual Basic strictly enforces regarding object names and programming elements. These rules include:

- Names must begin with either an alphabetic character or the underscore character (_).
- Names can only consist of alphabetic characters, numbers, and the underscore character (_).
- Names cannot match Visual Basic keywords.

When coming up with names to assign to controls, variables, and other objects in your applications, use a consistent naming scheme. Moving forward, I'll use words that are descriptive and that help to identify what an element is. Also, I'll employ camelCase spelling. Using camelCase, you use one or more words or abbreviations to generate element names. The first word or abbreviation begins with a lowercase character, and the first letter of all remaining words or abbreviations is spelled with an uppercase character.

Working with the default names that Visual Basic assigned to form controls can be difficult. I'll assign a descriptive name to form elements that describes their function. For example, I might assign a name of btnExit to a button that is responsible for exiting an application when clicked. Similarly, I might assign a name of txtInputName to a Textbox control intended to collect a user's name.

Let's begin customizing the form and the controls that you have added to it. We'll start by modifying the Form1, changing the properties listed in Table 3.12.

TABLE 3.12 PROPERTY CHANGES FOR THE FORM

Property	Value
FormBorderStyle	FixedSingle
Icon	Icon.ico
StartPosition	CenterScreen
Text	Speed Typing

You can download a copy of Icon.ico along with the source code for this project from the book's companion website located at http://www.courseptr.com/downloads.

Next, change the Name property of the ToolTip control to tipControl. Then change the Name property of the Timer control to tmrControl and set its Interval property to 1000.

Now, modify the properties belonging to the two TextBox controls, as shown in Table 3.13.

TABLE 3.13 PROPERTY CHANGES FOR THE TEXTBOX CONTROLS

Control	Property	Value
TextBox1	Name	txtDisplay
	ReadOnly	True
	ToolTip	Displays source text string
TextBox2	Name	txtEntry
	ReadOnly	True
	ToolTip	Type your text here

Modify the properties belonging to the three Label controls as shown in Table 3.14.

TABLE 3.14 PROPERTY CHANGES FOR THE LABEL CONTROLS

Control	Property	Value
Label1	Name	lblInstructions
	Text	Instructions: Click on Go to begin. You will have 15 seconds to type the text displayed in the Source Text field into the Enter Text Here field exactly as shown.
Label2	Name	lblSourceText
	Text	Source Text:
Label3	Name	lblEntryText
	Text	Enter Text Here:

Modify the properties belonging to the three Button controls as shown in Table 3.15.

Finally, add a StatusBar control to your form and change its Name property to stbControl. These are all the control property modifications that are required for the Speed Typing game.

TABLE 3.15	PROPERTY CHANGES FOR THE BUTTON CONTROLS	
Control	**Property**	**Value**
Button1	Name	btnGo
	Text	Go
	ToolTip	Display new text string
Button2	Name	btnDone
	Text	Done
	ToolTip	Check typing
Button3	Name	btnExit
	Text	Exit
	ToolTip	Exit game

Step 4: Adding a Little Programming Logic

Now it is time to start writing code. To make the Speed Typing game work, you are going to need to add code to five places, including the btnGo, btnDone, btnExit, and tmrControl controls. In addition, you'll need to add a few lines of code to define a few variables.

TRAP Because we haven't starting dissecting the statements that make up the Visual Basic programming language yet, you may not be able to understand everything that you'll see. So as with the previous two chapters, just key in what you see and follow along. We'll begin covering Visual Basic language elements in Chapter 5, "Storing and Retrieving Data in Memory," and by Chapter 8, "Enhancing Code Structure and Organization," you should be able to return to this chapter and fully understand all the details of the Speed Typing game.

For starters, double-click on the Code View icon in the Solution Explorer. The code editor will appear. The following two lines of code will already be displayed.

```
Public Class Form1

End Class
```

Add the following three statements between these two lines of code, as shown here:

```
Public Class Form1
    Dim intWrong As Integer = 0
    Dim intCount As Integer = 0
    Dim intTimer As Integer = 0
End Class
```

These three statements define the variables that the game will use to track the number of strikes made by the player, the number of tries the player has made, and amount of time that has elapsed for each turn.

Next, switch back to the form designer and then double-click on the btnGo button. This will switch you back to the code editor, where the following new code will have been added.

```
Private Sub btnGo_Click(ByVal sender As System.Object, _
    ByVal e As System.EventArgs) Handles btnGo.Click


End Sub
```

This code identifies the beginning and ending of the program statements that execute when the user clicks on the btnGo button. Modify this portion of your application by adding the programming statements shown below between these two statements.

```
Private Sub btnGo_Click(ByVal sender As System.Object, _
    ByVal e As System.EventArgs) Handles btnGo.Click

        If intCount = 0 Then txtDisplay.Text = _
          "Once upon a time there were three little pigs."
        If intCount = 1 Then txtDisplay.Text = _
          "In days gone by times were hard but the people were strong."
        If intCount = 2 Then txtDisplay.Text = _
          "Once in a while something special happens even to the " _
          & "worst of people."
        If intCount = 3 Then txtDisplay.Text = _
          "When injustice rears its head, it is the duty of all good " _
          & "citizens to object."
        If intCount = 4 Then txtDisplay.Text = _
          "It has been said that in the end there can be only one. " _
          & "Let that one be Mighty Molly."

        btnDone.Enabled = True
        btnGo.Enabled = False
        txtEntry.ReadOnly = False
        tmrControl.Enabled = True
        intTimer = 0
        txtEntry.Focus()


End Sub
```

The first five statements check to see what turn the game is currently executing (0 – 4) and displays the appropriate text in the txtDisplay control. For example, if this is the player's first turn then "Once upon a time there were three little pigs" will be displayed.

The next two statements enable the btnDone button and disable the btnGo button. Next, the txtEntry control's ReadOnly property is set equal to True in order to allow the player to begin typing text into it. Then the tmrControl is enabled and the value of intTimer is set equal to 0. This begins the 15-second countdown sequence. Finally, the cursor is automatically placed in the txtEntry field using the control's Focus() method.

TRICK The Focus method programmatically specifies which control you want to receive focus.

Return to the form designer windows and double-click on the btnDone button. This switches you back to the code editor, where code for the btnDone control's click event has been added, as shown here:

```
Private Sub btnDone_Click(ByVal sender As System.Object, _
        ByVal e As System.EventArgs) Handles btnDone.Click


End Sub
```

Add the following statements between these two statements:

```
stbControl.Text = ""
tmrControl.Enabled = False
```

The first statement clears out any text that might be displayed in the StatusBar. The second statement disables the game's Timer control.

Next, add the following statements just beneath the previous statements.

```
If txtEntry.Text = "" Then
  MessageBox.Show("Error: You must enter something!")
  txtEntry.Text = ""
  txtDisplay.Text = ""
  btnDone.Enabled = False
  btnGo.Enabled = True
  txtEntry.ReadOnly = True
  intTimer = 0
  btnGo.Focus()
  Return
End If
```

This set of statements checks to make sure that the player has typed something into the txtEntry field. If the user has not typed anything, the indented statements contained within the opening If and closing End If statements will execute, displaying an error message and resetting all the controls back to their initial settings. Note the use of the Return statement in the preceding group of statements. The Return statement tells Visual Basic to stop processing any of the remaining statements in the btnDone control's click event. This is appropriate because there is no point to performing any further processing if the player has not typed anything.

Next, add the following statement just beneath the previous statements.

```
If txtEntry.Text = txtDisplay.Text Then
  MessageBox.Show("Match - You typed in the string correctly!")
  intCount = intCount + 1
  intTimer = 0
Else
  MessageBox.Show("Strike " & intWrong + 1 _
    & " - You made at least one typo.")
  intWrong = intWrong + 1
  intTimer = 0
End If
```

These statements check to see if the text typed by the player exactly matches the text displayed by the game. In other words, does the text string currently stored in the txtEntry control match the text string stored in the txtDisplay control? If there is a match, the MessageBox.Show method is used to inform the player, and the game adds 1 to the number of turns of levels the player has completed and resets the variable used by the timer control (to track the number of seconds that a turn has lasted) back to 0. However, if the text stored in the two controls does not match, an error message is displayed, and the game adds 1 to the number of strikes made by the player before resetting the intTimer variable back to 0.

Now add the following statements just beneath the previous statements.

```
txtEntry.Text = ""
txtDisplay.Text = ""
btnDone.Enabled = False
btnGo.Enabled = True
txtEntry.ReadOnly = True
btnGo.Focus()
```

These statements reset the form's controls back to their default settings and sets the focus back to the btnGo control, in order to prepare the game for the player's next attempt.

Add the following statements just beneath the previous statements.

```
If intWrong = 3 Then
  If intCount < 2 Then
    MessageBox.Show("Game over. Your typing skill level " _
      & "is: Beginner. Please play again!")
    intCount = 0
    intWrong = 0
    Return
  End If
  If intCount < 4 Then
    MessageBox.Show("Game over. Your typing skill level " _
      & "is: Intermediate. Please play again!")
    intCount = 0
    intWrong = 0
    Return
  End If
  If intCount < 5 Then
    MessageBox.Show("Game over. Your typing skill level " _
      & "is: Advanced. Please play again!")
    intCount = 0
    intWrong = 0
    Return
  End If
End If

If intCount = 5 Then
  MessageBox.Show("Game complete. Your typing skill level " _
    & "is: Expert. Please play again!")
  intCount = 0
  intWrong = 0
End If
```

Each time the player clicks on the btnDone button, the game checks to see if the player has struck out or if all five levels have been completed. These statements are responsible for determining whether or not the player won the game and for assigning the player's typing skill level. If the player got three strikes, or was only able to complete the first level of the game, the game assigns a skill level rating of beginner. If the player managed to complete the second or third level, a skill level of intermediate is assigned. If the player manages to complete four levels, a skill level of advanced is assigned. Finally, if the player manages to complete all five levels, a skill level of expert is assigned.

Now it's time to add code to the btnExit control, as shown here:

```
Private Sub btnExit_Click(ByVal sender As System.Object, _
    ByVal e As System.EventArgs) Handles btnExit.Click
        Application.Exit()
End Sub
```

The last control that you need to provide code for is the game's Timer control. Switch back to the form designer and then double-click on the tmrControl control. This will switch you back to the code editor where the following new code will have been added.

```
Private Sub Timer1_Tick(ByVal sender As System.Object, _
    ByVal e As System.EventArgs) Handles tmrControl.Tick


End Sub
```

Modify this section of your application by adding the following statements inside these two statements.

```
intTimer = intTimer + 1
stbControl.Text = "Seconds remaining: " & (15 - intTimer)

If intTimer = 15 Then

  intWrong = intWrong + 1
  tmrControl.Enabled = False
  stbControl.Text = ""

  MessageBox.Show("Strike " & intWrong & " - Time is up. " _
    & "Please try again.")

  txtEntry.Text = ""
  txtDisplay.Text = ""
  btnDone.Enabled = False
  btnGo.Enabled = True
  txtEntry.ReadOnly = True
```

```
btnGo.Focus()

If intWrong = 3 Then
  If intCount < 2 Then
    MessageBox.Show("Game over. Your typing skill " _
       & "level is: Beginner. Please play again!")
    intCount = 0
    intWrong = 0
    Return
  End If
  If intCount < 4 Then
    MessageBox.Show("Game over. Your typing skill " _
       & "level is: Intermediate. Please play again!")
    intCount = 0
    intWrong = 0
    Return
  End If
  If intCount < 5 Then
    MessageBox.Show("Game over. Your typing skill " _
       & "level is: Advanced. Please play again!")
    intCount = 0
    intWrong = 0
    Return
  End If
End If

If intCount = 5 Then
  MessageBox.Show("Game complete. Your typing skill " _
     & "level is: Expert. Please play again!")
  intCount = 0
  intWrong = 0
End If

End If
```

The first statement adds 1 to the variable used by the Timer control to track the number of seconds that the current play has lasted. The second statement displays this information in the status bar located at the bottom of the window. The Timer control automatically executes every second. In its third statement, it checks to see if the 15 seconds have passed. If this is the case, it declares a strike by adding 1 to the variable used to track the number of failed attempts. The Timer control then disables itself, clears out any text displayed on the status bar, and uses the MessageBox.Show method to tell the player that time has expired.

The rest of the code that you added to the tmrControl control's click event checks to see if the game is over and assigns a skill level to the player using the same logic that you previously added to the btnDone control's click event.

Step 5: Testing the Execution of the Speed Typing Game

Okay, that's it. The Speed Typing game should be ready to go. Press F5 to give it a try. If any errors occur, go back and double-check the code statements that you added to make sure that you did not make any typos.

SUMMARY

In this chapter, you learned a great deal about how to jazz up your Windows application interfaces. This included learning how to implement a number of standard Windows features, such as status bars, ToolTips, customized icons, and System Tray icons. You also learned how to control where Windows opens your applications and the border style of your application windows. On top of all this, you learned how to work with the MessageBox.Show method and the InputBox function as well as learning how to create splash screens.

Now, before you move on to Chapter 4, take a few minutes and enhance the Speed Typing game by implementing the following challenges.

CHALLENGES

1. For starters, add additional levels to the game, making sure that each additional level is more challenging than the one that precedes it.
2. Modify the game so that it displays an icon in the System Tray whenever it is minimized. Provide the ability to redisplay the game when the player clicks on its System Tray icon.
3. Create a splash screen for the game and use the PictureBox control to include a suitable graphic image.

WORKING WITH
MENUS AND TOOLBARS

In this chapter, you will learn how to enhance your Visual Basic applications by adding professional-looking menus and toolbars. You will learn how to create menus and populate them with menu items. You will also learn how to create submenus and execute program code when users click on menu items. This chapter will show you how to make your menu systems easier to work with by adding shortcuts and access keys. You will also learn how to enable and disable menu items as well as how to make them appear and disappear. In addition to all this, this chapter will show you how to create context menus for specific controls and how to provide easy access to your application's most commonly used commands using toolbars. Finally, you will get the chance to get some hands-on experience with menus through the completion of this chapter's game project, the Lottery Assistant game.

Specifically, you will learn how to:

- Add a menu system to your application
- Add shortcuts and access keys to menu items
- Control when users can access menu items
- Create context menus for individual controls
- Add toolbars to your applications

PROJECT PREVIEW: THE LOTTERY ASSISTANT GAME

In this chapter, you will learn how to create a Visual Basic game called the Lottery Assistant that is designed to assist users in generating a list of randomly selected lottery numbers. Players will have control over a number of game settings, including the size of the font used to display game output and the game window's background color.

Different lottery games require the selection of numbers from various ranges. For example, one lottery game may require the selection of numbers in the range of 1 to 44, whereas another may set the range as 1 to 50. In addition, lottery games vary in the quantity of lottery numbers that must be selected to play. For example, for some games you may need to select five numbers, and for other games you might be required to pick six numbers. Therefore, the Lottery Assistant game provides players with the ability to specify:

- The range of numbers
- The quantity of lottery numbers required
- How many sets of lottery numbers they want generated

To play the game, the player must supply the information listed above into text fields. Then, to make the game run, the player will have to click on the appropriate menu item. Figures 4.1 through 4.6 demonstrate the overall execution of the Lottery Assistant game.

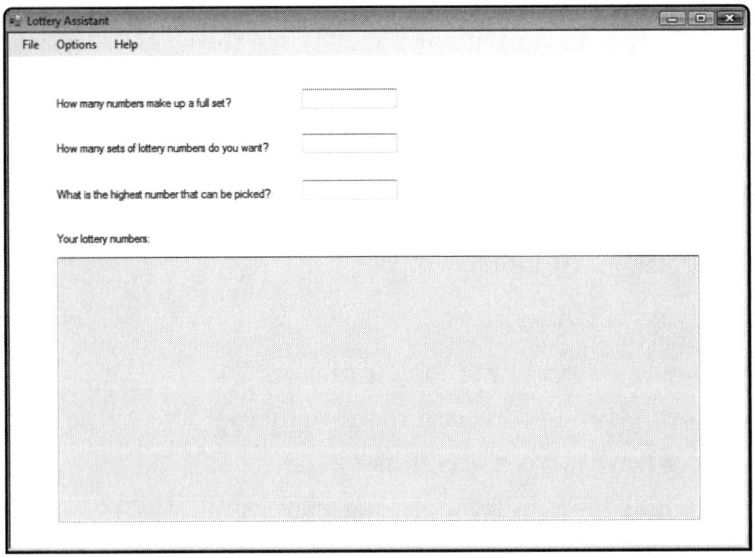

FIGURE 4.1

The Lottery Assistant game begins by collecting player input.

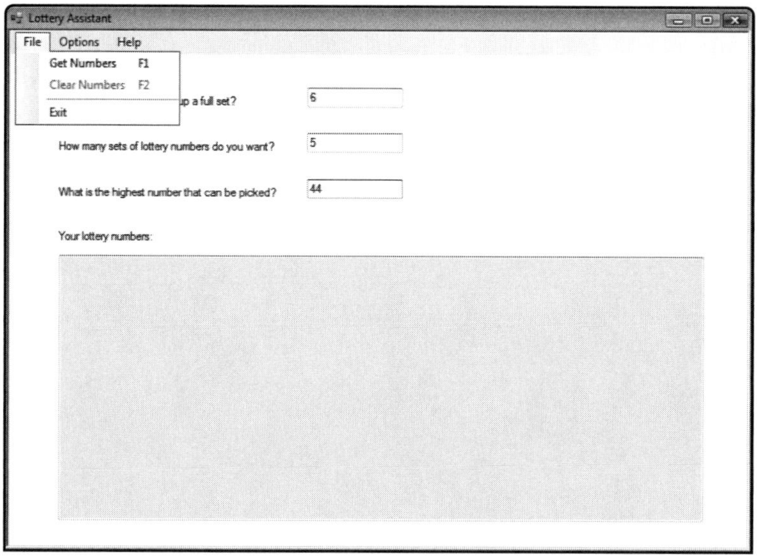

FIGURE 4.2

Players control the game using its menu system.

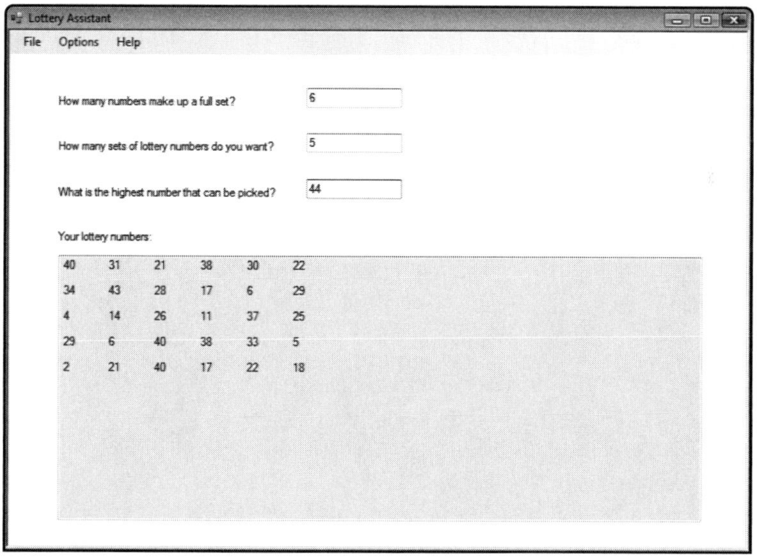

FIGURE 4.3

Up to 10 sets of lottery numbers can be generated at a time.

FIGURE 4.4

Players can configure the game's background color.

FIGURE 4.5

Using the Font Size submenu, the user can specify the font size used to display lottery numbers.

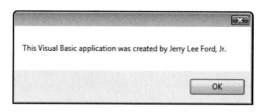

FIGURE 4.6

By clicking on the About menu item located on the Help menu, players can learn more about the game and its developer.

By the time you have created and run this game, you'll have learned how to create your own menu system, complete with menus, menu items, submenus, access keys, and shortcuts.

DESIGNING A MENU SYSTEM

One of the most basic features of any Windows application is its menu system. A menu system provides an intuitive and convenient means for organizing the commands that make your Visual Basic applications work.

A menu system is also a great space saver. It sits conveniently at the top of your application window and takes up very little space. In fact, it only takes up space when you access it, and then it closes back up automatically when you are done with it. A menu system frees up valuable space by allowing you to remove buttons and other types of controls that would otherwise be required.

Figure 4.7 shows a typical Windows application's menu system. As you can see, it consists of many different features.

Windows application menu systems generally consist of one or more of the following six menu features, each of which is visible in Figure 4.7.

- **Menus.** These are the first, or high-level, menu items that are immediately visible from the menu bar (for example, File, Edit, Help, and so on).
- **Menu items.** These are additional menu items residing under menus, each of which represents a choice that can be made by users.
- **Submenus.** These are collections of menu items accessed through a parent menu item. Submenus can be identified by the black arrow on the right end of the menu item that provides access to them.
- **Shortcuts.** These are keyboard characters, such as the F1 key, that can be used to access menu items.

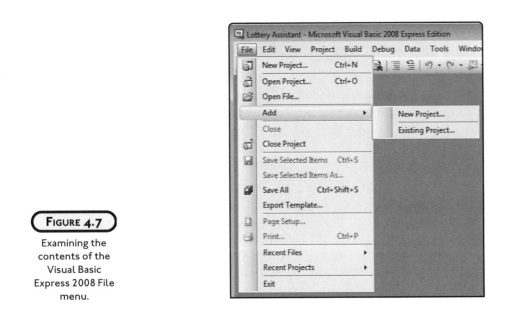

FIGURE 4.7

Examining the contents of the Visual Basic Express 2008 File menu.

- **Access Keys.** These are keyboard keys that, when used in conjunction with the Alt key, activate a menu or menu item.
- **Separators.** These are horizontal lines used to organize menu items into logical groups.

IN THE REAL WORLD

Today, most users are sophisticated and experienced enough with Microsoft Windows that they have come to expect that all Windows applications work in certain ways. Any application that fails to meet these expectations, no matter how good it may be, runs the risk of disappointing its target audience. One expectation that most Windows users have is that all Windows application menus should follow a predictable formula. By this I mean that users expect to see menu headings such as File, Edit, and Help. For example, the File menu is generally listed first, and Help is listed last. Menu items for opening, closing, printing, exiting, and so on typically are located on the File menu. In addition, the last menu item on the File menu should be an Exit command. Unless you have a compelling reason for not following this formula, I strongly recommend against varying from it.

ADDING MENUS, MENU ITEMS, AND SUBMENUS

The first step in adding a menu system to a Visual Basic application is to add the MenuStrip control located in the Toolbox. Doing so adds an instance of the control to the component tray. Once you have done this, you can begin defining menus, as demonstrated in Figure 4.8.

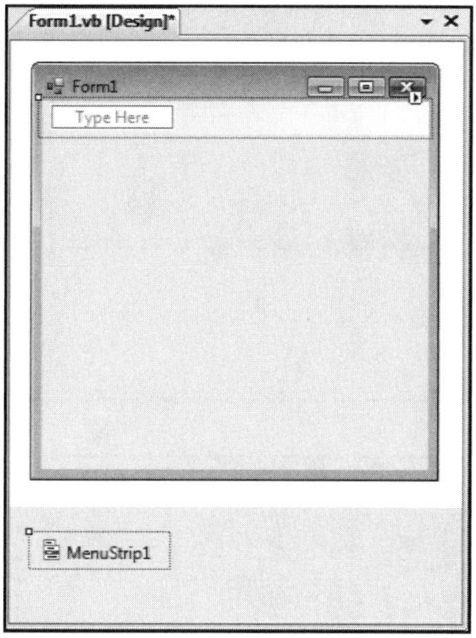

FIGURE 4.8

Using the MenuStrip control to add a menu system to a Visual Basic application.

The following procedure outlines the steps involved in adding a menu system to your Visual Basic applications.

1. Open your Visual Basic application and select the form to which you want to add a menu system.
2. Add the MenuStrip control to your form.
3. Click on the Type Here text that is displayed, and type the name of the first menu that you want to define, as demonstrated in Figure 4.9.
4. To create an additional menu, click on the Type Here text shown just to the right of the first menu heading and type the name of the menu, as demonstrated in Figure 4.10.
5. To add a menu item under a particular menu, click on the menu, click on the Type Here text that appears just underneath it, and type in the name of the menu item, as demonstrated in Figure 4.11.

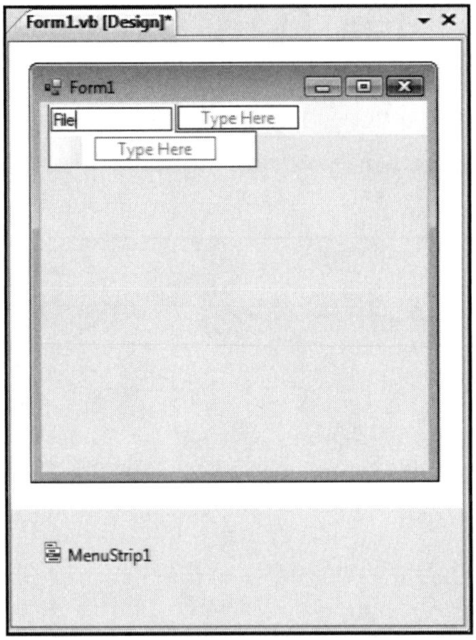

FIGURE 4.9

Defining the first menu heading in the application's menu system.

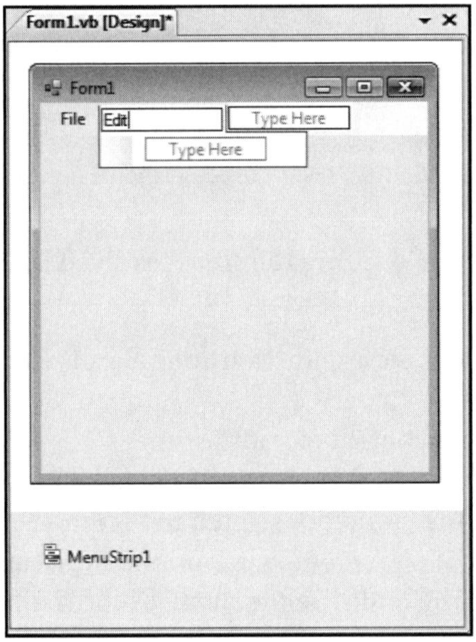

FIGURE 4.10

Adding a menu to the application's menu system.

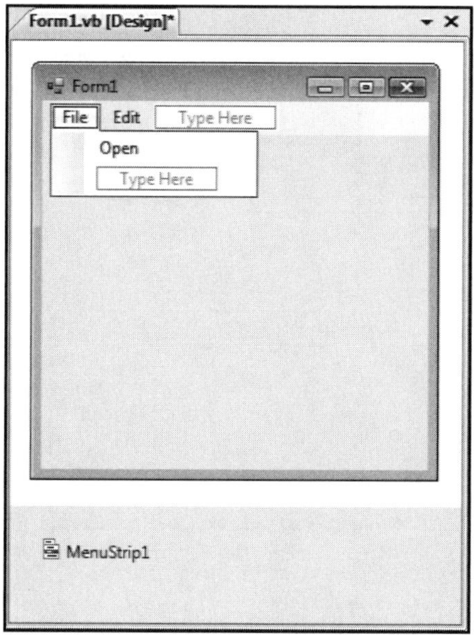

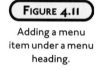

FIGURE 4.11

Adding a menu item under a menu heading.

6. To create a submenu, select the menu item that will provide access to the submenu. Then click on the Type Here text located just to the right of the menu item and type in the name of the first menu item in the submenu. Then, to complete the submenu, continue clicking on the Type Here text displayed under each new menu item in the submenu, adding as many menu items as required, as demonstrated in Figure 4.12.

7. Repeat steps 4 through 6 as many times as necessary to assemble your application's menu system.

One important point to think about when adding menus and menu items is spelling consistency. Always make the first letter in each menu or menu item a capital letter. Also, add three ellipses (...) to the end of any menu name that, when selected, will provide access to another window.

TRICK

You can quickly rearrange the contents of your menu systems by using drag-and-drop to move a menu item to a new location. You can also select a menu item, right-click on it, and select Delete to remove it.

TRICK

If you want, Visual Basic can help you start putting together a generic menu system that includes menus and menu items standard to most Windows applications. To take advantage of this feature, add the MenuStrip control to a form, right-click on the control, and select Insert standard items. In response, you'll end up with a preconfigured menu system like the one shown in Figure 4.13.

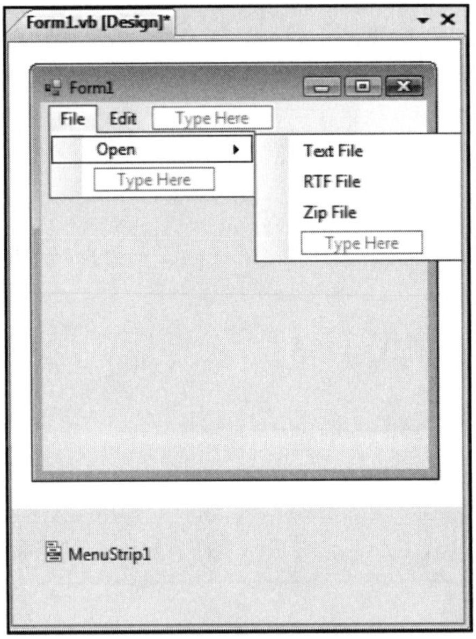

FIGURE 4.12

Adding a submenu item to the menu system.

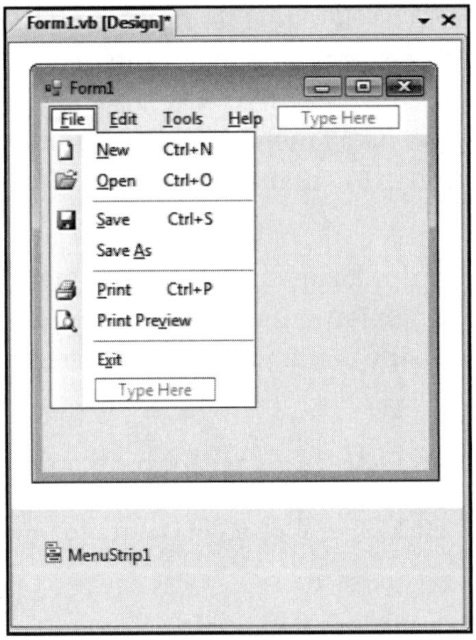

FIGURE 4.13

Inserting a preconfigured menu system to a form.

Associating Code Statements with Menus and Menu Items

As you may have guessed, all that you have to do to associate Visual Basic programming statements with a given menu or menu item is to double-click on it. When you do this, the IDE opens up the code editor, creates a new click event procedure for the selected menu or menu item, and positions the cursor so that you can begin entering your code statements.

For example, Figure 4.14 shows an example of the code associated with the Exit menu.

```
Form1.vb*  Form1.vb [Design]*                                      ▾ ✕
ExitToolStripMenuItem                      ▾   Click                ▾
☐ Public Class Form1

      Private Sub ExitToolStripMenuItem_Click(ByVal sender As System.Object, _
         ByVal e As System.EventArgs) Handles ExitToolStripMenuItem.Click

            Application.Exit()

         End Sub
  End Class
```

FIGURE 4.14

Adding code to the Exit menu item that will close the application when the user clicks on it.

Enhancing Windows Menus

As shown in the following list, you can do a number of things to make your menu systems easier and more convenient for users:

- Add shortcut keys
- Add access keys
- Add and remove check marks
- Organize menu items using separator bars

Adding Shortcut Keys

Shortcut keys provide users with the ability to access menu items using only the keyboard. Shortcuts can be used for fast access to commonly used application commands. Examples of shortcut keys include all of the function keys (F1 to F12) and keystroke combinations such as Ctrl + N and Ctrl + O.

TRAP A number of shortcut keys are so commonly used that they have become a de facto standard for Windows applications. Examples include Ctrl + S for saving and Ctrl + X for exiting an application. Make sure that you use these shortcuts when appropriate in your applications.

Adding a shortcut to a menu item is very straightforward, as outlined by the following procedure.

1. Select the menu containing the menu item that you want to work with.
2. Select the appropriate menu item.
3. Click on the value field associated with the Shortcut property (in the Properties window) and select one of the shortcuts displayed in the drop-down list, as demonstrated in Figure 4.15.

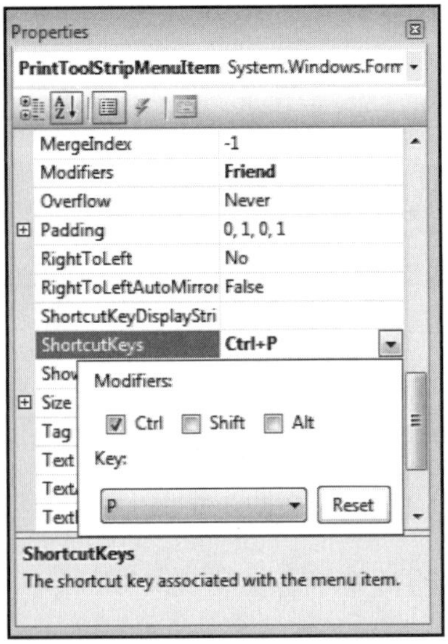

FIGURE 4.15

Specifying the shortcut you want to assign to a menu or menu item.

4. Once selected, the shortcut will be immediately visible, as demonstrated in Figure 4.16.

Adding Access Keys

Access keys also allow users to activate specific menu items using their keyboard. To set up an access key, you must designate one of the characters in a menu's or menu item's name as an access key. Access keys are identified by the presence of an underscore character under the letter that represents the access key. For example, the letter F is generally used as the access key for the File menu.

To use an access key, all the user has to do is press and hold the Alt key while simultaneously pressing the appropriate letter key. For example, to active the File menu in Visual Basic Express 2008, press and hold Alt and F at the same time. While the File menu is displayed, you can release the Alt key and press the access key for any menu item located under the File menu to access it.

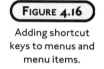

FIGURE 4.16

Adding shortcut keys to menus and menu items.

The following procedure outlines the steps involved in adding access keys to your Visual Basic menu and menu items.

1. Select the menu heading or menu item that you want to work with.
2. Position the cursor in front of the letter in the menu or menu item name that you want to designate as the access key.
3. Add the ampersand (&) character just in front of the selected letter (for example &File or E&xit). The results will be immediately visible, as demonstrated in Figure 4.17.

Adding and Removing Check Marks

Another feature that you may want to implement when creating a menu system for your applications is the use of check marks. Check marks are used to identify the status of menu items that can be toggled on and off. The presence of a check mark indicates that the menu item has been selected or enabled. Similarly, the absence of a check mark indicates that the menu item has been deselected or disabled. For example, later in this chapter when you develop the Lottery Assistant game, you will use check marks to show the player which font and background colors have been selected.

You can set an initial check mark setting at design time using the following procedure:

1. Select the menu item that you want to work with.
2. Click on the small arrow just to the right of the menu item. An Actions window appears. Click on the Checked option, as demonstrated in Figure 4.18.

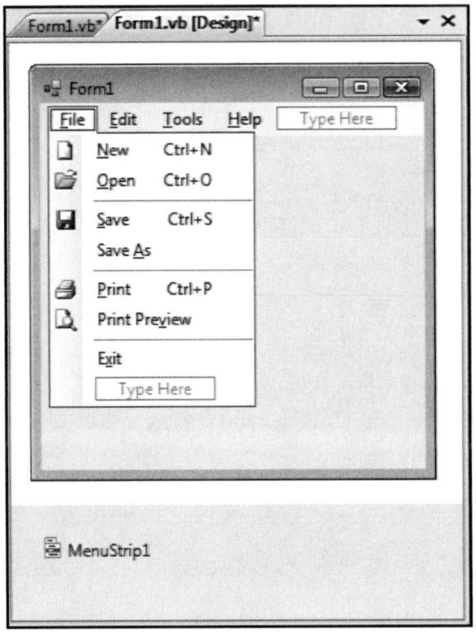

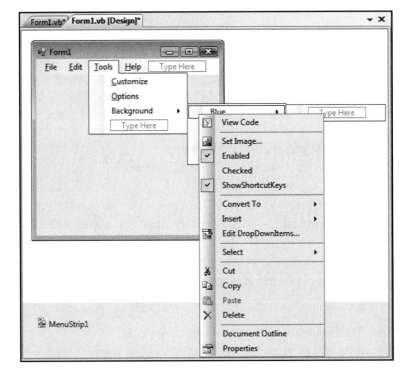

FIGURE 4.17

Adding access
keys to menus and
menu items.

FIGURE 4.18

Using a check mark
to indicate when a
menu item has
been selected.

TRICK You can also set the check mark value by selecting the appropriate menu item and then setting the Checked property in the Properties window to True.

Any menu item that can be checked can also be unchecked. When clicked, it is appropriate to switch the checked status of a menu item. Therefore, you will need to know how to programmatically change the checked status of your menu items at run-time, as demonstrated in the following example.

```
Private Sub GrayToolStripMenuItem_Click(ByVal sender As System.Object, _
    ByVal e As System.EventArgs) Handles GrayToolStripMenuItem.Click

        GrayToolStripMenuItem.Checked = True
        YellowToolStripMenuItem.Checked = False
        WhiteToolStripMenuItem.Checked = False

End Sub
```

Here the statement marks the Gray menu item as checked whenever the user clicks on it and removes check marks from the Yellow and White menu items. Alternatively, if the user comes back later and clicks on the Yellow menu item, it's appropriate to remove the check mark from the Gray and White menu items and add it to the White menu item, as demonstrated here:

```
Private Sub YellowToolStripMenuItem_Click(ByVal sender As System.Object, _
    ByVal e As System.EventArgs) Handles YellowToolStripMenuItem.Click

        GrayToolStripMenuItem.Checked = False
        YellowToolStripMenuItem.Checked = True
        WhiteToolStripMenuItem.Checked = False
End Sub
```

Organizing Menu Items Using Separator Bars

To make a lengthy list of menu items easier for users to work with, you can visually group related menu items together. For example, in Microsoft Excel, menu items for opening and closing files, saving files, printing files, and closing the application are all grouped separately.

Of course, in order to use the separator bar to organize menu items, you must have grouped them together in the first place. The following procedure outlines the steps involved in adding a separator bar between your menu items.

1. Begin creating your menu items.
2. When you get to a point where you want to insert a separator bar, add a temporary menu item at this location.
3. Click on the small arrow just to the right of the temporary menu item. An Actions window appears. Click on the drop-down list in the Type file and select `ToolStripSeparator`, as demonstrated in Figure 4.19.

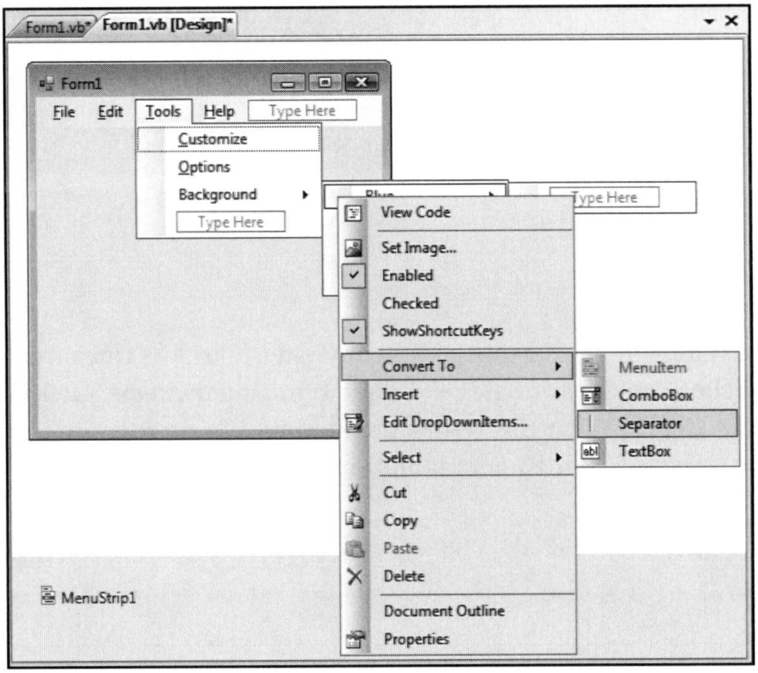

FIGURE 4.19

Using separator bars to visually group related menu items together.

Enabling and Disabling Menus and Menu Items

Based on the current status of your application, there may be times when you want to prevent a user from being able to click on a given menu item. For example, later in this chapter you will work on developing the Lottery Assistant game. This game will be controlled by its menu system, which will include Get Numbers and Clear Numbers menu items on its File menu. The game will enable and disable access to the Get Numbers menu item based on whether or not the user has entered all the data required to retrieve lottery numbers.

When a menu item is disabled, it will appear to the user to be grayed out and won't respond when clicked. By default, menu items are enabled. However, you can disable menu items at design time using the following procedure.

1. Select the menu or menu item that you want to work with.
2. Using the Properties window, set the Enabled property for the menu or menu item to True to enable the menu or menu item (the default) or set it to False to disable it. The results will be immediately visible, as demonstrated in Figure 4.20.

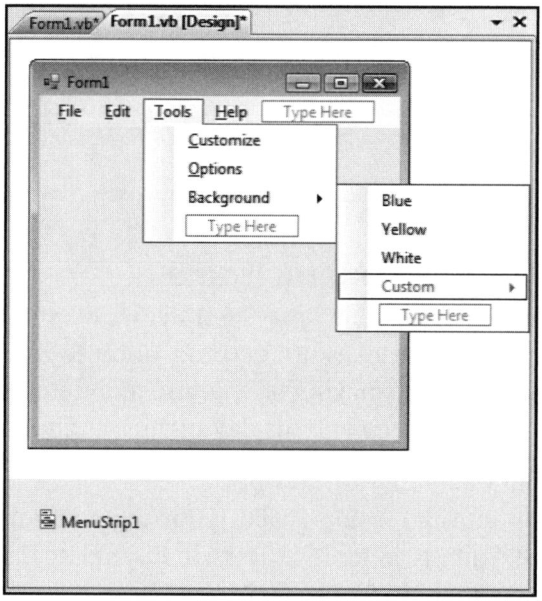

FIGURE 4.20

Disabling a menu item at design time.

Of course, for things to work, you need to add program statements to your code that enable your menu items at the appropriate time. Doing so is straightforward, as demonstrated here:

```
Private Sub Button1_Click(ByVal sender As System.Object, _
  ByVal e As System.EventArgs) Handles Button1.Click


    CustomToolStripMenuItem1.Enabled = True


End Sub
```

TRAP

If you disable a menu heading or a menu item that provides access to a submenu, then all menu items and submenus underneath it will be hidden from view, as demonstrated in Figure 4.21.

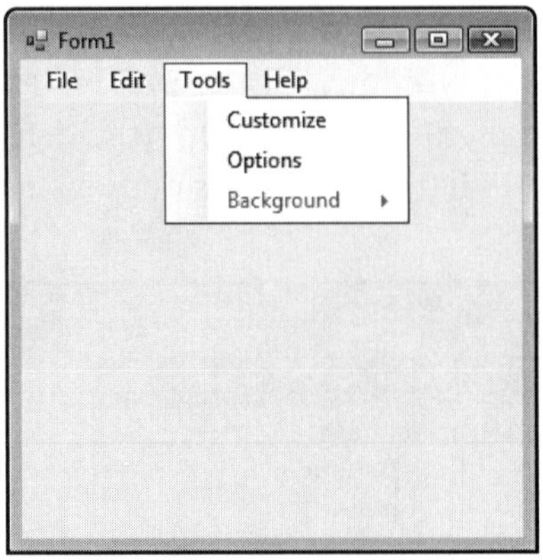

FIGURE 4.21

Disabling a menu item and its associated submenu.

Hiding and Displaying Menus and Menu Items

Depending on what your application is doing, there may be times where you feel that simply enabling and disabling menus and menu items is not enough. In these circumstances, you can go a step further by hiding and later redisplaying menus and menu items. The following procedure outlines the steps involved in hiding and displaying menus and menu items.

1. Select the menu or menu item that you want to work with.
2. Using the Properties window, set the Visible property for the menu or menu item to True to enable its display (the default) or set it to False to disable it. The results will be immediately visible, as demonstrated in Figure 4.22.

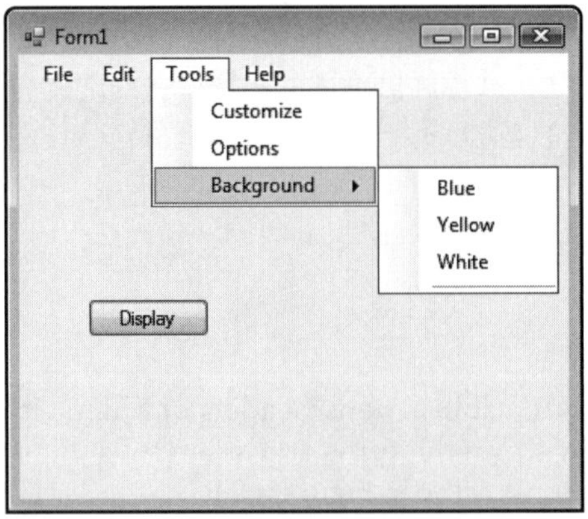

FIGURE 4.22

Making the Custom submenu item invisible on the Background submenu.

If you hide a menu or a menu item that provides access to a submenu, then all menu items and submenus underneath it will be hidden from view.

Once hidden, you'll need to add program statements to your code that make menu or menu items visible later on. Doing so is straightforward, as demonstrated here:

```
Private Sub Button1_Click_1(ByVal sender As System.Object, _
  ByVal e As System.EventArgs) Handles Button1.Click

        CustomToolStripMenuItem1.Visible = True

End Sub
```

As Figure 4.23 demonstrates, the Custom menu item is visible again once this above procedure has been executed.

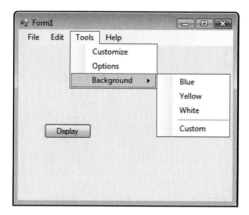

FIGURE 4.23

You can also control user access to menu items by hiding and redisplaying them when appropriate.

CONTEXT MENUS

A second type of menu system that you may want to add to your Visual Basic applications is a context menu. Context menus are hidden from view, only appearing when the user right-clicks on the form or control with which the context menu is associated.

DEFINITION A *context menu* is a menu system that you can attach to a form or control to provide users with easy access to common commands or options made available by your application.

The following procedure outlines the steps involved in setting up a context menu.

1. Double-click on the ContextMenuStrip control located in the Toolbox to add it to the component tray.
2. Add menu items to it by keying in text on top of the Type Here text, as demonstrated in Figure 4.24.

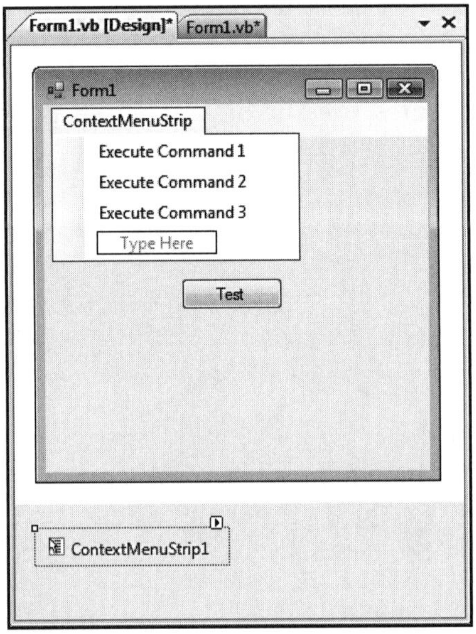

FIGURE 4.24

Configuring the menu items for a context menu.

3. Double-click on each of the menu items in the context list and add your program code, as demonstrated below. For example, you might add the following statement to the click event for the first context menu:

```
Private Sub ExecuteCommand1ToolStripMenuItem_Click(ByVal sender _
    As System.Object, ByVal e As System.EventArgs) _
    Handles ExecuteCommand1ToolStripMenuItem.Click

    MessageBox.Show("Command 1 should execute now.")

End Sub
```

Similarly, you might add the following code to the click event for the second context menu item:

```
Private Sub ExecuteCommand2ToolStripMenuItem_Click(ByVal sender _
    As System.Object, ByVal e As System.EventArgs) _
    Handles ExecuteCommand2ToolStripMenuItem.Click

    MessageBox.Show("Command 2 should execute now.")

End Sub
```

Finally, you could assign the following code to the click event for the third context menu item, as shown here:

```
Private Sub ExecuteCommand3ToolStripMenuItem_Click(ByVal sender As _
    System.Object, ByVal e As System.EventArgs) _
    Handles ExecuteCommand3ToolStripMenuItem.Click

    MessageBox.Show("Command 3 should execute now.")

End Sub
```

4. Select the control for which you created the context menu and set its ContextMenuStrip property equal to the name of the context menu that you just created.

Once you have finished configuring the form or control's ContextMenuStrip property, you can run your application and access the ContextMenu by right-clicking on the form or control, as demonstrated in Figure 4.25.

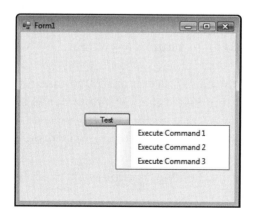

FIGURE 4.25

Examining the contents of Button control's associated context menu.

ADDING CONVENIENCE WITH TOOLBARS

Another feature commonly found on most Windows applications is toolbars. Toolbars display a collection of buttons, each of which when clicked executes a particular application command. By default, when you add a toolbar to a window, Visual Basic automatically places it at the top of the window, just below the menu, if one is present. However, you can move the toolbar to the bottom, right, or left side of the window if you prefer by setting the Dock property.

Typically, programmers use toolbars to give users single-click access to an application's most commonly used commands. Toolbar buttons can display either text, graphics, or both text and graphics.

The following procedure outlines the steps involved in adding a toolbar to a Visual Basic application and identifies various options that are available to you.

TRICK

The first step in adding a toolbar to a Visual Basic application is to add the ToolBar control located in the Toolbox to a form. However, by default, the ToolBar control is not found in the Toolbox window. But you can add it by right-clicking on the Toolbox window and selecting the Choose items option. This opens the Choose Toolbox Items dialog. Make sure that the .NET Framework Components property sheet is selected, and scroll down until you see ToolBar control. Select the ToolBar control and click on OK. The control will now be visible in the Toolbox window.

1. Drag and drop the ToolBar control onto your form.
2. Select the ToolBar control, locate the Buttons property in the Properties window, and click on the (Collection) ellipses button located in its property's value field. The ToolBarButton Collection Editor appears, as shown in Figure 4.26.
3. Click on the Add button to add as many buttons as you want to the toolbar. Each time you click on the Add button, an entry for the button is displayed in the Members pane located on the left-hand side of the editor, as demonstrated in Figure 4.27.
4. To display a text string on the button, select the Text property and type in a string as its value.
5. To add a ToolTip to the button, select the ToolTipText property and type in the text that you want to be displayed.
6. Modify the Style property to specify the style that you want to apply to the button. The following options are available:

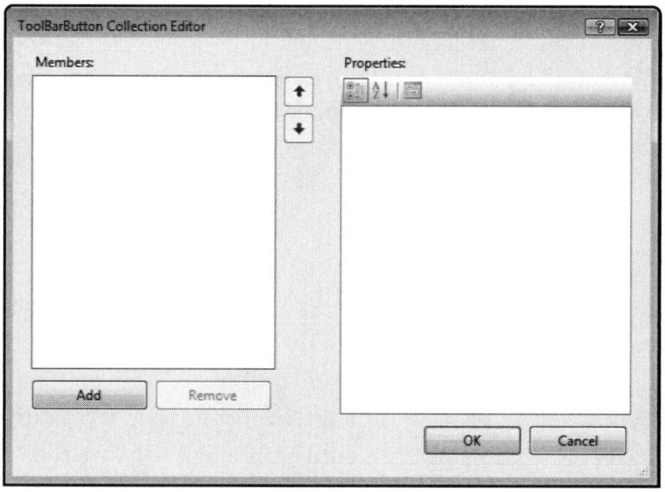

FIGURE 4.26

Adding and removing buttons to a toolbar.

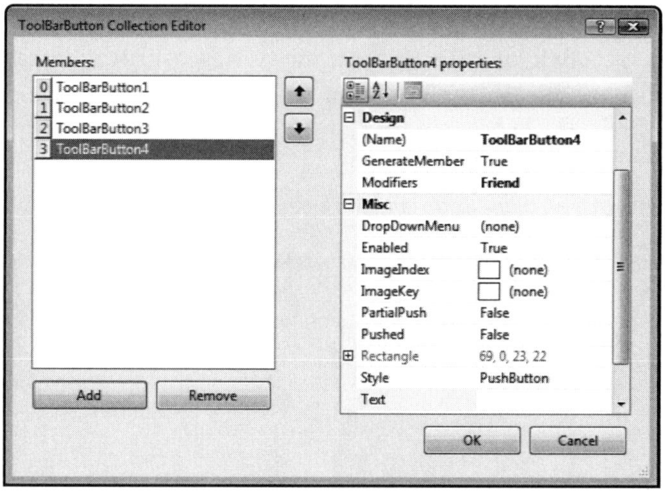

FIGURE 4.27

Use the up and down arrows to configure the order in which buttons are displayed on the toolbar.

- PushButton. Displays the three-dimensional button.
- ToggleButton. Toggles the button's appearance between a depressed and normal state each time the user clicks on it.
- Separator. Changes the button into a separator bar.
- DropDownButton. Modifies the button to behave as a drop-down control that displays menu items.

7. Click on OK to close the ToolBarButton Collection Editor.

TRICK   If you are adding text to your toolbar buttons, you may need to specify toolbar button width, depending on the amount of text you plan on displaying. To change the width or height of toolbar buttons, select the ToolBar control's ButtonSize property and specify a new size for your toolbar buttons.

Adding Graphics to Your Toolbars

Instead of displaying text in your toolbar buttons, you can display graphic images. But to do so, you have to take a few extra steps before you can actually associate a graphic with a button. For starters, you must add an ImageList control from the Toolbox to your application. Using this control, you will identify all of the graphic images that you plan on adding to your toolbars. Once added to the ImageList, you can then configure each of your toolbar buttons to display one of the graphic images defined in the ImageList.

The following procedure identifies the steps that are involved in making all this work.

1. Add an ImageList control to your form.
2. In the Properties window, click on the (Collection) ellipses button located in the Images property's value field. The ImageCollection Collection Editor appears as shown in Figure 4.28.

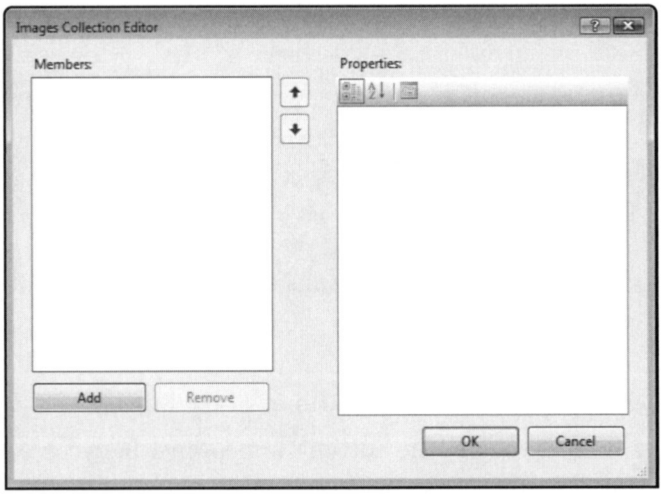

Images Collection Editor

Members:

Properties:

Add   Remove

OK   Cancel

FIGURE 4.28

Identifying the images that you plan on using to add graphics to your toolbar.

3. Click on the Add button and specify the name of an image to be added to the ImageList. Repeat this step as many times as necessary and make sure that you take note of the index number that is assigned to each image that you add.

4. Click on OK to close the ImageCollection Collection Editor.

Once you have finished adding images to the `ImageList` control, go back and select the `ImageList` property for your `ToolBar` control and specify the name of the `ImageList` that you just created. Then open the ToolBarButton Collection Editor by clicking on the `Button` property's `(Collection)` ellipses button. Modify the `ImageIndex` property for each button to associate the button with a given graphic image's index number within the `ImageList` control. For example, Figure 4.29 shows a toolbar under development with an image added to its first button.

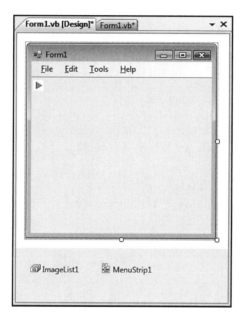

FIGURE 4.29

Adding a graphic image to a `ToolBar` control button.

Associating Program Statements with Toolbar Buttons

Unfortunately, individual toolbar buttons do not have their own click event. There is just a single click event for the entire `ToolBar` control. Therefore, it is up to you to programmatically figure out which button the user clicked on and then to execute the appropriate program statements. Fortunately, it is not too hard to make this happen.

The `ToolBarButtonClickEventArgs` object's `Button` property is automatically passed to the `ButtonClick` event handler at run-time. If you look back at Figure 4.27, you will see that just to the left of each toolbar button, there is a number that uniquely identifies the button's indexed position within the toolbar. By querying the `Button` property and comparing it to the button index numbers, you can identify which button was clicked.

To see how this all comes together, let's look at an example. For starters, access the toolbar's click event by double-clicking on it. The following code will appear in the code editor.

```
Private Sub ToolBar1_ButtonClick(ByVal sender As System.Object, _
      ByVal e As System.Windows.Forms.ToolBarButtonClickEventArgs) _
      Handles ToolBar1.ButtonClick


End Sub
```

In addition to defining the click event for the toolbar, this code automatically receives an argument that identifies the index number of the clicked button, which can then be accessed by your code as e.Button, as demonstrated in the following example.

```
Private Sub ToolBar1_ButtonClick(ByVal sender As System.Object, _
      ByVal e As System.Windows.Forms.ToolBarButtonClickEventArgs) _
      Handles ToolBar1.ButtonClick


      If ToolBar1.Buttons.IndexOf(e.Button) = 0 Then
          MessageBox.Show("You clicked on " & e.Button.Text)
      End If
      If ToolBar1.Buttons.IndexOf(e.Button) = 1 Then
          MessageBox.Show("You clicked on " & e.Button.Text)
      End If
      If ToolBar1.Buttons.IndexOf(e.Button) = 2 Then
          MessageBox.Show("You clicked on " & e.Button.Text)
      End If


End Sub
```

In this example, e.Button is an argument representing the index number of the button clicked by the user. The first three statements check to see if the first toolbar button was clicked. The next three statements check to see if the second toolbar button was clicked, and the last three statements check to see if the third toolbar button was clicked.

Figure 4.30 shows the output displayed when the previous example is executed and the user clicks on a button that is named Start.

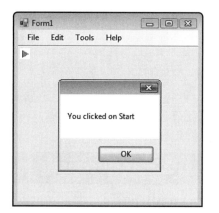

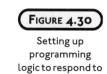

FIGURE 4.30

Setting up programming logic to respond to button clicks.

TRICK Because toolbar buttons generally represent commonly used commands already found in a menu, you can speed up application development using the `MenuItem` object's `PerformClick()` method to set up the button so that it executes the corresponding menu's click event, just as if the user had clicked it. For example, the following statements execute the click event for a menu item named `newToolStripMenuItem` in the event the user clicks on the first toolbar button:

```
Private Sub ToolBar1_ButtonClick(ByVal sender As System.Object, _
    ByVal e As System.Windows.Forms.ToolBarButtonClickEventArgs) _
    Handles ToolBar1.ButtonClick

        If ToolBar1.Buttons.IndexOf(e.Button) = 0 Then
            newToolStripMenuItem.PerformClick()
        End If
        If ToolBar1.Buttons.IndexOf(e.Button) = 1 Then
            MessageBox.Show("You clicked on " & e.Button.Text)
        End If
        If ToolBar1.Buttons.IndexOf(e.Button) = 2 Then
            MessageBox.Show("You clicked on " & e.Button.Text)
        End If

End Sub
```

BACK TO THE LOTTERY ASSISTANT GAME

Now it is time to turn your attention back to this chapter's game project. You will create the Lottery Assistant game using the five development steps that you have followed in previous chapters. By the time you have finished creating this game, you will have demonstrated your ability to modify your Visual Basic applications by adding fully functional menu systems to your forms.

Designing the Game

The Lottery Assistant game is played on a single form. Therefore, it consists of a single form, upon which you add the nine controls listed in Table 4.1.

TABLE 4.1 FORM CONTROLS FOR THE LOTTERY ASSISTANT GAME		
Control Type	**Control Name**	**Description**
Label	lblFullSet	Identifies the TextBox control where the player specifies how many numbers constitute a full set of lottery numbers.
Label	lblNoPics	Identifies the TextBox control where the player specifies how many sets of lottery numbers the game should generate.
Label	lblNoRange	Identifies the TextBox control where the player specifies the range of numbers from which the game should generate lottery numbers.
Label	lblOutput	Identifies the TextBox control where the game displays the lottery numbers that it generates.
TextBox	txtFullSet	The TextBox control where the player specifies how many numbers constitute a full set of lottery numbers.
TextBox	txtNoPics	The TextBox control where the player specifies how many sets of lottery numbers the game should generate.
TextBox	txtNoRange	The TextBox control where the player specifies the range of numbers from which the game should generate lottery numbers.
TextBox	txtOutput	The TextBox control where the game displays the lottery numbers that it generates.
MenuStrip	mnuStrip1	The name of the MenuStrip control that will be used to create the game's menu system.

Step 1: Creating a New Visual Basic Project

The first step in developing the Lottery Assistant game is to start Visual Basic and open a new project, as outlined here:

1. If you have not already done so, start up Visual Basic 2008 Express and then click on File and select New Project. The New Project dialog will appear.

2. Select Windows Application template.
3. Type **Lottery Assistant** as the name of your new application in the Name field located at the bottom of the New Project window.
4. Click on OK to close the New Project dialog.

In response, Visual Basic creates a new project for you and displays a blank form on which you will design the game's user interface.

Step 2: Creating the User Interface

The next step in the creation of the Lottery Assistant game is to assemble the game's interface. To begin, let's review the overall layout of the game's user interface, as shown in Figure 4.31.

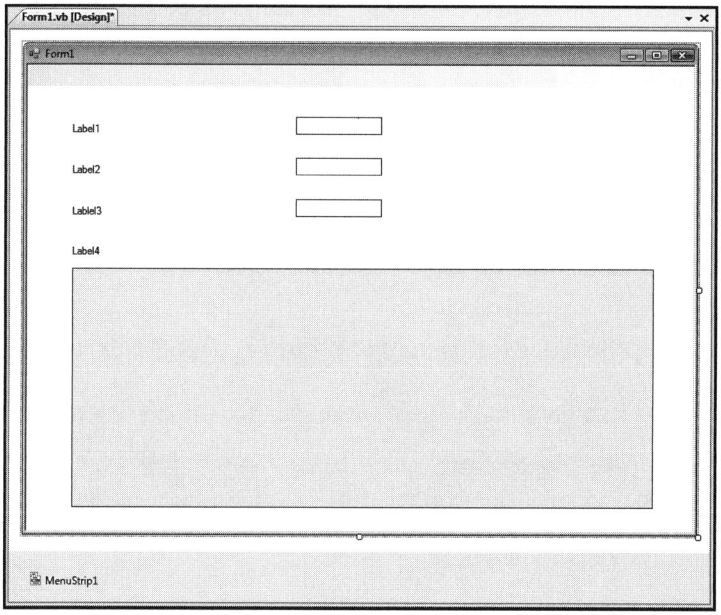

FIGURE 4.31

Completing the interface design for the Lottery Assistant game.

1. Begin by adding a MenuStrip control to the form. By default, Visual Basic assigns the name MenuStrip1 to the control.
2. Add four Label controls to the form and line them up as shown in Figure 4.31. By default, Visual Basic names them Label1 to Label4.
3. Add three TextBox controls to the form and line them up horizontally with the first Label controls. By default, Visual Basic names these controls TextBox1 to TextBox3.
4. Finally, add a fourth TextBox control to the form just under the Label4 control and resize it so that it covers most of the bottom half of the form, as shown in Figure 4.31. By default, Visual Basic assigns this control the name TextBox4.

The layout of the Visual Basic form is now complete. All controls should be visible on the form except for the MenuStrip1 control, which is displayed in a Component Tray just below the form.

Step 3: Customizing Form and Control Properties

Before you start customizing the properties associated with the controls that you just added to the form, you need to modify a few properties belonging to the form itself. The properties that need to be changed, along with their new value assignments, are listed in Table 4.2.

TABLE 4.2   PROPERTY VALUE ASSIGNMENTS FOR THE LOTTERY ASSISTANT GAME'S FORM

Property	Value
Name	ltaForm
BackColor	White
FormBorderStyle	Fixed3D
StartPosition	CenterScreen
Text	Lottery Assistant

Next, let's set the Name and Text properties for each of the four Label controls, as specified in Table 4.3.

TABLE 4.3   PROPERTY CHANGES FOR EACH OF THE LABEL CONTROLS

Control	Property	Value
Label1	Name	lblFullSet
	Text	How many numbers make up a full set?
Label2	Name	lblNoPics
	Text	How many sets of lottery numbers do you want?
Label3	Name	lblNoRange
	Text	What is the highest number that can be picked?
Label4	Name	lblOutput
	Text	Your lottery numbers:

Now let's make modifications belonging to each of the TextBox controls as listed in Table 4.4.

TABLE 4.4   PROPERTY CHANGES FOR EACH OF THE TEXTBOX CONTROLS

Control	Property	Value
TextBox1	Name	txtFullSet
TextBox2	Name	txtNoPics
TextBox3	Name	txtNoRange
TextBox4	Name	txtOutput
	ReadOnly	True
	ScrollBars	Vertical
	TabStop	False

Setting the ReadOnly property to True for the fourth TextBox control prevents the player from attempting to enter text into it. Setting the ScrollBars property to Vertical adds a scrollbar to the text box to allow the player to scroll up and down when more sets of lottery numbers are generated than can be displayed at one time. Setting the TabStop property to False takes the fourth TextBox control out of the tab index.

The last control that requires property modification is the MenuStrip control. For starters, click on the control and change its name to mnuStrip. Next, configure the MenuStrip control to create a menu system composed of the menus outlined in Table 4.5.

TABLE 4.5   MENUS FOR THE LOTTERY ASSISTANT GAME

Text Property	Resulting Menu Name	Description
&File	FileToolStripMenuItem	Contains commands that control the game's execution.
&Options	OptionsToolStripMenuItem	Contains commands that configure the game's display.
&Help	HelpToolStripMenuItem	Provides access to additional information about the game.

Once you have created each of the menus listed in Table 4.5, it is time to configure each menu by adding menu items. Table 4.6 lists the menu items that you'll need to add to the FileToolStripMenuItem menu.

TABLE 4.6   MENU ITEMS RESIDING UNDER THE FILE MENU

Text Property	Resulting Menu Name	Description
&Get Numbers	GetNumbersToolStripMenuItem	Retrieves randomly generated lottery numbers.
&Clear Numbers	ClearToolStripMenuItem	Clears out any text displayed in the game's TextBox controls.
E&xit	ExitToolStripMenuItem1	Terminates game execution.

The Clear Number menu item will be used to execute programming statements that remove any text that may currently be stored in the form's TextBox controls. When the form is first displayed, there won't be any text displayed in the TextBox controls. Therefore, it is appropriate to initially disable this Clear Number menu item at design time. Later, when the application is running and the player begins to key in text, you'll add programming logic to enable this menu item. So, to disable the Clear Numbers menu item, select it and then set its Enabled property (in the Properties window) to False.

Table 4.7 lists the menu items that you are to add to the OptionsToolStripMenuItem menu.

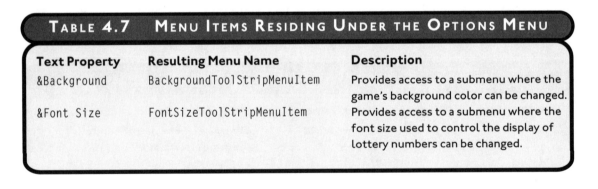

TABLE 4.7   MENU ITEMS RESIDING UNDER THE OPTIONS MENU

Text Property	Resulting Menu Name	Description
&Background	BackgroundToolStripMenuItem	Provides access to a submenu where the game's background color can be changed.
&Font Size	FontSizeToolStripMenuItem	Provides access to a submenu where the font size used to control the display of lottery numbers can be changed.

Table 4.8 lists the menu item that you are to add to the HelpToolStripMenuItem menu.

At this point, you have defined all three of the game's menus, as well as the menu items that reside underneath them. However, you are not done yet. Both the Background and Font Size menu items need to be set up to provide access to their own submenus. Table 4.9 outlines the contents of the Background submenu.

Table 4.10 outlines the contents of the Font Size submenu.

TABLE 4.8   MENU ITEMS RESIDING UNDER THE HELP MENU

Text Property	Resulting Menu Name	Description
&About	AboutToolStripMenuItem	Executes code that displays information about the game in a pop-up window.

TABLE 4.9   MENU ITEMS RESIDING ON THE BACKGROUND SUBMENU

Text Property	Resulting Menu Name	Description
&White	WhiteToolStripMenuItem	Sets the form's background color to white.
&Yellow	YellowToolStripMenuItem	Sets the form's background color to yellow.
&Gray	GrayToolStripMenuItem	Set the form's background color to gray.

TABLE 4.10   MENU ITEMS RESIDING ON THE FONT SIZE SUBMENU

Text Property	Resulting Menu Name	Description
8	ToolStripMenuItem1	Sets the font size displayed in the txtOutput control to 8.
10	ToolStripMenuItem2	Sets the font size displayed in the txtOutput control to 10.
12	ToolStripMenuItem3	Sets the font size displayed in the txtOutput control to 12.

Before you call it quits with the Lottery Assistant game's menu system, let's add just a few more bells and whistles. For starters, add the access key F1 to the Get Numbers menu item located under the File menu. Then add the access key F2 to the Clear Numbers menu item, which is also located under the File menu. Then set the Checked property for the White submenu item under the Options menu to True, indicating that it is the default menu item, and then do the same things for the Checked property belonging to the first menu item on the Font Size submenu.

That's all the property modifications that are required for the Lottery Assistant game's controls and menu system. Now it is time to add the program statements required to make the game work.

Step 4: Adding a Little Programming Logic

All of the Lottery Assistant game's program code is controlled by the game's menu system. Unlike the game projects that you worked on in previous chapters, there are no Button controls for the player to click on in this game. To keep things straightforward, let's begin by adding the programming statements for each menu item one by one, starting with the first menu item located on the File menu and finishing up with the last menu item under the Help menu.

Adding Code to the Get Numbers Menu Item

The easiest way to associate programming statements with a menu item is to double-click on the menu item. When you do, Visual Basic automatically opens the code editor and creates a couple of lines of initial code for you. So, for starters, double-click on the Get Numbers menu item located under the File menu. The following code will be automatically generated and displayed in the code editor.

```
Private Sub GetNumbersToolStripMenuItem_Click(ByVal sender _
     As System.Object, ByVal e As System.EventArgs) _
     Handles GetNumbersToolStripMenuItem.Click


End Sub
```

You will key in all the programming statements that are to be executed when the Get Numbers menu item is clicked between these two statements. For starters, add the following statements. These statements define variables and an array used by the application to store and manipulate the data it needs to execute. For now, just key in these statements exactly as shown. In Chapter 5, "Storing and Retrieving Data in Memory," you will learn all about variables and arrays.

```
Dim intForLoopCtr As Integer = 0
Dim blnFullSetComplete As Boolean = False
Dim intRndNo As Integer = 0
Dim strDisplayString As String = ""
Dim intNoOfValidPics As Integer = 0
Dim aintLotteryArray(10) As Array
Dim intNumberCount As Integer = 0
Dim strTestString As String = "_"
```

Next add the following statements, which check to see if the player has supplied valid input into the first TextBox control and displays an error message if this is not the case. Note the Return statement, which prevents Visual Basic from processing any of the remaining statements associated with the Get Numbers menu item click event.

```
If txtFullSet.Text = "" Then
    MessageBox.Show("You must specify how many numbers " & _
    "make up a full set.")
    Return
End If
```

The next set of statements checks to ensure that that the player entered numeric data into the first TextBox control and displays an error message if this is not the case.

```
If IsNumeric(txtFullSet.Text) = False Then
    MessageBox.Show("You must specify numeric input when " & _
    "specifying how many numbers make up a full set.")
    Return
End If
```

 TRICK You can use Visual Basic's IsNumeric function to test whether a value is numeric or not.

The next set of statements to be added check to see if the player entered a number greater than 10 in the first TextBox control and displays an error message if this is the case.

```
If Int32.Parse(txtFullSet.Text) > 10 Then
    MessageBox.Show("The maximum number of numbers in a full " & _
      "set is 10. Please enter a number between 3 - 10.")
    Return
End If
```

TRICK By default, anything the player types into a TextBox control is seen by Visual Basic as a text string. You can use Visual Basic's Int32.Parse method to convert a text string value to an integer.

Now add the following statements, which check to make sure that the user specified a number of no less than 3 in the first TextBox control.

```
If Int32.Parse(txtFullSet.Text) < 3 Then
    MessageBox.Show("The minimum number of numbers in a full " & _
      "set is 3. Please enter a number between 3 - 10.")
    Return
End If
```

Let's add program statements that validate the contents of the second TextBox control. These statements display error messages if the player fails to supply any text, if the player does not supply numeric input, or if the player tries to specify a number less than 1 or greater than 10.

```
If txtNoPics.Text = "" Then
    MessageBox.Show("You must specify how many sets of " & _
        "lottery numbers you want.")
    Return
End If

If IsNumeric(txtNoPics.Text) = False Then
    MessageBox.Show("You must specify numeric input when " & _
        "specifying how many sets of lottery numbers you want.")
    Return
End If

If Int32.Parse(txtNoPics.Text) > 10 Then
    MessageBox.Show("The maximum number of lottery tickets " & _
        "that can be generated is 10. Please enter a number " & _
        "between 1 - 10.")
    Return
End If

If Int32.Parse(txtNoPics.Text) < 1 Then
    MessageBox.Show("The minimum number of lottery tickets " & _
        "that can be generated is 1. Please enter a number " & _
        "between 1 - 10.")
    Return
End If
```

Now let's add program statements that validate the contents of the third TextBox control. These statements display error messages if the player fails to supply any text, if the player does not supply numeric input, or if the player tries to specify a number that is less than 9 or greater than 50.

```
If txtNoRange.Text = "" Then
    MessageBox.Show("You must specify the highest number " & _
        " that can be picked.")
    Return
```

```
End If

If IsNumeric(txtNoRange.Text) = False Then
    MessageBox.Show("You must specify numeric input when " & _
      "specifying the highest number that can be picked.")
    Return
End If

If Int32.Parse(txtNoRange.Text) > 50 Then
    MessageBox.Show("The maximum value for the highest number " & _
      "that can be picked is 50. Please enter a number " & _
      "less than or equal to 50.")
    Return
End If

If Int32.Parse(txtNoRange.Text) < 9 Then
    MessageBox.Show("The minimum value for the highest number " & _
      "that can be picked is 9. Please enter a number greater " & _
      "than or equal to 9.")
    Return
End If
```

Next add the following statements. These statements include a For loop and a Do loop, which you will learn more about in Chapter 7, "Processing Lots of Data with Loops." The For loop executes once for each set of lottery numbers that the player wants generated. The Do loop executes repeatedly until a complete set of numbers has been generated.

```
For intForLoopCtr = 1 To CInt(txtNoPics.Text)

    Do Until blnFullSetComplete = True

        Randomize()

        intRndNo = _
            FormatNumber(Int((txtNoRange.Text * Rnd()) + 1))


        If InStr(strTestString, _
            Convert.ToString("_" & intRndNo & "_")) = 0 Then
```

```
        strDisplayString = strDisplayString & " " & _
            intRndNo & ControlChars.Tab
        intNoOfValidPics = intNoOfValidPics + 1
        strTestString = strTestString & intRndNo & "_"
    End If

    If intNoOfValidPics = Int32.Parse(txtFullSet.Text) Then
        blnFullSetComplete = True

        strDisplayString = strDisplayString & _
            ControlChars.NewLine & ControlChars.NewLine
        strTestString = "_"
    End If

Loop

blnFullSetComplete = False
intNoOfValidPics = 0

Next
```

The basic logic used in the statements wrapped inside the Do loop is as follows:

- Get a randomly generated number.
- Add that number to a string representing a list of lottery numbers, but don't allow duplicate numbers to be added to the list.
- Format the display string so that a new line is generated for each set of lottery numbers.

The programming logic used in these statements is more than a little involved. I'll defer further discussion on this group of statements at this point until after you have had the chance to read Chapters 5 through 8.

The last program statements that you will add to the code that executes in response to the Get Numbers menu item's click event is shown here:

```
txtOutput.Text = strDisplayString
GetNumbersToolStripMenuItem.Enabled = False
ClearToolStripMenuItem.Enabled = True
```

The first of these three statements assigns the list of randomly generated lottery numbers created by the two previous loops to the txtOutput control's Text property, thus making the numbers visible to the player. The last two statements disable the Get Numbers menu item and enable the Clear Numbers menu item.

Adding Code to the Clear Numbers Menu Item

Now, switch back to the designer view, drill down into the File menu, and try to double-click on the Clear Numbers menu item. You may be surprised to see that you cannot use this technique to access the menu item's click event. This is because the menu item has been disabled. However, you can still access this menu item's click event by remaining in the code editor and selecting `ClearToolStripMenuItem` from the drop-down list located in the upper-left side of the code editor. Once selected, all the events associated with this menu item become accessible in the drop-down list located on the upper-right side of the code editor. Use this drop-down list to select the click event. The code editor will respond by generating the following code for you.

```
Private Sub ClearToolStripMenuItem_Click(ByVal sender _
    As System.Object, ByVal e As System.EventArgs) _
    Handles ClearToolStripMenuItem.Click


End Sub
```

Add the following statement between the two statements shown above. The first four statements clear out any text displayed in the four `TextBox` controls. The next statement places the cursor in the first `TextBox` control, and the last two statements enable the Get Numbers menu item and disable the Clear Numbers menu item.

```
txtFullSet.Text = ""
txtNoPics.Text = ""
txtNoRange.Text = ""
txtOutput.Text = ""
txtFullSet.Focus()
GetNumbersToolStripMenuItem.Enabled = True
ClearToolStripMenuItem.Enabled = False
```

Adding Code to the Exit Menu Item

Now return to the designer view and double-click on the Exit menu item located under the File menu. Modify the code that is generated for you by inserting the `Application.Exit()` statement as shown here:

```
Private Sub ExitToolStripMenuItem1_Click(ByVal sender _
    As System.Object, ByVal e As System.EventArgs) _
    Handles ExitToolStripMenuItem1.Click
```

```
        Application.Exit()

End Sub
```

Adding Code to the White Menu Item

Now it is time to start adding the program statements required to make the menu items on the Background submenu work. Start by accessing the click event for the White menu item and modify the code that is automatically generated as shown here:

```
Private Sub WhiteToolStripMenuItem_Click(ByVal sender _
     As System.Object, ByVal e As System.EventArgs) _
     Handles WhiteToolStripMenuItem.Click

        Me.BackColor = Color.White
        WhiteToolStripMenuItem.Checked = True
        YellowToolStripMenuItem.Checked = False
        GrayToolStripMenuItem.Checked = False

End Sub
```

As you can see, you are adding four statements. The first statement changes the background color of the parent object (the form) to white. The next statement places a check mark to the right of the White menu item. The last two statements make sure that the Yellow and Gray menu items do not display a check mark.

Adding Code to the Yellow Menu Item

Next access the click event for the Yellow submenu item and modify the code that is automatically generated as shown here:

```
Private Sub YellowToolStripMenuItem_Click(ByVal sender _
     As System.Object, ByVal e As System.EventArgs) _
     Handles YellowToolStripMenuItem.Click

        Me.BackColor = Color.Yellow
        WhiteToolStripMenuItem.Checked = False
        YellowToolStripMenuItem.Checked = True
        GrayToolStripMenuItem.Checked = False

End Sub
```

As you can see, the only difference between this and the code that you added to the White menu item is that this code changes the background color to yellow and sets the check mark for the Yellow menu item.

Adding Code to the Gray Menu Item

Now access the click event for the Gray menu item and modify the code that is automatically generated as shown here:

```
Private Sub GrayToolStripMenuItem_Click(ByVal sender _
    As System.Object, ByVal e As System.EventArgs) _
    Handles GrayToolStripMenuItem.Click

        Me.BackColor = Color.LightGray
        WhiteToolStripMenuItem.Checked = False
        YellowToolStripMenuItem.Checked = False
        GrayToolStripMenuItem.Checked = True


End Sub
```

Adding Code to the First Font Size Submenu Item

Let's add the code that will execute when the menu items on the Font Size submenu are clicked. For starters, access the click event for the first menu item in the Font Sizes submenu (the menu items that set the font size to 8) and modify the code that is automatically generated as shown here:

```
Private Sub ToolStripMenuItem1_Click(ByVal sender _
    As System.Object, ByVal e As System.EventArgs) _
    Handles ToolStripMenuItem1.Click

        txtOutput.Font = New Font("Microsoft Sans Serif", 8)
        ToolStripMenuItem1.Checked = True
        ToolStripMenuItem2.Checked = False
        ToolStripMenuItem3.Checked = False


End Sub
```

As you can see, the first statement that you added sets the Font property or the txtOutput control to Microsoft Sans Serif and specifies a font size of 8. The next three statements control the placement of the check mark.

Adding Code to the Second Font Size Submenu Item

Now access the click event for the second menu item in the Font Size submenu (the menu item that sets the font size to 10) and modify the code that is automatically generated as shown here:

```
Private Sub ToolStripMenuItem2_Click(ByVal sender As System.Object, _
     ByVal e As System.EventArgs) Handles ToolStripMenuItem2.Click

        txtOutput.Font = New Font("Microsoft Sans Serif", 10)
        ToolStripMenuItem1.Checked = False
        ToolStripMenuItem2.Checked = True
        ToolStripMenuItem3.Checked = False


End Sub
```

Adding Code to the Third Font Size Submenu Item

Finally, access the click event for the third menu item in the Font Size submenu (the menu item that sets the font size to 12) and modify the code that is automatically generated as shown here:

```
Private Sub ToolStripMenuItem3_Click(ByVal sender As System.Object, _
     ByVal e As System.EventArgs) Handles ToolStripMenuItem3.Click

        txtOutput.Font = New Font("Microsoft Sans Serif", 12)
        ToolStripMenuItem1.Checked = False
        ToolStripMenuItem2.Checked = False
        ToolStripMenuItem3.Checked = True


End Sub
```

Adding Code to the About Menu Item

Now let's add the program statements for the last remaining menu item by accessing the click event for the About menu item located under the Help menu. Modify the code that is automatically generated as shown here:

```
Private Sub AboutToolStripMenuItem_Click(ByVal sender _
     As System.Object, ByVal e As System.EventArgs) _
     Handles AboutToolStripMenuItem.Click

        MessageBox.Show("This Visual Basic application was created " & _
```

```
    "by Jerry Lee Ford, Jr.")
```

```
End Sub
```

As you can see, the `MessageBox.Show` method is executed whenever the player clicks on the About menu item, displaying information about the application and its author.

That's the last of this application's program statements. In the next four chapters, you will learn about the programming statements that make up the Visual Basic programming language. So if there is anything in this project that you had trouble understanding, bookmark it and then come back and look over the example again once you have read Chapters 5 through 8.

Step 5: Testing the Execution of the Click Race Game

Okay. That's it. It's time to test your newest creation. Press F5 and see how it runs. If you run into any errors, go back and check your typing and fix any typos that you may have made. Once you think you have the game running smoothly, share it with friends and ask them to test it out as well.

SUMMARY

In this chapter, you learned how to put finishing touches on your Visual Basic application's interfaces through the addition of a menu and toolbars. This included learning how to create menus, menu items, and submenus. You also learned how to enhance your menu system through the addition of shortcuts, access keys, and separator bars. On top of all this, you learned how to create context menus and how to associate them with controls. Finally, you learned how to provide single-click access to your Visual Basic application's most commonly used commands through the creation of toolbars.

Now, before you move on to Chapter 5, take a few minutes and enhance the Lottery Assistant game by implementing the following challenges.

CHALLENGES

1. Add a menu item under the Help menu that provides instructions for using the Lottery Game using the `MessageBox.Show` method.
2. Add a toolbar to the Lottery Assistant game and define buttons for each of the menu items found under the File and Options menus.
3. Going back to the material that you learned in Chapter 3, "Creating an Application Interface," create ToolTips for each `TextBox` and add a status bar to your application.

CHAPTER 5

STORING AND RETRIEVING DATA IN MEMORY

When you interact with a computer application, the information that you provide and the actions that you take are processed by the application. In order to be able to work with this information, the application needs to be able to store data as it collects it so that it can later retrieve and modify the data. In this chapter, you will learn how to store and retrieve data in memory using constants, variables, structures, and arrays. I'll also cover a couple of extra items, including how to embed comments inside your program code and how to work with the ProgressBar control. In addition, you will get the chance to work on a new game project, the Story of Mighty Molly game.

Specifically, you will learn how to:

- Define constants, variables, structures, and arrays
- Properly specify data types
- Convert data from one data type to another
- Specify variable scope

PROJECT PREVIEW: THE STORY OF MIGHTY MOLLY

In this chapter, you will learn how to create a Visual Basic game called the Story of Mighty Molly. In this game, the player helps to tell the story by providing answers to questions that are designed to collect specific data that is then used to complete the story. Figures 5.1 through 5.5 provide a sneak preview of the Story of Mighty Molly and demonstrate the overall execution of the game.

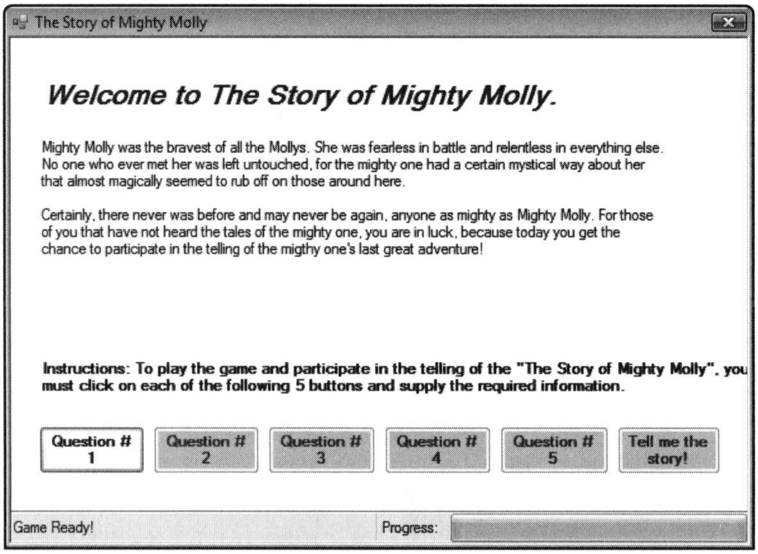

FIGURE 5.1

The Story of Mighty Molly game begins by prompting the player to click on each of six buttons that are designed to collect player input and tell the story.

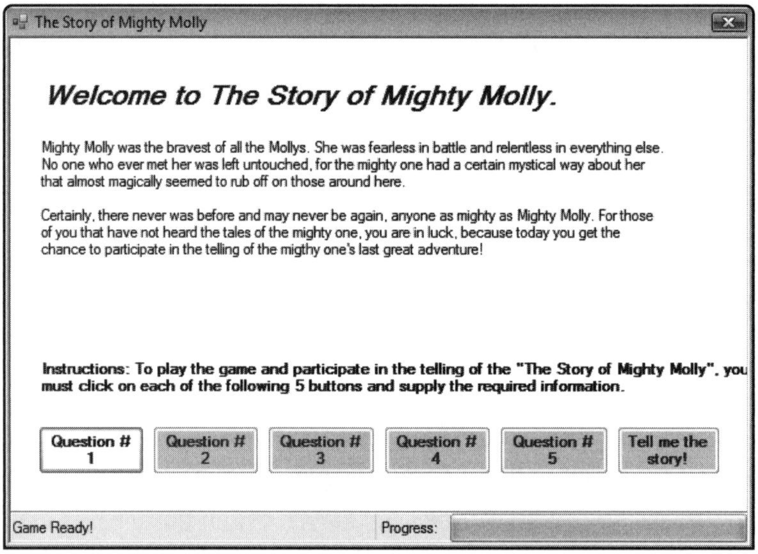

FIGURE 5.2

Players' input is collected using the InputBox() function.

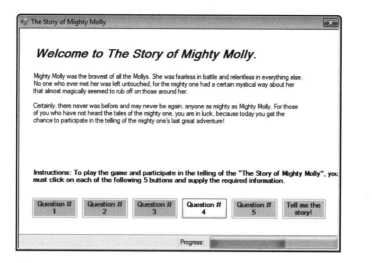

FIGURE 5.3

Buttons change colors to indicate that the player has already supplied the associated input.

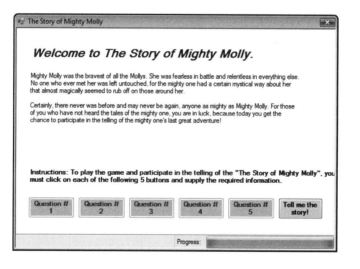

FIGURE 5.4

A progress bar located on the status bar indicates when all required information has been collected.

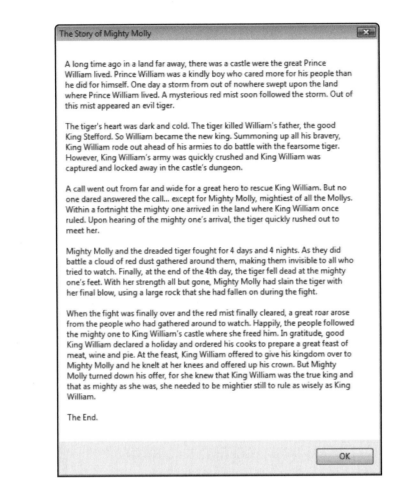

The Story of Mighty Molly

A long time ago in a land far away, there was a castle were the great Prince William lived. Prince William was a kindly boy who cared more for his people than he did for himself. One day a storm from out of nowhere swept upon the land where Prince William lived. A mysterious red mist soon followed the storm. Out of this mist appeared an evil tiger.

The tiger's heart was dark and cold. The tiger killed William's father, the good King Stefford. So William became the new king. Summoning up all his bravery, King William rode out ahead of his armies to do battle with the fearsome tiger. However, King William's army was quickly crushed and King William was captured and locked away in the castle's dungeon.

A call went out from far and wide for a great hero to rescue King William. But no one dared answered the call... except for Mighty Molly, mightiest of all the Mollys. Within a fortnight the mighty one arrived in the land where King William once ruled. Upon hearing of the mighty one's arrival, the tiger quickly rushed out to meet her.

Mighty Molly and the dreaded tiger fought for 4 days and 4 nights. As they did battle a cloud of red dust gathered around them, making them invisible to all who tried to watch. Finally, at the end of the 4th day, the tiger fell dead at the mighty one's feet. With her strength all but gone, Mighty Molly had slain the tiger with her final blow, using a large rock that she had fallen on during the fight.

When the fight was finally over and the red mist finally cleared, a great roar arose from the people who had gathered around to watch. Happily, the people followed the mighty one to King William's castle where she freed him. In gratitude, good King William declared a holiday and ordered his cooks to prepare a great feast of meat, wine and pie. At the feast, King William offered to give his kingdom over to Mighty Molly and he knelt at her knees and offered up his crown. But Mighty Molly turned down his offer, for she knew that King William was the true king and that as mighty as she was, she needed to be mightier still to rule as wisely as King William.

The End.

OK

FIGURE 5.5

Data input collected from the player is then plugged into the story line and displayed for the player to enjoy.

ENHANCING YOUR CODE WITH COMMENTS

As your Visual Basic applications get bigger and more complicated, so will the number and complexity of the programming statements that you add to them. As the amount of code in an application grows, it becomes increasingly harder to follow. Program code that makes perfect sense to you as you write it today may be very difficult for you to come back to a year or two later and try to work with again. It can be especially difficult for someone else who may have to follow behind you and make modifications or enhancements to the application.

So, like Hansel and Gretel, to make things easier on yourself or on someone who may have to follow behind you, it's a good idea to leave a trail of breadcrumbs. You can leave this trail in the form of comments. By embedding comments at key points in your applications, you can leave behind notes that explain why you did things the way you did.

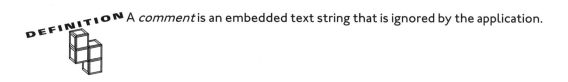

DEFINITION A *comment* is an embedded text string that is ignored by the application.

In Visual Basic, comments start with the ' character, as demonstrated here:

```
'Define an integer type variable named intCounter
Dim intCounter As Integer = 0
```

As you can see, the first statement in the previous example documents what the following statement does. When executed, Visual Basic ignores the first statement, only executing the second line of code. Visual Basic also allows you to add comments to the end of other statements, as demonstrated here:

```
MessageBox.Show("The date is: " & Now())  'Display current date and time
```

STORING AND RETRIEVING DATA

Like any programming language, Visual Basic requires the ability to store data and then later to retrieve and process it. You've seen numerous examples of this in game projects from earlier chapters. In this chapter, I'll explain your options for storing and retrieving data in Visual Basic.

DEFINITION *Data* is information collected by your application that it stores, retrieves, and modifies during execution.

Alternative Ways of Storing Data

Visual Basic is an extremely flexible programming language, often offering you many different ways of performing a particular task. Such is the case when it comes to working with data. In fact, Visual Basic provides a number of different data management options, each of which is uniquely suited to different situations. The options that you decide to use will vary from situation to situation, because the best method for storing data varies based on the manner in which the data is used.

- **Constants.** There will be times when you develop applications that need to work with known values that do not change during the execution of the applications. A good example would be an application that performs various mathematical calculations, using known values such as pi. Because the value of pi does not change, you can assign it to a constant.

- **Variables.** Constants are fine for storing limited amounts of data. However, in most cases, the data that your applications process will change during program execution. In these situations, you will need to use variables to store the data.

- **Arrays.** Sometimes, you may find that you need to store and work with collections of related information, such as a list of user names. In these situations, you can load the entire list into an array, which is an indexed list of related information.

- **Structures.** A structure is a user-defined data type that allows you to group together related variables into a single entity. For example, if you were creating an application that needed to work with people's names, addresses, and phone numbers, you could define a structure containing variables representing each of these pieces of information. Then, later in your application, you could create an array based on that structure and use it to store and process all three pieces of data for each person at the same time.

TRICK As discussed in Chapter 9, another option that is available to you for managing data is to define your own customized Class.

Data Types

Visual Basic is capable of storing and working with many different data types. Table 5.1 lists each of the data types supported by Visual Basic.

As Table 5.1 shows, Visual Basic supports a large collection of data types. Each data type, except the Object data type, is capable of storing a specific type of data. As Table 5.1 also shows, the amount of memory required to store data varies based on its data type. Visual Basic is very flexible. If you don't tell Visual Basic what the data type is for a particular piece of data, it assigns the data a default data type of Object.

TRAP Using the Object data type is not the most efficient option and will cause your application to consume additional memory. I recommend you always specify the data type for your variables.

TRICK When you specify the correct data types, you set up your Visual Basic programs to run more efficiently. However, I wouldn't invest too much time in analyzing the optimum data type for every variable you create. You can strike a balance between efficiency and memory usage versus development time by using String, Integer, Double, Boolean, and Date.

TABLE 5.1　VISUAL BASIC SUPPORTED DATA TYPES

Data Type	Storage Requirements (in Bytes)	Value Range
Boolean	2	True or False
Byte	1	0 to 255
Char	2	0 to 65535
Date	8	January 1, 0001 to December 31, 9999
Decimal	16	0 to +/-79,228,162,514,264,337,593,543,950,335
Double	8	-1.79769313486231570E+308 to -4.94065645841246544E-324 for negative number and 4.94065645841246544E-324 to 1.79769313486231570E +308 for positive numbers
Integer	4	-2,147,483,648 to 2,147,483,647
Long	8	-2,147,483,648 to 2,147,483,647
Object	4	Any type of variable
Sbyte	1	-128 to 127
Short	2	-32,768 to 32,767
Single	4	-3.402823E+38 to -1.401298E-45 for negative numbers and 1.401298E-45 and 3.4028235E+E38 for positive numbers
String	Varies	Up to two billion characters
UInteger	4	0 to 4,294,967,295
Ulong	8	0 to 18,446,744,073,709,551,615
UShort	2	0 to 65,535

By specifying a data type, you tell Visual Basic what range of values are allowable for a variable as well as what actions can be performed on the variable. For example, by specifying one of the numeric data types, you tell Visual Basic that it can perform mathematic calculations using the variable.

WORKING WITH CONSTANTS

When deciding whether to use a constant, variable, array, or structure to store a piece of data, it is best to first look at how the data is to be used. Data that is known at design time and that will not change during the execution of the application should be defined as a constant, allowing Visual Basic to more efficiently store and process the data.

Within Visual Basic, there are two sources of constants. You can define your own constants and assign data to them, or Visual Basic makes available to you a number of predefined constants.

Declaring Your Own Constants

By assigning data to a constant instead of to a variable, you eliminate the possibility that you might accidentally change the data later on in your application, which can happen in cases where you declare two very similarly named variables. If you try to change the data assigned to a constant, Visual Basic will flag it as an error when you test the execution of your application.

Constants make your application code easier to read. Your applications will also run faster because constants require less memory than variables.

To declare a constant within Visual Basic, you must use the Const keyword using the syntax outlined here:

```
Const ConstName As DataType = Expression
```

ConstName represents the name that you assign to the constant. DataType identifies the type of data that will be assigned to the constant, and Expression represents the value that is being assigned. To demonstrate how constants work, take a look at the following example:

```
Public Class Form1

    Const cTitleBarMsg As String = "The Story of Mighty Molly"

    Private Sub Form1_Load(ByVal sender As System.Object, _
        ByVal e As System.EventArgs) Handles MyBase.Load

            MessageBox.Show("Mighty Molly was the bravest of ......", _
                cTitleBarMsg)

    End Sub

End Class
```

In this example, a constant named cTitleBarMsg is declared with a date type of String and is assigned a value of "The Story of Mighty Molly". It is declared outside of any procedure and therefore can be accessed from anywhere within the Public Class Form1 and End Class statements. This is demonstrated when the MessageBox.Show method uses it as an argument specifying the pop-up window's title bar message, as shown in Figure 5.6.

TRICK As a matter of convention, I have added the letter c to the beginning of constants to make them easier to identify.

When assigning data to constants or variables, it is important that you package it appropriately. The following example demonstrates how to define a constant for a numeric type value:

```
Const cMaxValue As Integer = 999
```

To assign a `String` data type value to a constant, you must enclose the string within a pair of matching quotation marks, as shown here:

```
Const cCompanyname = "Inner IV Enterprises, Inc."
```

Finally, to assign a `Date` data type value to a constant, you must enclose the string within a pair of matching pound signs, as shown here:

```
Const cBirthday = #November 20, 1964#
```

Using Visual Basic Built-in Constants

Visual Basic provides access to all sorts of predefined constants. For example, in Chapter 3, "Creating an Application Interface," you learned how to work with constants that specified what types of buttons and icons should appear in pop-up windows displayed by the `MessageBox.Show` method. Table 5.2 lists a number of Visual Basic constants that you are likely to use over time to control the output of text strings.

TABLE 5.2 VISUAL BASIC CONSTANTS FOR FORMATTING STRINGS

Constant	Description
ControlCharsCr	Executes a carriage return.
ControlCharsCrLf	Executes a carriage return and a line feed.
ControlCharsFormFeed	Executes a form feed.
ControlCharsLf	Executes a line feed.
ControlCharsNewLine	Adds a newline character.
ControlCharsTab	Executes a horizontal tab.

You can see some of these string constants in action in the following example.

```
Private Sub Form1_Load(ByVal sender As System.Object, _
     ByVal e As System.EventArgs) Handles MyBase.Load


    Dim strStoryMsg As String = ""
    strStoryMsg &= "Once it was believed that the world was flat."
    strStoryMsg &= ControlChars.NewLine & "Later, it was found "
    strStoryMsg &= "that the world was round." & ControlChars.NewLine
    strStoryMsg &= "Who knew?" & ControlChars.NewLine
    strStoryMsg &= ControlChars.NewLine & ControlChars.Tab & "The End"
    MessageBox.Show(strStoryMsg)


End Sub
```

As you can see, the ControlCharsNewLine and ControlCharsTab constants were embedded within the string text to control when line breaks occurred and to execute a tab operation. This example displays the pop-up window shown in Figure 5.7.

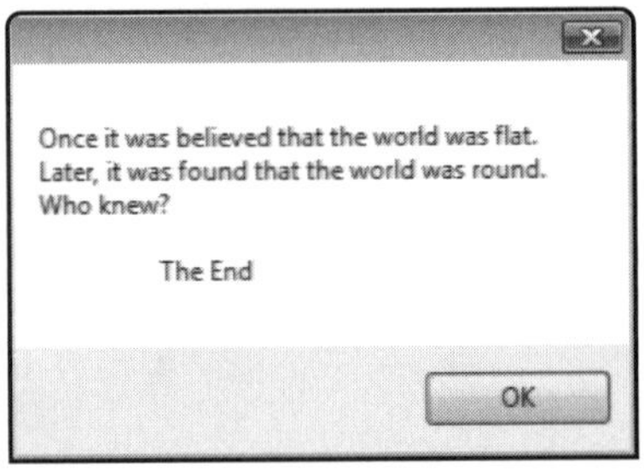

FIGURE 5.7

Using string constants to specify the output format of a string.

WORKING WITH VARIABLES

Constants are great for storing data that does not change during program execution. However, most of the time, you will need to store data that may change as your application runs. In these situations, you will need to use variables to store the data.

A variable is a pointer or logical reference to a location in memory where a piece of data is stored. Therefore, a variable doesn't actually store the data, it only keeps track of where the data resides.

 DEFINITION A *variable* stores data that may change during program execution.

Variables provide your Visual Basic applications with the ability to process all kinds of data. For example, in previous chapter game projects, you have seen where applications have used text boxes to collect player input, which were then stored in variables and later processed.

There are two steps to working with variables, as listed here:

- **Variable declaration.** This involves the naming of a variable and the identification of the type of data that it will store.
- **Variable assignment.** This is the process of assigning a value to a variable.

Defining Variables

After working on the game projects in the first four chapters, you've probably figured out by now that one way to declare a variable is to use the `Dim` keyword, as demonstrated here:

```
Dim intCounter
```

The `Dim` keyword is used to reserve space in memory. In this example, I have declared a new variable named `intCounter`. A variable declared in this manner is considered to be *loosely typed*, meaning that because you did not tell Visual Basic what type of data it will store, Visual Basic has, by default, assigned the variable and data type of `Object`. As a general rule, it's a good idea to *strongly type* variables. This is done by adding the `As` keyword to the end of a `Dim` statement and then specifying a data type, as demonstrated here:

```
Dim intCounter As Integer
```

In this example, I declared a variable named `intCounter` indicating that it will be used to store an `Integer`. By specifying a data type, I also told Visual Basic how much memory will be required to store the `intCounter` variable. If you refer back to Table 5.1, you'll see that an `Integer` type variable requires four bytes of memory.

By default, Visual Basic 2008 Express requires that all variables be explicitly declared. However, by adding the following statement as the first statement in your application's program code, you can disable this requirement.

```
Option Explicit Off
```

When this declaration requirement is disabled, you are allowed to implicitly declare variables, which means that you will be able to create new variables by simply referencing them for the first time, without previously declaring them, as demonstrated here:

```
strPlayerName = "Alexander Ford"
```

However, I strongly advise against implicitly declaring variables in your Visual Basic applications. Explicit variable declaration helps make your program code easier to read and is good programming practice.

If you want, Visual Basic allows you to save space by declaring multiple variables of the same data type on a single line, as demonstrated here:

```
Dim strFirstname, strMiddleName, strLastName As String
```

When developing Visual Basic applications that target .NET 3.0, Visual Basic 2008 Express provides a new capability referred to as *local type interference*, which means that you can now declare variables without explicitly specifying their data type. For example, using local type interference, you might define the following variable.

```
Dim intAge = 44
```

In response, Visual Basic 2008 Express will make its own determination as to the variable's data type. In the case of the above example, Visual Basic will strongly type the variable's value as an integer.

Assigning Data to Variables

Once a variable has been declared, you can assign a value to it, as demonstrated here:

```
Dim dteMyBirthday As Date
dteMyBirthday = #November 20, 1964#
```

If you don't assign a value to your variables when you first declare them, Visual Basic automatically assigns them a default value. A zero is automatically assigned to variables with a numeric data type. An empty string ("") is automatically assigned to a variable with a data type of String, and a date of January 1, 0001 is automatically assigned to a variable with a data type of Date. Unless you want these default value assignments, you'll need to make sure that you remember to assign a value to your variables either when you first declare them or at least before the first time your application tries to use them.

To save space, you can also combine variable declarations and assignments into one statement, as demonstrated here:

```
Dim dteMyBirthday As Date = #November 20, 1964#
```

You can even declare and assign values to multiple variables in the same statement, as demonstrated here:

```
Dim intMinimumAge As Integer = 16, intMaximumAge As Integer = 21
```

You can also mix and match data types when declaring variables and making value assignments, as shown here:

```
Dim strPlayerName As String = "Alexander Ford", intPlayerAge As Integer = 7
```

Defining Local Variables

A local variable is one that is declared at the block or procedure level using the `Dim` keyword. Local variables can only be referenced within the block or procedure where they are defined and are therefore not accessible to other parts of a Visual Basic application.

 **DEFINITION** A *block* is a collection of statements that are processed as a unit. Blocks are created using the `If` statement and various looping statements.

For example, the following statements demonstrate how to declare and assign data to a local variable name `blnGameOver` within a block.

```
If intCounter > 10 Then
    Dim blnGameOver As Boolean
    blnGameOver = True
End If
```

Because the `blnGameOver` variable is defined within a block, it cannot be referenced from anywhere outside the block. Similarly, the following example demonstrates how to declare and assign data to a local variable named `strMessage` within a procedure.

```
Private Sub Button1_Click(ByVal sender As System.Object, _
    ByVal e As System.EventArgs) Handles Button1.Click
```

```
        Dim strMessage As String
        strMessage = "Hello World!"
        MessageBox.Show(strMessage)

End Sub
```

Local variables exist only while the block or procedure that declares them is executing. Once the block or procedure ends, Visual Basic destroys any local variables, freeing up the memory that they used. Thus, using local variables can help reduce the overall amount of memory used by your application when compared to static and module variables, which have a longer lifetime.

Defining Static Variables

A static variable is one that is declared at the block or procedure level using the `Static` keyword. Static variables can only be referenced within the block or procedure where they are defined and therefore cannot be accessed by other parts of a Visual Basic application. However, unlike local variables, a static variable continues to exist after the block or procedure that contains it has finished executing. In fact, a static variable exists as long as your application runs. The following example demonstrates how to use a static variable.

```
Private Sub Button1_Click(ByVal sender As System.Object, _
       ByVal e As System.EventArgs) Handles Button1.Click

        Static intCounter As Integer
        intCounter += 1


End Sub
```

One good use for static variables is to create a procedure that behaves differently based on the number of times it has been executed. You can accomplish this by declaring a static variable with a data type of `Integer`, incrementing its value by 1 each time the procedure executes and adding programming logic for the procedure to behave differently when the value of the static variable reaches a certain number.

Defining Variable Scope

A module variable is one that is declared inside a module, structure, or class but that is not inside a procedure. Module variables are declared using the following syntax:

```
Modifier VariableName As DataType
```

The ability to reference a module variable depends on which of the following modifiers is used to define it:

- **Private.** Accessible from within the module, structure, or class where it is declared
- **Public.** Accessible from anywhere within the project where it is declared
- **Friend.** Accessible from anywhere within the solution where it is defined

As an example, the following statements define a module variable named strMessage that can be accessed from anywhere within the Form1 class where it is defined. In this example, however, Form1 represents the form or window within the application. If the application consisted of more than one form and there was a need to be able to access the variable from either form, then you would need to use the Public or Friend keyword to redefine the variable's scope.

```
Public Class Form1

    Private strMessage As String = "Hello World!"

    Private Sub Form1_Load(ByVal sender As System.Object, _
        ByVal e As System.EventArgs) Handles MyBase.Load

        MessageBox.Show(strMessage)

    End Sub


End Class
```

As a general rule, it is considered to be a good programming practice to limit the scope of your variables as narrowly as possible. This helps conserve memory and reduces the chances of accidentally changing the value assigned to a variable from a different location in a Visual Basic application.

Rules for Naming Variables

There are a few rules that you need to be aware of that govern the naming of variables. Failure to follow these rules, listed next, will result in an error.

- Variable names must begin with either an alphabetic or underscore character.
- Variable names cannot include spaces.
- Variable names cannot be reserved words.
- Variable names must be unique within their scope.

IN THE REAL WORLD

You may have noticed that I am preceding each variable name with a three-character prefix that helps to identify the type of data associated with the variable, making things easier to understand. I recommend that you do the same. For your convenience, you may want to use the prefixes shown in the following list.

- Boolean: bln
- Byte: byt
- Date: dtm
- Double: dbl
- Error: err
- Integer: int
- Long: lng
- Object: obj
- Single: sng
- String: str

Recognizing Variables as Objects

As you may recall from Chapter 1, "An Introduction to Visual Basic 2008 Express," Visual Basic is an object-oriented programming language. The object-oriented programming design is so strongly integrated into Visual Basic that even variables are treated like objects. To see what I mean, perform the following exercise.

1. Start Visual Basic and create a new Visual Basic application.
2. Double-click on the default form (form1) to open the code editor and access the form's Load event procedure.
3. By default, Visual Basic will generate the following code to set up the application's response to the Load event for you.

```
Public Class Form1

    Private Sub Form1_Load(ByVal sender As System.Object, _
      ByVal e As System.EventArgs) Handles MyBase.Load
```

```
    End Sub

End Class
```

4. Declare a variable name `strUserAge` as an `Integer` and assign it a value of 55 as shown here:

```
Dim strUserAge As Integer = 55
```

5. Next, type the following partial statement exactly as shown here:

```
MessageBox.Show(strUserAge.
```

6. Because Visual Basic treats variables as objects, IntelliSense kicks in and displays all of the properties and methods available, as shown in Figure 5.8.

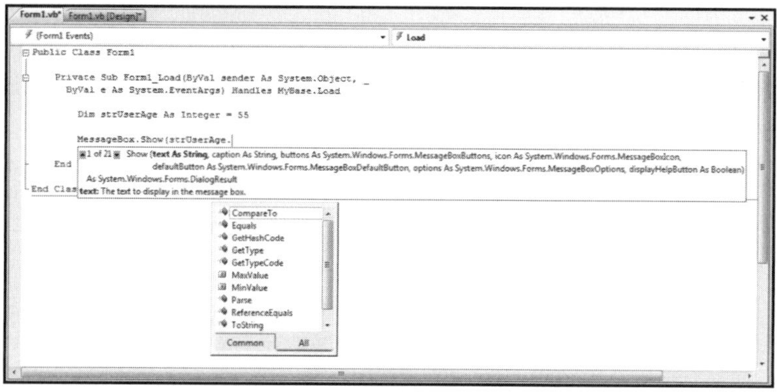

FIGURE 5.8

Using IntelliSense to view methods and properties associated with a variable object.

7. Click on `ToString` and press Enter. The statement should now look like the example shown here:

```
MessageBox.Show(strUserAge.ToString)
```

> **TRICK** You can use the `ToString` method to return a string showing the value for the specified variable, whether it is a number or a date.

Variable Conversion

Data typing is important because it tells Visual Basic how to store and handle the value that you assign. If you don't specify a variable's data type, Visual Basic assigns the variable a data type of `Object`. Then, later in your application when your program makes a change to the variable, Visual Basic takes its best guess as to how to convert the variable's data type assignment based on the action being taken. Most of the time, Visual Basic selects a data type that works just fine. However, it may not select the most efficient data type. And sometimes, the data type it selects causes problems. For example, if you declare a variable as an `Integer` but then assign a number that includes a decimal point, such as 5.1, to it, Visual Basic automatically rounds 5.1 to 5, which can lead to all sorts of problems. Instead of `Integer`, a value type of `Double` would have been the right choice in this example.

As you develop new Visual Basic applications, you are going to come across times when you will have to convert data from one type to another. There are two ways to convert a value's data type. One is to let Visual Basic do it for you automatically. However, as the following example demonstrates, sometimes Visual Basic gets things wrong.

```
Public Class Form1

    Private Sub Form1_Load(ByVal sender As System.Object, _
        ByVal e As System.EventArgs) Handles MyBase.Load

        Dim dblPI As Double = 3.14
        Dim intPI As Integer

        intPI = dblPI

        MessageBox.Show(intPI)

    End Sub

End Class
```

If you key in and run this example, you see that Visual Basic truncates .14, displaying a value of 3. This occurs because variables of the data type `Integer` are not able to store decimal information. Most likely, a conversion of this type will cause a problem in your applications. One way to prevent this type of problem is to add an `Option Strict On` statement to your program, as demonstrated here:

```
Option Strict On

Public Class Form1

    Private Sub Form1_Load(ByVal sender As System.Object, _
        ByVal e As System.EventArgs) Handles MyBase.Load
```

```
Dim dblPI As Double = 3.14
Dim intPI As Integer

intPI = dblPI

MessageBox.Show(intPI)

    End Sub

End Class
```

 Take note of the location of the Option Strict On statement. When used, Visual Basic requires that you place it before any declaration statements; therefore, it had to go before the Public Class Form1 statement. If you put it anywhere else in this example, you'll get an error.

Now, with the Option Strict On statement in place, press F5 and you see that Visual Basic displays a message indicating that an error has been detected. Visual Basic automatically displays the error message in the Error List window, as demonstrated in Figure 5.9.

FIGURE 5.9

Adding Option Strict On forces Visual Basic to alert you to variable conversion problems.

The first error displayed in the Error List window states that conversion from Double to Integer was disallowed. The following statement generated this conversion error when the example attempted to convert the value of pi from a data type of Double to a data type of Integer.

```
intPI = dblPI
```

The second error states that conversion from Integer to String was disallowed, as well. The following statement generated this conversion error, because the MessageBox.Show method can only display data of the String type.

```
MessageBox.Show(intPI)
```

Fortunately, Visual Basic supplies you with a large number of conversion methods and functions allowing you to tell it how you want to convert data from one type to another. To use the methods and functions, you must specify the data to be converted inside the opening and closing parentheses, as demonstrated in the following example.

```
Option Strict On

Public Class Form1

    Private Sub Form1_Load(ByVal sender As System.Object, _
        ByVal e As System.EventArgs) Handles MyBase.Load

        Dim dblPI As Double = 3.14
        Dim intPI As Integer

        intPI = CInt(dblPI)
        MessageBox.Show(Convert.ToString(intPI))

    End Sub

End Class
```

In this example, it is assumed that the truncation of .14 is acceptable. Therefore the value stored as a `Double` in the `dblPI` variable is converted to an `Integer` data type using the `Cint()` function. The `Convert.ToString()` method is used to convert the `Integer` data type associated with the `intPI` variable to a `String` so that it can be displayed by the `MessageBox.Show` method.

Functions and Methods for Manipulating Strings

A variable with a data type of `String` can be used to store up to two million characters. One of the many strengths of Visual Basic is the abundance of string manipulating functions and methods. In fact, Visual Basic provides so many different ways of manipulating strings that it is unlikely you will ever have to develop your own custom string handling functions.

 DEFINITION A *string* is a series of one or more characters, which may include alphabetic, numeric, and special characters, as well as spaces, that is defined within a pair of double quotation marks ("").

In previous chapters, you have seen a number of examples of how to work with strings using the ampersand (&) operator, which joins or concatenates two strings together. Visual Basic provides a number of other string manipulation tools, including the properties and methods listed in Table 5.3.

TABLE 5.3   STRING HANDLING PROPERTIES AND METHODS

String Object Methods	Description
String.ToLower	This method converts a string to all lowercase.
String.ToUpper	This method converts a string to all uppercase.
String.Length	This property is used to retrieve the length of a string.
String.SubString	This method extracts a portion of a string.
String.ConCat	This method combines two strings.
String.Chars	This property is used to search for one string within another string.
String.TrimStart	This method removes leading blank spaces from the left side of a string.
String.TimeEnd	This method removes trailing blank spaces from the right side of a string.

As a quick example of how to use these functions and methods, take a look at the following example.

```
Public Class Form1

    Private Sub Form1_Load(ByVal sender As System.Object, _
      ByVal e As System.EventArgs) Handles MyBase.Load

        Dim strMsg As String = "Once upon a time in a far away land."
        MessageBox.Show("String is " & strMsg.Length & " characters long.")

    End Sub

End Class
```

In this example, the Length property is used to display the number of characters that makes up the strMsg variable's value.

WORKING WITH ARRAYS

It can quickly become difficult to keep up with large numbers of variables. Many times, you'll find that the different pieces of data collected and processed by a Visual Basic program have a strong relationship to one another. For example, you might write an application that collects and processes a list of people's names. In this type of situation, you can organize and manage all the names collected by your application as a unit in an array.

 **DEFINITION** An *array* is an indexed list of data. The first piece of data stored in an array is assigned an index position of 0. The next piece of data is assigned an index position of 1, and so on. Any data stored in the array can be referenced based on its index position.

Defining Arrays

You can use the Dim keyword to create a single-dimension array using the following syntax.

```
Dim ArrayName(dimensions) As Integer
```

Dimensions represents a comma-separated list of numbers that specify how many dimensions make up the array. For example, the following statement defines an array named strCustomerNamesArray that can hold up to five names:

```
Dim strCustomerNamesArray(4) as String
```

Because an array begins with an index number of 0, I specified the number 4 in order to set up the array to hold five entries (0 through 4).

 TIP Take note from the previous example that I added the word Array to the end of the array name in order to identify it as an array. I also added a three-character string to the beginning of the array name to identify the type of data that array will hold.

Loading Array Elements

Once you have declared your array, you can populate it with data, as demonstrated here:

```
astrCustomerNamesArray(0) = "Markland B."
astrCustomerNamesArray(1) = "Mike M."
astrCustomerNamesArray(2) = "Nick C."
```

Once populated, you can reference pieces of data stored in the array by specifying the name of the array followed by an index number, as demonstrated here:

```
MessageBox.Show strCustomerNamesArray(2)
```

Retrieving Array Elements

Because data stored in an array is usually related, you can set up a loop to process the array contents using just a few lines of code. This is a lot faster and more efficient than trying to specify each piece of data in the array one at a time using its index number. For example, suppose you have an array that contains 1,000 names. It wouldn't be practical to reference each item in the array individually. Instead, a better way to process the contents of the array would be to set up a For...Next loop.

The syntax of the For...Next loop is outlined here:

```
For counter = begin To end
    statements
Next
```

counter represents a variable that will be used to control the execution of the loop. *begin* is a number specifying the starting value of the *counter* variable, and *end* specifies the ending value for the counter variable. To see how to use the For...Next loop to process the contents of an array, look at the following example.

```
Public Class Form1

    Private Sub Form1_Load(ByVal sender As System.Object, _
      ByVal e As System.EventArgs) Handles MyBase.Load

        Dim strMessage As String = ""
        Dim strCustomerNamesArray(4) As String
        Dim intCounter As Integer
        strCustomerNamesArray(0) = "Markland B."
        strCustomerNamesArray(1) = "Mike M."
        strCustomerNamesArray(2) = "Nick C."

        For intCounter = 0 To 2
            strMessage = strMessage & _
              strCustomerNamesArray(intCounter) & _
              ControlChars.NewLine
        Next intCounter
        MessageBox.Show(strMessage)

    End Sub

End Class
```

As you can see in this example, the `For...Next` loop was used to spin through each element in the `strCustomerNamesArray` and put together a display string, which was displayed by the `MessageBox.Show` method once the loop had finished running. You will find additional information on the `For..Next` loop in Chapter 7, "Processing Lots of Data with Loops."

Resizing Arrays

There may be times when you need to increase the size of an array to accommodate additional data. When you think this might be the case, you should declare the array without specifying its initial size, as demonstrated here:

```
Dim strCustomerNamesArray() As String
```

Then later, perhaps after you have queried the user as to how much information will be provided, you can resize the array using the `ReDim` keyword, as shown here:

```
ReDim strCustomerNamesArray(9)
```

At this point, you can begin populating the array with data. If, however, you find that you have not made the array big enough, you can always resize it again, as shown here:

```
ReDim Preserve strCustomerNamesArray(19)
```

Note that this time I added the keyword `Preserve` just before the array name. This keyword tells Visual Basic not to delete any data already stored in the array when resizing it. If you forget to add the `Preserve` keyword when resizing an array, you'll lose any already populated data.

 You can also make arrays smaller. If you do, you'll lose data if you resize the array smaller than the number of elements stored in it.

Erasing Arrays

Once your program has finished using the data stored in an array, it's a good idea to delete the array, thus freeing up memory. You can do this using the `Erase` keyword and the following syntax.

```
Erase ArrayName
```

For example, to delete `strCustomerNamesArray`, you would add the following statement at the appropriate location within your program code:

```
Erase strCustomerNamesArray
```

WORKING WITH STRUCTURES

As I stated earlier in this chapter, a structure is a user-defined entity. In other words, you name it, define the variables that make it up, and then populate it, usually by creating an array based on the structure. Structures can be declared within a module or class but not within a procedure. A `Structure` begins with the keyword `Structure` and ends with the `End Structure` statement. The basic syntax of a `Structure` is outlined here:

```
Structure StructureName
    Dim VariableName As DataType
    Dim VariableName As DataType
    .
    .
    .
End Structure
```

Once defined, every variable defined within a structure is treated as a method. To see how to really work with structures, let's look at an example.

1. Create a new Visual Basic project.
2. Double-click on `form1`. The code editor will appear, displaying code for the form's `Load` event.
3. Enter the following statements just below the `Public Class Form1` statement. These statements define a `Structure` that will hold employee data. The `Structure` is made up of two variables that store employee names and numbers.

   ```
   Structure EmployeeNames
       Dim EmployeeName As String
       Dim EmployeeNumber As Integer
   End Structure
   ```

4. Enter the following statements inside the `Load` event procedure for the form. These statements declare two variables used later to control a `For...Next` loop and a display string.

   ```
   Dim intCounter As Integer = 0
   Dim strMessage As String = "Employee Name" & ControlChars.Tab & _
     "Employee #" & ControlChars.CrLf
   ```

5. Create a small array based on the `EmployeeNames` structure that can hold information for three employees, as shown here:

```
Dim EmployeeDataArray(2) As EmployeeNames
```

6. Now populate the array with data for three employees, as shown here:

```
EmployeeDataArray(0).EmployeeName = "Alexander Ford"
EmployeeDataArray(0).EmployeeNumber = 12345
EmployeeDataArray(1).EmployeeName = "William Ford"
EmployeeDataArray(1).EmployeeNumber = 23456
EmployeeDataArray(2).EmployeeName = "Mollisa Ford"
EmployeeDataArray(2).EmployeeNumber = 22335
```

7. Finally, add the following statements, which will loop through the EmployeeDataArray and display its contents.

```
For intCounter = 0 To UBound(EmployeeDataArray)
    strMessage = strMessage & _
        EmployeeDataArray(intCounter).EmployeeName & ControlChars.Tab & _
        EmployeeDataArray(intCounter).EmployeeNumber & ControlChars.CrLf
Next
MessageBox.Show(strMessage)
```

 Ubound() is a built-in function that returns the upper limit of an array.

8. Press F5 to run your application and you'll see, as demonstrated in Figure 5.10, that all of the employee names and numbers have been processed.

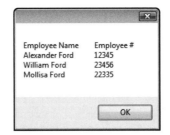

FIGURE 5.10

Managing large amounts of related data using an array based on a custom structure.

RESERVED WORDS

The Visual Basic programming language is made up of a large number of keywords (also referred to as reserved words) that have very specific meanings. An example of a reserved word is `Dim`, which is used to declare variables and arrays. Because it is a reserved word, you can only use the `Dim` keyword in your Visual Basic applications when you follow its syntax rules. In other words, you cannot use `Dim` as a variable name or as a name for any other programming construction (constants, arrays, structures, procedures, and so on). You will learn all about different reserved words as you make your way through this book.

 DEFINITION A *reserved word* is one that Visual Basic sets aside for a specific purpose. You may only use reserved words in your Visual Basic applications if you follow the rules that govern their usage.

BACK TO THE STORY OF MIGHTY MOLLY

Now it is time to turn your attention back to the development of this chapter's game project, the Story of Mighty Molly. To create this game, you will follow the same five development steps that you've used to create previous chapter projects.

Designing the Game

The Story of Mighty Molly will be played on a single window, although the `InputBox()` function and `MessageBox.Show` method will be used to collect and display stored input and output. The game will therefore be made up of one form and the 11 controls listed in Table 5.4.

TABLE 5.4	FORM CONTROLS FOR THE STORY OF MIGHTY MOLLY GAME	
Control Type	**Control Name**	**Description**
Label	lblWelcomeMsg	Displays the game's welcome message
Label	lblIntroText	Displays a brief prologue to the Story of Mighty Molly
Label	lblInstructions	Displays instruction for playing the game
Button	btnquestion1	Controls access to the game's first question
Button	btnquestion2	Controls access to the game's second question
Button	btnquestion3	Controls access to the game's third question
Button	btnquestion4	Controls access to the game's fourth question
Button	btnquestion5	Controls access to the game's fifth question
Button	btnPlayGame	Displays the game story
StatusBar	stbControl	Displays status information as the game progresses
ProgressBar	prbControl	Provides a graphical indication of the game's progress

Step 1: Creating a New Visual Basic Project

The first step in creating the Story of Mighty Molly is to start Visual Basic and open a new project.

1. If you have not already done so, start up Visual Basic 2008 Express and then click on File and select New Project. The New Project dialog will appear.
2. Select Windows Application template.
3. Type **The Story of Mighty Molly** as the name of your new application in the Name field located at the bottom of the New Project window.
4. Click on OK to close the New Project dialog.

Visual Basic will now create a new project for you, including an empty form, which you'll use to create the game's user interface.

Step 2: Creating the User Interface

Let's continue by adding the controls required to set up the game's user interface. The overall design of the game's interface is shown in Figure 5.11.

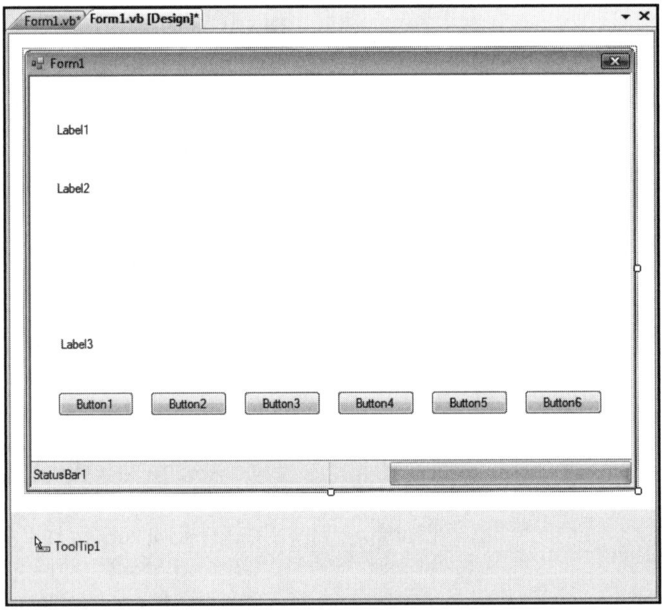

FIGURE 5.11

Completing the interface design for the Story of Mighty Molly game.

1. Begin by adding three Label controls to the form. By default, Visual Basic assigns the names Label1 through Label3 to these controls.
2. Add six Button controls to the form and line them up horizontally beneath the last Label control. By default, Visual Basic names these controls Button1 through Button6.
3. Add a StatusBar control to the form. By default, Visual Basic assigns this control the name StatusBar1.
4. Finally, add a ProgressBar control to the form and move it on top of the StatusBar control, as shown in Figure 5.11.

The overall layout for the application's form is now complete.

Step 3: Customizing Form and Control Properties

Now it is time to customize the form and its controls. By this point in the book, you should be comfortable with the steps involved in modifying form and control properties. So, instead of walking you through each step that is involved in modifying every control, I am going to provide tables for each control that identifies the property changes that need to be made and leave it up to you to make the changes. The property modifications that need to be made to form1 are listed in Table 5.5.

TABLE 5.5 PROPERTY CHANGES FOR FORM1	
Property	**Value**
Name	frmMain
BackColor	White
Cursor	Hand
FormBorderStyle	Fixed3D
MaximizeBox	False
MinimizeBox	False
StartPosition	CenterScreen
Text	The Story of Mighty Molly

The property changes for each of the form's three Label controls are listed in Table 5.6.

TABLE 5.6   PROPERTY CHANGES FOR THE LABEL CONTROLS

Control	Property	Value
Label1	Name	lblWelcomeMsg
	ForeColor	DarkBlue
	Text	Welcome to The Story of Mighty Molly.
Label2	Name	lblIntroText
	Text	Mighty Molly was the bravest of all the Mollys. She was fearless in battle and relentless in everything else. No one who ever met her was left untouched, for the mighty one had a certain mystical way about her that almost magically seemed to rub off on those around her. Certainly, there never was before and may never be again anyone as mighty as Mighty Molly. For those of you who have not heard the tales of the mighty one, you are in luck, because today you get the chance to participate in the telling of the mighty one's last great adventure!
Label3	Name	lblInstructions
	Font.Bold	True
	Text	Instructions: To play the game and participate in the telling of "The Story of Mighty Molly," you must click on each of the following 5 buttons and supply the required information.

The property changes for each of the six Button controls are listed in Table 5.7.

TABLE 5.7   PROPERTY CHANGES FOR THE BUTTON CONTROLS

Control	Property	Value
Button1	Name	btnQuestion1
	BackColor	LightYellow
	Font.Bold	True
	Text	Question # 1
	ToolTip	Click on button to answer the first question.
Button2	Name	btnQuestion2
	BackColor	LightGray
	Enabled	False
	Font.Bold	True
	Text	Question # 2
	ToolTip	Click on button to answer the second question.

```
Button3    Name         btnQuestion3
           BackColor    LightGray
           Enabled      False
           Font.Bold    True
           Text         Question # 3
           ToolTip      Click on button to answer the third question.
Button4    Name         btnQuestion4
           BackColor    LightGray
           Enabled      False
           Font.Bold    True
           Text         Question # 4
           ToolTip      Click on button to answer the fourth question.
Button5    Name         btnQuestion5
           BackColor    LightGray
           Enabled      False
           Font.Bold    True
           Text         Question # 5
           ToolTip      Click on button to answer the fifth question.
Button6    Name         btnPlayGame
           BackColor    LightGray
           Enabled      False
           Font.Bold    True
           Text         Tell me the story!
           ToolTip      Click on button to see the story.
```

The property changes for the StatusBar control are listed in Table 5.8.

TABLE 5.8   PROPERTY CHANGES FOR THE STATUSBAR CONTROL

Property	Value
Name	stbControl
Panels	StatusBarPanel1 (Text I Game Ready!)
	StatusBarPanel2 (Text I Progress:)
ShowPanels	True
Size.Height	24
SizingGrip	False

The property changes for the ProgressBar control are listed in Table 5.9.

TABLE 5.9 PROPERTY CHANGES FOR THE PROGRESSBAR CONTROL

Property	Value
Name	prbControl
Size.Height	22

Step 4: Adding a Little Programming Logic

Now that the game's user interface has been created and you have modified the appropriate form and control properties, it is time to begin coding. Start by double- clicking on `form1`. This will open the code editor and display code for the form's `Load` event. However, you don't need the code for the `Load` event, so you can delete it, leaving just the opening and closing `Class` statements, as shown here:

```
Public Class frmMain


End Class
```

Now add the following statements between these two statements.

```
'Declare constant used to specify titlebar message in pop-up Windows
Const cTitleBarMsg As String = "The Story of Mighty Molly"

'Declare variables used throughout the application
Private strCreature As String
Private strRoom As String
Private strColor As String
Private strWeapon As String
Private strFood As String
```

The first statement defines a constant that will be used to supply a title bar message for all the pop-up windows displayed by the game. The next five statements declare variables. Each variable will be used to store a piece of information supplied by the player. Notice that the `Friend` keyword is used to limit the scope of each variable to the class in which the variables were defined (such as `form1`). I could have just as easily used the `Dim` keyword and the application would have performed just the same. However, as a general rule, it is best to try to limit scope whenever possible.

Next, switch back to the form designer and double-click on the first `Button` control. Then modify the button's click event procedure, as shown here:

```
'This Sub procedure prompts the player to answer the 1st question
Private Sub btnQuestion1_Click(ByVal sender As System.Object, _
  ByVal e As System.EventArgs) Handles btnQuestion1.Click

    'Post message in the first panel on the statusbar
    StatusBarPanel1.Text = "Be Brave!"

    'Prompt player to answer the first question
    strCreature = InputBox("What creature scares you the most?", _
      cTitleBarMsg)

    'Make sure the player entered something
    If strCreature = "" Then
      MessageBox.Show("You must answer all questions to " & _
      "continue.", cTitleBarMsg)
    Else
      strCreature = strCreature.ToLower 'Convert input to lowercase
      StatusBarPanel1.Text = ""  'Clear statusbar
      btnQuestion1.Enabled = False  'Disable the 1st button control
      btnQuestion2.Enabled = True  'Enable the 2nd Button control
      btnQuestion1.BackColor = Color.LightPink  'Turn button pink
      btnQuestion2.BackColor = Color.LightYellow 'Turn button yellow
      prbControl.Value = 20  'Update the ProgressBar control
    End If

End Sub
```

The first statement inside the procedure sets the Text property of the StatusBarPanel1 to "Be Brave!" The next statement uses the InputBox() function to prompt the user to provide the name of a scary monster. The player's input is stored in a variable named strCreature. The next statement checks to make sure that the player did not click on the Cancel button or that the player did not click on the OK button without supplying any information. The MessageBox.Show method is used to display an error message if the player fails to provide input. Otherwise, the following actions are performed:

- The text string supplied by the player is converted to all lowercase using the ToLower method.

- The text displayed in the first status bar panel is cleared out.

- The btnQuestion1 button is disabled, preventing the player from clicking on it again.
- The btnQuestion2 button is enabled, allowing the player to click on it.
- The background color of the btnQuestion1 button is set to LightPink to indicate that the input collected from the player for the first question was accepted.
- The background color of the btnQuestion2 button is set to LightYellow to indicate that it is the currently active game button.
- The ProgressBar control is updated to show that the application has collected 20 percent of the input that is required to tell the story.

Now, access the procedure of the btnQuestion2 control and modify it as shown here:

```
'This Sub procedure prompts the player to answer the 2nd question
Private Sub btnQuestion2_Click(ByVal sender As System.Object, _
  ByVal e As System.EventArgs) Handles btnQuestion2.Click

    'Post message in the first panel on the statusbar
    StatusBarPanel1.Text = "Any Room Will Do!"

    'Prompt player to answer the second question
    strRoom = InputBox("What's the worst room in a castle?", _
      cTitleBarMsg)

    'Make sure the player entered something
    If strRoom = "" Then
      MessageBox.Show("You must answer all questions to " & _
      "continue.", cTitleBarMsg)
    Else
      strRoom = strRoom.ToLower  'Convert input to lowercase
      StatusBarPanel1.Text = ""  'Clear statusbar
      btnQuestion2.Enabled = False  'Disable the 2nd button control
      btnQuestion3.Enabled = True 'Enable the 3rd Button control
      btnQuestion2.BackColor = Color.LightPink  'Turn button pink
      btnQuestion3.BackColor = Color.LightYellow 'Turn button yellow
      prbControl.Value = 40  'Update the ProgressBar control
    End If

End Sub
```

As you can see, the code for the btnQuestion2 control is almost identical to the code that you added to the btnQuestion1 control, the only differences being:

- A different status bar message is displayed.
- A different question is asked.
- The player's response is stored in a different variable.
- This time, btnQuestion2 is disabled and btnQuestion3 is enabled.
- This time, the background color of btnQuestion2 is set to LightPink and the background of btnQuestion3 is set to LightYellow.

Now, access the procedure of the btnQuestion3 control and modify it as shown here:

```
'This Sub procedure prompts the player to answer the 3rd question
Private Sub btnQuestion3_Click(ByVal sender As System.Object, _
  ByVal e As System.EventArgs) Handles btnQuestion3.Click

    'Post message in the first panel on the statusbar
    StatusBarPanel1.Text = "Any Color Will Do!"

    'Prompt player to answer the third question
    strColor = InputBox("What is your favorite color?", _
      cTitleBarMsg)

    'Make sure the player entered something
    If strColor = "" Then
      MessageBox.Show("You must answer all questions to " & _
        "continue.", cTitleBarMsg)
    Else
      strColor = strColor.ToLower  'Convert input to lowercase
      StatusBarPanel1.Text = ""  'Clear statusbar
      btnQuestion3.Enabled = False 'Disable the 3rd button control
      btnQuestion4.Enabled = True  'Enable the 4th Button control
      btnQuestion3.BackColor = Color.LightPink  'Turn button pink
      btnQuestion4.BackColor = Color.LightYellow 'Turn button yellow
      prbControl.Value = 60  'Update the ProgressBar control
    End If


End Sub
```

Next, access the procedure of the btnQuestion4 control and modify it as shown here:

```
'This Sub procedure prompts the player to answer the 4th question
Private Sub btnQuestion4_Click(ByVal sender As System.Object, _
  ByVal e As System.EventArgs) Handles btnQuestion4.Click

    'Post message in the first panel on the statusbar
    StatusBarPanel1.Text = "Better be enough to kill a " & _
      strCreature & "!"

    'Prompt player to answer the fourth question
    strWeapon = InputBox("Name something that can be used as " & _
      "weapon that you might find on the ground.", cTitleBarMsg)

    'Make sure the player entered something
    If strWeapon = "" Then
      MessageBox.Show("You must answer all questions to " & _
        "continue.", cTitleBarMsg)
    Else
      strWeapon = strWeapon.ToLower 'Convert input to lowercase
      StatusBarPanel1.Text = ""  'Clear statusbar
      btnQuestion4.Enabled = False 'Disable the 4th button control
      btnQuestion5.Enabled = True  'Enable the 5th Button control
      btnQuestion4.BackColor = Color.LightPink  'Turn button pink
      btnQuestion5.BackColor = Color.LightYellow 'Turn button yellow
      prbControl.Value = 80  'Update the ProgressBar control
    End If

End Sub
```

Access the procedure of the btnQuestion5 control and modify it as shown here:

```
'This Sub procedure prompts the player to answer the 5th question
Private Sub btnQuestion5_Click(ByVal sender As System.Object, _
  ByVal e As System.EventArgs) Handles btnQuestion5.Click

    'Post message in the first panel on the statusbar
    StatusBarPanel1.Text = "What's Your Preference?"

    'Prompt player to answer the fifth question
```

```
      strFood = InputBox("What is your favorite thing to eat?", _
        cTitleBarMsg)

      'Make sure the player entered something
      If strFood = "" Then
        MessageBox.Show("You must answer all questions to " & _
          "continue.", cTitleBarMsg)
      Else
        strFood = strFood.ToLower 'Convert input to lowercase
        StatusBarPanel1.Text = ""  'Clear statusbar
        btnQuestion5.Enabled = False 'Disable the 5th button control
        btnPlayGame.Enabled = True  'Enable the last Button control
        btnQuestion5.BackColor = Color.LightPink  'Turn button pink
        btnPlayGame.BackColor = Color.LightGreen 'Turn button green
        prbControl.Value = 100   'Update the ProgressBar control
      End If


End Sub
```

Finally, modify the code for the btnPlayGame control as shown here:

```
'This Sub procedure is responsible for displaying the game's story
Private Sub btnPlayGame_Click(ByVal sender As System.Object, _
  ByVal e As System.EventArgs) Handles btnPlayGame.Click


    'Declare local variable used to store the game's story
    Dim strText As String = ""

    'Post message in the first panel on the statusbar
    StatusBarPanel1.Text = "Let's Rock!"

    'Assemble the game's story
    strText &= "A long time ago in a land far away, there "
    strText &= "was a castle where the great Prince William lived. "
    strText &= "Prince William was a kindly boy who cared more for "
    strText &= "his people than he did for himself. One day a storm "
    strText &= "from out of nowhere swept upon the land where "
    strText &= "Prince William lived. A mysterious " & strColor
    strText &= " mist soon followed the storm. Out of this mist "
```

```
strText &= "appeared an evil " & strCreature & "."
strText &= ControlChars.NewLine & ControlChars.NewLine
strText &= "The " & strCreature & "'s heart was dark and cold. "
strText &= "The " & strCreature & " killed William's father, the "
strText &= "good King Stefford. So William became the new king. "
strText &= "Summoning up all his bravery, King William rode out "
strText &= "ahead of his armies to do battle with the fearsome "
strText &= strCreature & ". However, King William's army was "
strText &= "quickly crushed and King William was captured and "
strText &= "locked away in the castle's " & strRoom & "
strText &= ControlChars.NewLine & ControlChars.NewLine
strText &= "A call went out from far and wide for a great hero "
strText &= "to rescue King William. But no one dared answer "
strText &= "the call except for Mighty Molly, mightiest of all "
strText &= "the Mollys. Within a fortnight the mighty one "
strText &= "arrived in the land where King William once ruled. "
strText &= "Upon hearing of the mighty one's arrival, the "
strText &= strCreature & " quickly rushed out to meet her."
strText &= ControlChars.NewLine & ControlChars.NewLine
strText &= "Mighty Molly and the dreaded " & strCreature
strText &= " fought for 4 days and 4 nights. As they did battle "
strText &= "a cloud of " & strColor & " dust gathered around "
strText &= "them, making them invisible to all who tried to "
strText &= "watch. Finally, at the end of the 4th day, the "
strText &= strCreature & " fell dead at the mighty one's feet. "
strText &= "With her strength all but gone, Mighty Molly had "
strText &= "slain the " & strCreature & " with her final "
strText &= "blow, using a large " & strWeapon & " that she had "
strText &= "fallen on during the fight." & ControlChars.NewLine
strText &= ControlChars.NewLine & "When the fight was finally "
strText &= "over and the " & strColor & "mist finally cleared, "
strText &= "a great roar arose from the people who had gathered "
strText &= "around to watch. Happily, the people followed the "
strText &= "mighty one to King William's castle where she "
strText &= "freed him. In gratitude, good King William declared "
strText &= "a holiday and ordered his cooks to prepare a great "
strText &= "feast of meat, wine, and " & strFood & ". At the "
strText &= "feast, King William offered to give his kingdom over "
```

```
      strText &= "to Mighty Molly and he knelt at her knees and "
      strText &= "offered up his crown. But Mighty Molly turned down "
      strText &= "his offer, for she knew that King William was the "
      strText &= "true king and that as mighty as she was, she needed "
      strText &= "to be mightier still to rule as wisely as King "
      strText &= "William." & ControlChars.NewLine
      strText &= ControlChars.NewLine & "The End."

    'Display the fully assembled story
     MessageBox.Show(strText, cTitleBarMsg)

    'Get the game ready to tell another story
    StatusBarPanel1.Text = "Game Ready!" 'Update statusbar message
    btnPlayGame.Enabled = False     'Disable the Button labeled Play

    'Reset variables to prepare the game to allow the player to create
    'a new story
    strCreature = ""
    strRoom = ""
    strColor = ""
    strWeapon = ""
    strFood = ""

    'Reset Button controls back to their original colors
    btnQuestion1.BackColor = Color.LightYellow
    btnQuestion2.BackColor = Color.LightGray
    btnQuestion3.BackColor = Color.LightGray
    btnQuestion4.BackColor = Color.LightGray
    btnQuestion5.BackColor = Color.LightGray
    btnPlayGame.BackColor = Color.LightGray

    'Reset the ProgressBar control's value property to zero
    prbControl.Value = 0

    'Enable the first Button control
    btnQuestion1.Enabled = True

End Sub
```

The first statement in this procedure declares a variable named strText, which will be used to hold the game's story line. The second statement posts a message of "Let's Rock!" in the left-hand status bar pane. The next series of statements builds the game's story line using the &= operator to append the lines of the story together. If you look closely at the text of the story, you see where the variables that contain the input provided by the player have been inserted throughout the story line. The MessageBox.Show method is then used to display the fully assembled story.

TRICK   The &= operator can be used as a shortcut for concatenating a text string to a String variable. It can be used as shown here:

```
strText &= "Once upon a time..."
```

Once the player has finished reading about Mighty Molly's adventure and clicked on the OK button displayed by the MessageBox.Show method's pop-up window, the remainder of the statements in the procedure execute and perform the following actions:

- Display the string text "Game Ready!" in the left status bar pane.
- Disable the btnPlayGame button.
- Reset the value stored in each of the game's variables to "".
- Set the background color of btnQuestion1 to LightYellow and the background of all the other buttons to LightGray.
- Reset the Value property of the ProgressBar control to 0.
- Enable the btnQuestion1 button.

Step 5: Testing the Execution of the Story of Mighty Molly Game

Okay. That's it. The Story of Mighty Molly should be ready to run. Press F5 and put the game through its paces. If you find any errors, double-check your typing. Once you think you have things working the way you want, try testing the game again, this time feeding data that the game doesn't expect to receive and see how it handles it.

SUMMARY

In this chapter, you learned how to store and retrieve data using a number of different programming constructs, including constants, variables, arrays, and structures. You learned how to specify data type, to convert data from one data type to another, and to control variable scope. You also learned how to add comments to your Visual Basic applications and to work with the ProgressBar control. Before you move on to Chapter 6, "Applying Conditional Logic," take a look at the following challenges and see if you can improve the Story of Mighty Molly.

CHALLENGES

1. Modify the story by allowing the players to change background colors and font types and sizes.
2. Create a unique looking icon for the game, display the icon on the application's title bar, and put an icon in the system tray when the game is running.
3. Modify the game so that the player can specify additional story inputs, including the name of the story's main character.

APPLYING CONDITIONAL LOGIC

In order to create truly effective applications, a programming language must be able to distinguish between two different situations and make a choice based on the results of that analysis. By examining user input, for example, you can use conditional logic to alter the execution flow of your Visual Basic applications. This allows you to develop applications that react dynamically and provide an interactive user experience. This chapter will provide you with instruction on how to apply conditional logic using variations of the If…Then and Select Case statements. In addition, you will get the chance to develop some advanced conditional logic of your own through the creation of the chapter's game project, the Guess a Number game.

Specifically, you will learn how to:

- Test two logical conditions
- Provide for alternative courses of action
- Embed conditional statements to create more complicated conditional logic tests
- Rest multiple conditions against a single value

PROJECT PREVIEW: THE GUESS A NUMBER GAME

In this chapter, you will learn how to create a Visual Basic game called the Guess a Number game. The development of this game will provide you with plenty of opportunities to apply your knowledge of conditional logic. Figures 6.1 through 6.4 provide a sneak preview of the Guess a Number game and demonstrate the game's overall execution.

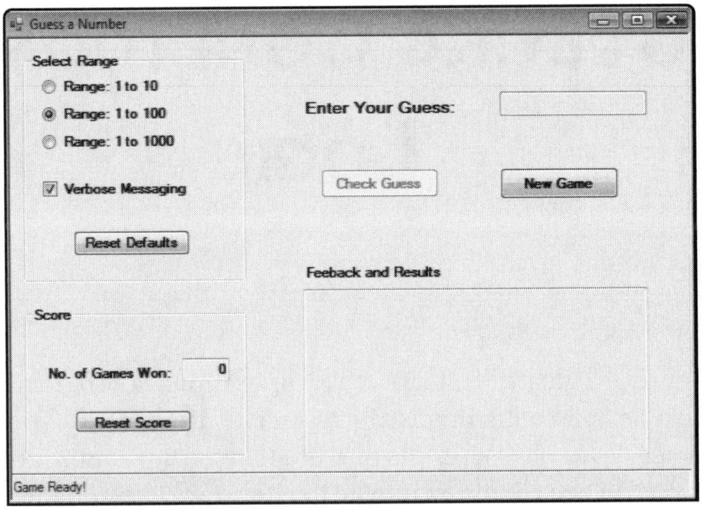

FIGURE 6.1

The game begins by allowing the player to specify configuration options, including the range of numbers to pick from and the amount of information the game will display.

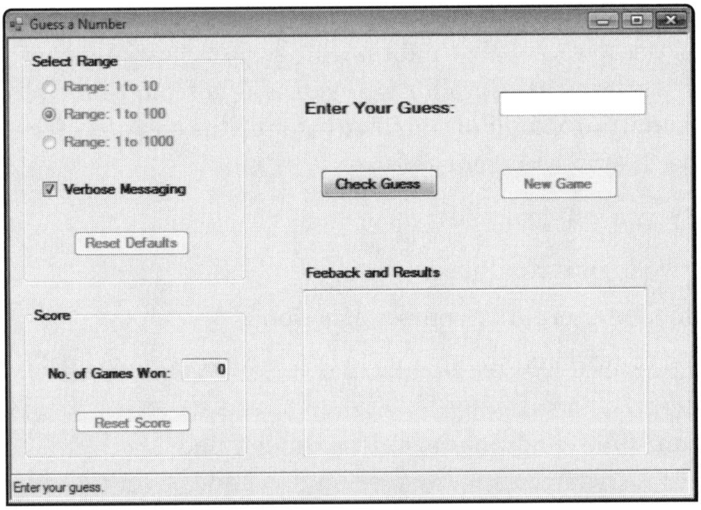

FIGURE 6.2

Once game play starts, the player's access to the configuration options is disabled and the player is prompted to make the first guess.

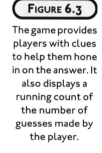

FIGURE 6.3

The game provides players with clues to help them hone in on the answer. It also displays a running count of the number of guesses made by the player.

FIGURE 6.4

At the end of each game, the player gets a chance to modify the game's configuration options and reset the score.

APPLYING CONDITIONAL LOGIC

Conditional logic is something that we apply all the time in our everyday lives. For example, based on the price of a particular item, you may decide either to put it back on the shelf or to purchase it. Likewise, based on how cold it feels when you wake up in the morning, you may decide whether to get up or sleep in. At the core of any conditional logic test is a determination as to whether the condition being tested is true or false. Based on the results of this analysis, different actions may be taken. To help facilitate the development of conditional logic, Visual Basic provides two different statements, each of which is suited to different situations. These statements are as follows:

- If…Then. This statement tests a condition and then alters the execution flow of your application based on the result of that test.
- Select Case. This statement performs a number of tests against a single value and performs one of a series of possible actions based on the result.

THE IF…THEN STATEMENT

You have already seen various implementations of the If…Then statement in previous chapter game projects. It is practically impossible to develop a useful application without using the If…Then statement. For example, in the Speed Typing game, which you created in Chapter 3, you used the If…Then statement numerous times. This included the use of five If…Then statements, which were used to determine which text statements the game should display, as shown here:

```
If intCount = 0 Then txtDisplay.Text = _
    "Once upon a time there were three little pigs."
If intCount = 1 Then txtDisplay.Text = _
    "In days gone by times were hard but the people were strong."
If intCount = 2 Then txtDisplay.Text = _
    "Once in a while something special happens even to the " _
    & "worst of people."
If intCount = 3 Then txtDisplay.Text = _
    "When injustice rears its head, it is the duty of all good " _
    & "citizens to object."
If intCount = 4 Then txtDisplay.Text = _
    "It has been said that in the end there can be only one. " _
    & "Let that one be Mighty Molly."
```

To better understand how If…Then statements work, look at the following example.

```
If it is below 32 degrees outside
  Then I'll stay in bed another hour
Else
  I'll get up and read the newspaper
EndIf
```

This English-like or pseudocode outline demonstrates how to apply a variation of the If…Then statements to your everyday life. In this example, the first line sets up the conditional test. If the tested condition turns out to be true, then the actions specified by the second statement are executed. Otherwise, an alternative course of action is taken.

DEFINITION *Pseudocode* is a rough, English-like outline or sketch of one or more program statements. The pseudocode, in effect, becomes an initial-level draft version of your application.

Now that you have seen several examples of the If...Then statement in action, let's spend some time dissecting it and exploring all its variations.

If...Then Statement Syntax

The If...Then statement provides the ability to test two or more conditions and to alter program statement flow based on the outcome of those tests. The If...Then statement supports many variations, as demonstrated by the following syntax.

```
If condition Then
     statements
ElseIf condition Then
    statements
Else
    statements
End If
```

Within this overall structure, there are many variations of the If...Then statements. We'll explore these variations in the sections that follow.

The Single Line If...Then Statement

In its simplest form, the If...Then statement tests a single condition and performs a single command when the tested condition proves true, as demonstrated here:

```
Dim intCounter As Integer = 0
If intCounter = 0 Then MessageBox.Show("We have a match.")
```

Here the condition being tested is whether the value assigned to intCounter equals 0. If the value assigned to intCounter is equal to 0, the result of the conditional test is true and therefore the MessageBox.Show method will execute and display a message. However, if the test proves false, the MessageBox.Show method will not execute and the application continues on, processing any remaining programming statements.

The advantage of the single line If...Then statement is that it allows you to set up a simple conditional test and to perform a single action only if the test proves true. This allows you to keep your code simple and to place both the conditional test and the resulting action on the same line.

Multiline If...Then Statements

More often than not, the logic that you'll need to use when testing logical conditions will be too complicated or large to fit into a single statement. When this is the case, you'll need to use the If...Then statement in the format demonstrated here:

```
Dim intCounter As Integer = 0
If intCounter = 0 Then
    intCounter += 1
    MessageBox.Show("The value of intCounter is " & intCounter)
End If
```

In this example, the number of commands to be executed by the If...Then statement are too numerous to be placed in a single statement. Therefore, the If...Then statement had to be expanded into a code block by adding an End If statement to the end. When used in this manner, you can place any number of statements between the opening If...Then statement and the closing End If statement, and they will all be executed if the condition being tested proves true.

The If...Then...Else Statement

The two previous examples demonstrate how to execute one or more commands when a tested condition proves true. But what do you do when the tested condition proves false, and as a result, you want to execute an alternate set of commands? One option is to write a second If...Then statement. For example, suppose you created a small Visual Basic application as depicted in Figure 6.5.

FIGURE 6.5

Validating player age before allowing the game to be played.

In this example, the application consists of a form with a `Label`, a `TextBox`, and a `Button` control. The application requires that the player type an age and click on the button labeled Play before being allowed to play the game. The following statements show the program code that has been added to the `Button` control's click event.

```
Public Class Form1

    Private Sub Button1_Click(ByVal sender As System.Object, _
      ByVal e As System.EventArgs) Handles Button1.Click

        If Int32.Parse(TextBox1.Text) < 18 Then
            MessageBox.Show("Thanks for playing!")
        End If
        If Int32.Parse(TextBox1.Text) >= 18 Then
            MessageBox.Show("Sorry. You are too old to play this game!")
            Application.Exit()
        End If

    End Sub

End Class
```

TRICK `Int32.Parse()` is a method that is used to convert a `String` value to an `Integer` value. Since, in the previous example, the `TextBox` control was used to collect the user's input, I converted its contents to `Integer` before trying to use it.

As you can see, two different `If…Then` statements have been set up. The first `If…Then` statement checks to see if the player is less than 18 years old. The second `If…Then` statement checks to see if the player is greater than or equal to 18 years of age. If the player is less than 18 years old, a friendly greeting message is displayed. Otherwise, the player is told that he is too old and the game is terminated. Note that for this example to work correctly, the user is required to enter a numeric value. Otherwise, an error will occur. Later, in this chapter's game project, you'll see examples of how to perform input validation to prevent incorrect user input from causing errors.

Although these two sets of `If…Then` statements certainly get the job done, a better way to accomplish the same thing would be to set up an `If…Then…Else` statement, as demonstrated here:

```
Public Class Form1

    Private Sub Button1_Click(ByVal sender As System.Object, _
      ByVal e As System.EventArgs) Handles Button1.Click

        If Int32.Parse(TextBox1.Text) < 18 Then
            MessageBox.Show("Thanks for playing!")
        Else
            MessageBox.Show("Sorry. You are too old to play this game!")
            Application.Exit()
        End If


    End Sub


End Class
```

As you can see, the If…Then…Else version of this example is slightly smaller and requires one less conditional test, making the programming logic simpler and easier to follow. Graphically, Figure 6.6 provides a visual flowchart view of the logic used in this example.

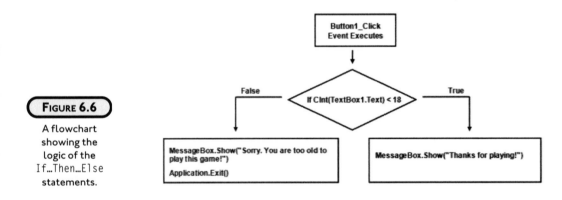

FIGURE 6.6

A flowchart showing the logic of the If…Then…Else statements.

DEFINITION A *flowchart* is a graphical depiction of the logic flow in a computer application.

IN THE REAL WORLD

Professional programmers often develop flowcharts that outline the overall execution of an application that they are about to develop. This helps them by providing a visual map that lays out the application's overall design while also helping to organize the programmer's thoughts. If an application is particularly large, a team of programmers may develop it. Using a flowchart, the programmers could divide up the work with one person focusing on the development of a specific part of the application.

The If…Then…ElseIf Statement

If you want, you can add the ElseIf keyword one or more times to expand the If…Then statement. Each instance of the ElseIf keyword allows you to set up a test for another alternative condition. To better understand how the If…Then…ElseIf statement works, take a look at the following example, shown in Figure 6.7.

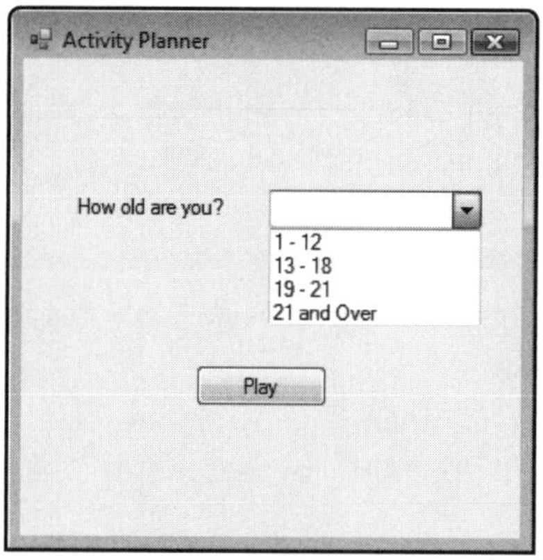

FIGURE 6.7

Using an If…Then…ElseIf statement to process the contents of a ComboBox control.

In this example, a new Visual Basic application has been created, consisting of a form with a Label, a Button, and a ComboBox control.

TRICK

The ComboBox control provides a drop-down list from which the user can select a single option. After adding a ComboBox to a form at design time, you can populate it with choices by locating its Items property in the Properties window and clicking on the (Collection) entry in the value column. This opens the String Collection Editor, as shown in Figure 6.8. All you have to do now is enter the choices that you want to display in the ComboBox control, making sure to type each option on its own line.

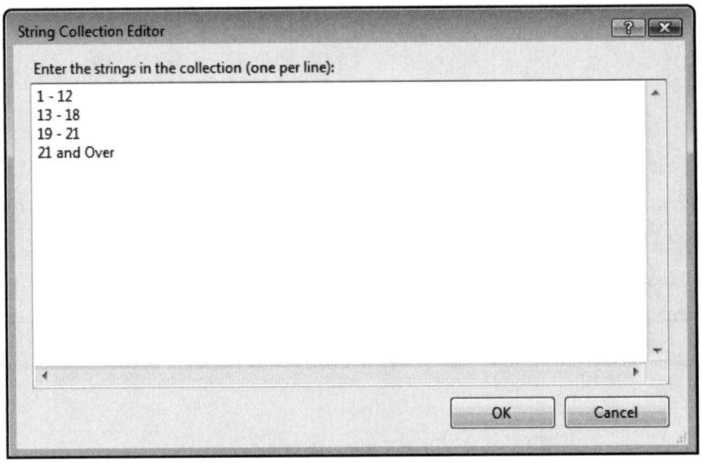

FIGURE 6.8

Using the String
Collection Editor
at design time to
populate the
contents of a
ComboBox control.

To make a selection, the user must select one of the choices displayed in the ComboBox control
and then click on the form's Button control. When this occurs, the code assigned to this control's click event, shown below, will execute.

```
Public Class Form1

    Private Sub Button1_Click(ByVal sender As System.Object, _
      ByVal e As System.EventArgs) Handles Button1.Click

        If ComboBox1.Text = "1 - 12" Then
            MessageBox.Show("There is a skateboard park just " & _
              "down the street.")
        ElseIf ComboBox1.Text = "13 - 18" Then
            MessageBox.Show("There is a 99 cent movie theater " & _
              "2 blocks over.")
        ElseIf ComboBox1.Text = "19 - 21" Then
            MessageBox.Show("A new dance club has opened downtown " & _
              "on 3rd street.")
        Else
            MessageBox.Show("OH, You must be tired. How about a nap.")
        End If

    End Sub

End Class
```

As you can see, by adding multiple ElseIf keywords, you are able to set up a conditional logic that can test for multiple possible conditions.

NESTING CONDITIONAL LOGIC

Sometimes the logic that you are developing may be too complicated to be represented using the different variations of the If…Then statements. However, you can greatly extend the power of the If…Then statements by nesting them within one another. This enables you to develop logic that tests for one condition and then further tests other conditions based on the result of the previous test.

 DEFINITION *Nesting* is the process of embedding one statement within another statement of the same type, such as when you embed If…Then statements in order to develop more complicated conditional logic.

TRAP You can embed as many If…Then statements as you want within one another. However, the deeper you go, the more difficult your program code will be to read and maintain.

THE SELECT CASE STATEMENT

In many cases, you'll want to compare one value or expression to a whole series of possible values. One way to accomplish this is by setting up as many If…Then statements as are required to make all the comparisons. However, a better way to tackle this type of situation is to use the Select Case statement.

The syntax for the Select Case statement is shown here:

```
Select Case expression
  Case value
    statements
    .
    .
    .
  Case value
    statements
  Case Else
    statements
End Select
```

As you can see, you use the Select Case statement to set up a block of code that begins with a Select Case statement and ends with the End Select statement. Between these two statements, you insert one or more Case statements, each of which defines a value or expression to be tested. You can also include a Case Else statement as a sort of catchall. The Case Else statement will execute in the event that all of the previous Case statements failed to result in a match. To better understand how the Select Case statement works, look at the following pseudocode example.

```
Select Case Temperature
   Case If it is below 32 degrees stay in bed
   Case If it is exactly 32 degrees play the lottery
   Case Else Just read the newspaper
End Select
```

In this example, one value, the temperature, is compared to a number of different values. If any of the values, as defined by a Case statement, are equal to the value of the temperature, then the programming logic associated with that value is executed.

As you can see, functionally the Select Case and the If…Then…Else statements are fairly similar. However, the Select Case statement is easier to read and is perfect for performing multiple tests against a single value or expression.

In most cases, you'll be able to reduce the number of lines of code that you need to perform a conditional test when you use a Select Case code block in place of a series of If…Then statements. As an example, look at the following code, which represents a rewrite of the example presented earlier in this chapter in the section that covered the nesting If…Then statements.

```
Select Case intWrong = 3
    Case intCount < 2
            MessageBox.Show("Game over. Your typing skill level " _
                & "is: Beginner. Please play again!")
            intCount = 0
            intWrong = 0
            Return
    Case intCount < 4
            MessageBox.Show("Game over. Your typing skill level " _
                & "is: Intermediate. Please play again!")
            intCount = 0
            intWrong = 0
            Return
    Case intCount < 5
```

```
        MessageBox.Show("Game over. Your typing skill level " _
            & "is: Advanced. Please play again!")
        intCount = 0
        intWrong = 0
        Return
End Select
```

As you can see, this example is not only a few lines shorter than the previous example, but it's also easier to read and follow along.

Comparison Operators

Up to this point in the book, most of the conditional tests that you have seen involved comparing two values or expressions to see if they were equal. Although this is certainly a powerful type of test, there are times when you need to test the relationship between values and expressions in different ways. For example, you may want to know if one value is less than, greater than, or equal to another value. To accomplish these types of comparisons, you can use any of the comparison operators listed in Table 6.1.

TABLE 6.1   VISUAL BASIC COMPARISON OPERATORS

Operator	Description
=	Equal
<>	Not equal
<	Less than
>	Greater than
<=	Less than or equal to
>=	Greater than or equal to

To get a better feel for how to use these operators, take a look at the following example.

```
Dim intSecretNumber As Integer = 6
Dim intPlayerGuess As Integer

intPlayerGuess = InputBox("Type a number between 1 and 10.")

If intPlayerGuess < intSecretNumber Then
    MessageBox.Show("Your guess is too low.")
```

```
End If
If intPlayerGuess = intSecretNumber Then
    MessageBox.Show("Your guess is correct.")
End If
If intPlayerGuess > intSecretNumber Then
    MessageBox.Show("Your guess is too high.")
End If
```

As you can see, three If…Then statements have been set up. The first If...Then statement uses the less than operator (<) to see if the value entered by the player is less than intSecretNumber (which is 6). Likewise, the second If…Then statement checks to see if the player's guess is equal to intSecretNumber. Finally, the third If…Then statement uses the greater than operator (>) to see if the number supplied by the user is greater than intSecretNumber.

BACK TO THE GUESS A NUMBER GAME

Let's get started on the development of this chapter's game project, the Guess a Number game. To create this game, you will follow the same five development steps that you've used to create previous chapter projects.

Designing the Game

The Guess a Number game is played on a single window. Unlike previous applications where data was collected from the user using the InputBox() function, this game will collect the player's input by adding radio buttons and a check box to the user interface. In addition, instead of displaying output using the MessageBox.Show method, the game will display information messages for the player to read in a TextBox control located on the user interface.

The advantage of collecting player input and displaying game output on the user interface is that it will make the game run smoother, meaning that the player won't have to constantly stop and respond to pop-up windows as the game runs. In order to create the user interface, you'll have to learn how to work with several new types of controls, including the GroupBox, RadioButton, and CheckBox controls.

The Guess a Number game is made up of one form and the 17 controls listed in Table 6.2.

TABLE 6.2   FORM CONTROLS FOR THE GUESS A NUMBER GAME

Control Type	Control Name	Description
GroupBox1	grpRange	Contains radio buttons, a check box, and a button that control the game's configuration settings
GroupBox2	grpScore	Displays the number of games won by the player and contains a button that is used to reset the score
RadioButton1	rbnControl10	Sets the range of game numbers from 1 through 10
RadioButton2	rbnControl100	Sets the range of game numbers from 1 through 100
RadioButton3	rbnControl1000	Sets the range of game numbers from 1 through 1000
CheckBox1	chkVerbose	Determines the level of messaging displayed by the game
Label1	lblGamesWon	Identifies the TextBox control where the total number of games won is displayed
Label2	lblInstructions	Identifies the TextBox control where the player enters guesses
Label3	lblFeedback	Identifies the TextBox control where game output is displayed
Button1	btnDefaults	Resets default RadioButton and CheckBox control settings
Button2	btnReset	Resets the number of games won back to zero in order to start a new game session
Button3	btnCheckGuess	Processes the player's guess to see if the player guessed low, high, or won the game
Button4	btnNewGame	Starts a new game
TextBox1	txtGamesWon	Displays the number of games that the player has won
TextBox2	txtInput	Collects and displays player guesses
TextBox3	txtOutput	Displays output messages generated during game play
StatusBar1	stbControl	Displays information messages during game play

Step 1: Creating a New Visual Basic Project

The first step in creating the Guess a Number game is to open up Visual Basic and create a new project as outlined here:

1. If you have not already done so, start up Visual Basic 2008 Express and click on File and select New Project. The New Project dialog will appear.
2. Select the Windows Forms Application template.
3. Type **Guess a Number** as the name of your new application in the Name field located at the bottom of the New Project window.
4. Click on OK to close the New Project dialog.

Visual Basic will now create a new project for you and display a new form upon which you will design the game's user interface.

Step 2: Creating the User Interface

The first step in laying out the user interface is adding controls to the form and moving and resizing them to the appropriate locations. The following procedure outlines the overall steps involved in creating the game's user interface. As you go through each step, make sure that you reference Figure 6.9 so that you'll know where each control should be placed.

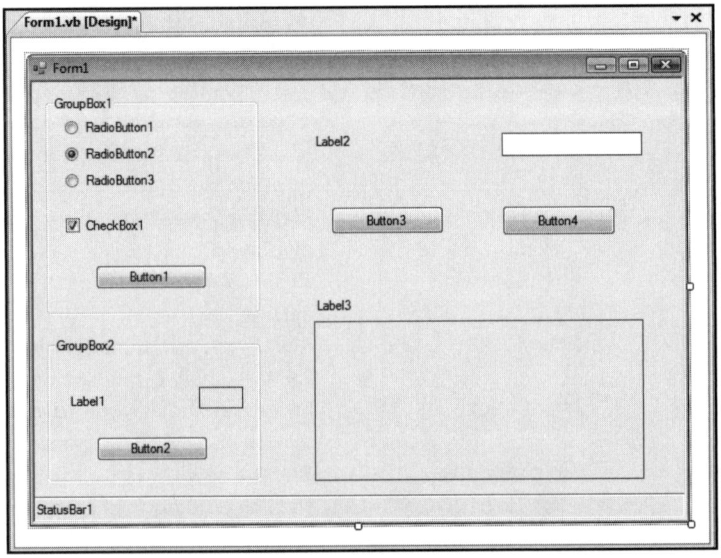

FIGURE 6.9

Completing the interface design for the Guess a Number game.

1. Start by adding two GroupBox controls to the form. Position and resize them as shown in Figure 6.9.

   DEFINITION A GroupBox control is a container that is used to organize other controls. The GroupBox control displays a caption, set using its Text property, and displays a visible border.

2. Add three RadioButton controls to the form and move them into the first GroupBox control, as shown in Figure 6.9.

A RadioButton control collects True/False or On/Off information. RadioButton controls are used together in groups to provide users with the ability to pick between mutually exclusive choices.

3. Add a CheckBox control to the form and move it just underneath the last RadioButton control.

 A CheckBox control collects True/False or On/Off information. Unlike RadioButton controls, CheckBox controls can be used individually. When selected, the CheckBox control displays an x.

4. Add a Button control to the first GroupBox control and reduce its size as shown in Figure 6.9.
5. Now, add a Label, TextBox, and Button control to the second GroupBox and resize and position them, as shown in Figure 6.9.
6. Add two additional Label controls and position them toward the middle of the form, as shown in Figure 6.9.
7. Add a TextBox control to the right of the first Label control and increase its width by approximately 30 percent.
8. Add another TextBox control underneath the second Label control and resize it until it takes up most of the remaining space in the lower-right side of the form.
9. Add two more Button controls on the right-hand side of the form between the two Label and TextBox controls.
10. Lastly, add a StatusBar control to the bottom of the form.

The overall layout of your new application's form is now complete.

Step 3: Customizing Form and Control Properties

Now it is time for you to customize various properties belonging to the form and the controls that you have placed on it. Begin by changing the form properties listed in Table 6.3.

TABLE 6.3   PROPERTY CHANGES FOR FORM1

Property	Value
Name	frmMain
Cursor	Hand
FormBorderStyle	Fixed3D
StartPosition	CenterScreen
Text	Guess a Number

Next, make changes shown in Table 6.4 to the GroupBox controls.

TABLE 6.4   PROPERTY CHANGES FOR THE GROUPBOX CONTROLS

Control	Property	Value
GroupBox1	Name	grpRange
	Text	Select Range
GroupBox2	Name	grpScore
	Text	Score

Make the changes shown in Table 6.5 to the RadioButton controls.

TABLE 6.5   PROPERTY CHANGES FOR THE RADIOBUTTON CONTROLS

Control	Property	Value
RadioButton1	Name	rbnControl10
	Text	Range: 1 to 10
RadioButton2	Name	rbnControl100
	Checked	True
	Text	Range: 1 to 100
RadioButton3	Name	rbnControl1000
	Text	Range: 1 to 1000

Make the changes shown in Table 6.6 to the `CheckBox` control.

TABLE 6.6   PROPERTY CHANGES FOR THE CHECKBOX CONTROL

Property	Value
Name	chkVerbose
Checked	True
CheckState	Checked
Text	Verbose Messaging

Make the changes shown in Table 6.7 to the `Button` controls.

TABLE 6.7   PROPERTY CHANGES FOR THE BUTTON CONTROLS

Control	Property	Value
Button1	Name	btnDefaults
	Text	Reset Defaults
Button2	Name	btnReset
	Text	Reset Score
Button3	Name	btnCheckGuess
	Enabled	False
	Text	Check Guess
Button4	Name	btnNewGame
	Text	New Game

Make the changes shown in Table 6.8 to the `Label` controls.

Make the changes shown in Table 6.9 to the `TextBox` controls.

Make the changes shown in Table 6.10 to the `StatusBar` control.

TABLE 6.8 PROPERTY CHANGES FOR THE LABEL CONTROLS

Control	Property	Value
Label1	Name	lblGamesWon
	Font.Bold	True
	Text	No. of Games Won:
Label2	Name	lblInstructions
	Font.Bold	True
	Font.Size	10
	Text	Enter Your Guess:
Label2	Name	lblFeedback
	Font.Bold	True
	Text	Feedback and Results

TABLE 6.9 PROPERTY CHANGES FOR THE TEXTBOX CONTROLS

Control	Property	Value
TextBox1	Name	txtGamesWon
	ReadOnly	True
	TabStop	False
TextBox2	Name	txtInput
	Enabled	False
TextBox3	Name	txtOutput
	ReadOnly	True
	TabStop	False

TABLE 6.10 PROPERTY CHANGES FOR THE STATUSBAR CONTROL

Property	Value
Name	stbControl
SizingGrip	False
Text	Game Ready!

That's it. At this point, you have configured all the form and control properties that need to be set at design time.

Step 4: Adding a Little Programming Logic

Let's begin by double-clicking on the form and adding the following statement just beneath the `Public Class frmMain` statement, as shown here:

```
Public Class frmMain

    'Declare variable used to store the game's randomly generated number
    Private intRandomNumber As Integer

End Class
```

The `intRandomNumber` variable will be used through the application to store the game's randomly generated secret number. Next, modify the form's `Load` event procedure as shown here:

```
'This Sub procedure executes when the game's interface is loaded
Private Sub Form1_Load(ByVal sender As System.Object, _
  ByVal e As System.EventArgs) Handles MyBase.Load

    txtGamesWon.Text = 0  'Set number of games won to zero
    btnNewGame.Focus()   'Set focus to the Button labeled New Game

End Sub
```

The first statement displays a value of 0 in the `txtGamesWon` control, and the second statement places focus on the `btnNewGame` control. Next, we need to add logic to the `btnDefaults` control that will reset the game's default settings, as controlled by the `RadioButton` and `CheckBox` controls located in the first `GroupBox` control. Do so by modifying the click event procedure for the `btnDefaults` control, as shown here:

```
'This Sub procedure executes when the btnDefaults Button is clicked
Private Sub btnDefaults_Click(ByVal sender As System.Object, _
  ByVal e As System.EventArgs) Handles btnDefaults.Click

    rbnControl100.Checked = True  'Check the rbnConrol100 radio button
    chkVerbose.Checked = True   'Turn on verbose messaging
    txtInput.Focus()   'Set focus to txtInput

End Sub
```

The first statement selects the `RadioButton` that represents the range of 1 to 100. The second statement selects (by placing an x inside) the `chkVerbose` `CheckBox` control, and the third statement sets the focus to the txtInput control (to save the player the trouble of having to put it there before typing in the next guess).

Next, let's add logic to the btnReset control so that the player can reset the value that tracks the number of games won to 0. Also, take note that the value used to track the number of games won is not assigned to a variable. Instead, it is stored and managed within the txtGameWon control's Text property.

```
'This Sub procedure executes when the player clicks the Reset Defaults
Private Sub btnReset_Click(ByVal sender As System.Object, _
   ByVal e As System.EventArgs) Handles btnReset.Click

     txtGamesWon.Text = 0   'Set number of games won to zero

End Sub
```

Next, add the following statements to the TextChanged event for the txtInput control.

```
'This Sub procedure executes as soon as the player types in a guess
Private Sub txtInput_TextChanged(ByVal sender As System.Object, _
   ByVal e As System.EventArgs) Handles txtInput.TextChanged

     btnCheckGuess.Enabled = True 'Enable the Button labeled Check Guess
     btnNewGame.Enabled = False   'Disable the Button labeled New Game

End Sub
```

The TextChanged event is automatically triggered whenever the user keys something into the TextBox control associated with the event. It is used in the Guess a Number game to control when the btnCheckGuess button is enabled and when the btnNewGame is disabled.

Now we need to add logic to the application that randomly generates the game's secret number. To do so, I have decided to create a new procedure named GetRandomNumber() and place the logic to generate the random number in it. You won't be able to automatically generate this procedure by double-clicking on an object in the form designer. Instead, you'll need to key it in entirely by hand as shown below. You'll learn more about how to work with procedures in Chapter 8, "Enhancing Code Structure and Organization," including how to create your own custom procedures. For now, just key in the procedure as shown here:

```
'This Sub procedure retrieves the game's random number
Public Sub GetRandomNumber()
```

```
'Declare variable representing the random number's maximum value
Dim intUpperLimit As Integer

'Instantiate a Random object
Dim objRandom As New Random

'If the 1st radio button is selected set the maximum value to 10
If rbnControl10.Checked = True Then
    intUpperLimit = 10
End If

'If the 2nd radio button is selected set the maximum value to 100
If rbnControl100.Checked = True Then
    intUpperLimit = 100
End If

'If the 3rd radio button is selected set the maximum value to 1000
If rbnControl1000.Checked = True Then
    intUpperLimit = 1000
End If

'Use the Random object's Next() method to generate a random number
intRandomNumber = objRandom.Next(intUpperLimit)
```

End Sub

When called by the btnNewGame control's click event procedure, the GetRandomNumber procedure instantiates a new Random object called objRandom and checks to see which RadioButton control is currently selected so that it will know what range to use when generating the game's secret number. It then executes Random object's Next() method, in order to generate the random number. The Next() method is passed the value stored in the intUpperLimit variable to specify the maximum range from which the random number should be selected (between 0 and the value of intRandomNumber).

TRICK

The Random object's Next() method is used to generate a random number. If called without passing it any parameters, the Next() method generates a non-negative whole number. If passed a single integer value, the Next() method generates a random number between zero and the value of the integer argument. If passed two integer values, the Next() method will generate a random number within the specified range.

Now let's add the code required for the click event belonging to the btnCheckGuess control, as shown here:

```vb
'This Sub procedure executes when the player clicks on the button
'labeled Check Guess
Private Sub btnCheckGuess_Click(ByVal sender As System.Object, _
  ByVal e As System.EventArgs) Handles btnCheckGuess.Click

    Dim intPlayerGuess As Integer 'Declare variable to store guess
    Static intNoOfGuesses As Integer 'Declare variable to keep track
                                'of the number of guesses made

  If txtInput.Text.Length > 0 Then  'Make sure player typed something
      If IsNumeric(txtInput.Text) = True Then 'Ensure input is numeric

          'Convert String input to Integer data type
          intPlayerGuess = Int32.Parse(txtInput.Text)
          btnCheckGuess.Enabled = True 'Enable Check Guess button

          'See if player's guess is correct
          If intPlayerGuess = intRandomNumber Then
              txtInput.Text = ""  'Clear the TextBox control
              intNoOfGuesses += 1  'Increment variable by one

              'See if player enabled verbose messaging
              If chkVerbose.Checked = True Then
                  txtOutPut.Text = "Congratulations!" & _
                    ControlChars.CrLf & ControlChars.CrLf & _
                  "You have won the Guess a Number Game. " & _
                  ControlChars.CrLf & ControlChars.CrLf & _
                  "Number of guesses made = " & intNoOfGuesses
              Else
                  txtOutPut.Text = "Congratulations! You Win."
              End If

              intNoOfGuesses = 0  'Reset variable to zero
              txtInput.Enabled = False  'Disable TextBox control
```

```
            'Update the display of the total number of games won
            txtGamesWon.Text = txtGamesWon.Text + 1
            'Disable the Button labeled Check Guess
            btnCheckGuess.Enabled = False
          'Enable the Button labeled New Game
            btnNewGame.Enabled = True '

            'Enable all Radio buttons
            rbnControl10.Enabled = True
            rbnControl100.Enabled = True
            rbnControl1000.Enabled = True

            'Enable the two reset buttons
            btnDefaults.Enabled = True
            btnReset.Enabled = True

            stbControl.Text = "Game Ready!"  'Post statusbar message

    End If

    'See if the player's guess was too low
    If intPlayerGuess < intRandomNumber Then
        txtInput.Text = ""  'Clear the TextBox control
        intNoOfGuesses += 1  'Increment variable by one

        'See if player enabled verbose messaging
        If chkVerbose.Checked = True Then
            txtOutPut.Text = "The number that you " & _
            "entered was too low. Enter higher number " & _
            "and try again." & _
            ControlChars.CrLf & ControlChars.CrLf & _
            "Number of guesses taken so far = " & _
            intNoOfGuesses
        Else
            txtOutPut.Text = "Too low."
        End If
    End If
```

```vb
            'See if the player's guess was too high
            If intPlayerGuess > intRandomNumber Then
                txtInput.Text = ""  'Clear the TextBox control
                intNoOfGuesses += 1  'Increment variable by one

                'See if player enabled verbose messaging
                If chkVerbose.Checked = True Then
                    txtOutPut.Text = "The number that you " & _
                    "entered was too high. Enter lower number " & _
                    "and try again." & _
                    ControlChars.CrLf & ControlChars.CrLf & _
                    "Number of guesses taken so far = " & _
                    intNoOfGuesses
                Else
                    txtOutPut.Text = "Too high. Try again."
                End If
            End If

        Else
            txtInput.Text = ""  'Clear the TextBox control

            'Display message if player fails to provide numeric input
            If chkVerbose.Checked = True Then
                txtOutPut.Text = "Sorry but you entered a " & _
                "non-numeric guess. Please try again and be " & _
                "sure to enter a number this time."
            Else
                txtOutPut.Text = "Numeric input required. Try again."
            End If
        End If

    Else
        txtInput.Text = ""  'Clear the TextBox control

        'Display error if player fails to provide input
        If chkVerbose.Checked = True Then
            txtOutPut.Text = "Sorry but to play you must enter a " & _
            "number. Please enter a number and try again."
        Else
```

```
            txtOutPut.Text = "No input provided. Try again."
        End If
    End If


    txtInput.Focus()  'Set focus to the TextBox control

End Sub
```

As you can see, this procedure is rather long and contains the bulk of the application's programming logic. It begins by declaring two variables. The first variable is `intPlayerGuess` and is used to store and process the input provided by the player. A new value will be assigned to this variable each time the player clicks on the `Button` control labeled Check Guess. Therefore, it is declared as a local variable. However, the second variable, which is named `intNoOfGuesses`, is defined as a `Static` variable, making its lifetime last for as long as the game runs, so that it can be used to maintain a count of the number of guesses that the player makes during each game.

Next, an `If…Then…Else` block is set up that determines what statements in the procedure will execute based on whether the player entered any input. If no input was provided, an error message is displayed in the `txtOutput` control. Otherwise, a second nested `If…Then…Else` block executes and checks to see if the input supplied by the player is numeric. If the input is not numeric, an error message is displayed in the `txtOutput` control; otherwise, one of three nested `If…Then` blocks execute. The first `If…Then` block checks to see if the player won the game by guessing the secret number. The second `If…Then` block checks to see if the player's guess was too low, and the third `If…Then` block checks to see if the player's guess was too high.

If the player's guess was too high or too low, an error message is displayed in the `txtOutput` control. The message that is displayed depends on whether the `chkVerbose` control is checked. If the player guesses correctly, she wins the game and a congratulatory message is displayed in the `txtOutput` control. In addition, the following actions are taken to prepare the game for another play:

- The value of `intNoOfGuesses` is reset to zero.
- The value indicating the number of games won is incremented by adding 1 to the value stored in the `txtGamesWon` control's text property.
- The Check Guess button is disabled and the New Game button is enabled.
- The game's `RadioButton` controls are enabled, allowing the player to make changes to them if desired.
- The game's Reset Default button is also enabled.
- The message displayed in the game's `StatusBar` control is updated.

Last but not least, it is time to add some code to the btnNewgame control's click event procedure, as shown here:

```
'This Sub procedure executes when the New Game button is clicked
Private Sub btnNewGame_Click(ByVal sender As System.Object, _
  ByVal e As System.EventArgs) Handles btnNewGame.Click

    GetRandomNumber()  'Call the GetRandomNumber procedure

    txtOutPut.Text = ""  'Clear the TextBox control
    txtInput.Text = ""  'Clear the TextBox control
    btnNewGame.Enabled = False  'Enable the New Game button
    btnCheckGuess.Enabled = True  'Disable the Check Guess button
    txtInput.Enabled = True  'Enabled the TextBox control

    'Disable all Radio buttons
    rbnControl10.Enabled = False
    rbnControl100.Enabled = False
    rbnControl1000.Enabled = False

    'Disable the two reset buttons
    btnDefaults.Enabled = False
    btnReset.Enabled = False

    stbControl.Text = "Enter your guess."  'Display instructions
    txtInput.Focus()  'Set focus to the TextBox control

End Sub
```

When clicked, the code for the button labeled New Game clears out any text display in the txtInput and txtOutput controls. Next, the btnNewGame control is disabled, and the btnCheckGuess control is enabled. Then the txtInput control is enabled to allow the player to enter a guess, and the game's RadioButton control and btnReset control are all disabled, preventing the player from making configuration changes while a new game is being played. Lastly, an instructional message is displayed on the game's StatusBar control, and the cursor is placed in the txtInput control.

Step 5: Testing the Execution of the Guess a Number Game

That's it. The Guess a Number game is ready to run. Press F5 and see how it works. If you have any errors, double-check your typing. Otherwise, pass it on to your friends and ask them to play and to report any problems back to you if they run into one.

SUMMARY

In this chapter, you learned how to apply conditional logic to your Visual Basic applications using variations of the If...Then statement and the Select Case statement. This included learning how to set up conditional tests to test for one or more possible outcomes and developing alternative execution flows in the event that the conditional tests proved false. In addition, you learned how to work with the GroupBox, RadioButton, CheckBox, and ComboBox controls.

Before you jump into Chapter 7, "Processing Lots of Data with Loops," and learn how to apply advanced looping logic to your Visual Basic applications, take a few extra moments to review the following challenges and see if you can improve the Guess a Number game.

CHALLENGES

1. Modify the Guess a Number game by providing better clues as the player's guesses begin to get closer to the secret number. For example, you might add text that tells the player when they are getting "warm," "warmer," and "hot."

2. Add logic to the game to display the average number of guesses that it takes the player to guess the secret number and display this information in the grpScore control (GroupBox).

3. Modify the Guess a Number game so that the game ends if the player has not guessed the secret number after a certain number of tries and display the number of games lost in the grpScore control (GroupBox). Also, display the secret number in the txtOutput control (TextBox) when the player loses a game.

PROCESSING LOTS OF DATA WITH LOOPS

As you have already seen in previous chapter projects, there are times when you need to create loops within your applications to repeatedly perform a number of steps. Loops are also essential for processing large amounts of data without requiring a large number of programming statements. Loops are a great option for processing the contents of arrays and controls, such as the ComboBox and ListBox, which store collections of data. In this chapter, you will learn how to use a number of Visual Basic statements to create different kinds of loops. In addition, you will get the chance to apply what you'll learn through the development of the chapter's game project, the Dice Poker game.

Specifically, you will learn how to:

- Create Do...While and Do...Until loops
- Create For...Next and For Each...Next loops
- Create While loops
- Use variations of the Exit keyword to break out of loops

PROJECT PREVIEW: THE DICE POKER GAME

In this chapter's project, you will apply your new knowledge of iterative processing to the development of the Dice Poker game. In addition, you'll get your first taste of working with and controlling graphics by learning how to work with the ImageList and PictureBox controls.

Figures 7.1 through 7.5 show examples from the Dice Poker game, demonstrating its functionality and overall execution flow.

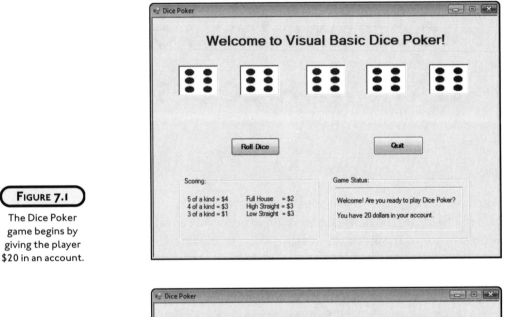

FIGURE 7.1

The Dice Poker game begins by giving the player $20 in an account.

FIGURE 7.2

Players can elect to hold onto specific dice before rolling the dice a second time.

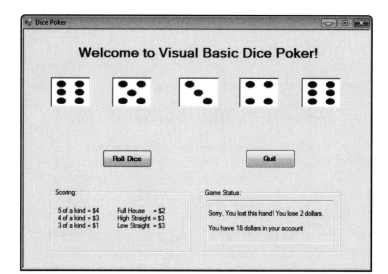

FIGURE 7.3

Two dollars are deducted from the player's account for each losing hand.

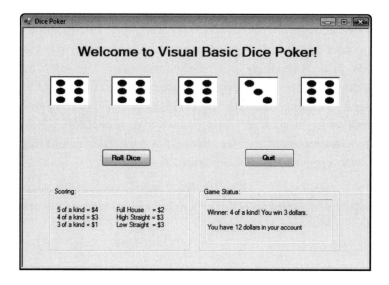

FIGURE 7.4

Winning hands are rewarded with additional credits to the player's account.

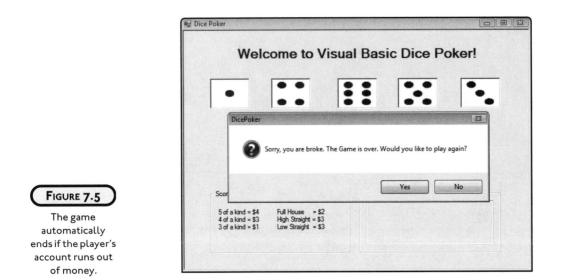

FIGURE 7.5

The game automatically ends if the player's account runs out of money.

ITERATIVE PROCESSING

Loops allow programmers to do a lot of work with a little code. Thanks to loops, it is possible to process dozens, hundreds, or tens of thousands of elements using the same number of programming statements. Loops are especially adept at processing the contents of arrays and collections, such as the collection associated with the ListBox control. Loops can also be set up to drive any form or iterative logic, such as when you want to repeatedly prompt a user to supply additional information, or when you want to run a particular group of programming statements over and over again until a certain result is achieved.

DEFINITION A *loop* is a group of programming statements that are executed repeatedly. Loops provide an effective tool for processing large amounts of data.

Do Loops

You can set up Do loops to iterate until or while a specific condition is true. Do loops are well suited to situations where you know in advance what specific condition must occur in order for the tested condition to become true. For example, you might set up a Do…Until or Do…While loop to allow a user to enter as much input as desired, terminating the loop's execution only when the user enters a trigger word such as "Quit" or "Exit."

Do…While

A Do…While loop iterates as long as a specified condition remains true. Visual Basic allows you to construct a Do…While loop in either of two formats. The syntax of the first format is shown here:

```
Do While condition
   statements
Loop
```

condition represents an expression that is tested upon each iteration of the loop, as demonstrated in the following example.

```
Dim intCounter As Integer = 0
Do While intCounter < 10
   intCounter += 1
Loop
```

In this example, an Integer type variable named intCounter is declared and then used to control the iteration of a Do…While loop. The loop iterates for as long as the value of intCounter is less than 10. As you can see, the value of intCounter is increased by 1 at the end of each iteration, causing the loop to iterate 10 times. However, if the value of intCounter had been set to a value greater than or equal to 10 at the beginning of the example, the loop would never have executed, because the While keyword and the tested expression have been placed on the same line as the Do keyword. The syntax for the second format of the Do...While statement is shown here:

```
Do
   statements
Loop While condition
```

As you can see, the While keyword and the tested condition have been moved to the end of the loop and placed on the same line as the Loop keyword. The result is that the loop will always execute at least once, even if the tested condition is initially false. To get a better feel for how to work with the Do…While loop, take a look at the following example.

```
Public Class Form1

    Private Sub Button1_Click(ByVal sender As System.Object, _
       ByVal e As System.EventArgs) Handles btnBooks.Click

        Dim strTitleAndAuthor As String = "", strInput As String = ""
        Do While strInput.ToLower <> "quit"
```

```
        strInput = InputBox("Enter a book title or type Quit to " & _
          "exit the application.", "Book Tracker")
        If strInput.ToLower <> "quit" Then
            strTitleAndAuthor = strTitleAndAuthor & strInput & _
            ControlChars.CrLf
        End If
    Loop
    MessageBox.Show(strTitleAndAuthor, "New Book Entries")
End Sub

End Class
```

In this example, a Do...While loop was set up to collect names of books using the
InputBox() function. Each new book name is added to the end of a variable string, which is
formatted so that it will display each book's title on its own line when later displayed. The
loop has been set up to iterate until the user enters the word "Quit." Take note of the use of
the ToLower method to translate the user's input to all lowercase letters when the example
checks to see if the player entered the word "Quit." By converting the player's input to all
lowercase like this, the example eliminates any concerns over the case the user might choose
to use when typing in the word "Quit."

Figures 7.6 and 7.7 show the interaction between the above example and the user when
executed.

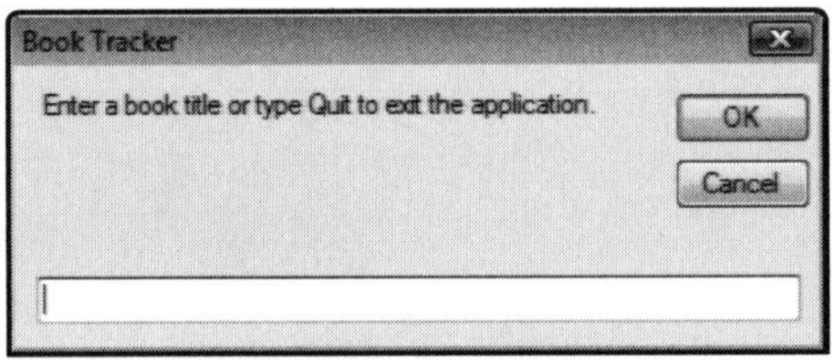

FIGURE 7.6

Processing the
names of books
using a
Do...While loop.

FIGURE 7.7

Displaying the
information that
was collected by
the Do...While
loop.

In this example, the first format of the Do…While loop was used. However, you could just as easily rewrite this example and move the While keyword and the tested expression to the end of the loop, as demonstrated below. Regardless, the results are the same.

```
Public Class Form1

    Private Sub Button1_Click(ByVal sender As System.Object, _
        ByVal e As System.EventArgs) Handles btnBooks.Click

        Dim strTitleAndAuthor As String = ""
        Dim strInput As String = ""

        Do
            strInput = InputBox("Enter a book title or type Quit to" & _
                "exit the application.", "Book Tracker")
            If strInput.ToLower <> "quit" Then
                strTitleAndAuthor = strTitleAndAuthor & strInput & -
                ControlChars.CrLf
            End If
        Loop While strInput.ToLower <> "quit"

        MessageBox.Show(strTitleAndAuthor, "New Book Entries")

    End Sub

End Class
```

Do…Until

The Do…Until loop iterates as long as a condition is false. In other words, it iterates until a condition becomes true. As with the Do…While loop, Visual Basic supports two different forms of the Do…Until loop. The syntax of the first format is shown here:

```
Do Until condition
    statements
Loop
```

To get a better feel for how the Do…Until loop works, look at the following example.

```
Public Class Form1

    Private Sub Button1_Click(ByVal sender As System.Object, _
      ByVal e As System.EventArgs) Handles Button1.Click

        Dim strPlayerInput As String = ""
        Dim blnStopGame As Boolean = False

        Do Until blnStopGame = True
            strPlayerInput = MessageBox.Show("Do you want to quit?", _
              "Continue?", MessageBoxButtons.YesNo, _
              MessageBoxIcon.Question)
            'Check to see if the user clicked on Yes when prompted to quit
            If Int32.Parse(strPlayerInput) = 6 Then
                blnStopGame = True
            Else
                MessageBox.Show("Oh, I see...")
            End If
        Loop

        Application.Exit()

    End Sub

End Class
```

In this example, a loop has been set up that requires the user to enter the word "Quit" in order to terminate the application. If the user enters the word "Quit," the application stops; otherwise, refusing to give up, this stubborn little example continues to prompt the user to type "Quit." Figures 7.8 and 7.9 demonstrate the interaction between the above example and the user when executed.

FIGURE 7.8

Using a Do…Until loop to prompt the player to terminate the game.

Oh, I see...

OK

FIGURE 7.9

The game sarcastically responds to the player when he or she fails to enter the word "Quit."

The syntax for the second form of the `Do...Until` statement is outlined here:

```
Do
    statements
Loop Until condition
```

As you can see, the `Until` keyword and the *condition* to be tested have been placed on the third line just after the `Loop` keyword.

For...Next

The `For...Next` loop is an excellent choice when you know in advance how many times a loop will need to execute. The For…Next loop executes a specific number of times as determined by a counter, which can increase or decrease based on the logic you are implementing.

The syntax for the `For...Next` statement is shown here:

```
For counter [As DataType] = begin To end [Step StepValue]
    statements
Next
```

counter is a variable that controls the execution of the loop. *DataType* is an optional parameter allowing you to define the loop's counter within the loop itself. If you choose not to supply the `DataType` here, you will still have to define it elsewhere in your application. *begin* specifies the starting value of the *counter* variable, and *end* specifies its ending value. *StepValue* is optional. When supplied, *StepValue* specifies an increment value to be used by the `For...Next` statement when incrementing the value assigned to the *counter* variable. If you don't specify a value for *StepValue*, a value of 1 is assumed.

The following example demonstrates how to use a For…Next loop to iterate through the contents of an array.

```
Public Class Form1

    Private Sub Form1_Load(ByVal sender As System.Object, _
        ByVal e As System.EventArgs) Handles MyBase.Load
```

```
        Dim strMessage As String = ""
        Dim intCounter As Integer = 0

        Dim strCustomerNamesArray(4) As String
        strCustomerNamesArray(0) = "Markland B."
        strCustomerNamesArray(1) = "Mike M."
        strCustomerNamesArray(2) = "Nick C."

        For intCounter = 0 To 2
            strMessage &= strCustomerNamesArray(intCounter) & _
            ControlChars.NewLine
        Next intCounter
        MessageBox.Show(strMessage)

    End Sub

End Class
```

In this example, the For…Next loop is set up to iterate three times (from 0 to 2). Upon each iteration, the value assigned to intCounter is automatically incremented by 1. By plugging in the intCounter variable in place of a number (strCustomerNamesArray(intCounter)), a display string is assembled that shows all of the contents of the array.

It is important to understand that the value assigned to the StepValue can be something other than just 1. You could set it equal to 2 to skip every other element stored in an array, or as the following example demonstrates, you could assign it a negative number to process the array in reverse order.

```
For intCounter = 2 To 0 Step -1
    strMessage &= strCustomerNamesArray(intCounter) & _
    ControlChars.NewLine
Next intCounter
```

You can also use the For…Next loop to work with Visual Basic controls that have collections, such as the ListBox control. The following example demonstrates how to use a For…Next loop to add elements to a ListBox control at run-time.

DEFINITION   A ListBox is a control that displays a list of items from which a selection can be made.

The first step in working with the ListBox control is to add an instance of the control from the Toolbox window to a form. Once added to a form, you can populate and access the contents of a ListBox using the methods and properties belonging to its Items property. The Items property is actually a collection and any items that you add to a ListBox are referenced by their index position within the Items collection. You can add items to a ListBox control using the Items collection's Add() method. You can then refer to any item in the Items collection using the Item property.

```
Public Class frmMain

    Private Sub Button1_Click(ByVal sender As System.Object, _
        ByVal e As System.EventArgs) Handles Button1.Click

        Static intSheep As Integer = 0
        For intCounter As Integer = 0 To 9 Step 1
            intSheep += 1
            lbxNumbers.Items.Add(intSheep.ToString & "  Sheep")
        Next

    End Sub

End Class
```

In this example, a Visual Basic application was created that consists of a Button control and a ListBox control. The application promises to help the user get to sleep by counting sheep, 10 at a time, whenever the user clicks on the Button control.

The For...Next loop in this example will iterate 10 times (0 to 9). Within the loop, the value of an Integer type variable named intSheep is incremented by 1, and the ListBox control's (lbxNumbers) Items property's (which itself is an object or collection) Add() method is used to load new items into the ListBox. Figure 7.10 shows output that is produced after this application is started and the user clicks on the button for the first time.

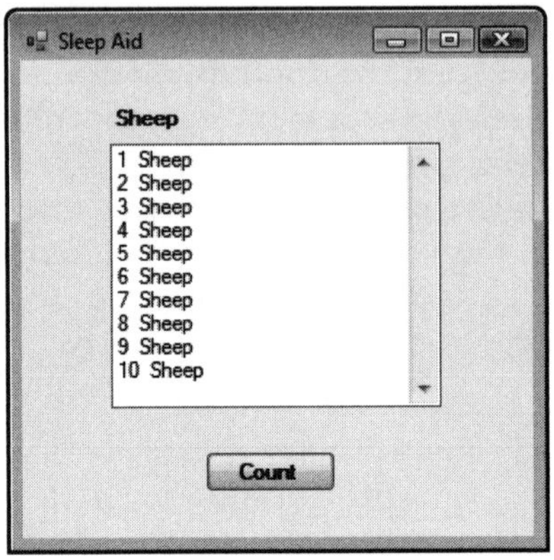

FIGURE 7.10

Using a For…Next
loop to populate
the contents of a
ListBox.

In addition to adding elements to a control's collection, you can use the For…Next loop to retrieve elements from a collection, as demonstrated in the next example.

```
Public Class Form1

    Private Sub Button2_Click(ByVal sender As System.Object, _
      ByVal e As System.EventArgs) Handles btnExit.Click

        Application.Exit()

    End Sub

    Private Sub Button1_Click(ByVal sender As System.Object, _
      ByVal e As System.EventArgs) Handles btnDisplay.Click

        Dim strMessage As String = ""
        Dim intCounter As Integer

        For intCounter = 1 To lbxCustomers.Items.Count - 1
            strMessage &= lbxCustomers.Items.Item(intCounter) & _
              ControlChars.CrLf
        Next

        MessageBox.Show("Customer List: " & ControlChars.CrLf & _
          ControlChars.CrLf & strMessage, "Customer Listing")
```

```
    End Sub

End Class
```

As you can see, this time, the For…Next loop uses the ListBox (lbxCustomers) control's Items collection's Item property to retrieve an element, using its index number from the ListBox control. Figures 7.11 and 7.12 demonstrate the operation of this application.

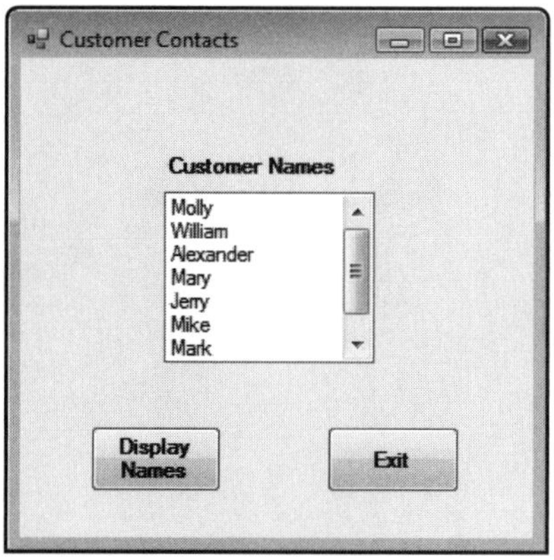

FIGURE 7.11

You can set up a For…Next loop that processes all of the contents of a ListBox control.

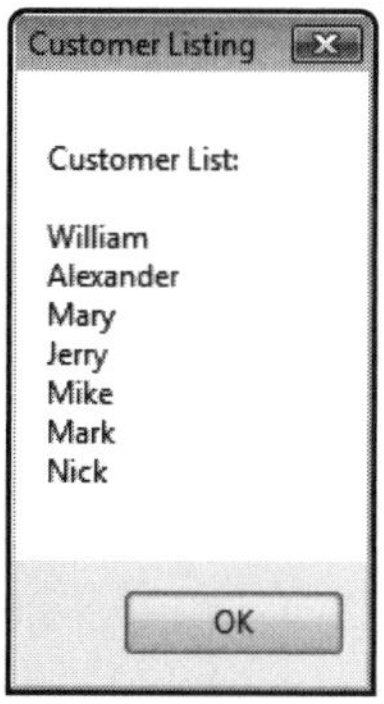

FIGURE 7.12

The For…Next loop spins through the contents of the ListBox and uses the data to display a list of customers.

For…Each…Next

The For…Each…Next loop is perfect for processing the contents of arrays and collections when you don't know in advance the exact number of elements that are being stored. The For…Each…Next loop automatically iterates through each member and alleviates any concern regarding the tracking of index numbers.

The syntax of the For…Each…Next statement is shown here:

```
For Each element [As DataType] In collection
    statements
Next [element]
```

element is a variable that represents a property (that is, a member) associated with the specified *collection*. The DataType parameter is optional. When used, it allows you to define the *element* variable's data type within the loop itself. If you choose not to supply the DataType parameter here, you still have to define it elsewhere in your application.

The following example demonstrates how to set up a For…Each…Next loop to process the contents of an array.

```
Public Class Form1

    Private Sub Form1_Load(ByVal sender As System.Object, _
    ByVal e As System.EventArgs) Handles MyBase.Load

        Dim strMessage As String = ""
        Dim strName As String = ""
        Dim strCustomerNamesArray(4) As String
        strCustomerNamesArray(0) = "Markland B."
        strCustomerNamesArray(1) = "Mike M."
        strCustomerNamesArray(2) = "Nick C."
        strCustomerNamesArray(3) = "Jerry F."
        strCustomerNamesArray(4) = "Rocky B."

        For Each strName In strCustomerNamesArray
            strMessage &= strName & ControlChars.NewLine
        Next strName

        MessageBox.Show(strMessage, "Customer Contact Names")

    End Sub

End Class
```

As you can see from this example, the For…Each…Next loop automatically iterates through each element in the array without requiring the use of a counter or any additional logic. Figure 7.13 shows the output that is generated when this example is executed.

FIGURE 7.13

Using a
For...Each...Next
loop to process
the contents of an
array.

While

One last type of loop that I want to introduce you to is the While loop. The While loop is designed to run as long as a stated condition is true. The While loop has the following syntax.

```
While condition
        statements
End While
```

condition is expressed in the form of an expression, as demonstrated here:

```
Dim strUserResponse As String, blnTerminateFlag As Boolean = False

While blnTerminateFlag = False
    strUserResponse = InputBox("Enter Quit to stop the application.")
    If strUserResponse.ToLower = "quit" Then
        blnTerminateFlag = True
    Else
        MessageBox.Show("The current date and time is " & Now())
    End If
End While
```

In this example, the user is prompted to enter the word "Quit" in order to stop the application from continuing to execute. If the user enters anything other than the word "Quit," or if the user clicks on the pop-up window's Cancel button, the While loop displays the current date and time and then iterates and continues prompting the user to enter the word "Quit."

The previous example demonstrates that the While loop requires its tested condition to be checked at the beginning of the loop. Although useful, the While loop is not as flexible as the Do...While and Do...Until loops, which can test a condition before or after initial loop execution and provide the same capabilities as the While loop.

ENDLESS LOOPS

One of the concerns to be aware of when working with loops is an endless loop. Endless loops occur when you apply faulty logic that results in the loop running forever (or until you forcefully terminate your application).

 DEFINITION An *endless loop* is a loop that has no means for terminating, causing the loop to run forever and draining computer resources.

 TRICK If, while testing the execution of your Visual Basic application, you think you may have an endless loop, you can stop the program from running by opening the Debug menu and clicking on the Stop Debug menu item.

The following example demonstrates how easy it is to accidentally set up an endless loop.

```
Dim intCounter As Integer = 0
Do While intCounter < 5
  intCounter = intCounter - 1
  MessageBox.Show(intCounter)
Loop
```

In this example, a Do…While loop is set up to iterate as long as the value of intCounter is less than 5. However, instead of incrementing the value of intCounter by 1 upon each iteration of the loop, I accidentally decremented the value of intCounter by -1. As a result, the value of intCount will never reach 5 and the loop will never terminate on its own. The lesson here is to always double-check the way that you have set up your loops and to test your applications thoroughly so that if you do accidentally introduce a situation where an endless loop can occur, you'll catch it.

BREAKING OUT OF LOOPS

Sometimes you may find situations in which you will want to break out of a loop before it finishes processing, based on some condition that occurs. To deal with this type of situation, you can use either of two types of Exit statements to force an immediate termination of a loop. Once executed, the Exit statement transfers control to the next statement following the loop within the application.

Exit For

You can use the Exit statement to break out of any For...Next or For Each...Next loop. The syntax for this form of the Exit statement is shown here:

```
Exit For
```

The following example demonstrates how to use the Exit For statement to break out of the processing of a loop.

```
Private Sub Form1_Load(ByVal sender As System.Object, _
    ByVal e As System.EventArgs) Handles MyBase.Load

    Dim intCounter As Integer
    Dim strResponse As String
    Dim UserArray(4) As String

    For intCounter = 0 To 4
        strResponse = InputBox("Enter a name or type Quit to exit.")
        If strResponse.ToLower = "quit" Then
            MessageBox.Show("Data collection has been terminated.")
            Exit For
        End If
        UserArray(intCounter) = strResponse
    Next

End Sub
```

In this example, a For...Next loop has been set up to collect five names that the user supplies by entering them into a pop-up window generated by an InputBox() function. However, if at any point during the collection process the user decides to enter the word "Quit," the Exit For statement executes and terminates the data collection process.

Exit Do

You can also use the Exit statement to break out of any Do...Until or Do...While loop. The syntax for this form of the Exit statement is shown here:

```
Exit Do
```

The following example demonstrates how to use the Exit Do statement to break out of the processing of a loop.

```
Private Sub Form1_Load(ByVal sender As System.Object, _
  ByVal e As System.EventArgs) Handles MyBase.Load

    Dim intCounter As Integer = 0
    Dim intOverFlow As Integer = 50
    Dim strResponse As String = ""
    Dim blnTerminate As Boolean = False
    Dim UserArray(49) As String

    Do Until blnTerminate = True
        strResponse = InputBox("Enter a name or type Quit to exit.")
        If strResponse.ToLower = "quit" Then
            MessageBox.Show("Data collection has been terminated.")
            blnTerminate = True
        Else
            UserArray(intCounter) = strResponse
            intCounter += 1
            If intCounter = intOverFlow Then
                MessageBox.Show("Error: Array overflow, max size = 50")
                Exit Do
            End If
        End If
    Loop

End Sub
```

BACK TO THE DICE POKER GAME

It is time to turn your attention back to the development of this chapter's game project, the Dice Poker game. You will create this game by following the five basic development steps that you've used to create all the previous chapter projects.

Designing the Game

The Dice Poker game is played on a single window and is made up of one form and the 20 controls listed in Table 7.1.

Control Type	Control Name	Description
Label	lblWelcome	Displays the game's welcome message
PictureBox	pbxDie1	Displays the image for the first die
PictureBox	pbxDie2	Displays the image for the second die
PictureBox	pbxDie3	Displays the image for the third die
PictureBox	pbxDie4	Displays the image for the fourth die
PictureBox	pbxDie5	Displays the image for the fifth die
CheckBox	chkDie1	Determines whether the first die should be held at the end of the first roll
CheckBox	chkDie2	Determines whether the second die should be held at the end of the first roll
CheckBox	chkDie3	Determines whether the third die should be held at the end of the first roll
CheckBox	chkDie4	Determines whether the fourth die should be held at the end of the first roll
CheckBox	chkDie5	Determines whether the fifth die should be held at the end of the first roll
CheckBox	chkKeepAll	Determines whether the CheckBox controls representing all five dice should be checked
Button	btnRollDice	Controls the logic that rolls the dice for the game
Button	btnExit	Controls the termination of the game
GroupBox	grpScoring	Provides a container for storing the Label control that displays the game's scoring rules
GroupBox	grpOutput	Provides a container for storing the TextBox control that displays the output messages
Label	lblLegend	Displays the game's scoring rules
TextBox	txtOutput	Displays status messages during the game's execution
Imagelist	imlDiceList	Stores a list of bitmap images representing each of the six sides of a die
Timer	tmrRoll	Controls the logic that spins each of the game's five die

TABLE 7.1   FORM CONTROLS FOR THE DICE POKER GAME

Step 1: Creating a New Visual Basic Project

The first step in creating the Dice Poker game is to open up Visual Basic and create a new project, as outlined here:

1. If you have not already done so, start up Visual Basic 2008 Express and then click on File and select New Project. The New Project dialog will appear.
2. Select the Windows Application template.

3. Type **Dice Poker** as the name of your new application in the Name field located at the bottom of the New Project window.

4. Click on OK to close the New Project dialog.

Visual Basic will create a new project for you and display a new form upon which you will design the game's user interface.

Step 2: Creating the User Interface

The first step in laying out the user interface is to add controls to the form and move and resize them to the appropriate locations. As you go through each step, make sure that you reference Figure 7.14 so that you'll know where each control needs to be placed and what size it needs to be.

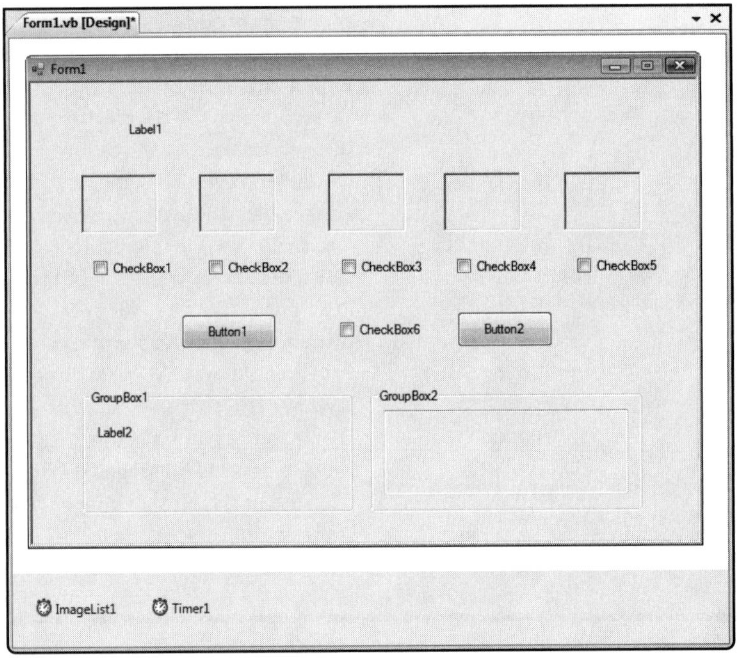

FIGURE 7.14

Completing the interface design for the Dice Poker game.

1. Begin by resizing form1 until it is about 7.25 inches wide and 5.5 inches tall.

2. Next, add a Label control near the top of the form. You'll use this control to display the game's welcome message.

3. Add five PictureBox controls to the form and space them out evenly just under the Label control.

 **DEFINITION** A `PictureBox` control displays a graphical image (.gif, .jpg, .jpeg, .bmp, .wmf, and .png) on a Visual Basic form.

4. Add six `CheckBox` controls to the form. Place each of the first five controls under one of the five `PictureBox` controls. Place the sixth `CheckBox` control in the middle of the form about .5 inch below the third `CheckBox` control.

5. Add two `Button` controls, one on each side of the sixth `CheckBox` control.

6. Next, add two `GroupBox` controls under the two `Button` controls and enlarge and resize each `GroupBox` control until they take up most of the space at the bottom of the form.

7. The first `GroupBox` control displays a text string showing the player how winning hands are scored. Therefore, you need to add a `Label` inside the first `GroupBox` control.

8. The second `GroupBox` control displays informational messages that identify winning and losing hands and tell the player how many dollars are in the account. To display this text, you need to add a `TextBox` control inside the second `GroupBox` control and resize it until it almost fills the `GroupBox` control.

9. In order to control the rolls of each die, you need to add a `Timer` control to your application. Once added, the `Timer` control is displayed in a component tray.

10. Finally, you need to add an `ImageList` control to your application. Once added, the `ImageList` control is also displayed in the component tray.

 DEFINITION An `ImageList` control is used to store images, which can then be displayed by other controls, such as the `PictureBox` control.

At this point, the overall layout of the Dice Poker game's user interface is now complete and you can begin modifying form and control properties.

Step 3: Customizing Form and Control Properties

Let's begin by making the required changes to properties belonging to the `Form` object, as listed in Table 7.2.

TABLE 7.2   PROPERTY CHANGES FOR FORM1

Property	Value
Name	frmMain
Cursor	Hand
FormBorderStyle	Fixed3D
MaximizeBox	False
StartPosition	CenterScreen
Text	Dice Poker

Make the property changes shown in Table 7.3 to the Label controls.

TABLE 7.3   PROPERTY CHANGES FOR LABEL CONTROLS

Control	Property	Value
Label1	Name	lblWelcome
	ForeColor	Blue
	Text	Welcome to Visual Basic Dice Poker!
Label2	Name	lblLegend
	Text	5 of a kind = $4 Full House = $2
		4 of a kind = $3 High Straight = $3
		3 of a kind = $1 Low Straight = $3

Make the property changes shown in Table 7.4 to the PictureBox controls.

TABLE 7.4   PROPERTY CHANGES FOR PICTUREBOX CONTROLS

Control	Property	Value
PictureBox1	Name	pbxDie1
	BorderStyle	Fixed3D
	Size Mode	StretchImage
PictureBox2	Name	pbxDie2
	BorderStyle	Fixed3D

PictureBox3	Size Mode	StretchImage
	Name	pbxDie3
	BorderStyle	Fixed3D
PictureBox4	Size Mode	StretchImage
	Name	pbxDie4
	BorderStyle	Fixed3D
PictureBox5	Size Mode	StretchImage
	Name	pbxDie5
	BorderStyle	Fixed3D
	Size Mode	StretchImage

Make the property changes shown in Table 7.5 to the CheckBox controls.

TABLE 7.5   PROPERTY CHANGES FOR CHECKBOX CONTROLS

Control	Property	Value
CheckBox1	Name	chkDie1
	Text	Keep
	Visible	False
CheckBox2	Name	chkDie2
	Text	Keep
	Visible	False
CheckBox3	Name	chkDie3
	Text	Keep
	Visible	False
CheckBox4	Name	chkDie4
	Text	Keep
	Visible	False
CheckBox5	Name	chkDie5
	Text	Keep
	Visible	False
CheckBox6	Name	ChkKeepAll
	Text	Keep All
	Visible	False

Make the property changes shown in Table 7.6 to the Button controls.

TABLE 7.6 PROPERTY CHANGES FOR BUTTON CONTROLS

Control	Property	Value
Button1	Name	btnRollDice
	Font.Bold	True
	Text	Roll Dice
Button2	Name	btnExit
	Text	Quit
	Font.Bold	True

Make the property changes shown in Table 7.7 to the GroupBox controls.

TABLE 7.7 PROPERTY CHANGES FOR GROUPBOX CONTROLS

Control	Property	Value
GroupBox1	Name	grpScoring
	Text	Scoring:
GroupBox2	Name	grpOutput
	Text	Game Status:

Make the property changes shown in Table 7.8 to the TextBox control.

TABLE 7.8 PROPERTY CHANGES FOR TEXTBOX CONTROL

Property	Value
Name	txtOutput
ReadOnly	True

Now, change the Name property for the Timer control to tmrRoll, and change the Name property of the ImageList control to imlDiceList. At this point, all that remains is to load the images representing each side of a die into the ImageList control's Images property (Collection) as outlined in Table 7.9. You'll find copies of each of the bitmap image files along with the source code for this chapter's game project at this book's companion website (www.courseptr.com/downloads). The dice images were created using Microsoft Paint and saved as 24-bit color images.

 Once you have loaded all of the application's bitmap images into the ImageList control, you'll be able to programmatically reference those images as demonstrated here:

```
PbxDie1.Image = imlDiceList.Images(3)
```

In this example, the fourth bitmap image stored in the ImageList control named imlDiceList is loaded into a PictureBox control named pbxDie1 using the PictureBox control's Image property.

TABLE 7.9	BITMAP IMAGES TO ADD TO THE IMAGELIST CONTROL'S IMAGES COLLECTION	
Property	**File**	**Index No.**
Name	1.bmp	1
Name	2.bmp	2
Name	3.bmp	3
Name	4.bmp	4
Name	5.bmp	5
Name	6.bmp	6

 You don't have to worry about packaging and distributing the six bitmap images of the game's dice. Visual Basic will automatically save copies of the bitmap files inside your application's binary file.

Step 4: Adding a Little Programming Logic

The first task to perform in putting together the program code for the Dice Poker game is to define class (or module) level constants and variables, as shown here:

```
'Declare constants and variables used throughout the application

'Controls the amount of time that it takes for the dice to roll
Private Const cintRollPeriod As Integer = 5
```

```
'Stores titlebar message
Private Const cTitleBarMsg As String = "DicePoker"

'Used to control display of Checkbox controls
Private blnExcludeList As Boolean

'Number of dollars in player's account
Private intTotalDollars As Integer = 20
Private intNoOfRolls As Integer  'Tracks the number of die rolls
Private intCounter As Integer  'Counter variable

Private intDice1 As Integer  'Number 1 die
Private intDice2 As Integer  'Number 2 die
Private intDice3 As Integer  'Number 3 die
Private intDice4 As Integer  'Number 4 die
Private intDice5 As Integer  'Number 5 die
```

Next, access the `Load` event procedure for the form and add the statements shown here:

```
'Load blank images at form load and display welcome message
Private Sub Form1_Load(ByVal sender As System.Object, _
   ByVal e As System.EventArgs) Handles MyBase.Load

    pbxDie1.Image = imlDiceList.Images(5)
    pbxDie2.Image = imlDiceList.Images(5)
    pbxDie3.Image = imlDiceList.Images(5)
    pbxDie4.Image = imlDiceList.Images(5)
    pbxDie5.Image = imlDiceList.Images(5)

    'Display greeting & the number of dollars in the player's account
    txtOutput.Text = ControlChars.CrLf & "Welcome! Are you ready " & _
        "to play Dice Poker?" & ControlChars.CrLf & _
        ControlChars.CrLf & "You have " & intTotalDollars & _
        " dollars in your account."

End Sub
```

The first five statements load the image of the number six side of a die into the five PictureBox controls. The next statement displays a welcome message in the TextBox control and tells the player how many dollars are in the account.

Next, modify the click event procedure for the form's first Button control, as shown here:

```
'This Sub procedure manages the first and second rolls of the die
Private Sub Button1_Click(ByVal sender As System.Object, _
  ByVal e As System.EventArgs) Handles btnRollDice.Click

    If intNoOfRolls = 2 Then  'See if the die have been rolled twice
        btnRollDice.Text = "Roll Dice"  'Change button's display text
        intNoOfRolls = 0  'Reset to 0 to get game ready for new hand
    End If

    'If the first roll has been made toggle the display of the
    'CheckBox control and keep track of the number of rolls
    If btnRollDice.Text = "Roll Dice" Then
        blnExcludeList = False
        intNoOfRolls += 1
    Else
        blnExcludeList = True
        intNoOfRolls += 1
    End If

    tmrRoll.Enabled = True  'Start the Timer control

End Sub
```

These statements use an Integer type variable named intNoOfRolls to keep track of whether the player is about to make the first or second roll. If the value of intNoOfRolls is equal to 2, then the text string "Roll Dice" is displayed on the first Button control and the value of intNoOfRolls is reset back to 0. The following If…Else statement checks to see whether a Boolean type variable named blnExcludeList should be set to True or False based on the text displayed on the first Button control and increments the value of intNoOfRolls by 1. The btnExcludeList variable is used later in the application to determine whether to display the CheckBox controls that allow the player to hold on to dice before making the second roll. The last statement begins the dice rolling process by enabling the Timer control (tmrRoll).

Next, create the following subroutine procedure as shown below. Visual Basic won't create this procedure for you. You have to create this procedure from scratch.

```
'This Sub procedure controls the rolling of the die
Private Sub RollTheDice(ByVal x As Integer)
    'Stores randomly generated number representing the role of a die
    Dim intRoll As Integer
    'These variables are used to track which die the player chooses
    'to hold onto over his/her first roll
    Dim blnSkipCase1 As Boolean = False
    Dim blnSkipCase2 As Boolean = False
    Dim blnSkipCase3 As Boolean = False
    Dim blnSkipCase4 As Boolean = False
    Dim blnSkipCase5 As Boolean = False

    If blnExcludeList = True Then    'Flag die the player wants to hold
        If chkDie1.Checked = True Then blnSkipCase1 = True
        If chkDie2.Checked = True Then blnSkipCase2 = True
        If chkDie3.Checked = True Then blnSkipCase3 = True
        If chkDie4.Checked = True Then blnSkipCase4 = True
        If chkDie5.Checked = True Then blnSkipCase5 = True
    End If

    Randomize()   'Ensure a random number is generated
    intRoll = Int(Rnd() * 6) + 1   'Simulate a 6-sided die

        'Test the random value to determine what graphic to display
        Select Case intRoll

            Case 1 'Update image for the first die as it spins
                If blnSkipCase1 = False Then 'Player elected not to hold
                    If x = 1 Then pbxDie1.Image = imlDiceList.Images(0)
                    If x = 2 Then pbxDie1.Image = imlDiceList.Images(1)
                    If x = 3 Then pbxDie1.Image = imlDiceList.Images(2)
                    If x = 4 Then pbxDie1.Image = imlDiceList.Images(3)
                    If x = 5 Then pbxDie1.Image = imlDiceList.Images(4)
                    If x = 6 Then pbxDie1.Image = imlDiceList.Images(5)
                    intDice1 = x
```

```
        End If

    Case 2 'Update image for the second die as it spins
        If blnSkipCase2 = False Then 'Player elected not to hold
            If x = 1 Then pbxDie2.Image = imlDiceList.Images(0)
            If x = 2 Then pbxDie2.Image = imlDiceList.Images(1)
            If x = 3 Then pbxDie2.Image = imlDiceList.Images(2)
            If x = 4 Then pbxDie2.Image = imlDiceList.Images(3)
            If x = 5 Then pbxDie2.Image = imlDiceList.Images(4)
            If x = 6 Then pbxDie2.Image = imlDiceList.Images(5)
            intDice2 = x
        End If

    Case 3 'Update image for the third die as it spins
        If blnSkipCase3 = False Then 'Player elected not to hold
            If x = 1 Then pbxDie3.Image = imlDiceList.Images(0)
            If x = 2 Then pbxDie3.Image = imlDiceList.Images(1)
            If x = 3 Then pbxDie3.Image = imlDiceList.Images(2)
            If x = 4 Then pbxDie3.Image = imlDiceList.Images(3)
            If x = 5 Then pbxDie3.Image = imlDiceList.Images(4)
            If x = 6 Then pbxDie3.Image = imlDiceList.Images(5)
            intDice3 = x
        End If

    Case 4 'Update image for the fourth die as it spins
        If blnSkipCase4 = False Then 'Player elected not to hold
            If x = 1 Then pbxDie4.Image = imlDiceList.Images(0)
            If x = 2 Then pbxDie4.Image = imlDiceList.Images(1)
            If x = 3 Then pbxDie4.Image = imlDiceList.Images(2)
            If x = 4 Then pbxDie4.Image = imlDiceList.Images(3)
            If x = 5 Then pbxDie4.Image = imlDiceList.Images(4)
            If x = 6 Then pbxDie4.Image = imlDiceList.Images(5)
            intDice4 = x
        End If

    Case 5 'Update image for the fifth die as it spins
        If blnSkipCase5 = False Then 'Player elected not to hold
            If x = 1 Then pbxDie5.Image = imlDiceList.Images(0)
```

```
            If x = 2 Then pbxDie5.Image = imlDiceList.Images(1)
            If x = 3 Then pbxDie5.Image = imlDiceList.Images(2)
            If x = 4 Then pbxDie5.Image = imlDiceList.Images(3)
            If x = 5 Then pbxDie5.Image = imlDiceList.Images(4)
            If x = 6 Then pbxDie5.Image = imlDiceList.Images(5)
            intDice5 = x
        End If

    End Select

End Sub
```

Note that when this procedure is called, it is passed a variable identifying which die (1 through 6) is being rolled, which it stores in a variable of its own named x. The procedure begins by defining local variables needed for the procedure's execution.

An If…Then statement that contains five embedded If…Then statements is then executed. All of these statements execute only if the value assigned to blnExcludeList is equal to True, indicating that the player has already taken the first roll. Each of the nested If…Then statements checks to see if the player has elected to hold on to any of the dice from the first roll (by selecting the CheckBox control for the associated die).

Next, the Randomize() function is executed, and a random number with a value between 1 and 6 is created and assigned to a variable named intRoll. A Select Case block is then used to associate the randomly generated number to the die passed to the procedure (represented by the variable named x). For example, if the randomly generated number is 2, then the program statements associated with Case 2 are executed. Then, if the value passed to the procedure is 3, indicating that the roll is for the third die, the third embedded If…Then statement executes and assigns the image of the number 2 die to the third PictureBox control.

Next, access the Tick event procedure for the Timer1 control and modify it as shown here:

```
'This Sub procedure controls the overall execution of the game
Private Sub Timer1_Tick(ByVal sender As System.Object, _
   ByVal e As System.EventArgs) Handles tmrRoll.Tick


    Dim I As Integer 'Declare variable used to control loop

    'Loop six times calling RollTheDice() upon each iteration
    For I = 1 To 6
```

```
    RollTheDice(I)
Next

intCounter += 1  'Increment counter by one

'Disable timer & display CheckBox controls at the end of each roll
If intCounter > cintRollPeriod Then
    intCounter = 0  'Reset counter
    tmrRoll.Enabled = False  'Disable timer control
    If intNoOfRolls = 1 Then  'Prepare game for second roll
        btnRollDice.Text = "Roll Again"
        chkDie1.Visible = True  'Enable Checkbox controls
        chkDie2.Visible = True
        chkDie3.Visible = True
        chkDie4.Visible = True
        chkDie5.Visible = True
        chkKeepAll.Visible = True
    End If

    If intNoOfRolls = 2 Then  'Prepare game for a new hand
        btnRollDice.Text = "Roll Dice"
        chkDie1.Checked = False  'Disable CheckBox controls
        chkDie2.Checked = False
        chkDie3.Checked = False
        chkDie4.Checked = False
        chkDie5.Checked = False
        chkKeepAll.Visible = False
        chkDie1.Visible = False  'Hide CheckBox controls
        chkDie2.Visible = False
        chkDie3.Visible = False
        chkDie4.Visible = False
        chkDie5.Visible = False
        chkKeepAll.Checked = False

        TotalTheScore() 'Call procedure that keeps track of score

        'Call procedure that displays the player's account status
        UpdateAccountStatus()
```

```
            If intTotalDollars <= 0 Then  'See if player has gone broke
                EndOfGame()  'Call procedure to see if game is over
            End If

        End If

    End IF

End Sub
```

This procedure begins by declaring a variable that will be used to control the execution of a For...Next loop. The loop iterates six times, calling the RollTheDice procedure and passing the procedure a number (e.g., I) representing one of the sides of the die. Next, the value assigned to the intCounter variable, which is used to control how long the Timer control is enabled, is incremented by 1.

An If...Then block is then executed to determine whether it's time to disable the Timer control. In addition, two embedded If...Then blocks execute, based on whether the player has made his first roll, enabling or disabling the display of the CheckBox controls.

Next, the procedure calls on the TotalTheScore and UpdateAccountStatus procedures before checking the number of dollars in the player's account to determine whether the EndOfGame procedure should be called.

The next procedure that you'll work on is the TotalTheScore procedure. This is another procedure that you will have to create from scratch, as shown here:

```
'This Sub procedure keeps track of the player's score
Private Sub TotalTheScore()

    'Declare array to be used to keep count of number in each hand
    Dim intDieArray(6) As Integer

    'Declare variable used to control loop execution
    Dim intCounter As Integer = 1

    'Iterate six times and keep count of the total number of
    '1s, 2s, 3s, 4s, 5s and 6s that have been rolled
    For intCounter = 1 To 6
        If intDice1 = intCounter Then intDieArray(intCounter) += 1
        If intDice2 = intCounter Then intDieArray(intCounter) += 1
```

```
        If intDice3 = intCounter Then intDieArray(intCounter) += 1
        If intDice4 = intCounter Then intDieArray(intCounter) += 1
        If intDice5 = intCounter Then intDieArray(intCounter) += 1
Next

'Iterate six times looking for winning hands
For intCounter = 1 To 6

    'See if the player has 5 of a kind
    If intDieArray(intCounter) = 5 Then
        intTotalDollars += 4  'Update player's account
        txtOutput.Text = ControlChars.CrLf & "Winner: 5 of " & _
          "a kind! You win 4 dollars."
        Return
    End If

    'See if the player has 4 of a kind
    If intDieArray(intCounter) = 4 Then
        intTotalDollars += 3  'Update player's account
        txtOutput.Text = ControlChars.CrLf & "Winner: 4 of " & _
          "a kind! You win 3 dollars."
        Return
    End If

    'See if the player has 3 of a kind or a full house
    If intDieArray(intCounter) = 3 Then 'Player has 3 of a kind
        Dim intCounter2 As Integer = 1
        For intCounter2 = 1 To 6 'See if player has a full house
            If intDieArray(intCounter2) = 2 Then
                intTotalDollars += 2  'Update player's account
                txtOutput.Text = ControlChars.CrLf & "Winner:" & _
                  " Full house!  You win 2 dollars."
                Return
            End If
        Next
        intTotalDollars += 1  'Update player's account
        txtOutput.Text = ControlChars.CrLf & "Winner: 3 of a " & _
          "kind! You win 1 dollar."
```

```
            Return
        End If

Next


'Iterate through die 2 - 6 looking for a High Straight
For intCounter = 2 To 6
    If intDieArray(intCounter) <> 1 Then
        Exit For  'No need to keep looking any further
    Else
        If intCounter = 6 Then
            intTotalDollars += 3  'Update player's account
            txtOutput.Text = ControlChars.CrLf & "Winner: " & _
              "High Straight! You win 3 dollars."
            Return
        End If
    End If
Next


'Iterate through die 1 - 5 looking for a Low Straight
For intCounter = 1 To 5
    If intDieArray(intCounter) <> 1 Then
        Exit For  'No need to keep looking any further
    Else
        If intCounter = 5 Then
            intTotalDollars += 3  'Update player's account
            txtOutput.Text = ControlChars.CrLf & "Winner: Low" & _
              " Straight! You win 3 dollars."
            Return
        End If
    End If
Next

intTotalDollars -= 2   'Update player's account
txtOutput.Text = ControlChars.CrLf & "Sorry, You lost this " & _
```

```
"hand! You lose 2 dollars."
```

```
End Sub
```

This procedure begins by defining an array that will be used to store the total number of 1s, 2s, 3s, 4s, 5s, and 6s in the player's hand. Then a local variable named intCounter is set up for use as a counter in the For…Next statement that follows. The For…Next loop iterates six times incrementing the appropriate array index value for each dice roll.

Next, another For…Next loop executes a series of embedded If…Then statements. The first If…Then code block checks to see if the player's hand is 5 of a kind by examining the value stored in each element of the intDieArray. The second If...Then code block looks for 4 of a kind, and the third If…Then block first looks for 3 of a kind. If he or she does have 3 of a kind, a second For…Next loop is executed to see if the player has a full house.

 TRICK If you look closely at the code in the TotalTheScore procedure, you'll see that even though the intDieArray has six elements, the procedure does not store any data in the first element of the array. I did this in order to simplify things by pairing up the index position 1 in the array with the die value of 1, the index position of 2 in the array with the die value of 2 and so on. Then, when I set up the procedure's For…Next loops, I made sure that I specified the correct starting and ending index numbers, so that the loops never processed the array's first index value (e.g., intDieArray(0)).

If the player does not have 3, 4, or 5 of a kind, the procedure checks to see if he has a high straight (e.g., 2–6) using another For…Next loop to iterate through each of the values stored in the intDieArray. Next, if the player does not have a high straight, another For…Next loop is set up to look for a low straight. Finally, if the player doesn't have a winning hand, two dollars are subtracted from his account. The logic used to develop this portion of code is fairly involved. To help make it easier to follow along, I have provided the flowchart shown in Figure 7.15, which shows the overall logical flow involved in analyzing the player's hand.

The next procedure that you'll work on is the EndOfGame procedure. You'll have to create this procedure from scratch, as shown here:

```
'This Sub procedure prompts the player to play another hand and
'controls game termination
Private Sub EndOfGame()

    'Declare variable used to hold player response
    Dim intPlayAgain As Integer
```

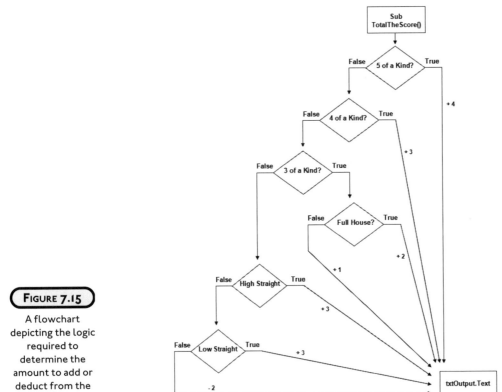

FIGURE 7.15

A flowchart depicting the logic required to determine the amount to add or deduct from the player's account.

```
txtOutput.Text = ""  'Clear out any status messages

'Prompt player to try again
intPlayAgain = MessageBox.Show("Sorry, you are " & _
  "broke. The Game is over. Would you like to " & _
  "play again?", cTitleBarMsg, _
  MessageBoxButtons.YesNo, MessageBoxIcon.Question, _
  MessageBoxDefaultButton.Button1)

'If player clicks on Yes set up a new game
If intPlayAgain = 6 Then
    intTotalDollars = 20   'Reset the player's bank account
    pbxDie1.Image = imlDiceList.Images(5) 'Load blank images
    pbxDie2.Image = imlDiceList.Images(5)
```

```
        pbxDie3.Image = imlDiceList.Images(5)
        pbxDie4.Image = imlDiceList.Images(5)
        pbxDie5.Image = imlDiceList.Images(5)
        txtOutput.Text = ControlChars.CrLf & "Welcome! Are you " & _
          "ready to play Dice Poker?" & ControlChars.CrLf & _
          ControlChars.CrLf & "You have " & intTotalDollars & _
          " dollars in your account."
    Else 'If player clicks on No end the game
        Application.Exit()
    End If

End Sub
```

This procedure begins by declaring a variable used to hold the player's response when asked to play a new game. The player is prompted to play again using the MessageBox.Show method. If the player clicks on Yes, his bank account is reset to 20 dollars and an image of a blank die is loaded into each of the PictureBox controls. If the player clicks on No, the game is terminated.

The next procedure that you'll work on is the UpdateAccountStatus procedure which you will have to create from scratch, as shown here:

```
'This Sub procedure updates the display of the player's account status
Private Sub UpdateAccountStatus()

    txtOutput.Text &= ControlChars.CrLf & ControlChars.CrLf & _
      "You have " & intTotalDollars & " dollars in your account."

End Sub
```

This procedure is called from the Timer1_Tick procedure to append a string of text, showing the player's account balance, to the text displayed in the txtOutput TextBox control.

Next, access the click event procedure for the game's Exit button and modify it as shown here:

```
Private Sub btnExit_Click(ByVal sender As System.Object, _
  ByVal e As System.EventArgs) Handles btnExit.Click

    Application.Exit()

End Sub
```

Lastly, access the `CheckedChange` event procedure for the `chkKeepAll` CheckBox control and modify it as shown here:

```
'This Sub procedure executes when the player selects the CheckBox
'control labeled KeepAll
Private Sub chkKeepAll_CheckedChanged(ByVal sender _
  As System.Object, ByVal e As System.EventArgs) _
  Handles chkKeepAll.CheckedChanged

    'If the player selects the CheckBox labeled KeepAll, select
    'the other CheckBox controls
    If chkKeepAll.Checked = True Then
        btnRollDice.Text = "Stick"
        chkDie1.Checked = True
        chkDie2.Checked = True
        chkDie3.Checked = True
        chkDie4.Checked = True
        chkDie5.Checked = True
    Else
    'If the player clears the CheckBox labeled KeepAll, clear the
    'other CheckBox controls
        btnRollDice.Text = "Roll Again"
        chkDie1.Checked = False
        chkDie2.Checked = False
        chkDie3.Checked = False
        chkDie4.Checked = False
        chkDie5.Checked = False
    End If

End Sub
```

This procedure allows the player to hold on to all of the dice from the first roll, which makes sense in situations when the player gets a high or low straight or five of a kind on the first roll. The procedure also changes the text display on the first Button control to either "Stick" or "Roll Again" based on whether the player selected the `chkKeepAll` button.

Step 5: Testing the Execution of the Dice Poker Game

That's it. The Dice Poker game is now ready to run. Go ahead and run the game by pressing F5 and make sure that everything works like it is supposed to. If you run into any problems, go back and double-check your typing. Once things are in order, pass it around to a few of your friends and ask them what they think.

SUMMARY

In this chapter, you learned how to work with variations of the Do and For loops. You also learned how to set up a While loop. You learned how to use loops to collect and process user input and to process the contents of arrays and controls, such as the ListBox. In addition, you learned about endless loops and how to use variations of the Exit keyword to break out of loops. On top of all this, you created the Dice Poker game.

Now, before you move on to Chapter 8, "Enhancing Code Structure and Organization," and start learning how to work with procedures, take a few extra minutes and improve the Dice Poker game by completing the following challenges.

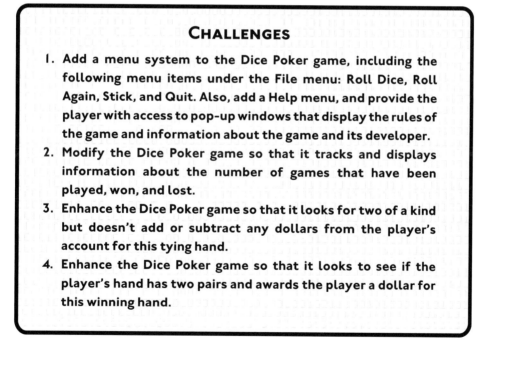

CHALLENGES

1. Add a menu system to the Dice Poker game, including the following menu items under the File menu: Roll Dice, Roll Again, Stick, and Quit. Also, add a Help menu, and provide the player with access to pop-up windows that display the rules of the game and information about the game and its developer.

2. Modify the Dice Poker game so that it tracks and displays information about the number of games that have been played, won, and lost.

3. Enhance the Dice Poker game so that it looks for two of a kind but doesn't add or subtract any dollars from the player's account for this tying hand.

4. Enhance the Dice Poker game so that it looks to see if the player's hand has two pairs and awards the player a dollar for this winning hand.

CHAPTER 8

ENHANCING CODE STRUCTURE AND ORGANIZATION

Whether you have realized it or not, every application that you have developed so far in this book has relied on procedures to organize and store program code. In this chapter, you will learn how to create your own custom procedures. You will learn how to create Sub and Function procedures and will understand the difference between the two. You will also learn how to pass data to your procedures for processing and how to return data from Function procedures. In addition, you will get plenty of chances to create and work with custom procedures when you create this chapter's game project, the Hangman game.

Specifically, you will learn how to:

- Organize the programming logic that makes up your applications into procedures in order to make them easier to develop and maintain
- Create custom procedures
- Pass and return data to and from procedures
- Streamline your applications by placing reusable code within procedures
- Develop procedures that can process optional data

PROJECT PREVIEW: THE HANGMAN GAME
In this chapter's project, you will apply your new knowledge of how to work with different types of procedures to the development of the Hangman game.

Figures 8.1 and 8.2 show examples from the Hangman game, demonstrating its functionality and overall execution flow.

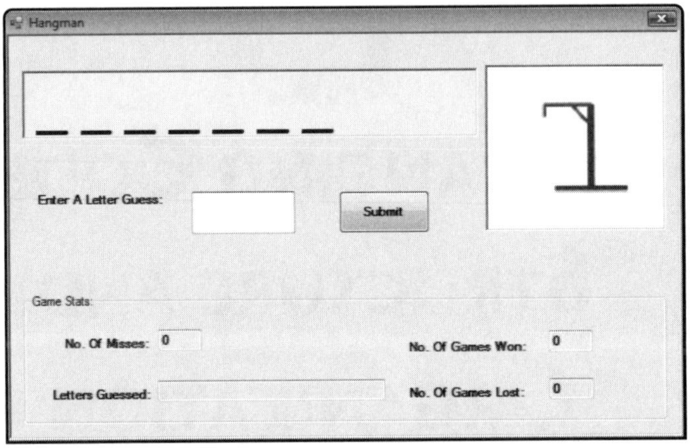

FIGURE 8.1

When first started, the game displays a graphic showing an empty hangman's gallows and a series of underscore characters representing the secret word.

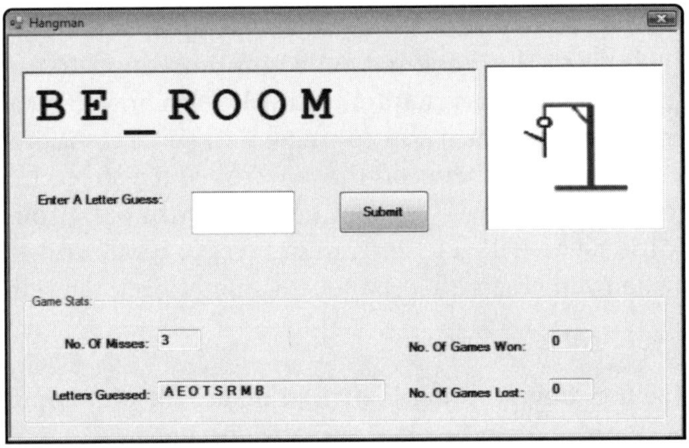

FIGURE 8.2

As the game progresses, each correct guess is displayed at the top of the window, and a visual record of every letter guessed is displayed at the bottom of the window.

The game automatically validates player input, ensuring that only one letter is entered at a time, that numeric guesses are rejected, and that only one character at a time is submitted. A correct guess is displayed as part of the game's mystery word. Each incorrect guess causes the picture of the hangman gallows to become more complete. Game play ends when the player successfully guesses every letter that makes up the mystery word or when the picture of the gallows is complete. At the end of each round of play, the player is encouraged to play again.

CREATING PROCEDURES

In the previous chapter's project, the Dice Poker game, you were required to create two custom procedures in which you added code to manage the process of rolling the game's virtual die and totaling the game score. By creating these two procedures and assigning the code statements that performed specific tasks, you were able to simplify the logic in the click procedure for the btnRollDice control. This made the overall development of the game a lot easier. As your applications continue to grow in size and complexity, it will become increasingly difficult to write them without using custom procedures.

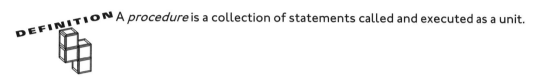

DEFINITION A *procedure* is a collection of statements called and executed as a unit.

Procedures make application development easier by breaking applications down into small pieces, allowing you to group related statements and to write applications one procedure at a time.

Because a procedure can be called and executed repeatedly as needed, procedures also facilitate code reduction, resulting in applications that are easier to maintain. Anytime that you find yourself adding code to perform the same set of steps over again, it's a good idea to create a single procedure that performs the task and then to call upon that procedure as needed.

Sub and Function Procedures

Procedures begin with a declaration statement (Sub or Function) and end with an End statement. When called, program flow is transferred from the statement that calls the procedure to the procedure itself. Once the procedure finishes executing, program flow is returned back to the calling statement, as demonstrated in Figure 8.3.

Procedures make for better organization of application logic by allowing you to group logical tasks together and isolating those tasks from other tasks. Procedures also facilitate the development of smaller applications by providing a means of creating reusable tasks that you can call as many times as necessary. On top of all this, procedures help make code maintenance a lot easier by allowing you to isolate and streamline your code. For example, you will find it a lot easier to make a change to a single procedure that performs a common task than it would be to make the same change over and over again to code that otherwise might be replicated at various points within an application.

Handling Events

With the exception of declaration statements, all Visual Basic code has to be stored inside a procedure. As I have already stated, you have been working with procedures in all of the chapter projects that you have completed so far in this book. For example, in many of the chapter game projects, you have added code to perform tasks that executed when the application was first loaded. Before adding this code, you double-clicked on the game project's form when viewing it in the form designer in order to get Visual Basic to automatically generate a Load event procedure for you, which was then displayed in the code editor.

```
Public Class frmMain

    Private Sub Form1_Load(ByVal sender As System.Object, _
        ByVal e As System.EventArgs) Handles MyBase.Load

        Load_Word_Array()

        Initialize_Game_Stats()

        Start_The_Game()

    End Sub


    Sub Load_Word_Array()

        astrWordList(0)  = "ELEPHANT"
        astrWordList(1)  = "CARRIAGE"
        astrWordList(2)  = "ENVELOPE"
        astrWordList(3)  = "PRESIDENT"
        astrWordList(4)  = "ELLIPTICAL"
        astrWordList(5)  = "MARKER"
        astrWordList(6)  = "BATTLESHIP"
        astrWordList(7)  = "TERMINATE"
        astrWordList(8)  = "REJOICE"
        astrWordList(9)  = "LIBERTY"
        astrWordList(10) = "CLASSIC"
        astrWordList(11) = "REFLEX"
        astrWordList(12) = "AIRPLANE"
        astrWordList(13) = "DWELLING"
        astrWordList(14) = "APARTMENT"
        astrWordList(15) = "RENTAL"
        astrWordList(16) = "FAUCET"
        astrWordList(17) = "BEDROOM"
        astrWordList(18) = "VOLLEY"
        astrWordList(19) = "WHISTLE"

    End Sub

End Class
```

FIGURE 8.3

A procedure returns program flow control back to the statement that calls it once it finishes executing.

Sub Procedures

Each procedure, whether it is a Sub or a Function procedure, must be assigned a unique name when it is declared. A Sub procedure is declared using the Sub and End Sub statements. Sub procedures are designed to group related statements together, which can then be executed as a unit. Sub procedures execute without returning any results back to the statement that calls them. Once its execution is completed, a Sub procedure returns processing control back to its calling statement.

The syntax that you'll use when defining your own custom Sub procedure is outlined here:

```
[Public | Private | Friend] Sub name [(arglist)]
    statements
End Sub
```

Private is an optional keyword that limits access to the procedure to the class or module where it is declared. Public is an optional keyword that makes the procedure available without restriction. Friend is an optional keyword that makes the procedure available throughout an entire application. Name represents the name that you will assign to the Sub procedure. Arglist is a list made up of one or more comma-separated arguments that can be passed to the Sub procedure for processing. Statements represent one or more code statements that you insert inside the Sub procedure.

Just like variable names, a Sub procedure's name must be unique within its defined scope, otherwise an error will occur.

Defining a Custom Sub Procedure

Let's take a look at an example of a small Sub procedure named GoodBye().

```
Public Sub GoodBye()
    MessageBox.Show("Please play again soon.", "Good_Bye Demo")
End Sub
```

Because the Public keyword was added to the beginning of the Sub procedure declaration, the procedure is accessible from anywhere within the application. When called, the Sub procedure displays a message in a pop-up window and then returns control back to the statement that called it.

If you declare a procedure without specifying the Public, Private, or Friend keyword, Visual Basic automatically makes the procedure Public. Doing so is considered poor programming practice so be sure to always use the appropriate keyword when defining your own custom procedures.

Calling a Custom Sub Procedure

To execute a Sub procedure, you type the name of the procedure followed by a pair of parentheses. For example, the following statement can be used to call the GoodBye() Sub procedure defined above.

```
GoodBye()
```

 You can also call on or execute a procedure using the `Call` keyword as demonstrated here:

```
Call GoodBye()
```

However, the `Call` keyword is considered to be a legacy statement, meaning that it is no longer required and seldom used anymore.

 You can force the early termination of a `Sub` procedure using the following statement.

```
Exit Sub
```

Function Procedures

A `Function` procedure is declared using the `Function` and `End Function` statements. `Function` procedures work almost exactly like `Sub` procedures. `Function` procedures incorporate all the capabilities of `Sub` procedures. In addition, `Function` procedures are capable of returning a result (a value) back to their calling statement.

The syntax that you'll use when creating a custom `Function` procedure is outlined here:

```
[Public | Private | Friend] Function name [(arglist)] As DataType
    statements
    [Return]
End Function
```

`Private` is an optional keyword that limits access to the procedure to the class or module where it is declared. `Public` is an optional keyword that makes the procedure available without restriction. `Friend` is an optional keyword that makes the procedure available throughout an entire application. `Name` represents the name that you will assign to the `Function` procedure. `Arglist` is a list made up of one or more comma-separated arguments that can be passed to the `Function` procedure for processing. `Statements` represent one or more code statements that you insert inside the `Sub` procedure. `DataType` specifies the data type of the value that the `Function` procedure will return to its calling statement. `Return` is a keyword used to specify a value that the `Function` is to pass back to the statement that called it.

The following example shows a `Function` procedure that displays a text message in a pop-up window without returning a result.

```
Public Function GoodBye() As String
    MessageBox.Show("Please play again soon.", "GoodBye Demo")
End Function
```

In this example, the Function procedure works exactly like the Sub procedure example you saw earlier. You can execute this procedure from anywhere in your application using the following statement.

```
GoodBye()
```

Function procedures can also return a result to their calling statements. This can be accomplished in two different ways. The first way is to create a variable with the same name as the Function procedure and assign it the value that is to be returned, as demonstrated here:

```
Public Function GetUserName() As String
        GetUserName = InputBox("Please enter your first and last " & _
            "name.", "User Name")
End Function
```

You can call this Function procedure using the statements shown here:

```
Dim strUserName As String
strUserName = GetUserName()
```

In this example, the value returned by the Function procedure is assigned to a variable named strUserName.

TRICK   Instead of setting up your Function procedures so that they can return a value, you have the option of defining module or class-level variables, which you can then modify from within your Sub and Function procedures. This negates the need to return a value in order to make that value available to another part of the application. However, all things being equal, it is better to return a value using a Function procedure and to leave your variables scoped as tightly as possible.

Note that in this example the value stored in the strUserName variable is not returned until the function finishes executing.

TRICK   You can force the early termination of a Function procedure using the following statement.

```
Exit Function
```

The Exit Function statement forces an immediate exit of the function and returns a value, if one has been specified.

The second way to set up a function to return a value is to use the Return statement to specify the value that you want returned, as demonstrated here:

```
Public Function GetUserName() As String
    Dim strUserName
    strUserName = InputBox("Please enter your first and last " & _
      "name.", "User Name")
    Return strUserName
End Function
```

Using the Return statement is the preferred method for returning a value back to a calling statement. It makes your code easier to read and I strongly recommend that you always use it.

TRAP If a Function procedure ends without setting a return value, Visual Basic will automatically supply a default value. For example, a 0 will be returned for a function with one of the numeric data types, and an empty string ("") will be returned for a function with a String data type. Unless you want your functions to return default values, you need to be sure that you set them up to return the appropriate value. Otherwise, if no return value is required, change your Function procedure to a Sub procedure.

You can also call on functions by referring to them as part of another statement, as demonstrated in the following example.

```
MessageBox.Show("Hello " & GetUserName())
```

PASSING ARGUMENTS

Procedures can be set up to process data that is passed to them in the form of arguments. These arguments are passed to a procedure and mapped to parameters that are defined as part of the procedure's declaration, as demonstrated here:

```
Public Sub DisplayMessage(ByVal strMessage As String)
    MessageBox.Show(strMessage, "Sample Message")
End Sub
```

TRICK You can set up your Sub procedures to process as many arguments as you choose to pass to it, as long as you separate each corresponding argument definition with a comma.

In this example, a Sub type procedure named DisplayMessage is defined. The procedure defines a single variable, a parameter named strMessage with a data type of String. The argument passed to the Sub procedure is automatically assigned to the strMessage variable. The argument is passed by value (ByVal), meaning that any change made to the value of strMessage will have no effect on the value assigned to the argument passed to the procedure. You can also pass an argument by reference (ByRef). However, this is not the default option. In fact, if you fail to specify ByVal or ByRef when you define your procedure, Visual Basic will automatically insert ByVal for you.

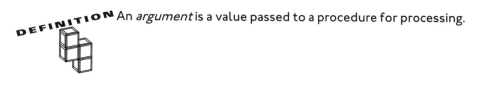 An *argument* is a value passed to a procedure for processing.

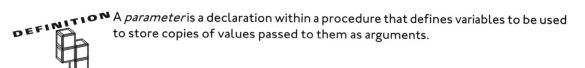 A *parameter* is a declaration within a procedure that defines variables to be used to store copies of values passed to them as arguments.

You can pass as many arguments as required to a procedure, as long as you separate each argument by a comma when calling the procedure, as demonstrated here:

```
DisplayMessage("Click on Yes to accept.", "Sample Message", "question")
```

Like Sub procedures, you can set up Function procedures to process data that is passed to the procedures in the form of arguments. These arguments are passed to a procedure and mapped to parameters that are defined as part of the procedure's declaration, as demonstrated here:

```
Public Function DisplayMessage(ByVal strMessage As String, _
  ByVal strTitle As String) As String

    Dim intResult As Integer = 0
    intResult = MessageBox.Show(strMessage, strTitle, _
      MessageBoxButtons.YesNo)

    If intResult = 6 Then
        Return "Yes"
    Else
        Return "No"
    End If

End Function
```

PASSING OPTIONAL ARGUMENTS

Visual Basic also allows you to set up procedures that can process optional arguments. There are a few rules that you need to be aware of when setting up a procedure to accept optional arguments. First of all, you must remember to define a default value for any Optional argument. The default value must be expressed as a constant value. In other words, you cannot use a variable or other type of value. Finally, any argument that follows an Optional argument must also be an Optional argument.

The following example demonstrates how to set up a procedure with an Optional argument.

```
Sub DisplayMessage(Optional ByVal strUserName As String = "")
        MessageBox.Show("Greetings " & strUserName)
End Sub
```

You can call the Sub procedure in the previous example without passing it an argument, as shown here:

```
DisplayMessage()
```

Alternatively, you can call the Sub procedure and pass it an argument, as demonstrated here.

```
DisplayMessage("Alexander Ford")
```

As mentioned above, you can set up your procedures to process more than one Optional argument at a time, as demonstrated here:

```
Public Sub DisplayMessage(ByVal strMessage As String, _
     Optional ByVal strTitleBarMessage As String = "", _
     Optional ByVal strIcon As String = "")


      If strIcon = "Exclamation" Then
         MessageBox.Show(strMessage, strTitleBarMessage, _
           MessageBoxButtons.OK, MessageBoxIcon.Exclamation)
      Else
         MessageBox.Show(strMessage, strTitleBarMessage, _
           MessageBoxButtons.OK, MessageBoxIcon.Information)
      End If


End Sub
```

You can call the previous Sub procedure in a number of different ways. For example, the following statement calls the procedure and passes it three arguments.

```
DisplayMessage("The current date and time are " & Now(), "Demo", _
   "Exclamation")
```

You can also call the procedure and pass it just two arguments, as shown here:

```
DisplayMessage("The current date and time are " & Now(), "Demo")
```

You can also call the procedure as shown here:

```
DisplayMessage("The current date and time are " & Now(), , _
   "Information")
```

In the last example, arguments representing the procedure's first and third parameters were passed. Notice that to make this work, I had to include a comma where the procedure's second parameter is defined.

Figure 8.4 shows how the pop-up windows produced by the three previous calling statements will look when displayed.

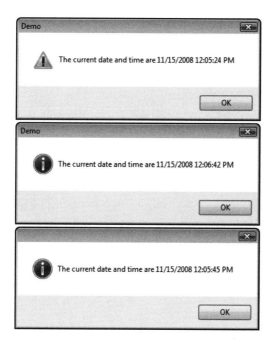

FIGURE 8.4

Using the `Optional` keyword, you can create flexible procedures that can process different numbers of arguments.

LEVERAGING THE POWER OF VISUAL BASIC'S BUILT-IN FUNCTIONS AND .NET OBJECTS

Although the ability to create your own procedures is a very powerful programming tool, allowing you to perform all sorts of tasks, it is not always necessary for you to develop all of the programming logic required to perform a given task. Instead, you can often take advantage of Visual Basic's built-in collection of functions as well as properties and methods provided by .NET objects. By leveraging the functionality provided by these functions and objects, you can save a lot of development time.

You've already learned how to work with a number of built-in Visual Basic functions. One good example has been the use of the InputBox() function as a means of collecting input from the player during game play. This function allows you to display a text string and to collect and return text input provided by the player, as demonstrated in the following example.

```
Dim strUserReply As String = ""
strUserReply = InputBox("Please enter your first name.", _
  "Data Collection example")
```

The pop-up window produced by this example is shown in Figure 8.5.

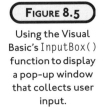

FIGURE 8.5

Using the Visual Basic's InputBox() function to display a pop-up window that collects user input.

You could, of course, create your own custom InputBox()-like function by adding a new form to a Visual Basic project and then adding a Label, a TextBox, and two Button controls to it, followed by the programming logic required to tie everything together. However, unless the InputBox() function fails to provide you with a particular piece of functionality that you absolutely must have when prompting the user for input, there is no reason to take the extra time to create your own function.

Date-Related Objects

The .NET Framework provides numerous objects that assist you in working with the date and time. For example, the DateTime object's Now() method can be used to retrieve the current system date and time, as demonstrated here:

```
MessageBox.Show(DateTime.Now())
```

DEFINITION The DateTimeObject is used to represent a moment in time. Its Now property retrieves the current date and time from the computer.

When executed, this statement produces the pop-up window shown in Figure 8.6.

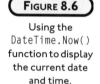

FIGURE 8.6

Using the DateTime.Now() function to display the current date and time.

1/7/2009 7:23:57 PM

OK

You can also use the Convert object's ToDateTime method to convert a string value to a Date data type, as demonstrated here:

```
Dim strDate As String
Dim dteDate As Date
strDate = "1/7/2009"
dteDate = Convert.ToDateTime(strDate)
MessageBox.Show(dteDate)
```

DEFINITION The Convert object converts or changes a data type from one type to another. Its ToDateTime method converts numerous data types to a Date data type.

The following example demonstrates how to use the TimeSpan object's Subtract method to determine the number of days that have elapsed from the specified date to the current date. In the case of this example the specified date is November 11, 1964.

```
Dim dteCurrentDate As Date = DateTime.Now
Dim dteBirthDate As Date = #11/20/1964#
Dim dteDateDiff As TimeSpan
dteDateDiff = dteCurrentDate.Subtract(dteBirthDate)
MessageBox.Show("I was born " & dteDateDiff.Days & " days ago.")
```

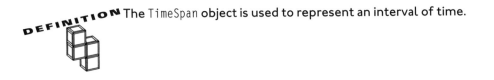

DEFINITION The TimeSpan object is used to represent an interval of time.

The first two statements in this example declare variables that store the current date and a date representing somebody's birthday. The third statement declares a variable named dteDateDiff as an instance of the TimeSpan object. The next statement uses the TimeSpan object's Subtract method. The Subtract method is used to determine the amount of time that has passed between the two time periods. The value assigned to dteDateDiff is then displayed in the final statement which uses the TimeSpan object's Days property to specify the unit of measurement to represent the time span between the two time frames.

Figure 8.7 shows the output produced by the previous example.

FIGURE 8.7

Using the
TimeSpan object's
Subtract method
to count the
number of days
between two
dates.

> I was born 16066 days ago.
>
> OK

Before moving on, let's take a look at one last example of how to programmatically work with date and time values using the DateTime object's ToString method. The ToString method converts a date/time value to a specified string format. For example, using the DateTime object's ToString method, you can create your own Visual Basic digital clock, as shown in Figure 8.8.

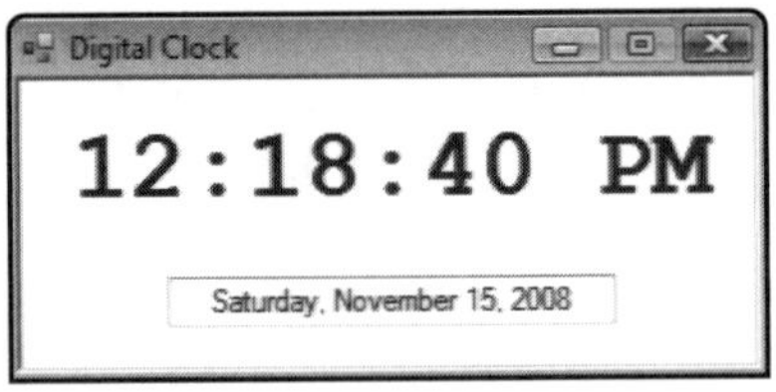

FIGURE 8.8

Using date-
related functions
to create a digital
clock.

> **Digital Clock**
>
> # 12:18:40 PM
>
> Saturday, November 15, 2008

The code associated with the digital clock example is shown next and is available for download from this book's companion website (www.courseptr.com/downloads).

```
Public Class Form1

    Private Sub Form1_Load(ByVal sender As System.Object, _
      ByVal e As System.EventArgs) Handles MyBase.Load

        txtDate.Text = DateTime.Now.ToString("D") 'Long Date pattern

    End Sub

    Private Sub Timer1_Tick(ByVal sender As System.Object, _
      ByVal e As System.EventArgs) Handles Timer1.Tick

        lblTime.Text = DateTime.Now.ToString("T")
        If DateTime.Now.ToString("T") = #12:00:00 AM# Then
            txtDate.Text = DateTime.Now.ToString("D")
        End If

    End Sub

End Class
```

In this example, the current date is displayed when the Form1_Load event procedure executes. The current date is collected using the DateTime object's Now method and then formatted using the object's ToString method. The ToString method is passed an argument of "D", specifying that the date be displayed in a long date format as shown in Figure 8.8.

The Timer_Tick event procedure updates the display of the current time every second by passing the ToString method an argument of "T," specifying a long time format. The Timer control that drives this procedure was enabled at design time, and its Interval property was set equal to 1000 so that the procedure starts executing the moment the application is loaded.

The Timer_Tick event procedure is also responsible for updating the display of the current date, which it changes automatically at one second past midnight.

String Manipulation Functions

Strings are a commonly used data type in Visual Basic applications. The .NET Framework provides Visual Basic with an abundance of different String object methods for manipulating strings. For example, using the ToString method, you can convert a value to a String data type, as demonstrated here:

```
Dim intValue As Integer = 12345
Dim strSample As String = intValue.ToString()
```

In this example, the `String` object's `ToString` method is used to convert the number 12345 to a string, which is then assigned to a variable named `strSample`. The following list provides a sampling of different types of methods and properties provided by the `String` object.

- `Trim`. A method used to remove leading and trailing blank spaces from a value.
- `ToUpper`. A method that retrieves an all uppercase version of a string.
- `ToLower`. A method that retrieves an all lowercase version of a string.
- `Length`. A property used to return the number of characters that make up a string.
- `Substring`. A method used to return a value indicating the starting location of one string within another.

The following example demonstrates how to use each of these `String` manipulation functions.

```
Dim strDataString As String = "   Once upon a time...   "
Dim strTestString As String = ""
Dim intLength As Integer = 0

strTestString = strDataString.Trim      'Assigns "Once upon a time..."
strTestString = strDataString.ToUpper   'Assigns "   ONCE UPON A TIME...   "
strTestString = strDataString.ToLower   'Assigns "   once upon a time...   "
intLength = strDataString.Length        'Assigns 25
strTestString = strDataString.Substring(3, 9)  'Displays "Once upon"
```

Note that the value that is assigned or displayed by each statement in the above example is shown as a comment that precedes each statement.

LAMBDA EXPRESSIONS

A new feature found in Visual Basic 2008 Express is the introduction of support for lambda expressions. A *lambda expression* is an inline function that can return a single value. Lambda expressions create unnamed functions. Lambda expressions are made possible through the introduction of .NET 3.0.

Lambda expressions were added primarily to support Language Integrated Queries (LINQ), another new feature in Visual Basic 2008 that facilitates the submission and processing of database queries. However, even without LINQ, you can still take advantage of lambda expressions within your Visual Basic applications. As an example, let's create a new application called Price Updater that takes a price, entered as numeric input, and updates it by a hundred dollars, rounding the final result when necessary to the nearest whole number.

Begin by creating a new Windows Forms application and set up its GUI so that it looks like the example shown in Figure 8.9.

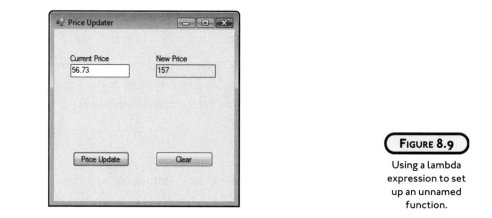

FIGURE 8.9

Using a lambda expression to set up an unnamed function.

Make sure that you add the necessary controls in the order presented, adding the left and then the right Label first, followed by the left and right TextBox controls, and then the left and right Button controls. Next, double-click on the first Button control and add the following statement to it.

```
If TextBox1.Text <> "" Then
    Dim Increment As Func(Of Integer, Integer) = _
        Function(x As Integer) x + 100
    Dim UnitCost = Increment(TextBox1.Text)
    TextBox2.Text = UnitCost.ToString
End If
```

Here, a lambda expression has been used to define a function that accepts a numeric argument and returns an integer value. Specifically, it adds 100 to the argument represented as x. Note that this example also introduces a new type of value known as Func. The Func data type is also a new Visual Basic 2008 feature and is required to set up the application's unnamed function. Next, click on the second Button control and add the following program statements to it.

```
TextBox1.Text = ""
TextBox2.Text = ""
```

Now, start your new application and type a number in the Current Price field and click on the Price Update button. In response, the application's unnamed function is executed and the value generated by lambda expression is posted in the New Price field. As this example demonstrated, lambda expressions develop and implement anonymous functions with a minimum of fuss, resulting in small, concise expressions that help produce more readable code.

BACK TO THE HANGMAN GAME

Now it is time to turn your attention back to this chapter's game project, the Hangman game. The Hangman game is based on a children's game in which the player attempts to guess a secret word. If the player guesses the word before making six incorrect guesses, the player wins. Otherwise, the game is lost.

Designing the Game

The Hangman game will be played within a single window. Therefore, it will be made up of one form and the 25 controls listed in Table 8.1.

TABLE 8.1 FORM CONTROLS FOR THE HANGMAN GAME

Control Type	Control Name	Description
Panel1	pnlLetters	A Panel control used to group Textbox controls that will be used to display guessed letters
TextBox1	txtLetter1	Displays the first letter in the game's secret word
TextBox2	txtLetter2	Displays the second letter in the game's secret word
TextBox3	txtLetter3	Displays the third letter in the game's secret word
TextBox4	txtLetter4	Displays the fourth letter in the game's secret word
Textbox5	txtLetter5	Displays the fifth letter in the game's secret word
TextBox6	txtLetter6	Displays the sixth letter in the game's secret word
TextBox7	txtLetter7	Displays the seventh letter in the game's secret word
TextBox8	txtLetter8	Displays the eighth letter in the game's secret word
TextBox9	txtLetter9	Displays the ninth letter in the game's secret word
TextBox10	txtLetter10	Displays the tenth letter in the game's secret word
Textbox11	txtMisses	Displays the number of misses that the player has made
TextBox12	txtGuesses	Displays the letters that the player has already guessed (both right and wrong)
TextBox13	txtGamesWon	Displays the number of games that the player has won
TextBox14	txtGamesLost	Displays the number of games that the player has lost

GroupBox1	grpStatus	Contains Label and TextBox controls that display game statistics
Label1	lblInput	Identifies the TextBox control where the player enters a letter guess
Label2	lblNoMissed	Identifies the TextBox control that displays the number of misses that the player has made
Label3	lblGuessed	Identifies the TextBox control that displays the letters that the player has already guessed (both right and wrong)
Label4	lblGamesWon	Identifies the TextBox control that displays the number of games that the player has won
Label5	lblGamesLost	Identifies the TextBox control that displays the number of games that the player has lost
Button1	btnSubmit	Executes code that checks to see if the player has guessed a letter in the secret word
PictureBox1	pbcHangmanBmp	Displays a graphic that shows how many letter guesses the player has missed
ImageList1	imlHangmanBmps	Stores an indexed collection of the hangman images that are displayed in the PictureBox control

Step 1: Creating a New Visual Basic Project

The first step in creating the Hangman game is to open up Visual Basic and create a new project as outlined here:

1. If you have not already done so, start up Visual Basic 2008 Express and then click on File and select New Project. The New Project dialog will appear.
2. Select Windows Application template.
3. Type **Hangman** as the name of your new application in the Name field located at the bottom of the New Project window.
4. Click on OK to close the New Project dialog.

Step 2: Creating the User Interface

Now let's begin work on laying out the game's user interface by adding controls to the form and moving and resizing them in the appropriate locations. Refer to Figure 8.10 as you go through each step so that you'll know how to resize and place the controls.

Examining the
layout of the
Hangman game's
user interface.

1. Begin by clicking on the form and setting its Size property to 655, 412.
2. Add a Panel control to the form and resize it as shown in Figure 8.10.

DEFINITION A Panel control stores and organizes other controls.

3. Add ten TextBox controls inside the Panel control and resize them as shown in Figure 8.10.
4. Add a Label control to the form. By default, Visual Basic will name it Label1.
5. Just to the right of the Label1 control, add a TextBox control and a Button control, as shown in Figure 8.10.
6. Add a GroupBox control at the bottom of the form and resize it until it takes up the bottom 30 percent of the form.
7. Inside the GroupBox control, add four Label and four TextBox controls, as shown in Figure 8.10.
8. Add a PictureBox control to the upper-right corner of the form and resize it until it is approximately 2 inches tall by 2 inches wide.
9. Lastly, add an ImageList control, which will appear in a component tray, located at the bottom of the form designer.

Step 3: Customizing Form and Control Properties

Let's begin by modifying properties associated with the game's form, as shown in Table 8.2.

TABLE 8.2 PROPERTY CHANGES FOR FORM1	
Property	**Value**
Name	frmMain
Cursor	Hand
FormBorderStyle	Fixed3D
MaximizeBox	False
MinimizeBox	False
Size	655, 412
StartPosition	CenterScreen
Text	Hangman

Next, modify the following properties associated with the Panel control, as shown in Table 8.3.

TABLE 8.3 PROPERTY CHANGES FOR THE PANEL CONTROL	
Property	**Value**
Name	pnlLetters
BackColor	WhiteSmoke
BorderStyle	Fixed3D

Next, modify the following properties associated with the GroupBox control, as shown in Table 8.4.

TABLE 8.4 PROPERTY CHANGES FOR THE GROUPBOX CONTROL	
Property	**Value**
Name	grpStatus
Text	Game Stats:

Now, modify the following properties associated with the TextBox controls, as shown in Table 8.5.

TABLE 8.5 PROPERTY CHANGES FOR THE TEXTBOX CONTROLS

Control	Property	Value
TextBox1	Name	txtLetter1
	AutoSize	False
	BackColor	WhiteSmoke
	BorderStyle	None
	Font.Name	Courier New
	Font.Size	36
	Font.Bold	True
	ForeColor	DarkBlue
	ReadOnly	True
	TabStop	False
TextBox2	Name	txtLetter2
	AutoSize	False
	BackColor	WhiteSmoke
	BorderStyle	None
	Font.Name	Courier New
	Font.Size	36
	Font.Bold	True
	ForeColor	DarkBlue
	ReadOnly	True
	TabStop	False
TextBox3	Name	txtLetter3
	AutoSize	False
	BackColor	WhiteSmoke
	BorderStyle	None
	Font.Name	Courier New
	Font.Size	36
	Font.Bold	True
	ForeColor	DarkBlue
	ReadOnly	True
	TabStop	False
TextBox4	Name	txtLetter4
	AutoSize	False
	BackColor	WhiteSmoke

	BorderStyle	None
	Font.Name	Courier New
	Font.Size	36
	Font.Bold	True
	ForeColor	DarkBlue
	ReadOnly	True
	TabStop	False
TextBox5	Name	txtLetter5
	AutoSize	False
	BackColor	WhiteSmoke
	BorderStyle	None
	Font.Name	Courier New
	Font.Size	36
	Font.Bold	True
	ForeColor	DarkBlue
	ReadOnly	True
	TabStop	False
TextBox6	Name	txtLetter6
	AutoSize	False
	BackColor	WhiteSmoke
	BorderStyle	None
	Font.Name	Courier New
	Font.Size	36
	Font.Bold	True
	ForeColor	DarkBlue
	ReadOnly	True
	TabStop	False
TextBox7	Name	txtLetter7
	AutoSize	False
	BackColor	WhiteSmoke
	BorderStyle	None
	Font.Name	Courier New
	Font.Size	36
	Font.Bold	True
	ForeColor	DarkBlue
	ReadOnly	True
	TabStop	False
TextBox8	Name	txtLetter8
	AutoSize	False
	BackColor	WhiteSmoke
	BorderStyle	None
	Font.Name	Courier New

	Font.Size	36
	Font.Bold	True
	ForeColor	DarkBlue
	ReadOnly	True
	TabStop	False
TextBox9	Name	txtLetter9
	AutoSize	False
	BackColor	WhiteSmoke
	BorderStyle	None
	Font.Name	Courier New
	Font.Size	36
	Font.Bold	True
	ForeColor	DarkBlue
	ReadOnly	True
	TabStop	False
TextBox10	Name	txtLetter10
	AutoSize	False
	BackColor	WhiteSmoke
	BorderStyle	None
	Font.Name	Courier New
	Font.Size	36
	Font.Bold	True
	ForeColor	DarkBlue
	ReadOnly	True
	TabStop	False
TextBox11	Name	txtInput
	AutoSize	False
	CharacterCasing	Upper
	Font.Size	18
	Font.Bold	True
TextBox12	Name	txtMisses
	AutoSize	False
	ReadOnly	True
	TabStop	False
TextBox13	Name	txtGuesses
	AutoSize	False
	ReadOnly	True
	TabStop	False
TextBox14	Name	txtGamesWon
	AutoSize	False
	ReadOnly	True
	TabStop	False

TextBox15	Name	txtGamesLost
	AutoSize	False
	ReadOnly	True
	TabStop	False

Now, modify the following properties associated with the Label controls, as shown in Table 8.6.

TABLE 8.6   PROPERTY CHANGES FOR THE LABEL CONTROLS

Control	Property	Value
Label1	Name	lblInput
	Text	Enter A Letter Guess:
	Font.Bold	True
Label2	Name	lblNoMissed
	Text	No. Of Misses:
	Font.Bold	True
Label3	Name	lblGuesses
	Text	Enter A Letter Guess:
	Font.Bold	True
Label4	Name	lblGamesWon
	Text	Enter A Letter Guess:
	Font.Bold	True
Label5	Name	lblGamesLost
	Text	Enter A Letter Guess:
	Font.Bold	True

Now, modify the following properties associated with the Button control, as shown in Table 8.7.

Now, modify the following properties associated with the PictureBox control, as shown in Table 8.8.

TABLE 8.7 PROPERTY CHANGES FOR THE BUTTON CONTROL	
Property	**Value**
Name	btnSubmit
Font.Bold	True
Text	Submit

TABLE 8.8 PROPERTY CHANGES FOR THE PICTUREBOX CONTROL	
Property	**Value**
Name	pbcHangmanBmp
BorderStyle	Fixed3D
SizeMode	StretchImage

Finally, change the name property of the ImageList control to imlHangmanBmps and add the following bitmap images to the Images property (collection) as shown in Table 8.9. Don't worry about having to create these bitmap images yourself. I have included copies of them with the source for the game project on the book's companion website (www.courseptr.com/downloads).

TABLE 8.9 BITMAP IMAGES TO ADD TO THE IMAGELIST CONTROL'S IMAGES COLLECTION		
Property	**File**	**Index No.**
Name	100.bmp	0
Name	80.bmp	1
Name	60.bmp	2
Name	40.bmp	3
Name	20.bmp	4
Name	10.bmp	5
Name	0.bmp	6

Step 4: Adding a Little Programming Logic

Begin coding the Hangman game by double-clicking on the game's form, thus opening the code editor and creating the form's Load event procedure as shown here:

```
Public Class frmMain


End Class
```

Just above the Load event procedure, add the following statements.

```
Const cTitleBarMsg As String = "HANGMAN"  'Titlebar message
Private astrWordList(19) As String  'Stores a list of game words
Private strGameWord As String = ""  'Stores the word currently in play
Private strWrong As String = ""  'Stores a list of missed guesses
Private intMisses As Integer = 0  'Keeps count of missed guesses
Private intNoRight As Integer = 0  'Keeps count of correct guesses
Private intPlayAgain As Integer = 0  'Track the player's response
Private intHangmanNo As Integer = 6 'Controls display of hangman image
```

These declaration statements define a constant, an array, and variables that are used by two or more procedures in the application. The array, strWordListArray, will be used to store secret words used to play the game. The rest of the variables will be used to hold the currently selected secret word and game statistics and to display a string of letters that have been guessed by the player.

Now, add the following statements to the Form1_Load procedure.

```
'This procedure executes when the game first starts
Private Sub Form1_Load(ByVal sender As System.Object, _
  ByVal e As System.EventArgs) Handles MyBase.Load

    LoadWordArray()  'Populate the array with words
    InitializeGameStats()  'Set up the game's starting values
    StartTheGame()  'Start the game

End Sub
```

The three statements inside the Form1_Load procedure set up game play by calling three custom procedures. The LoadWordArray procedure populates the strWordListArray array with 20 secret words. To create it, scroll down below the Form1_Load procedure and enter the following statements.

```
'This procedure loads words into the game's array
Sub LoadWordArray()

End Sub
```

Next, add the following statements inside the `LoadWordArray` procedure to populate each element of the array.

```
strWordListArray(0) = "ELEPHANT"
strWordListArray(1) = "CARRIAGE"
strWordListArray(2) = "ENVELOPE"
strWordListArray(3) = "PRESIDENT"
strWordListArray(4) = "ELLIPTICAL"
strWordListArray(5) = "MARKER"
strWordListArray(6) = "BATTLESHIP"
strWordListArray(7) = "TERMINATE"
strWordListArray(8) = "REJOICE"
strWordListArray(9) = "LIBERTY"
strWordListArray(10) = "CLASSIC"
strWordListArray(11) = "REFLEX"
strWordListArray(12) = "AIRPLANE"
strWordListArray(13) = "DWELLING"
strWordListArray(14) = "APARTMENT"
strWordListArray(15) = "RENTAL"
strWordListArray(16) = "FAUCET"
strWordListArray(17) = "BEDROOM"
strWordListArray(18) = "VOLLEY"
strWordListArray(19) = "WHISTLE"
```

The `InitializeGameStats` Sub procedure will set the game statistics displayed in the `GroupBox` control to zeroes. You'll need to create this Sub procedure from scratch by inserting it just under the `LoadWordArray` procedure. Once created, you will need to modify it as shown here:

```
'This procedure resets values stored in the game's TextBox controls
Sub InitializeGameStats()

    txtGamesWon.Text = 0
    txtGamesLost.Text = 0

End Sub
```

The `StartTheGame` Sub procedure is responsible for setting up the game to play a new round. It does so by making three `Sub` procedure calls, which reset variable defaults, retrieve a secret word, and format the word for display. The procedure ends by setting focus to the `txtInput` control to ready the game for the player input.

```
'This procedure preps the game for a new round of play
Sub StartTheGame()

    ResetDefaultSettings()  'Call procedure to reset game settings
    strGameWord = RetrieveWord()  'Get a word for the player to guess
    FormatGameWord()  'Format the display of the mystery word
    txtInput.Focus()  'Prepare the game to accept the player's guess

End Sub
```

Next, create the `ResetDefaultSettings` Sub procedure, shown below, to prepare the game to play a new round.

```
'This procedure resets variables and TextBox control values back to
'their starting values
Sub ResetDefaultSettings()

    intMisses = 0
    intNoRight = 0
    txtGuesses.Text = ""
    txtMisses.Text = intMisses
    txtInput.Text = ""
    intHangmanNo = 6
    pbcHangmanBmp.Image = imlHangmanBmps.Images.Item(6)

End Sub
```

Note that in addition to resetting variable default values, the last statement in the previous procedure displays an empty hangman's gallows graphic in the `PictureBox` control.

Now, create the `RetrieveWord` procedure. The procedure will retrieve a random number, use that number to select a word from the `strWordListArray` array, and then return the secret word to the statement that called the procedure. Therefore, you will need to define this procedure as a `Function` and return the secret word by assigning it to a variable that has the same name as the procedure.

```
'This procedure randomly retrieves a word for the player to guess
Function RetrieveWord() As String

      'Declare a variable to hold a randomly generated number
      Dim intRandomNo As Integer = 0
      Dim r As New Random  'Instantiate a Random object

      'Use the Random object's Next method to retrieve a number between
      'zero and the number of words in the array
      intRandomNo = r.Next(strWordListArray.Length)

      'Use the random number to select a word from the array and pass
      'the word back to the calling statement
      Return strWordListArray(intRandomNo)

End Function
```

Note the use of the Random object and its Next method in the RetrieveWord procedure. In previous chapters you've seen me use Visual Basic's built-in Randomize and Rnd functions. The functionality provided by these two functions has been duplicated by the .NET Framework's Random object and its Next method.

Next, create the FormatGameWord Sub procedure as shown below. The procedure begins by declaring an Integer type variable named intCounter. It then assigns an empty string to each of the ten TextBox controls that are used to display the letters that make up the game's secret word. The procedure then sets up a For...Next loop to display an underscore character for each letter in the secret word.

```
'This procedure formats the display of underscore characters
'representing the game's word
Sub FormatGameWord()

      'Define a variable to be used as a counter
      Dim intCounter As Integer = 1

      'Game words are limited to ten or fewer characters. Each letter is
      'stored in a separate TextBox control. Start by setting the value
      'stored in each TextBox control to a blank character
      txtLetter1.Text = ""
```

```
        txtLetter2.Text = ""
        txtLetter3.Text = ""
        txtLetter4.Text = ""
        txtLetter5.Text = ""
        txtLetter6.Text = ""
        txtLetter7.Text = ""
        txtLetter8.Text = ""
        txtLetter9.Text = ""
        txtLetter10.Text = ""

        'Use a For...Next loop to display an underscore character for each
        'letter that makes up the game's word
        For intCounter = 1 To strGameWord.Length
            If intCounter = 1 Then txtLetter1.Text = "_"
            If intCounter = 2 Then txtLetter2.Text = "_"
            If intCounter = 3 Then txtLetter3.Text = "_"
            If intCounter = 4 Then txtLetter4.Text = "_"
            If intCounter = 5 Then txtLetter5.Text = "_"
            If intCounter = 6 Then txtLetter6.Text = "_"
            If intCounter = 7 Then txtLetter7.Text = "_"
            If intCounter = 8 Then txtLetter8.Text = "_"
            If intCounter = 9 Then txtLetter9.Text = "_"
            If intCounter = 10 Then txtLetter10.Text = "_"
        Next

End Sub
```

You can create the next procedure, shown below, by returning to the form designer and double-clicking on the btnSubmit control and then modifying the procedure as shown here:

```
'This procedure executes each time the player clicks on the button
'control labeled Submit
Private Sub btnSubmit_Click(ByVal sender As System.Object, _
   ByVal e As System.EventArgs) Handles btnSubmit.Click

     Dim intCounter As Integer = 0 'Variable to be used as a counter
     Dim strWordLetter As String = "" 'Store the player's guess
     Dim strInputOk As String = "" 'Used when validating player input
```

```
strInputOk = ValidatePlayerInput() 'Call validation procedure
If strInputOk = "Error" Then
    Exit Sub 'Exit procedure if player's guess is invalid
End If


'Display an error if the player has already guessed the letter
If Strings.InStr(1, txtGuesses.Text, txtInput.Text.ToUpper, 1) _
  <> 0 Then
    MessageBox.Show("Error: Letter has already been guessed.")
Else 'See if the player guessed a letter in the word

    'Add letter to list of letters that have already been guessed
    txtGuesses.Text &= " " & txtInput.Text

    'Look for the letter in the word
    If Strings.InStr(1, strGameWord.ToUpper, _
      txtInput.Text.ToUpper, 1) = 0 _
      Then 'The player's guess was wrong

        'Append letter to the list of missed guesses
        strWrong &= " " & txtInput.Text.ToUpper
        intMisses += 1 'Add one to the number of missed guesses
        txtMisses.Text = intMisses 'Display # of missed guesses

        'Decrement variable used to keep track of which Hangman
        'graphic is to be displayed
        intHangmanNo -= 1
        pbcHangmanBmp.Image = _
           imlHangmanBmps.Images.Item(intHangmanNo) 'Display graphic

        If intMisses = 6 Then 'Game is over after 6 missed guesses
            txtGamesLost.Text += 1 'Increment counter
            'Call procedure to see if player wants to play again
            PromptForNewGame("Sorry. You have lost.")
        End If
    End If

    'Use For...Next loop to spin through each letter in the word
```

```
        For intCounter = 1 To strGameWord.Length
            'Select one letter at a time
            strWordLetter = Mid(strGameWord, intCounter, 1)
            'See if the letter matches the player's guess
            If strWordLetter.ToUpper = txtInput.Text.ToUpper Then
                intNoRight += 1  'Increment counter
                'Execute procedure to display a guessed letter
                FlipGameLetter(intCounter)
            End If
        Next

    End If

    'See if the player has guessed every letter in the word
    If intNoRight = strGameWord.Length Then
        txtGamesWon.Text += 1
        'Call procedure to see if player wants to play again
        PromptForNewGame("Congratulations. You have Won!")
    End If

    txtInput.Text = ""
    txtInput.Focus()

End Sub
```

The procedure begins by declaring three variables and then calls on the ValidatePlayerInput procedure to determine if the player's input is acceptable. If the input is okay, the procedure continues executing. Next, the procedure uses an If...Then...Else statement to see if the player has entered a letter guess that has already been tried. If this is a new guess, the letter is appended to the end of the test string displayed in the txtGuesses control.

An embedded If...Then statement then checks to see if the player's guess is wrong using the Strings object's Instr() function. If the player guesses incorrectly, the value stored in the txtMisses control is increased by 1 and the graphic displayed in the PictureBox control is changed to reflect the number of misses so far. A check is then made to see if the player has missed a total of six guesses, thus losing the game.

DEFINITION The Strings object provides access to methods that can be used to perform string operations. The Strings object's InStr method retrieves an Integer specifying the start position of one string within another.

If the game has not been lost, a For...Next loop is used to spin through the secret word and display each letter that matches the player's guess. Finally, a check is made to see if the player has guessed all of the letters that make up the secret word, thus winning the game. If the game has not been won, the txtInput control is cleared and given focus, thus preparing the game for the player's next guess.

Next, you will need to manually create the ValidatePlayerInput procedure. This procedure will need to return a value, so you will need to define it as a Function, as shown here:

```
'This procedure validates the player's guess
Function ValidatePlayerInput() As String

        'See if the player clicked on Submit without entering a guess
        If txtInput.Text = "" Then
            MessageBox.Show("Error: You must enter a letter.")
            txtInput.Text = ""
            txtInput.Focus()
            Return "Error" 'Return a value indicating an invalid guess
        End If

        'See if the player entered more than one character
        If txtInput.Text.Length > 1 Then
            MessageBox.Show("Error: You may only enter one letter per" & _
              "guess.")
            txtInput.Text = ""
            txtInput.Focus()
            Return "Error" 'Return a value indicating an invalid guess
        End If

        'See if the player entered a number
        If IsNumeric(txtInput.Text) = True Then
            MessageBox.Show("Error: Numeric entries are not valid.")
            txtInput.Text = ""
            txtInput.Focus()
```

```
        Return "Error" 'Return a value indicating an invalid guess
    End If

    Return "Passed" 'Return a value indicating a valid guess

End Function
```

The procedure performs three input validation tests to make sure the player has provided an acceptable guess. It accomplishes this using three If...Then statements. The first If...Then statement makes sure that the player enters something. The second If...Then statement makes sure that the player did not enter more than one character, and the third If...Then statement makes sure that the player didn't enter a number. Each time the player correctly guesses a letter, the FlipGameLetter Sub procedure is executed. You'll need to manually create this procedure, as shown here:

```
'This procedure is responsible for displaying uppercase letters in
'the appropriate TextBox controls
Sub FlipGameLetter(ByVal intLetterNumber As Integer)

    'Select the letter to be displayed based on the argument passed
    'to the procedure
    Select Case intLetterNumber
        Case 1
            txtLetter1.Text = txtInput.Text.ToUpper
        Case 2
            txtLetter2.Text = txtInput.Text.ToUpper
        Case 3
            txtLetter3.Text = txtInput.Text.ToUpper
        Case 4
            txtLetter4.Text = txtInput.Text.ToUpper
        Case 5
            txtLetter5.Text = txtInput.Text.ToUpper
        Case 6
            txtLetter6.Text = txtInput.Text.ToUpper
        Case 7
            txtLetter7.Text = txtInput.Text.ToUpper
        Case 8
            txtLetter8.Text = txtInput.Text.ToUpper
        Case 9
```

```
            txtLetter9.Text = txtInput.Text.ToUpper
        Case 10
            txtLetter10.Text = txtInput.Text.ToUpper
    End Select
```

```
End Sub
```

This procedure consists of a single Select Case statement, which compares the player's guess to each letter in the secret word and flips (that is, displays) any letters that match the guess.

The last procedure that you will need to create is the PromptForNewGame Sub procedure. You will need to manually define this procedure and then set it up as shown here:

```
'This procedure prompts the player to play again
Sub PromptForNewGame(ByVal strMessage As String)

    'Ask player to play again
    intPlayAgain = MessageBox.Show(strMessage & _
      " Would you like to play again?", _
      cTitleBarMsg, MessageBoxButtons.YesNo, MessageBoxIcon.Question)

    'The player clicked on Yes
    If intPlayAgain = 6 Then
        StartTheGame() 'Start a new game
    Else 'The player clicked on No
        Application.Exit() 'End the game
    End If

End Sub
```

The procedure uses the MesssageBox.Show method to ask if the player would like to play another round. If the player clicks on the Yes button, the StartTheGame procedure is executed. Otherwise, the Application.Exit statement executes and terminates the application.

Step 5: Testing the Execution of the Hangman Game

The Hangman game is now complete. Press F5 and test the game to make sure that everything is working properly. If you run into errors, then you have probably made one or more typing mistakes. Go back and double-check your code and see if you have made any errors. Before you pass the game along to your friends, make sure that you remember to test all aspects of the game, including feeding it good and bad input.

SUMMARY

In this chapter, you learned how to improve the overall organization and design of your Visual Basic applications using procedures. This included learning how to create your own custom Sub and Function procedures. You also learned how to pass arguments to your procedures and how to define optional parameters. In addition, you learned how to use the Panel control as a container for storing other controls. Before you move on to the next chapter, take a few extra minutes and see if you can improve on the Hangman game by implementing the following challenges.

CHALLENGES

1. Improve the Hangman game by separating the display of letters correctly guessed from letters incorrectly guessed.
2. Increase the size of the game's array and make the required modifications to the program's code that references it so that you can add additional words to it and provide a bigger pool from which secret words will be randomly chosen.
3. Add a CheckBox control to the game just under the PictureBox control and use it to give the player the option of displaying or hiding the GroupBox control and its contents. Adjust the size of the form as appropriate.

GETTING COMFORTABLE WITH OBJECT-ORIENTED PROGRAMMING

In this chapter, you will learn about Visual Basic object-oriented programming. This will include learning about a number of new programming concepts, including abstraction, encapsulation, inheritance, and polymorphism. You will also learn more about working with objects, including a look at examples of objects provided by Visual Basic and the .NET Framework, as well as how to create your own objects by creating custom classes. You will also learn how to store and protect the data stored in your custom objects and to provide access to it through the implementation of properties and methods. In addition, you will get the chance to create another Visual Basic application based on the classic children's rock, paper, scissors game.

Specifically, you will learn:

- About object-oriented programming concepts and terms
- How to define custom classes
- How to instantiate objects based on your custom classes
- How to set up method overloading within custom classes
- How to provide controlled access to the data stored within objects

PROJECT PREVIEW: THE ROCK, PAPER, SCISSORS GAME

This chapter's game project is the Rock, Paper, Scissors game, which you probably remember playing when you were a child. The rules of the game haven't changed. Each player attempts to outplay an opponent (in this case, the computer) by consistently selecting superior choices. The rules for scoring the game are listed here:

- Rock crushes scissors to win.
- Paper covers rock to win.
- Scissors cut paper to win.
- Everything else is a tie.

Figures 9.1 to 9.3 illustrate examples of the Rock, Paper, Scissors game in action, showing its functionality and overall execution flow.

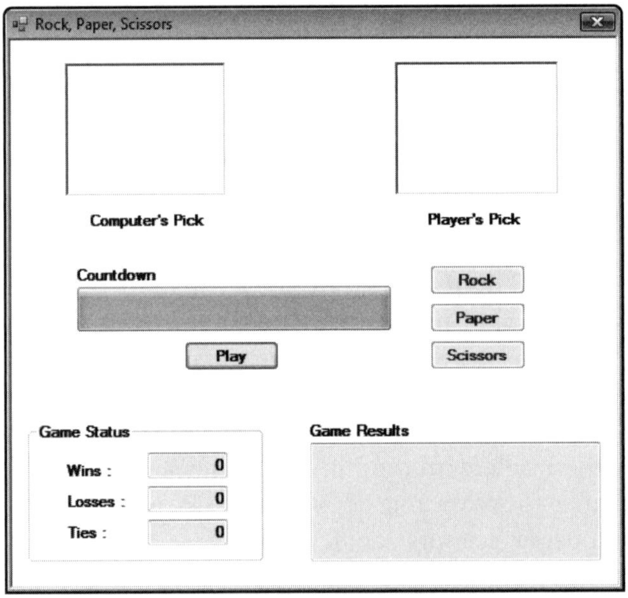

FIGURE 9.1

The Rock, Paper, Scissors game begins by displaying the game board.

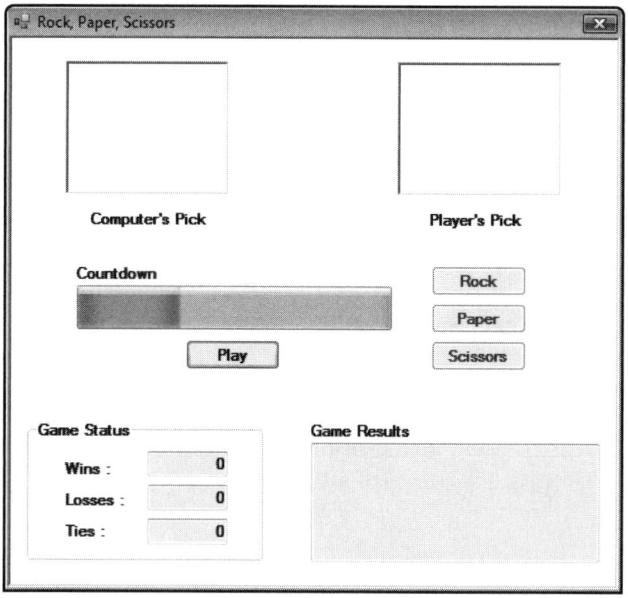

FIGURE 9.2

When the player clicks on the Play button, a 1.5-second countdown begins and the player gets a half-second at the end of the countdown to select a move.

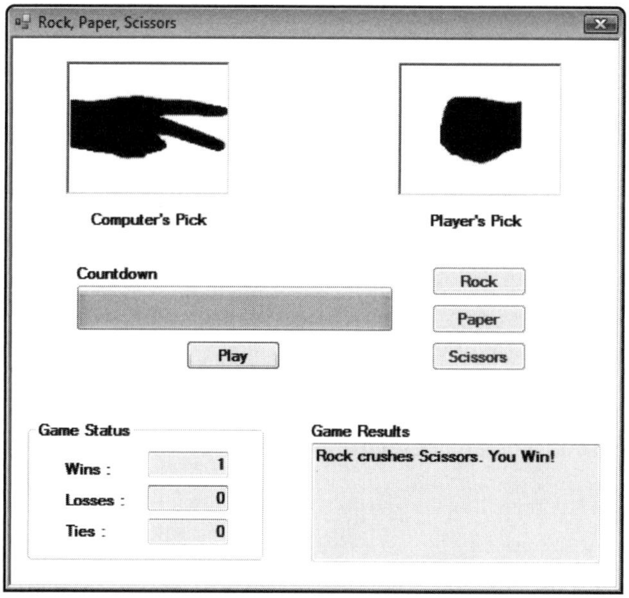

FIGURE 9.3

As soon as both the computer and the player have made their choices, the game displays graphics showing each move and determines who won.

OBJECT-ORIENTED PROGRAMMING

OOP (*object-oriented programming*) is a major feature of Visual Basic. In OOP, data and code are grouped together as objects. Objects are, in effect, self-contained entities. As an example, think about the Visual Basic forms and controls with which you have been working. Each of these represents a different type of object. Objects can store data and provide a carefully designed interface for accessing their data and exercising their functionality. This access is provided through object properties and methods. Objects also have the ability to validate any data that is passed to them and to reject it if it fails to meet certain predefined criteria. Thus, properly defined objects make applications more reliable.

Objects make things easier. Think about the Form object. Every chapter game project that you have worked on has used one, yet you never had to create one. Visual Basic makes forms available to you as classes. Forms have their own properties, such as background color and foreground color, which you do not have to define or validate. Forms have methods associated with them, such as maximize and minimize, which you do not have to define. All you have to know is how to add new controls to your forms in order to modify them. Forms also have events, like the Load event, to which they automatically know how to respond.

OOP Terms

In Visual Basic, objects are created from classes. A class provides a template that specifies data, properties, and methods that are available for working with the data.

 DEFINITION A *class* is a template that can be used to instantiate objects.

Visual Basic provides access to a large collection of classes. For example, the code behind a Form comes from the Form class, which is located in the System.Windows.Forms namespace. Examples of other classes include System.Windows.Forms.Button, where the Button class is defined, and System.Windows.Forms.CheckBox, where the CheckBox class is defined.

DEFINITION A *namespace* is an organized collection of classes. The .NET Framework provides access to numerous namespaces, which it makes available in its class library.

Whether you realized it or not up to this point, you have been working with classes in all of the chapter game projects that you have worked on in this book. Every time you have designed a new user interface, you have worked with classes provided by the .NET Framework. If you go back and look at your various chapter project applications, you'll notice that all of the code for the application is wrapped up inside an opening and closing Class statement. For example, the first and last statements in most Windows Forms Applications are shown here:

```
Public Class Form1

End Class
```

As simple as these statements look, they deserve a little extra explanation. The opening statement publicly defines a new `Class` called `Form1`, and the last statement defines the end of the class. However, there is more going on here than first meets the eye. Visual Basic 2008 Express makes things easy on you by hiding much of the work that it does behind the scenes on your behalf. To see what is really happening here, click on the Show All file icon in the Solution Explorer and then expand the `Form1.vb` entry and double-click on the `Form1.designer.VB` entry. You'll see a whole bunch of behind-the-scenes code that Visual Basic has automatically generated on your behalf. You can learn a lot from studying the code that you see here, but it isn't necessary that you understand everything that you see. Take a look at the first two statements that are displayed, as shown here:

```
Partial Class Form1
  Inherits System.Windows.Forms.Form
```

As you can now see, the form that Visual Basic has automatically provided you with is actually inherited (or cloned) from the `Form` class stored in the `System.Windows.Forms` namespace.

As should be obvious at this point, OOP simplifies the coding process by hiding many of the complexities of an application from the programmer. In addition, it promotes the reuse of code by making it possible to define a class once and then use it over and over again to create as many objects as required.

Visual Basic also allows you to create your own custom classes, which is much of the focus of this chapter. But before I get too deep into our discussion of OOP, let's stop for a minute and go over a few key terms and make sure that you understand the basic building blocks of OOP.

Abstraction

Abstraction is a process by which you define in program code a logical representation of a class. This includes the specification of the base functionality belonging to the class and the definition of properties and methods that are required for the proper operation of the class. Returning to the `Form` class as an example, base properties include the `Text`, `Size`, `BackColor`, and `ForeColor` properties.

Encapsulation

Encapsulation is the process whereby you package the base functionality of a class and provide access to the features of the class through a collection of properties and methods. When an object is created from a particular class, the inner workings of the object are hidden from the programmer. Again, consider the Form class. You don't know what the code behind it looks like or how it is written. You cannot directly access its internal code or data. You only know that to work with the form, you modify its properties, execute its methods, and provide code for its events. How the Form class was designed to make all these things work is hidden from you. Thus, encapsulation helps simplify program development and hide complexity.

Encapsulation also includes data protection, meaning that code can be added to process and verify the validity of any data passed to an object to ensure that it meets certain criteria.

Inheritance

Inheritance is the process whereby one class is derived from another. When you define a new class in your program code, such as when you define a new class for a Visual Basic Form, the class that you create inherits its features from a base class, which in the case of this example is System.Windows.Forms.Form.

Polymorphism

Polymorphism is the ability to create something in different forms. Within Visual Basic, polymorphism is accomplished through a programming technique know as overloading. For example, using overloading, a programmer might develop multiple versions of the same procedure (with the same procedure name), each of which is designed to handle a different combination of arguments. For example, one version of a procedure might be set up to process a single Integer argument, whereas another version of the procedure might be set up to process two arguments, one of which might be an Integer and the other a String.

DEFINITION *Overloading* is the process of defining the same method multiple times, each with a different argument list.

TRICK One really good example of overloading that you have already seen and worked with is the MessageBox class's Show method. This method supports multiple overloads, allowing it to accept various combinations of arguments and data types. To view the various combinations of arguments and data that you can pass to the MessageBox.Show method, open the Visual Basic code editor and type MessageBox.Show(. In response, IntelliSense will display a pop-up window showing the various options that are available to you. Click on the up and down arrows in the upper-left corner of the pop-up window to explore the various overload options that are available.

CLASSES AND OBJECTS

As I have already stated, a class is a template that defines all of the attributes, properties, methods, and events required to create an object. Using abstraction, programmers develop a design for a class. Using encapsulation, they implement a class's structure. One class can be established by inheriting it from another class. Finally, using overloading, programmers can extend procedures within classes to handle different sets of arguments.

For example, you might analogize the relationship between a class and an object as being akin to the relationship between a mold and Jell-O. The mold defines an overall form and shape of the Jell-O. Once poured into the mold and solidified, the new instance of Jell-O takes on the basic qualities of the mold. As another, more specific, example, the Form object is an instance of the Form class and has access to all the features provided by that class.

In order to use a class, you must first instantiate it. The instantiation process varies depending on the class you are working with. For example, to instantiate a Button or CheckBox class (control), all that you have to do is place a copy of it on a form. However, if you create your own custom class as part of a Visual Basic application, you will create a new class instance using the New keyword.

Creating a New Class

There are a number of ways that you can create a new class. First, as you have already seen, anytime you create a new Visual Basic application, a new class is created for you based on the System.Windows.Forms.Form class. In the case of the Dice Poker game, the new class was named frmMain.

You can also add a new class to an application by simply inserting its declaration under the existing class definition in the code editor, as shown here:

```
Public Class frmMain
    Private Sub frmMain_Load(ByVal sender As System.Object, _
        ByVal e As System.EventArgs) Handles MyBase.Load
    End Sub
End Class

Public Class Greeting

End Class
```

In this example, a new class named Greeting has been defined. At the moment, the class does not have any data members, properties, or methods defined to it.

DEFINITION A *data member* is a variable that is defined within a class. Ordinarily, data members are hidden from the outside world and used only within the class. However, data members can be made directly accessible from outside the class using the Public keyword.

Let's continue on with the previous example, adding a little code to give the Greeting class a little functionality. Modify the example as shown below, starting with the code in the Greeting class and then adding the two statements inside the frmMain_Load event procedure.

```
Public Class frmMain

    Private Sub frmMain_Load(ByVal sender As System.Object, _
        ByVal e As System.EventArgs) Handles MyBase.Load

        Dim SampleGreeting As New Greeting
        MessageBox.Show(SampleGreeting.Message)

    End Sub

End Class

Public Class Greeting

    Public Message As String = "Hello World!"

End Class
```

The statement that you added to the Greeting class sets up a data member. Data members are by default private, meaning that they cannot be accessed from outside of the class itself. However, in this example, I made the data member public just so that we could have a working example that does something.

By itself, the Greeting class does not do anything. You need to instantiate an object based on the class in order to be able to do something. The first statement in the frmMain_Load event procedure instantiates a new object named SampleGreeting using the New keyword, which follows the syntax shown here:

```
Dim ObjectName As New ClassName
```

Then the MessageBox.Show method is used to access and display the SampleGreeting object's Message data member.

Another way to add a new class to your application is to create it in its own code module, separate and distinct from the form's class code, as demonstrated in the following example.

1. Click on the Add Class option located on the Project menu. The Add New Item window appears, as shown in Figure 9.4.

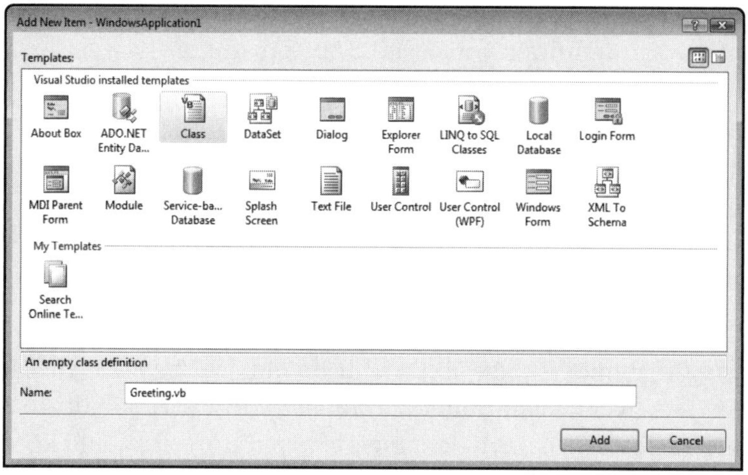

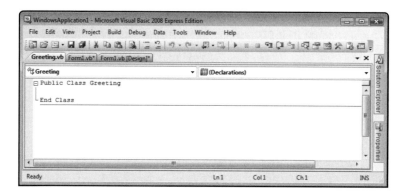

FIGURE 9.4

Defining a new class in its own code module.

2. Select the Class icon and type a name for the class that you are about to define in the Name field, and then click on the Add button.
3. A new tab will appear in the code editor, and the opening and closing class statements for the new class will be displayed, as shown in Figure 9.5.

FIGURE 9.5

Viewing the code that Visual Basic automatically created for the new class.

4. Modify the program code for the Greeting class as shown here:

```
Public Class Greeting

    Public Message As String = "Hello World!"

End Class
```

Now, if you run this example, you will find that it displays the same results as the example in which you embedded the Class definition beneath the bottom of the frmMain class.

Understanding Data Members

In the previous two examples that demonstrated how to create a new class, you learned how to define a new data member. By default, class data members are private, which means that they cannot be seen or accessed from outside the class. However, as the examples showed, you can make data members publicly available. You can also declare them as protected, in which case they can be accessed only by derived classes of the base class.

Although it is possible for data members to be accessed from outside the class, they are not properties of that class. However, when made publicly available, you lose the ability to restrict control over data members. Instead of making data members public, you should keep them private and set up properties to provide controlled access to any data stored in your classes.

Defining Class Properties

Properties can be used to set and retrieve values. To set up a property within a class, you start by declaring a private data member and then define a public property procedure that provides controlled access to the value stored in the data member. The following types of property procedures are supported by Visual Basic.

- **Get.** Retrieves the value assigned to a property
- **Set.** Assigns a value to a property

The following example demonstrates how to add a property to a class.

```
Public Class Greeting

    Private Message As String

    Public Property Text() As String
        Get
            Return Message
        End Get
```

```
        Set(ByVal Value As String)
            Message = Value
        End Set
    End property
End Class
```

As you have seen throughout this book, before you can use an object, you must instantiate it. You can then reference its properties by specifying the name of the object, followed by a period and the name of a particular property. When you assign a value to the Text property, the Set property procedure block executes. Note that the Set property procedure is automatically passed an argument named Value in which the data passed to the Set property procedure is stored. All you have to do to finish up the property assignment is to assign the data stored in Value to a private data member (Message). When you retrieve the value associated with the Text property, the Get procedure block is automatically executed.

The following statements demonstrate how to derive an object from the Greeting class and then set and retrieve the object's Text property. The first statement shown below instantiates a new object named SampleGreeting that is derived from the Greeting class. The next two statements assign a value to the object's Text property and then use the MessageBox.Show method to demonstrate that the property assignment was successful.

```
Dim objSample As New Greeting
objSample.Text = "Good Morning."
MessageBox.Show(objSample.Text)
```

As I mentioned earlier, the advantage of setting up properties, compared to simply making data members public, is that you can add code to your property procedures to perform data validation before allowing access to the data associated with a particular property. As a quick example of how this works, I have modified the previous example, shown below, to include such a check.

```
Public Property Text() As String
    Get
        Return Message
    End Get
    Set(ByVal Value As String)
        If Len(Value) > 2 Then
            Message = Value
        End If
    End Set
End Property
```

This new example now requires that a property assignment for the Text property be at least two characters in length.

Adding Class Methods

In addition to defining data members and properties in your custom classes, you can add your own methods. To add a method to a class, all you have to do is add a Sub or Function procedure, as demonstrated here:

```
Public Class Greeting

    Private Message As String

    Public Property Text() As String
        Get
            Return Message
        End Get
        Set(ByVal Value As String)
            If Len(Value) > 2 Then
                Message = Value
            End If
        End Set
    End Property

    Public Sub PostWelcome()
        MessageBox.Show("Welcome to my Visual Basic application!")
    End Sub

End Class
```

In this example, the Greeting class has been modified by the addition of a method named PostWelcome(). When executed, this method uses the MessageBox.Show method to display a text message. Like all of the other object methods that you have worked with, you can call on this method by specifying the name of its object followed by a period and the name of the method, as shown here:

```
Dim objSample As New Greeting
objSample.PostWelcome()
```

One of Visual Basic's object-oriented programming features is polymorphism. Polymorphism is implemented in Visual Basic by providing the ability to overload class methods. When you overload a method, as demonstrated below, Visual Basic makes sure that the correct method is executed based on the argument list that is passed.

```
Public Class DisplayMessage

    Public Overloads Sub Display(ByVal Message As String)
        MessageBox.Show(Message)
    End Sub

    Public Overloads Sub Display(ByVal Message As String, Title As String)
        MessageBox.Show(Message, Title)
    End Sub

End Class
```

In this example, two Sub procedures, both of which are named Display, are defined. Notice the use of the keyword Overloads in both Sub procedure definitions. The first Sub procedure is designed to process a single argument, whereas the second Sub procedure is designed to process two arguments.

 For overloading to work, you must provide each overloaded procedure with a unique set of arguments. You can vary the argument list by changing the number of arguments that are passed, by changing the types of arguments passed, or a combination of both.

Inheriting from Another Class

Anytime Visual Basic provides a new form, behind the scenes the new instance of the form is created by specifying the Inherits keyword and the name of the class that is to be inherited from, as shown here:

```
Partial Public Class frmMain
    Inherits System.Windows.Forms.Form
```

The derived class inherits its features from the base class. Anytime you add a control to a form, Visual Basic automatically handles the setup of the new instance of the control (object). In addition to inheriting from classes provided to you by Visual Basic and the .NET Framework, you can derive new classes from classes that you create. The following example demonstrates how to create a new class named GreetingTwo using the Greeting class as the base class.

```
Public Class GreetingTwo
    Inherits Greeting
```

```
Private Warning As String = "Action not allowed."

Public ReadOnly Property ErrMsg() As String
    Get
        Return Warning
    End Get
End Property
```

```
End Class
```

You'll notice that the GreetingTwo class not only inherits all of the properties and methods belonging to the Greeting class, but also extends this functionality by adding a new property of its own. In addition, you'll notice that the new ErrMsg property has been made read-only, meaning that it can be retrieved but not modified by calling statements.

Any objects created using the new GreetingTwo class automatically inherit all of the properties and methods from that, which itself includes methods and properties inherited from the Greeting class.

BACK TO THE ROCK, PAPER, SCISSORS GAME

It is time to turn your attention back to the development of this chapter's game project, the Rock, Paper, Scissors game. You will create this game by following the same basic set of steps that you've used to create all the previous chapter projects.

Designing the Game

The Rock, Paper, Scissors game is played on a single window and is made up of one form and the 22 controls listed in Table 9.1.

Step 1: Creating a New Visual Basic Project

The first step in creating the Rock, Paper, Scissors game is to open up Visual Basic and create a new project as outlined here:

1. If you have not already done so, start up Visual Basic 2008 Express and then click on File and select New Project. The New Project dialog will appear.
2. Select Windows Forms Application template.
3. Type **Rock, Paper, Scissors** as the name of your new application in the Name field located at the bottom of the New Project window.
4. Click on OK to close the New Project dialog.

TABLE 9.1   FORM CONTROLS FOR THE ROCK, PAPER, SCISSORS GAME

Control Type	Control Name	Description
PictureBox	pcbLeft	Displays an image showing the computer's selection
PictureBox	pcbRight	Displays an image showing the player's selection
Label	lblComputer	Identifies the PictureBox control where the computer's selection is displayed
Label	lblPlayer	Identifies the PictureBox control where the player's selection is displayed
Label	lblCountDown	Identifies the function of the ProgressBar control
ProgressBar	pgbCountDown	Displays a graphical 1.5-second countdown
Button	btnPlay	Starts game play by enabling the Timer control
Button	btnRock	Allows the player to select Rock
Button	btnPaper	Allows the player to select Paper
Button	btnScissors	Allows the player to select Scissors
GroupBox	grpStatus	Contains Label and TextBox controls that identify and display game statistics
Label	lblWins	Identifies the TextBox control that displays the number of games won
Label	lblLosses	Identifies the TextBox control that displays the number of games lost
Label	lblTies	Identifies the TextBox control that displays the number of games tied
TextBox	txtWins	Displays the number of games the player has won
TextBox	txtLosses	Displays the number of games the player has lost
TextBox	txtTies	Displays the number of games the player has tied
Label	lblResults	Identifies the TextBox control where the results of each game are displayed
TextBox	lblOutput	Displays a test string detailing the results of each game
ToolTip	tltControl	Provides the ability to assign ToolTips to individual controls
Timer	tmrControl	Controls the 1.5-second countdown sequence and the half-second windows in which the player gets to make a selection
ImageList	imlHands	Stores the bitmap images that are displayed in the PictureBox controls during game play

Step 2: Creating the User Interface

Let's begin the development of the Rock, Paper, Scissors game by laying out and resizing all of the controls that will be needed to set up the game's user interface. Refer to Figure 9.6 so that you'll know where to place each control and how to resize them.

1. Begin by clicking on the form and setting its Size property to 488, 456.
2. Add two PictureBox controls, one in the upper-left corner of the form and the other in the upper-right corner. Set the Size property for both PictureBox controls to 129,103.
3. Next, add a pair of Label controls to the form. Place the first one just under the first PictureBox control and the second one just under the second PictureBox control.
4. Add another Label control about an inch below the left-hand side of the first PictureBox control, and then add a ProgressBar control just beneath it, setting its Size property to 250, 34.
5. Add four Button controls to the form, as shown in Figure 9.6.
6. Add a GroupBox control to the lower-left corner of the form. Set its Size property to 187, 108, its Font to Bold, and its Text property to Game Status.
7. Add three Label controls and three TextBox controls inside the GroupBox control, as shown in Figure 9.6.
8. Add three more TextBox controls to the GroupBox control, just to the right of the three Label controls.

9. Add another `Label` control just to the right of the `GroupBox` control and then add a `TextBox` control underneath it. Set the `Size` property for the `TextBox` control to `229, 86`.

10. Finally, add `ToolTip`, `Timer`, and `ImageList` controls.

Step 3: Customizing Form and Control Properties

Okay, let's get to work on making the required changes to the game's form and control properties as listed in Table 9.2.

TABLE 9.2 PROPERTY CHANGES FOR FORM 1

Property	Value
Name	frmMain
BackColor	LightYellow
FormBorderStyle	Fixed3D
MaximizeBox	False
MinimizeBox	False
StartPosition	CenterScreen
Text	Rock, Paper, Scissors

Make the property changes shown in Table 9.3 to the `PictureBox` controls.

TABLE 9.3 PROPERTY CHANGES FOR PICTUREBOX CONTROLS

Control	Property	Value
PictureBox1	Name	pcbleft
	BorderStyle	Fixed3D
	SizeMode	StretchImage
PictureBox2	Name	pcbRight
	BorderStyle	Fixed3D
	SizeMode	StretchImage

Make the property changes shown in Table 9.4 to the `Label` controls.

Next, change the name of the `ProgressBar` control to `pgbCountDown`. Then make the property changes shown in Table 9.5 to the four `Button` controls.

TABLE 9.4	PROPERTY CHANGES FOR LABEL CONTROLS	
Control	**Property**	**Value**
Label1	Name	lblComputer
	Font.Bold	True
	Text	Computer's Pick
Label2	Name	lblPlayer
	Font.Bold	True
	Text	Player's Pick
Label3	Name	lblCountDown
	Font.Bold	True
	Text	Countdown
Label4	Name	lblWins
	Font.Bold	True
	Text	Wins :
Label5	Name	lblLosses
	Font.Bold	True
	Text	Losses :
Label6	Name	lblWins
	Font.Bold	True
	Text	Ties :
Label7	Name	lblResults
	Font.Bold	True
	Text	Game Results

TRICK The ProgressBar control is used to display a visual indication of the status of a process. Once added to a form, you can update the ProgressBar control's appearance by setting its Value property to zero to represent a process that has not started. You can then set the Value property anywhere between 0 and 100 to represent the current status of a process. Finally, you can set the Value property to 100 to represent a process that has completed.

Make the property changes shown in Table 9.6 to the four TextBox controls.

Next, change the name of the ToolTip control to tltControl. Then make the property changes shown in Table 9.7 to the Timer control.

TABLE 9.5   PROPERTY CHANGES FOR BUTTON CONTROLS

Control	Property	Value
Button1	Name	btnPlay
	BackColor	ButtonFace
	Font.Bold	True
	Text	Play
	ToolTip	Begin 1.5-second countdown
Button2	Name	btnRock
	BackColor	ButtonFace
	Enabled	False
	Font.Bold	True
	Text	Rock
	ToolTip	Select Rock
Button3	Name	btnPaper
	BackColor	ButtonFace
	Enabled	False
	Font.Bold	True
	Text	Paper
	ToolTip	Select Paper
Button4	Name	btnScissors
	BackColor	ButtonFace
	Enabled	False
	Font.Bold	True
	Text	Scissors
	ToolTip	Select Scissors

TABLE 9.6   PROPERTY CHANGES FOR TEXTBOX CONTROLS

Control	Property	Value
TextBox1	Name	txtWins
	Font.Bold	True
	ReadOnly	True
	TextAlign	Right
TextBox2	Name	txtLosses
	Font.Bold	True
	ReadOnly	True

	TextAlign	Right
TextBox3	Name	txtTies
	Font.Bold	True
	ReadOnly	True
	TextAlign	Right
TextBox4	Name	txtOutput
	Font.Bold	True
	ReadOnly	True

TABLE 9.7   PROPERTY CHANGES FOR TIMER CONTROL

Control	Property	Value
Timer1	Name	tmrControl
	Interval	500

Finally, change the name of the Name property for the ImageList control to imlHands and add the following bitmap images to its Images property (collection) as shown in Table 9.8. You'll find copies of the bitmap images required to complete this project, along with the source code, on this book's companion website (www.courseptr.com/downloads).

TABLE 9.8   BITMAP IMAGES TO ADD TO THE IMAGELIST CONTROL'S IMAGES COLLECTION

Property	File	Index No.
Name	Left-Paper.bmp	0
Name	Right-Paper.bmp	1
Name	Left-Rock.bmp	2
Name	Right-Rock.bmp	3
Name	Left-Scissors.bmp	4
Name	Right-Scissors.bmp	5
Name	Blank.bmp	6

Step 4: Adding a Little Programming Logic

The first task in putting together the program code for the Rock, Paper, Scissors game is to double-click on the game's form to open the code editor. In response, Visual Basic automatically defines a new Class for you called frmMain (the name you assigned to Form1). This derived class will inherit properties, methods, and events associated with the System.Windows.Forms base class.

Once the frmMain class has been defined, you can begin adding the program code. For starters, define a variable named intCounter with a data type of Integer as shown below. This variable will be used later in the application to keep track of a 1.5-second countdown process that controls the tempo of the game.

```
Public Class frmMain

    'Declare a variable to be used as a counter
    Private intCounter As Integer
End Class
```

There are a few one-time activities that need to be performed when the Rock, Paper, Scissors game first starts up. These activities include loading a blank bitmap image into both of the game's PictureBox controls and setting all of the Text properties for the three TextBox controls located in the GroupBox control to zero. To accomplish these activities, add the following code statements to the form's Load event.

```
'This procedure loads default settings when the form first loads
Private Sub Form1_Load(ByVal sender As System.Object, _
  ByVal e As System.EventArgs) Handles MyBase.Load

    pcbLeft.Image = imlHands.Images.Item(6) 'Load a blank Bitmap
    pcbRight.Image = imlHands.Images.Item(6) 'Load a blank Bitmap

    'Set game statistics stored in the game's Textbox control to zero
    txtWins.Text = 0
    txtLosses.Text = 0
    txtTies.Text = 0

End Sub
```

In order to initiate game play, the player must click on the Button control labeled Play. This button initiates the game's 1.5-second countdown process by setting the Value property of the ProgressBar control equal to 0 and then enabling the Timer control. This procedure also clears the display of any leftover text in the txtOutput (Textbox) control and sets the display of blank bitmap images in the game's two PictureBox controls. The code for the btnPlay_Click event Sub procedure is shown here:

```
'This procedure initiates the game's 1.5-second countdown
Private Sub btnPlay_Click(ByVal sender As System.Object, _
   ByVal e As System.EventArgs) Handles btnPlay.Click

    pgbCountDown.Value = 0 'Set ProgressBar to show 0 percent progress
    tmrControl.Enabled = True 'Start countdown by enabling the Timer
    txtOutput.Text = "" 'Clear out any text stored in the Textbox

    pcbLeft.Image = imlHands.Images.Item(6)  'Load a blank Bitmap
    pcbRight.Image = imlHands.Images.Item(6) 'Load a blank Bitmap

End Sub
```

The Timer control is responsible for controlling the timing of the game. It simulates the amount of time that it typically takes for two players to manually sync up by performing a 1.5-second countdown. The Timer controls Interval property was set at design time to 500, which equates to a half-second. The value of the intCounter variable is incremented by 1 upon each tick of the Timer control.

The tmrControl_Tick procedure, shown below, uses a Select Case block to keep track of time. Once the first half-second has passed, the value of intCounter will be 1 and the ProgressBar control's Value property is set to 33, in order to provide the player with a visual indicator that a third of the countdown has elapsed. After the passage of a full second, the second Case statement is triggered and the ProgressBar control's Value property is updated to show that two-thirds of the countdown has elapsed.

```
'This procedure controls the timing of game play
Private Sub tmrControl_Tick(ByVal sender As System.Object, _
   ByVal e As System.EventArgs) Handles tmrControl.Tick

    intCounter += 1  'Increment counter

    'Determine the actions to take based on the counter's value
    Select Case intCounter
        Case 1  'At .5 seconds
            pgbCountDown.Value = 33 'Set ProgressBar to show 33%
```

```
        Case 2   'At 1 second
             pgbCountDown.Value = 66 'Set ProgressBar to show 66%
        Case 3   'At 1.5 seconds
             pgbCountDown.Value = 100 'Set ProgressBar to show 100%
             'Enable the 3 game choice buttons
             btnRock.Enabled = True
             btnPaper.Enabled = True
             btnScissors.Enabled = True
        Case 4   'At 2 seconds
             intCounter = 0   'Set counter to zero
             tmrControl.Enabled = False 'Disable the Timer Control
             'Disable the 3 game choice buttons
             btnRock.Enabled = False
             btnPaper.Enabled = False
             btnScissors.Enabled = False
             pgbCountDown.Value = 0 'Set ProgressBar to show 0%
        Case Else
    End Select

End Sub
```

At 1.5 seconds, the ProgressBar control's Value property is updated to show that the count-down is complete. At this point, the buttons representing the Rock, Paper, and Scissors options are enabled, and the player has a half-second in which to make a choice of which button to click. Once the last half-second interval has elapsed, the last Case statement is triggered. As a result, the value of intCounter is reset to 0, the three option buttons are disabled, the Timer control is disabled, and the ProgressBar control is cleared by setting its Value property to 0.

The code for the Button control event representing the selection of the Rock option is shown below. It includes two Dim statements that define local variables used to store both the player's and the computer's choices. The last four statements in this procedure display a graphic representing the player's choice of Rock, sets the strPlayerPick variable equal to Rock, calls on the ComputerTurn() procedure function to retrieve the computer's choice, and then passes the player's and computer's choices to the CheckGameResults() procedure for processing (to determine the results of the game).

```
'This procedure executes when the player selects Rock
Private Sub btnRock_Click(ByVal sender As System.Object, _
  ByVal e As System.EventArgs) Handles btnRock.Click
```

```
    Dim strPlayerPick As String 'Used to store player's move
    Dim strComputerPick As String 'Used to store computer's move

    'Load Bitmap representing a Rock into the right-most PictureBox
    pcbRight.Image = imlHands.Images.Item(3)

    strPlayerPick = "Rock" 'Set the player's move equal to Rock

    'Run procedure that determines the computer's move
    strComputerPick = ComputerTurn()

    'Run procedure that determines who has won the game
    CheckGameResults(strPlayerPick, strComputerPick)

End Sub
```

The click event procedure for the Button control representing the Paper option is shown below. Its code is almost identical to that of the Button control for the Rock option, except that it reflects the player's choice of Paper as the move.

```
'This procedure executes when the player selects Paper
Private Sub btnPaper_Click(ByVal sender As System.Object, _
   ByVal e As System.EventArgs) Handles btnPaper.Click

    Dim strPlayerPick As String 'Used to store player's move
    Dim strComputerPick As String 'Used to store computer's move

    'Load Bitmap representing Paper into the right-most PictureBox
    pcbRight.Image = imlHands.Images.Item(1)

    strPlayerPick = "Paper" 'Set the player's move equal to Paper

    'Run procedure that determines the computer's move
    strComputerPick = ComputerTurn()

    'Run procedure that determines who has won the game
    CheckGameResults(strPlayerPick, strComputerPick)

End Sub
```

The code for the Button control representing the Scissors option is shown below. As you can see, it is only a slight variation of the previous two procedures.

```
'This procedure executes when the player selects Scissors
Private Sub btnScissors_Click(ByVal sender As System.Object, _
  ByVal e As System.EventArgs) Handles btnScissors.Click

    Dim strPlayerPick As String 'Used to store player's move
    Dim strComputerPick As String 'Used to store computer's move

    'Load Bitmap representing Scissors into the right-most PictureBox
    pcbRight.Image = imlHands.Images.Item(5)

    strPlayerPick = "Scissors" 'Set player's move equal to Scissors

    'Run procedure that determines the computer's move
    strComputerPick = ComputerTurn()

    'Run procedure that determines who has won the game
    CheckGameResults(strPlayerPick, strComputerPick)

End Sub
```

The ComputerTurn() procedure, shown below, is a custom-developed Function. Therefore, you will have to manually define it before you can begin coding it. It begins by defining a local variable that will be used to store the computer's selection. Then the Random class's Next method is used to generate a random number between 1 and 3.

```
'This procedure determines the computer's move
Function ComputerTurn() As String

    'Declare a variable to hold a randomly generated number
    Dim intRandomNumber As Integer

    'Declare a variable to hold the Computer's assigned move
    Dim strComputerMove As String = ""

    Dim r As New Random 'Instantiate a Random object

    'Use the Random class's Next method to get a number between 1 - 3
```

```
intRandomNumber = r.Next(1, 3)

If intRandomNumber = 3 Then   'Assign Rock as the computer's turn
    'Load Bitmap of Rock into left-most PictureBox
    pcbLeft.Image = imlHands.Images.Item(2)
    strComputerMove = "Rock"
End If

If intRandomNumber = 2 Then 'Assign Scissors as the computer's turn
    'Load Bitmap of Scissors into left-most PictureBox
    pcbLeft.Image = imlHands.Images.Item(4)
    strComputerMove = "Scissors"
End If

If intRandomNumber = 1 Then 'Assign Paper as the computer's turn
    'Load Bitmap of Paper into left-most PictureBox
    pcbLeft.Image = imlHands.Images.Item(1)
    strComputerMove = "Paper"
End If

Return strComputerMove

End Function
```

The rest of the ComputerTurn() procedure processes the randomly generated number using three If…Then statements. If the random number is equal to 3, the computer's choice is set equal to Rock and the appropriate graphic is loaded into the first PictureBox control. The second and third If…Then blocks are used to process the computer choice for Paper and Scissors.

The CheckGameResults() Sub procedure, shown below, processes two arguments. The arguments passed to it are the player's and the computer's choices. This procedure is made up of a Select Case block that compares the player's choice against each of the three possible options (Rock, Paper, and Scissors). Based on which of the three options match the player's choice, three embedded If…Then statements are executed to determine what choice the computer was assigned by the game. Once the player's and the computer's choices have been identified, the appropriate output string is posted in the txtOutput (TextBox) control, and the value stored in the TextBox controls that represent the number of games won, lost, and tied is incremented as appropriate.

```
'This procedure compares the player's move to the computer's move
Sub CheckGameResults(ByVal strPlayerPick As String, _
  ByVal strComputerPick As String)

    pgbCountDown.Value = 0 'Set the ProgressBar to show 0%

    Select Case strPlayerPick  'Process the player's move

        Case "Rock" 'Determine results if the player picks Rock
            If strComputerPick = "Rock" Then
                txtOutput.Text = "Rock versus Rock is a Tie!"
                'Add 1 to the TextBox that displays the # of ties
                txtTies.Text += 1
            End If
            If strComputerPick = "Scissors" Then
                txtOutput.Text = "Rock crushes Scissors. You Win!"
                'Add 1 to the TextBox that displays the # of wins
                txtWins.Text += 1
            End If
            If strComputerPick = "Paper" Then
                txtOutput.Text = "Paper covers Rock. You Lose!"
                'Add 1 to the TextBox that displays the # of losses
                txtLosses.Text += 1
            End If

        Case "Scissors" 'Determine results if the player picks Scissors
            If strComputerPick = "Rock" Then
                txtOutput.Text = "Rock breaks scissors. You Lose!"
                'Add 1 to the TextBox that displays the # of losses
                txtLosses.Text += 1
            End If
            If strComputerPick = "Scissors" Then
                txtOutput.Text = "Scissors versus Scissors is a Tie"
                'Add 1 to the TextBox that displays the # of ties
                txtTies.Text += 1
            End If
            If strComputerPick = "Paper" Then
                txtOutput.Text = "Scissors cut Paper. You Win!"
```

```
                  'Add 1 to the TextBox that displays the # of wins
                  txtWins.Text += 1
             End If
       Case "Paper" 'Determine results if the player picks Paper
             If strComputerPick = "Rock" Then
                  txtOutput.Text = "Paper covers Rock. You Win!"
                  'Add 1 to the TextBox that displays the # of wins
                  txtWins.Text += 1
             End If
             If strComputerPick = "Scissors" Then
                  txtOutput.Text = "Scissors cut Paper. You Lose!"
                  'Add 1 to the TextBox that displays the # of losses
                  txtLosses.Text += 1
             End If
             If strComputerPick = "Paper" Then
                  txtOutput.Text = "Paper versus paper is a Tie!"
                  'Add 1 to the TextBox that displays the # of ties
                  txtTies.Text += 1
             End If
    End Select

End Sub
```

Step 5: Testing the Execution of the Rock, Paper, Scissors Game

Okay, that's it. The Rock, Paper, Scissors game is now ready to run. Go ahead and run the game by pressing F5 and make sure that everything works like it is supposed to. If you run into any problems, go back and double-check your typing. Once things are in order, pass it around to a few of your friends and ask them what they think.

SUMMARY

In this chapter, you learned about Visual Basic classes and namespaces. You learned how to create your own custom classes. You then learned how to instantiate new objects using your custom classes. The custom objects that you created included their own properties and methods. You also learned how to overload object methods and how to provide controlled access to data stored within your objects. On top of all this, you created the Rock, Paper, Scissors game.

Now, before you move on to Chapter 10, "Graphics, Audio, and Animation," spend a few additional minutes improving the Rock, Paper, Scissors game by implementing the following challenges.

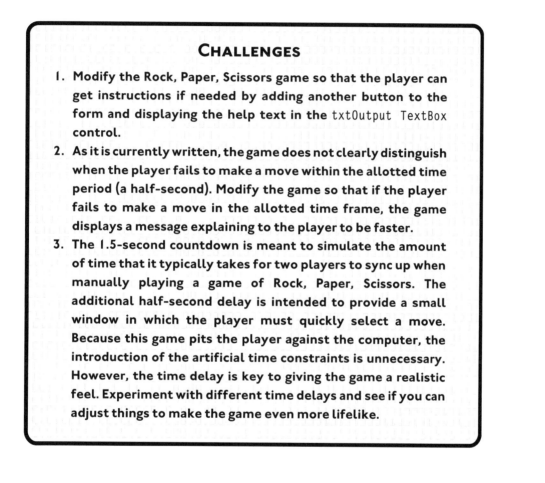

CHALLENGES

1. Modify the Rock, Paper, Scissors game so that the player can get instructions if needed by adding another button to the form and displaying the help text in the txtOutput TextBox control.

2. As it is currently written, the game does not clearly distinguish when the player fails to make a move within the allotted time period (a half-second). Modify the game so that if the player fails to make a move in the allotted time frame, the game displays a message explaining to the player to be faster.

3. The 1.5-second countdown is meant to simulate the amount of time that it typically takes for two players to sync up when manually playing a game of Rock, Paper, Scissors. The additional half-second delay is intended to provide a small window in which the player must quickly select a move. Because this game pits the player against the computer, the introduction of the artificial time constraints is unnecessary. However, the time delay is key to giving the game a realistic feel. Experiment with different time delays and see if you can adjust things to make the game even more lifelike.

INTEGRATING GRAPHICS AND AUDIO

This chapter will introduce you to various graphic and audio capabilities provided by Visual Basic 2008 Express. You will learn how to work with a number of new classes associated with the `System.Drawing.Graphics` namespace. Using objects created from classes stored in this namespace, you will learn how to draw custom graphics in your applications. You will also learn how to use the `SoundPlayer` control to enable playing sounds in your applications. In addition, you will learn how to work with the classes stored in the `My` namespace to create a small application called the Audio Jukebox. On top of all this, you will learn how to create this chapter's game project, the VB Doodle game.

Specifically, you will learn how to:

- Work with the `Graphics`, `Pen`, `Pens`, `Brush`, and `Brushes` classes
- Draw both graphics and text
- Work with the `SoundPlayer` class to add sounds to your applications
- Use classes in the `My` namespace to display a list of files and to play wave files

PROJECT PREVIEW: THE VB DOODLE GAME

In this chapter, you will demonstrate your knowledge and understanding of Visual Basic graphics capabilities by developing the VB Doodle game. VB Doodle is a drawing program that allows players to draw freehand images as well as providing assistance in drawing a number of predefined shapes, such as lines and rectangles. Figures 10.1 and 10.2 show examples from the VB Doodle game, demonstrating its functionality and overall execution flow.

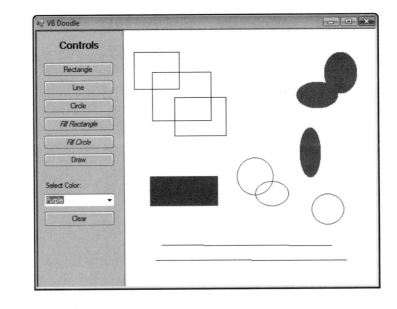

FIGURE 10.1

The user interface for the VB Doodle game consists of a control panel and a drawing area and provides a range of colors and shapes with which to work.

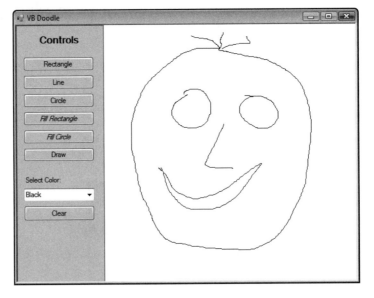

FIGURE 10.2

The player also has the option of making a freehand drawing using any combination of colors.

By the time you have finished the creation of the VB Doodle game, you will have demonstrated your understanding of the fundamentals of working with Visual Basic's built-in graphic drawing capabilities. You will be well prepared to move on and tackle more advanced graphics topics.

INTEGRATING GRAPHICS INTO YOUR VISUAL BASIC APPLICATIONS

Visual Basic 2008 Express provides graphic support based on GDI+ (*Graphics Device Interface*), which it implements in the form of properties and methods made available by classes organized in the System.Drawing namespace. GDI+ manages and displays graphic images, drawing vector graphics, and drawing text.

 DEFINITION *GDI+ (Graphics Device Interface)* creates graphics and draws text for video and print output.

GDI+ draws graphics using a coordinate system. Coordinates are measured using pixels. A graphic is rendered by specifying its starting position relative to coordinates (0,0) and other required coordinates to render a particular shape based on their distance from (0,0) on the X and Y axis, as depicted in Figure 10.3.

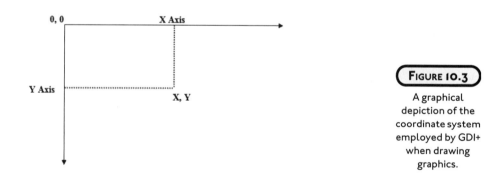

FIGURE 10.3

A graphical depiction of the coordinate system employed by GDI+ when drawing graphics.

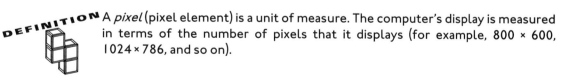 **DEFINITION** A *pixel* (pixel element) is a unit of measure. The computer's display is measured in terms of the number of pixels that it displays (for example, 800 × 600, 1024 × 786, and so on).

Working with Graphic Images

As you have seen in earlier chapters, Visual Basic makes it relatively easy to add the display of graphic images to applications using the PictureBox control. Other controls, such as the

Button control, also display bitmaps. Visual Basic provides built-in support for numerous types of graphic files, including .bmp, .jpeg, and .gif.

As you have already seen, you can configure the PictureBox control's Image property to display a graphic image. You also learned through the creation of the Dice Poker game, shown in Figure 10.4, that you can preload graphic images into an ImageList control and then display these images in any control capable of displaying them.

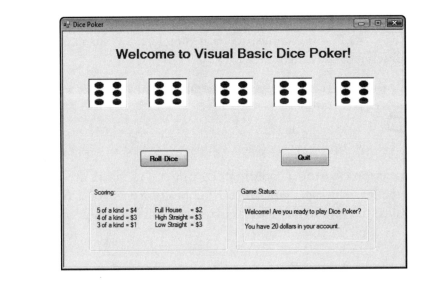

FIGURE 10.4

An example of an application that uses the PictureBox and ImageList controls to work with graphics.

GDI+ support for images also includes the ability to manipulate them in many different ways, including stretching, centering, and zooming.

Drawing Vector Graphics

Instead of simply rendering a copy of an already existing graphic image, GDI+ provides Visual Basic with the ability to draw (from scratch) images using coordinates passed to various methods. Visual Basic allows you to draw on various surfaces, including Button and Form backgrounds. You can execute methods that can draw lines, ellipses, rectangles, polygons, pie shapes, arcs, curved shapes, and so on. For example, to draw a rectangle, you only have to call on the appropriate method and pass it the coordinates of the starting and end points for the figure.

Working with the Graphics Class

In order to draw a graphic, you need a surface to draw it on, such as a Form or Button control. Before you can start drawing, you must create a Graphics object for the drawing surface you intend on using. The first step in completing this task is to set up an instance of the `Graphics` class within your application, as demonstrated here:

```
Dim MyGraphics As System.Drawing.Graphics
```

Once this has been done, you call on the `CreateObjects()` function to establish a pointer to the control or form to be used as the drawing surface, as demonstrated here:

```
Private Sub frmMain_Load(ByVal sender As System.Object, _
  ByVal e As System.EventArgs) Handles MyBase.Load


    FormGraphic = Me.CreateGraphics()


End Sub
```

In this example, the object variable `FormGraphic` has been set to use the `frmMain` form (`Me`) as a drawing surface. Once the `Graphics` class reference has been defined and the drawing surface established, you can begin drawing graphics within your application by calling on any of the `Graphics` class's methods, as listed in Table 10.1.

TABLE 10.1   DRAWING METHODS ASSOCIATED WITH THE SYSTEM.DRAWING.GRAPHICS CLASS

Method	Description
Clear	Clears the drawing surface
DrawArc	Draws an arc
DrawBezier	Draws a bezier curve
DrawBeziers	Draws a collection of bezier curves
DrawClosedCurve	Draws a closed curve
DrawCurve	Draws a curve
DrawEllipse	Draws an ellipse
DrawIcon	Draws an icon
DrawIconUnstretched	Draws the image without scaling its image
DrawImage	Draws an image
DrawImageUnscaled	Draws an image without scaling its size
DrawLine	Draws a line
DrawLines	Draws a collection of line segments
DrawPath	Draws a graphics path
DrawPie	Draws a pie shape

DrawPolygon	Draws a polygon
DrawRectangle	Draws a rectangle
DrawRectangles	Draws a collection of rectangles
DrawString	Draws a text string
FillClosedCurve	Draws a filled curve
FillEllipse	Draws a filled ellipse
FillPath	Draws a filled path
FillPie	Draws a filled pie
FillPolygon	Draws a filled polygon
FillRectangle	Draws a filled rectangle
FillRectangles	Draws a collection of filled rectangles
FillRegion	Draws a filled region

Working with the Pen Class

One way to draw a graphic using the Graphics class is with the Pen class, as demonstrated here:

```
FormGraphic.DrawLine(pen, Coordinates)
```

In this example, pen represents a Pen object and *Coordinates* represents the start and ending point for a line. The Pen class is located in the System.Drawing namespace. It allows you to specify how you want a given image to be drawn. One Pen property is Color, which allows you to specify the color of the line to be drawn. Another Pen property is Brush, which is used to retrieve or set a Brush object for the Pen. Using methods associated with the Brush class, you can draw filled-in shapes.

To specify a color when drawing shapes with the Pen class or filling in shapes with the Brush class, you can specify any of a large collection of predefined colors that are provided by these classes. In Table 10.2, you'll find a complete list of the colors provided by these two classes. The following example demonstrates the syntax involved in drawing a green line using the Pen class.

```
FormGraphic.DrawLine(Pen.Green, coordinates)
```

Similarly, the following syntax demonstrates how to formulate a statement that fills in a red rectangle shape using the Brush class.

```
FormGraphic.FillRectangle(Brush.Red, coordinates)
```

TABLE 10.2 PREDEFINED COLORS PROVIDED BY THE PENS AND BRUSHES CLASSES

AliceBlue	DarkTurquoise	LightSkyBlue	Peru
AntiqueWhite	DarkViolet	LightSlateGray	Pink
Aqua	DeepPink	LightSteelBlue	Plum
Aquamarine	DeepSkyBlue	LightYellow	PowderBlue
Azure	DimGray	Lime	Purple
Beige	DodgerBlue	LimeGreen	Red
Bisque	Firebrick	Linen	RosyBrown
Black	FloralWhite	Magenta	RoyalBlue
BlanchedAlmond	ForestGreen	Maroon	SaddleBrown
Blue	Fuchsia	MediumAquamarine	Salmon
BlueViolet	Gainsboro	MediumOrchid	SandyBrown
Brown	GhostWhite	MediumPurple	SeaGreen
BurlyWood	Gold	MediumSeaGreen	SeaShell
CadetBlue	Goldenrod		Sienna
Chartreuse	Gray	MediumSlateBlue	Silver
Chocolate	Green	MediumSpringGreen	SkyBlue
Coral	GreenYellow	MediumTurquoise	SlateBlue
CornflowerBlue	Honeydew	MediumVioletRed	SlateGray
Cornsilk	HotPink	MidnightBlue	Snow
Crimson	IndianRed	MintCream	SpringGreen
Cyan	Indigo	MistyRose	SteelBlue
DarkBlue	Ivory	Moccasin	Tan
DarkCyan	Khaki	NavajoWhite	Teal
DarkGoldenrod	Lavender	Navy	Thistle
DarkGray	LavenderBlush	OldLace	Tomato
DarkGreen	LawnGreen	Olive	Transparent
DarkKhaki	LemonChiffon	OliveDrab	Turquoise
DarkMagenta	LightBlue	Orange	Violet
DarkOliveGreen	LightCoral	OrangeRed	Wheat
DarkOrange	LightCyan	Orchid	White
DarkOrchid	LightGoldenrod	Yellow	PaleGoldenrod
	WhiteSmoke		
DarkRed	LightGray	PaleGreen	Yellow
DarkSalmon	LightGreen	PaleTurquoise	YellowGreen
DarkSeaGreen	LightPink	PaleVioletRed	
DarkSlateBlue	LightSalmon	PapayaWhip	
DarkSlateGray	LightSeaGreen	PeachPuff	

Drawing Basic Shapes

The best way to learn how to work with the Graphics class is to experiment with it. Let's begin with a couple of quick examples. The first example, shown next, demonstrates how to draw a green square.

```
Public Class frmMain

    Private Sub btnDraw_Click(ByVal sender As System.Object, _
      ByVal e As System.EventArgs) Handles btnDraw.Click

        'Declare an object based on the Graphics class
        Dim FormGraphic As System.Drawing.Graphics

        'Declare and instantiate an object based on the Pen class and
        'set its color and width
        Dim MyPen As New Pen(Color.Green, 3)

        'Declare and instantiate an object based on the Rectangle class
        'and set its coordinates
        Dim MyRectangle As New Rectangle(20, 20, 250, 250)

        'Set the form's background as the drawing surface
        FormGraphic = Me.CreateGraphics()

        'Draw the shape
        FormGraphic.DrawRectangle(MyPen, MyRectangle)

    End Sub

End Class
```

In this example, the program statements that draw the square shape are executed after the user clicks on the Button control labeled Draw. As you can see, it does not take many lines of code to create this simple drawing. The first statement defines an object variable named FormGraphic based on the System.Drawing.Graphics class. The second statement defines an object variable named MyPen as a Pen object, setting the object's Color property equal to green and its line width to 3 pixels (the default width is 1 pixel). The third statement defines an object variable named MyRectangle as a Rectangle object, passing the object the coordinates of the drawing's starting location (20, 20) and its length position (250, 250) relative to the upper-left corner of the drawing surface (frmMain). Take note of the use of the New keyword in the second and third statements. By adding this keyword, you are able to declare and instantiate an object in the same statement. The fourth statement sets the form's background as the drawing surface. The last statement executes the Graphics class's DrawRectangle method, passing it the object variables representing the Pen object and Rectangle object.

TRICK Even though this example draws a square shape, I had to use the Rectangle **class and the** DrawRectangle **method because there is no** Square **object or** DrawSquare **method.**

Figure 10.5 shows the drawing that is produced when this example is executed.

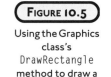

FIGURE 10.5

Using the Graphics class's DrawRectangle method to draw a square.

The next example demonstrates how to draw a filled-in circle. As you can see, it is very similar to the previous example.

```
Public Class frmMain

    Private Sub btnDraw_Click(ByVal sender As System.Object, _
        ByVal e As System.EventArgs) Handles btnDraw.Click

        'Declare an object based on the Graphics class
        Dim FormGraphic As System.Drawing.Graphics
        'Declare and instantiate a SolidBrush and set its color
        Dim MyBrush As New SolidBrush(Color.Blue)
```

```
        'Declare and instantiate a Rectangle and set its coordinates
        Dim MyRectangle As New Rectangle(20, 20, 250, 250)

        'Set the form's background as the drawing surface
        FormGraphic = Me.CreateGraphics()

        FormGraphic.FillEllipse(MyBrush, MyRectangle)    'Draw the shape

    End Sub

End Class
```

Like the previous example, this example draws a filled-in circle only after the user has clicked on the Button control labeled Draw. The first statement defines an object variable named FormGraphic based on the System.Drawing.Graphics class. The second statement defines an object variable named MyBrush based on the SolidBrush class, setting the object's Color property equal to Blue. The third statement defines an object variable named MyRectangle based on the Rectangle class, passing the object the coordinates of the drawing's starting location (20, 20) and its length position (250, 250). I had to use the Rectangle class to outline the starting location and dimensions of the drawing because the .NET Framework does not provide an Ellipse class. Fortunately, an ellipse is drawn using the same set of coordinates as those required to draw a rectangle shape. The last statement executes the Graphics class's DrawEllipse method, passing it the object variables representing the SolidBrush object and Rectangle object.

 TRICK Even though this example draws a circle shape, I had to use the Ellipse class and the Graphics class's FillEllipse method because there is no Circle class or FillCircle method.

Figure 10.6 shows the drawing that is produced when this example is executed.

Drawing a filled-in
circle using the
`Graphics` object's
`FillEllipse`
method.

Drawing Text

In addition to displaying and drawing graphic images, Visual Basic's GDI+ draws text as a graphic image using the `Graphics` class's `DrawString` method. For example, one way to call on this method is shown here:

```
Dim objName As System.Drawing.Graphics
objName(TextString, FontType, BrushColor, Coordinates)
```

`ObjName` is the name that you choose to assign to the new instance of the `Graphics` class. `TextString` represents the string to be written as a graphic. `FontType` identifies the type of font to be used (Arial, Courier, and so on). `BrushColor` specifies the color to be used and `Coordinates` represents the X and Y coordinates for the upper-left side of the starting position of the text image.

The following statement shows you how to create a text graphic drawing.

```
Public Class frmMain

    Private Sub frmMain_Paint(ByVal sender As Object, _
      ByVal e As System.Windows.Forms.PaintEventArgs) Handles Me.Paint

        'Declare and instantiate a Font and specify property settings
        Dim MyFont = New Font("Arial", 32, FontStyle.Bold)

        'Draw the specified text and set its color and coordinates
```

```
      e.Graphics.DrawString(DateTime.Now(), MyFont, Brushes.Red, 10, 50)

   End Sub

End Class
```

In this example, the statements that draw the text image have been placed inside the frmMain_Paint procedure. This event procedure automatically executes anytime a form needs to be repainted, including when the form is first displayed. In this example's first statement, a Font object variable named MyFont is instantiated and passed arguments that set its font type, font size, and font style. The second statement draws a text string using the Graphics class's DrawString method. Notice that the Graphics class is referenced as e.Graphics in this example. I was able to set up the reference to the Graphics class this way because the Paint event procedure automatically generates a reference to the System.Drawing class in the form of a variable named e.

The graphic text to be written is supplied by the DateTime class's Now() method. Font information is supplied by passing the DrawString method the MyFont object. Finally, the Brushes.Red argument is used to specify the color of the text, and the coordinates (10, 50) are passed in order to specify the location where the graphic text should start being written.

Figure 10.7 shows the output generated when this example is run.

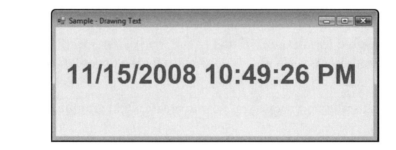

FIGURE 10.7

Visual Basic allows you to draw text as a graphic.

DRAWING USING POWER PACK CONTROLS

In addition to programmatically drawing lines and shapes at run-time using Graphics, Pen, Pens, Brush, and Brushes classes, you can hand-draw lines and shapes at development time within the IDE using controls provided by the Visual Basic Power Packs. In previous editions of Visual Basic, you had the option of downloading and installing Visual Basic Power Packs. However, beginning with Visual Basic 2008 Express, the Visual Basic Power Packs are automatically installed as part of the Visual Basic installation process.

Included as part of Visual Basic Power Packs are the following controls.

- LineShape. Draws a line between two points.
- OvalShape. Draws ellipse and circle shapes.
- RectangleShape. Draws rectangle and square shapes.

To work with any of these controls, just click on them, and then using the mouse, draw the specified shaped on your form. Figure 10.8 shows an example of how shapes can be drawn on a form while still designing within the IDE.

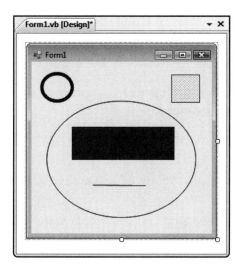

FIGURE 10.8

Using Visual Basic Power Packs controls to draw lines and shapes.

Once drawn, you can specify different property settings for lines and shapes, modifying such things as FillColor, FillGradientStyle, and BorderWidth.

 WPF applications do not support Visual Basic Power Packs controls. However, you can still manually draw on application windows using WPF controls supplied as part of Visual Basic 2008 Express. These controls include the Ellipse and Rectangle controls.

ADDING SOUNDS TO YOUR APPLICATIONS

Many Windows applications use sound to communicate with users. Some applications play a sound to indicate when a specific event occurs, such as when the application has finished loading or has run into a problem. Visual Basic 2008 Express provides support for playing sounds in the form of wave files.

DEFINITION A *wave* file is a digital audio file with a `.wav` file extension that was originally developed by Microsoft.

There are plenty of different sources of wave files at your disposal. For example, you can download an untold number of wave files from the Internet. You will also find an assortment of wave files on your computer. Windows Vista and Windows XP, for example, store a number of wave files in the C:\Windows\Media folder.

You can play a wave file within your applications using the `SoundPlayer` class, which can be instantiated as demonstrated here:

```
Dim MySound As New SoundPlayer
```

Once instantiated, you can use the `MySound` variable to access properties and methods belonging to the `SoundPlayer` class, including those listed here:

- `SoundLocation`. A `SoundPlayer` property that is used to specify the location of the wave file to be played
- `Play()`. A `SoundPlayer` method that plays the wave file specified by the `SoundPlayer` class's `SoundLocation` property
- `PlayLooping()`. A `SoundPlayer` method that repeatedly plays the wave file specified by the `SoundPlayer` class's `SoundLocation` property
- `Stop()`. A `SoundPlayer` method that stops playing any currently executing sound

The following example demonstrates how to instantiate an object based on the `SoundPlayer` class and then use it to repeatedly play a wave file when the application loads.

```
Public Class frmMain

    'Declare and instantiate the SoundPlayer
    Private MySound As New SoundPlayer

    Private Sub frmMain_Load(ByVal sender As System.Object, _
      ByVal e As System.EventArgs) Handles MyBase.Load

        'Specify the location of the wave file
        MySound.SoundLocation = "C:\Windows\Media\chimes.wav"
```

```
      MySound.PlayLooping()  'Repeatedly play the sound file

   End Sub

End Class
```

RAD DEVELOPMENT WITH THE MY NAMESPACE

One of the most handy features in Visual Basic 2008 Express is the My namespace, which provides easy access to methods and properties belonging to the most commonly used Visual Basic classes. As such, the My namespace is particularly adept at facilitating rapid application development. Accessing classes stored within the My namespace is easy; just type My followed by a period and IntelliSense Everywhere will appear and help you formulate your code statements.

The My namespace is organized into a series of high-level classes. These classes include:

- My.Application. Gets information about the currently running application, such as its name and version
- My.Computer. Gets information about the local computer, including its hardware
- My.User. Gets information about the current user, including username and domain name
- My.Forms. Gets information regarding any currently open application forms

Among the many different types of things you can do with the classes that make up the My namespace, you can use properties and methods belonging to the My.Computer class to quickly and easily add the ability to play wave audio files in your Visual Basic applications. To demonstrate this, let's develop a new application called the Audio Jukebox. This application will use properties and methods belonging to the My.Computer class to play .wav files. Specifically, it will use the Play method belonging to the Audio class, which is a subclass of the My.Computer class, to play a wave file. It will also use the FileSystem subclass's GetFiles method to generate a list of wave files and the FileSystem class's CurrentDirectory property to specify the location of these wave files. Figure 10.9 shows what the application will look like when you have finished building it.

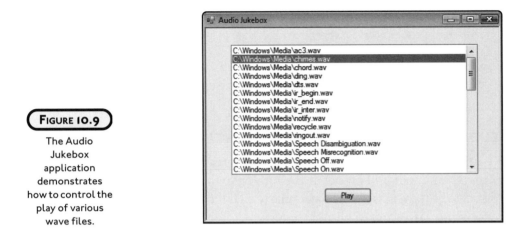

FIGURE 10.9

The Audio
Jukebox
application
demonstrates
how to control the
play of various
wave files.

The application's user interface is made up of a form with a ListBox and Button control. Assign a name of lbxWaveFiles to the ListBox control and a name lf btnPlay to the Button control. Then, add the following code to the application as shown here:

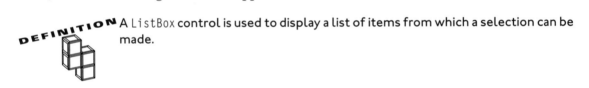

DEFINITION A ListBox control is used to display a list of items from which a selection can be made.

TRICK One way to populate a ListBox control with a list of items is to use the ListBox class's DataSource property. Once populated, you can use the ListBox class's SelectedItem property to determine which item is selected by the user. The Audio Jukebox application demonstrates how to use the DataSource property to display a list of wave files and the SelectedItem property to determine which wave file is selected for play.

```
Public Class frmMain

    Private Sub frmMain_Load(ByVal sender As System.Object, _
    ByVal e As System.EventArgs) Handles MyBase.Load

        'Specify the location of the wave files to be displayed by the
        'application
        My.Computer.FileSystem.CurrentDirectory = "C:\Windows\Media"

        'Load a list of wave files into the ListBox control
```

```
    lbxWaveFiles.DataSource = My.Computer.FileSystem.GetFiles _
      (My.Computer.FileSystem.CurrentDirectory, _
      FileIO.SearchOption.SearchTopLevelOnly, "*.wav")

  End Sub

  Private Sub btnPlay_Click(ByVal sender As System.Object, _
    ByVal e As System.EventArgs) Handles btnPlay.Click

      'Play the selected wave file
      My.Computer.Audio.Play(lbxWaveFiles.SelectedItem.ToString)

  End Sub

End Class
```

The first statement requires a little explanation. It begins with the My class. This class provides access to the Computer class. The Computer class has a property named FileSystem, which provides access to the FileSystem class, which in turn has a property named CurrentDirectory, which is set equal to "C:\Windows\Media".

The second statement populates the ListBox control with a list of wave files located in the "C:\Windows\Media" folder. This statement also requires some additional explanation. This statement works by executing the My.Computer.FileSystem.GetFiles method, which is passed three arguments in the following order: target folder, a value specifying search depth, and a string specifying the files to be retrieved. In the case of this example, all files with a .wav file extension are displayed.

In order to use the application, the user must select one of the wave files displayed in the ListBox control and then click on the Button control labeled Play, which then uses the Audio class's Play method to play the selected wave file. As you can see, the My namespace and the objects that can be generated from its classes allow you to perform complex tasks with very little coding and offer yet another alternative for adding sound to your Visual Basic application.

BACK TO THE VB DOODLE GAME

It is time to turn your attention back to the development of this chapter's game project, the VB Doodle game. The VB Doodle game is a drawing program. You will create it by following the five basic development steps that have been used in the creation of all the previous chapter game projects.

Designing the Game

The VB Doodle game is executed using a single window and is made up of one form and the 11 controls listed in Table 10.3.

TABLE 10.3	FORM CONTROLS FOR THE VB DOODLE GAME	
Control Type	**Control Name**	**Description**
Panel1	pnlControl	Panel control located on the left-hand side of the user interface where game controls are displayed
Label1	lblControls	Identifies the location of the controls for the VB Doodle application
Label2	lblColor	Identifies the ComboBox control where the player makes color selections
Button1	btnRectangle	Initiates the process of drawing a rectangle
Button2	btnLine	Initiates the process of drawing a line
Button3	btnCircle	Initiates the process of drawing an ellipse
Button4	btnFillRectangle	Initiates the process of drawing a filled-in rectangle
Button5	btnFillCircle	Initiates the process of drawing a filled-in ellipse
Button6	btnDraw	Initiates the process of making a freehand drawing
Button7	btnClear	Initiates the clearing of the drawing area
ComboBox1	cbxColor	Lists the available color choices provided by the application

Step 1: Creating a New Visual Basic Project

The first step in creating the VB Doodle game is to open up Visual Basic and create a new project as outlined here:

1. Start up Visual Basic 2008 Express and then click on File and select New Project. The New Project dialog will appear.
2. Select the Windows Forms Application template.
3. Type **VB Doodle** as the name of your new application and click on OK to close the New Project dialog.

Step 2: Creating the User Interface

The first step in designing the game's user interface is to add the appropriate controls to the form and then move and resize them to the right locations. Use Figure 10.10 as a reference as you go through each of the following steps to make sure that you know where each control should be placed and their approximate sizes.

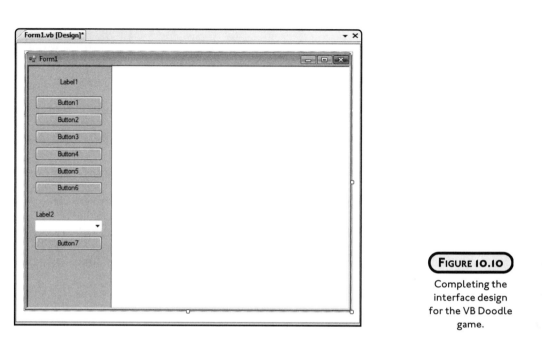

Figure 10.10

Completing the interface design for the VB Doodle game.

1. Resize Form1 by setting its Size property to 586, 458.
2. Add a Panel control to the left-hand side of the form and resize it until it takes up approximately 25 percent of the available form space.
3. Add and center a Label control on the top of the Panel control.
4. Add six Button controls under the Label control.
5. Add a second Label control beneath the last button that you added to the Panel control.
6. Add a ComboBox control just under the second Label control.
7. Finally, add one more Button control on the Panel control.

Step 3: Customizing Form and Control Properties

Now let's start customizing the properties associated with the form and its controls. Start by changing the form properties listed in Table 10.4.

Next, modify the properties listed in Table 10.5 for the Panel control.

TABLE 10.4   PROPERTY CHANGES FOR FORM1

Property	Value
Name	frmMain
BackColor	White
FormBorderStyle	Fixed3D
Size	586, 458
StartPosition	CenterScreen
Text	VB Doodle

TABLE 10.5   PROPERTY CHANGES FOR PANEL CONTROL

Property	Value
Name	pnlControl
Anchor	Top, Bottom, Left
BackColor	LightGray
BorderStyle	FixedSingle

 TRICK Take special note of the Anchor property setting. It has been set so that the Panel control will automatically resize itself if the form is resized. This allows the player to change the size of the drawing area without affecting the size and appearance of the Panel control.

Next, modify the properties listed in Table 10.6 for the two Label controls.

TABLE 10.6   PROPERTY CHANGES FOR LABEL CONTROLS

Control	Property	Value
Label1	Name	lblControls
	Font.Bold	True
	Text	Controls
Label2	Name	lblColor
	Font.Bold	True
	Text	Select Color:

Now, modify the properties listed in Table 10.7 for the seven Button controls.

TABLE 10.7   PROPERTY CHANGES FOR BUTTON CONTROLS

Control	Property	Value
Button1	Name	btnRectangle
	Text	Rectangle
Button2	Name	btnLine
	Text	Line
Button3	Name	btnCircle
	Text	Circle
Button4	Name	btnFillRectangle
	Text	Fill Rectangle
Button5	Name	btnFillCircle
	Text	Fill Circle
Button6	Name	btnDraw
	Text	Draw
Button7	Name	btnClear
	Text	Clear

Now modify the properties listed in Table 10.8 for the ComboBox control.

TABLE 10.8   PROPERTY CHANGES FOR COMBOBOX CONTROL

Property	Value
Name	cbxColor
Items	Red
	Green
	Blue
	Black
	Yellow
	Purple
Text	Red

Step 4: Adding a Little Programming Logic

The first step in writing the code for the VB Doodle game is to define class-level variables that the application will need in order to run, as shown here:

```
Public Class frmMain

    'Declare a variable representing the System.Drawing.Graphics class
    Private FormGraphic As Graphics

    'Declare variables representing the Point class
    Private StartPoint As Point
    Private EndPoint As Point

    'Declare a variable that will be used to store and track the drawing
    'option selected by the player
    Private strCurrentAction As String = "Line"

    'Declare a variable to be used as a counter
    Private intCounter As Integer = 0

    Private apntArray() As Point    'Declare an array

End Class
```

The first declaration statement defines an object variable that will be used to represent the Graphics class. The second and third statements define object variables that will be used to represent the Point class. The third statement defines a string variable name, strCurrentAction, that will be used by the application to keep track of the currently selected drawing option. The last two statements are used to define a variable that will be used to keep track of the number of elements stored in an array named apntArray.

One of the procedures within the application allows the player to make a freehand drawing. This is accomplished by storing coordinates representing the location of the pointer in the apntArray as the player moves the mouse around when drawing freehand and then passing these coordinates to the DrawLines method.

 DEFINITION A Point class is a member of the System.Drawing namespace. The Point class can be used as a mechanism for storing sets of coordinates.

Next, set up the application so that it associates the `FormGraphic` object variable with its drawing surface (the form), which you can do by modifying the `frmMain_Load` procedure as shown here:

```
'This procedure executes when the VB Doodle game loads
Private Sub frmMain_Load(ByVal sender As System.Object, _
  ByVal e As System.EventArgs) Handles MyBase.Load

    'Create an instance of the Graphics class
    objFormGraphic = Me.CreateGraphics

End Sub
```

Regardless of which type of drawing operation the player wants to make, such as drawing a line, a rectangle, or a freehand image, everything begins when the player clicks on the mouse button to set the starting point for whatever shape is being drawn. Therefore, you will need to modify the `frmMain_MouseDown` procedure as shown here to capture this initial set of coordinates and assign it to the `StartPoint` variable.

```
'This procedure captures the coordinates used to draw shapes
Private Sub frmMain_MouseDown(ByVal sender As Object, _
  ByVal e As System.Windows.Forms.MouseEventArgs) Handles Me.MouseDown

    'Create an instance of the point class and assign coordinates
    StartPoint = New Point(e.X, e.Y)

End Sub
```

The next procedure to set up is the `frmMain_MouseMove` Sub procedure, shown here:

```
'This procedure captures coordinates for freehand drawings
Private Sub frmMain_MouseMove(ByVal sender As Object, _
  ByVal e As System.Windows.Forms.MouseEventArgs) Handles Me.MouseMove

    'The button labeled Draw was clicked
    If strCurrentAction = "Draw" Then
        'The player must press and hold down the left mouse button
        If e.Button = Windows.Forms.MouseButtons.Left Then
            'Create an instance of the Point class and assign a set
            'of coordinates
            Dim DrawPoint As New Point(e.X, e.Y)
```

```
                    'Resize the array and keep all existing data
                    ReDim Preserve apntArray(intCounter)

                    'Add the most recently collected set of coordinates
                    apntArray(intCounter) = objPoint
                    intCounter += 1   'Increment the counter

                    'A minimum of 2 sets of coordinates is required to draw
                    If intCounter >= 2 Then
                        'Call procedure that does the actual drawing
                        SelectAndDraw("Draw", apntArray)
                    End If
                End If
            End If

    End Sub
```

This procedure is responsible for collecting the coordinates of the mouse as the player moves it around the form when creating a freehand image (when the value of strCurrentAction is equal to "Draw"). However, coordinates are only recorded if the player is holding down the left mouse button when the mouse is being moved (if e.Button = Windows.Forms. MouseButtons.Left Then). Individual coordinates are stored as object variables named DrawPoint and then assigned to the apntArray. The intCounter variable, which is incremented by one with the addition of every new set of coordinates, is used to assign the index number of each new array entry.

The coordinates stored in the apntArray are then passed on to the SelectAndDraw procedure, where the Graphics class's DrawLines method will be used to draw the image on the form. The DrawLines method requires a minimum of two sets of coordinates in order to execute. Therefore, the SelectAndDraw procedure is only called if the value of intCounter is greater than or equal to 2.

The player can release the left mouse button at any time when making a freehand drawing to change colors or to reposition the pointer to a new location to add another freehand drawing to the form. Therefore, whenever the player releases the mouse button, the application will need to reset the intCounter variable to 0 and reinitialize the apntArray array. In addition, the application will need to capture the location of the last set of coordinates for the freehand image. You can set all this up by modifying the frmMain_MouseUp procedures as shown here:

```
'This procedure runs when the player releases the left mouse button
Private Sub frmMain_MouseUp(ByVal sender As Object, _
  ByVal e As System.Windows.Forms.MouseEventArgs) Handles Me.MouseUp

    intCounter = 0  'Reset the counter to zero
    ReDim apntArray(intCounter)  'Reset the array
    EndPoint = New Point(e.X, e.Y)  'Capture last set of coordinates
    DrawGraphic()  'Call procedure that draws the shape

End Sub
```

As you can see, the apntArray is reset using the ReDim keyword (without using the Preserve keyword). Once the coordinates of the pointer's last location (when the left mouse button was released) have been captured, a procedure named DrawGraphic is called.

The DrawGraphic procedure, shown next, is responsible for laying out the required coordinates for a drawing based on the value assigned to the strCurrentAction variable.

```
'This procedure assembles the coordinates required to draw shapes
Private Sub DrawGraphic()

    'Assemble coordinates for a rectangle drawing
    If strCurrentAction = "Rectangle" Then
        'Declare variable representing a rectangle
        Dim ShapeCoordinates As Rectangle
        'Instantiate a rectangle object and assign its coordinates
        ShapeCoordinates = _
          New Rectangle(Math.Min(EndPoint.X, StartPoint.X), _
            Math.Min(EndPoint.Y, StartPoint.Y), _
            Math.Abs(EndPoint.X - StartPoint.X), _
            Math.Abs(EndPoint.Y - StartPoint.Y))
        'Call procedure to draw shape
        SelectAndDraw("Rectangle", ShapeCoordinates)
    End If

    If strCurrentAction = "Line" Then
        SelectAndDraw("Line")    'Call procedure to draw a line
    End If
```

```
'Assemble coordinates for a circle drawing
If strCurrentAction = "Circle" Then
    'Declare variable representing a rectangle
    Dim ShapeCoordinates As Rectangle
    'Instantiate a rectangle object and assign its coordinates
    ShapeCoordinates = _
    New Rectangle(Math.Min(EndPoint.X, StartPoint.X), _
      Math.Min(EndPoint.Y, StartPoint.Y), _
      Math.Abs(EndPoint.X - StartPoint.X), _
      Math.Abs(EndPoint.Y - StartPoint.Y))
    'Call procedure to draw shape
    SelectAndDraw("Ellipse", ShapeCoordinates)
End If


'Assemble coordinates for a filled rectangle drawing
If strCurrentAction = "FillRectangle" Then
    'Declare variable representing a rectangle
    Dim ShapeCoordinates As Rectangle
    'Instantiate a rectangle object and assign its coordinates
    ShapeCoordinates = _
      New Rectangle(Math.Min(EndPoint.X, StartPoint.X), _
      Math.Min(EndPoint.Y, StartPoint.Y), _
      Math.Abs(EndPoint.X - StartPoint.X), _
      Math.Abs(EndPoint.Y - StartPoint.Y))
    'Call procedure to draw shape
    SelectAndDraw("FillRectangle", ShapeCoordinates)
End If


'Assemble coordinates for a filled circle drawing
If strCurrentAction = "FillCircle" Then
    'Declare variable representing a rectangle
    Dim ShapeCoordinates As Rectangle
    'Instantiate a rectangle object and assign its coordinates
    ShapeCoordinates = _
      New Rectangle(Math.Min(EndPoint.X, StartPoint.X), _
      Math.Min(EndPoint.Y, StartPoint.Y), _
      Math.Abs(EndPoint.X - StartPoint.X), _
      Math.Abs(EndPoint.Y - StartPoint.Y))
```

```
        'Call procedure to draw shape
        SelectAndDraw("FillCircle", ShapeCoordinates)
    End If

End Sub
```

For example, if `strCurrentAction` is equal to `Rectangle`, an object variable named `ShapeCoordinates` is declared representing the `Rectangle` class. The coordinates for the drawing are then laid out and the `SelectAndDraw` procedure is called and passed a string representing the shape to be drawn and the coordinates required to draw it.

TRICK   The way that the coordinates are assembled for a rectangle shape requires a little extra examination. As you can see, both the `Math` class's `Min` and `Abs` methods are used. To understand what is going on here, you must first remember that the rectangle will be drawn from left to right, and that the point in its upper-left corner is determined based on its relationship to the (0,0) coordinates. This is true even if the player decides to draw the rectangle right to left.

The first use of `Math.Min` determines whether `EndPoint.X` or `StartPoint.X` is the leftmost coordinates by returning a value representing the lower of the two coordinates. Likewise, the second use of `Math.Min` determines whether the `EndPoint.Y` or the `StartPoint.Y` coordinates is the topmost coordinate. Once the coordinate of the top-left corner is identified, the first `Math.Abs` method is used to retrieve an absolute number representing the length of the rectangle along the X axis by subtracting the difference between `EndPoint.X` and `StartPoint.X`. Likewise, the length of the rectangle's Y axis is determined by returning the absolute value of `EndPoint.Y` minus `StartPoint.Y`.

DEFINITION   An *absolute number* is a non-negative number. For example, the absolute value of -9 is 9. By the same token, the absolute value of 9 is also 9.

Now it is time to begin adding code to the click event for each of the game's `Button` controls. The code for the `btnRectangle_Click` procedure is shown below. When selected, it sets the value of `strCurrentAction` equal to `"Rectangle"` to allow the player to indicate what type of drawing to make.

```
'This procedure runs when the button labeled Rectangle is clicked
Private Sub btnRectangle_Click(ByVal sender As System.Object, _
  ByVal e As System.EventArgs) Handles btnRectangle.Click
```

```
    strCurrentAction = "Rectangle"

End Sub
```

The code for the btnLine_Click procedure is shown here:

```
'This procedure runs when the button labeled Line is clicked
Private Sub btnLine_Click(ByVal sender As System.Object, _
  ByVal e As System.EventArgs) Handles btnLine.Click

    strCurrentAction = "Line"

End Sub
```

The code for the btnCircle_Click procedure is shown here:

```
'This procedure runs when the button labeled Circle is clicked
Private Sub btnCircle_Click(ByVal sender As System.Object, _
  ByVal e As System.EventArgs) Handles btnCircle.Click

    strCurrentAction = "Circle"

End Sub
```

The code for the btnFillRectangle_Click procedure is shown here:

```
'This procedure runs when the button labeled Fill Rectangle is clicked
Private Sub btnFillRectangle_Click(ByVal sender As System.Object, _
  ByVal e As System.EventArgs) Handles btnFillRectangle.Click

    strCurrentAction = "FillRectangle"

End Sub
```

The code for the btnFillCircle_Click procedure is shown here:

```
'This procedure runs when the button labeled Fill Circle is clicked
Private Sub btnFillCircle_Click(ByVal sender As System.Object, _
  ByVal e As System.EventArgs) Handles btnFillCircle.Click

    strCurrentAction = "FillCircle"

End Sub
```

The code for the `btnDraw_Click` procedure is shown here:

```
'This procedure runs when the button labeled Draw is clicked
Private Sub btnDraw_Click(ByVal sender As System.Object, _
  ByVal e As System.EventArgs) Handles btnDraw.Click

    strCurrentAction = "Draw"

End Sub
```

The code for the `btnClear_Click` procedure is shown below. Instead of setting a variable as was done in the other `Button` object click event procedures, this procedure executes the `Graphics` object's `Clear` method, passing it `Me.BackColor` to clear out the drawing area (the form's background).

```
'This procedure runs when the button labeled Clear is clicked
Private Sub btnClear_Click(ByVal sender As System.Object, _
  ByVal e As System.EventArgs) Handles btnClear.Click

    FormGraphic.Clear(Me.BackColor)

End Sub
```

The last procedure that you'll need to set up for the VB Doodle game is the `SelectAndDraw` Sub procedure, which is shown below. This procedure uses a `Select Case` block to process the `strShape` argument that is passed to it. Then, based on the appropriate match, a call is made to the appropriate `Graphics` object method.

```
'This procedure draws the selected shape
Private Sub SelectAndDraw(ByVal strShape As String, _
  Optional ByVal Coordinates As Object = "")

    'Declare and instantiate a Pen object and assign its color
    Dim Pen1 As New Pen(Color.FromName(cbxColor.Text))

    'Declare and instantiate a SolidBrush object and assign its color
    Dim Brush1 As New SolidBrush(Color.FromName(cbxColor.Text))

    'Process the procedure arguments and draw
    Select Case strShape
    Case "Line"
```

```
            FormGraphic.DrawLine(Pen1, StartPoint, EndPoint)
                Case "Rectangle"
            FormGraphic.DrawRectangle(Pen1, Coordinates)
                Case "Ellipse"
            FormGraphic.DrawEllipse(Pen1, Coordinates)
                Case "FillRectangle"
            FormGraphic.FillRectangle(Brush1, Coordinates)
                Case "FillCircle"
            FormGraphic.FillEllipse(Brush1, Coordinates)
                Case "Draw"
            FormGraphic.DrawLines(Pen1, Coordinates)
        End Select

End Sub
```

Step 5: Testing the Execution of the VB Doodle Game

Okay, that's it. The VB Doodle game is now ready to run. Go ahead and run the game by pressing F5, and make sure that everything works like it is supposed to. If you run into any problems, go back and double-check your typing.

SUMMARY

In this chapter, you learned how to work with various classes and objects that provide graphics and audio. This included learning how to work with the `System.Drawing.Graphics` namespace. You learned how to instantiate the `Graphics` object as well as the `Pens` and `Brushes` objects and to use their properties and methods to create various drawing applications. You learned how to add sound to your Visual Basic applications using the `SoundPlayer` class. You also learned a little about the `My` namespace and how to use properties and methods belonging to the `My.Computer` class to play wave files. On top of all this, you learned how to create the VB Doodle game.

Before you move on to Chapter 11, "Debugging Visual Basic Applications," take a few extra minutes to improve the VB Doodle game by completing the following challenges.

CHALLENGES

1. As the game is currently written, it is not always clear what type of shape the player is working with. To make the application easier to use, add a `StatusBar` control and use it to display a string identifying the currently selected shape.

2. The `Graphics` class creates many other shapes besides rectangles, ellipses, and lines. Enhance the VB Doodle game to support other shapes, such as the pie, arc, and polygon. You can get information on the arguments that need to be supplied to create each of the shapes using Visual Basic's Help system.

3. The Visual Basic `Pens` and `Brushes` classes provide access to dozens of predefined colors. Expand the VB Doodle game's list of supported colors to give the player additional choices.

11

DEBUGGING VISUAL BASIC APPLICATIONS

Welcome to the final chapter in this book. In this chapter, you will learn how to deal with syntax, logic, and run-time errors. This includes learning how to set up breakpoints to track variable status and program flow. You will learn how to work with a number of debugging windows. You also will learn how to develop custom exception-handling routines. In addition, you will get the chance to apply what you learn to the development of the chapter's game project, the Tic-Tac-Toe game.

Specifically, you will learn:

- About the different types of errors that can occur
- How to set breakpoints and to step through code execution
- How to use various debugging windows
- How to create exception-handling routines

PROJECT PREVIEW: THE TIC-TAC-TOE GAME

As this chapter's game project, you will develop a two-player Visual Basic version of the Tic-Tac-Toe game. You will track and validate player moves and determine when a game is won, lost, or tied. Figures 11.1 and 11.2 show examples from the Tic-Tac-Toe game in action.

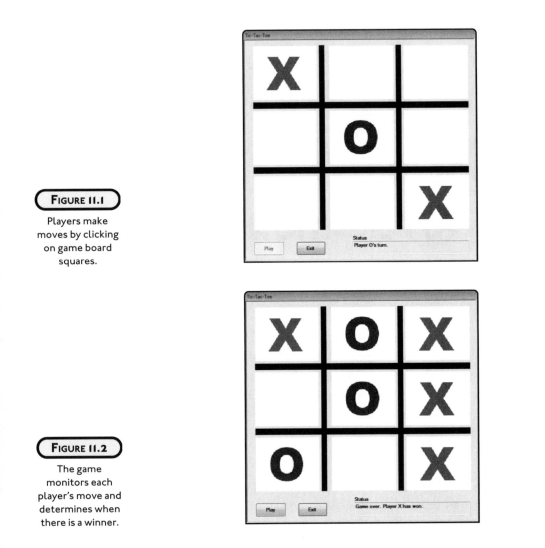

FIGURE 11.1

Players make moves by clicking on game board squares.

FIGURE 11.2

The game monitors each player's move and determines when there is a winner.

By the time you have created and run this game, you will have completed the last game project in this book and will be well on your way to becoming a Visual Basic programmer.

DEALING WITH ERRORS

As your Visual Basic programs grow larger and more complex, errors are going to happen. That is just the way things work. Even the most experienced programmers run into errors all the time. Visual Basic applications are subject to many different types of errors. The occurrence of an error causes an application to behave inappropriately and is often referred to as a bug. Your job as a programmer is to seek out and remove (or handle) these bugs.

There are many things that you can do to minimize the number of errors in your applications. For starters, you can sit down and plan out the overall design of your applications before you start writing them. Once created, you should test your applications extensively to look for bugs. Other good programming practices that you should consider include:

- Creating a simple and easy-to-use interface
- Providing users with clear instructions
- Validating user input data before accepting it
- Using consistent naming schemes for constants, variables, objects, arrays, and `Function` and `Sub` procedures
- Anticipating specific situations where errors might occur and trying to deal with them programmatically

There are three basic categories of errors that you will experience when developing Visual Basic applications. These are as follows:

- Syntax errors
- Logical errors
- Run-time errors

Syntax Errors

The most common type of error is a syntax error. A syntax error occurs when you key in a statement that does not conform to Visual Basic's rules. Syntax errors are often the result of typos, such as when you accidentally mistype a keyword or leave out a required parameter.

Visual Basic identifies syntax errors in your programming statements as you finish typing them by underlining the errors, as demonstrated in Figure 11.3. Because syntax errors are identified for you as you key in your Visual Basic program statements, they are easy to locate and correct. You can also view syntax errors from the Error List window, as shown at the bottom of Figure 11.3. This window will automatically open during application development if you attempt to run a Visual Basic application that has a syntax error in it. The window shows each error, provides a brief description of the error, and identifies the line number of the statement that contains the error. If you want, you can double-click on an error listed in the Error List window and Visual Basic will respond by locating the statement that contains it in the code editor.

DEFINITION

A *syntax* error is an error that occurs when you do not write a code statement according to the rules of the programming language.

FIGURE 11.3

The compiler flags Visual Basic syntax errors by underlining them with a jagged blue line.

As demonstrated in Figure 11.3, sometimes you see a small red rectangle displayed under the last letter in the word where an error has been flagged. This rectangle is a *smart tag* and its purpose is to let you know that Visual Basic has some suggestions for fixing the problem. To view these suggestions, move the pointer over the smart tag. In response, an exclamation point in a red circle is displayed. Click on the red circle and Visual Basic will display its proposed solutions, as demonstrated in Figure 11.4.

FIGURE 11.4

Click on the red exclamation point to get advice on how to fix errors.

TRICK Sometimes you might miss when Visual Basic flags a syntax error in your code. To help prevent this from happening, you might want to keep the Error List window open while you are writing code. You can do this by clicking on the View menu and then selecting the Error List menu item.

Logical Errors

Logical errors are errors caused by a mistake on the programmer's part. For example, you might accidentally add together two numbers that should have been subtracted. The end result is that everything runs fine but the output is not what you expect. Another example of a logical error is when you accidentally set up an endless loop.

DEFINITION A *logical* error is created when the programmer makes a mistake in laying out the logic used to perform a given task.

Visual Basic won't be able to flag or report your logical errors. The best way to deal with logical errors is to try to prevent them in the first place by taking extra care in the formulation of your programming logic. Organize your Visual Basic applications into procedures by assigning each procedure one specific task to perform. Then do your best to test out each procedure as you go. However, even the best laid plans often go awry, and when this occurs, there is no substitute for careful testing as a means of identifying logical errors.

Run-Time Errors

A third category of errors is the run-time error, which occurs whenever a statement attempts to do something that is not possible. For example, a run-time error will occur if an application attempts to access a disk drive that does not exist or if a broken network connection prevents the access of a network file.

DEFINITION A *run-time* error occurs when an application attempts to perform an illegal action.

Unlike syntax errors, the compiler won't flag run-time errors for you. In fact, if a seldom-used procedure contains code that might produce a run-time error and you don't carefully test the functionality provided by that procedure, you may not catch the run-time error at all, in which case, the user will be left to discover it.

If you come across a run-time error when running your Visual Basic application in debug mode, you'll receive an error message like the one shown in Figure 11.5. However, if you don't catch the run-time error during testing and development, your application may or may not display an error message when its release version is being executed. Worse still, your application might simply lock up and stop responding.

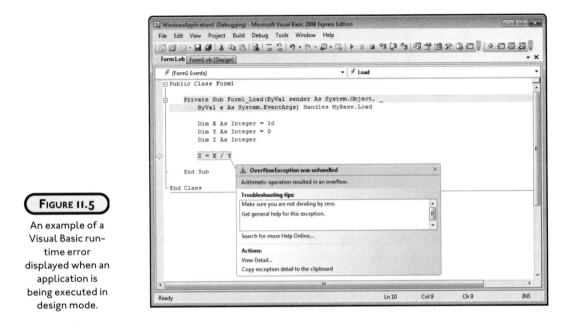

FIGURE 11.5

An example of a Visual Basic run-time error displayed when an application is being executed in design mode.

A run-time error can also occur if the user passes your application some unanticipated input. Therefore, it is important that you add logic to your applications to validate, as much as possible, all user input. It is also critical to test all of the functionality provided by your Visual Basic applications as thoroughly as possible to minimize the possibility of running into unexpected run-time errors. However, try as you may, there is no way to completely avoid run-time errors. For example, sometimes hardware just fails or the network goes down. If your application requires these resources to execute, then run-time errors will eventually occur. However, as you'll learn later in this chapter, Visual Basic allows you to develop exception handlers so that you can recover from or at least gracefully respond to unavoidable run-time errors.

ESTABLISHING BREAKPOINTS

Visual Basic 2008 Express has tools for tracking down and dealing with errors. Using these tools, you can track down errors by monitoring your program code statements as they execute in order to examine variable and property values and to observe the execution flow of your application.

Up to this point in the book, you have executed your Visual Basic applications mostly in design mode by pressing the F5 key within the Visual Basic IDE. However, you also learned how to create standalone executable versions of your Visual Basic applications, known as run-time mode. Now it's time to learn about a third mode of application execution, break mode.

In break mode, you are able to pause the execution of your application and examine its status before resuming execution. This can be a very effective tool for tracking down and locating statements that may be incorrectly setting variable and property values. Break mode allows you to step through each line of your program code, to see what procedures have been called, and to examine variable and property values.

Setting Up Breakpoints

To set up a breakpoint within your application, click on the left-hand margin of the code editor on the line where you want to place the breakpoint. Once the breakpoint has been set, a circular marker is displayed in the margin, and the line of code where the breakpoint is set is highlighted, as demonstrated in Figure 11.6.

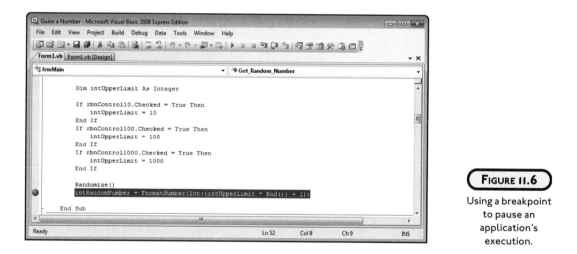

FIGURE 11.6

Using a breakpoint to pause an application's execution.

Place your breakpoints at locations within your applications where you suspect a problem may be occurring. You can set as many breakpoints as you want. When you press F5 to run your application and a breakpoint is reached, program execution pauses and the circular marker for the current breakpoint changes to display an arrow, as demonstrated in Figure 11.7.

```
Dim intUpperLimit As Integer

If rbnControl10.Checked = True Then
    intUpperLimit = 10
End If
If rbnControl100.Checked = True Then
    intUpperLimit = 100
End If
If rbnControl1000.Checked = True Then
    intUpperLimit = 1000
End If

Randomize()
intRandomNumber = FormatNumber(Int((intUpperLimit * Rnd()) + 1))

End Sub
```

FIGURE 11.7

The Visual Basic
IDE changes the
highlight of the
currently active
breakpoint.

    Once you have resolved any errors that you may have and no longer need any
breakpoints, you can remove them by clicking on the circular markers located in
the left-hand margin.

You can learn a lot about what is going on in your application by setting a breakpoint and
then examining the value of properties and variables to see what they have been set to. For
example, at the bottom of Figure 11.7, you can see that the Locals window and the Immediate
window have been opened. The Locals window displays information about variables within
the current context, including their current value and type. If you want, you can even change
the value assigned to a variable displayed in the Locals window.

If the Locals and Immediate windows are not automatically displayed, you
can open them yourself by clicking on Debug > Windows > Locals and Debug
> Windows > Immediate.

You can also use the Immediate window to query the value of a variable or property. For
example, if you look at the Immediate window in Figure 11.7, you will see where I checked
on the value assigned to the intUpperLimit variable by typing in a question mark followed by
the name of the variable.

By using breakpoints and the windows mentioned above, you can track down many errors by locating the statements in your applications that inappropriately modify variable or property values.

Stepping through Code Execution

Another important feature provided by Visual Basic when executing an application in break mode is the ability to step through program statements. This allows you to identify a section of code where you think an error may be located (by setting a breakpoint) and then to step through and execute each subsequent statement a line at a time. This lets you follow the execution flow of an entire process, pausing at any point along the way to check on the value of related variables and properties.

Visual Basic offers three different ways to step through your program statements, as listed here:

- **Step Into.** Executes the breakpoint statement and then pauses before the execution of statements that follow
- **Step Over.** Executes entire procedures, pausing before the execution of the next procedure
- **Step Out.** Used inside a procedure to return to the calling procedure where program flow is then paused

You can selectively choose which of these step options you want to use at any moment by clicking on their icons, which are located in the Visual Basic standard toolbar, as shown in Figure 11.8.

FIGURE 11.8

Using the Debug icons on the standard toolbar to step through program statements.

Edit and Continue

When you come across a statement with an error in it when debugging an application, the usual thing to do is stop the debugging session, fix the error, and then rebuild and execute the application again to see if things work properly. However, Visual Basic 2008 introduces a new feature called Edit and Continue which can save you time by allowing you to apply changes to your application when paused at a breakpoint and then to resume the application's execution to see the effects of your change right away.

To use this new feature, locate the yellow arrow, which identifies the next statement to be executed in your debug session, and place your cursor over it. When you do, a transparent arrow will appear. Once visible, you can drag and drop the yellow arrow to a new location in your program, allowing you to resume the application's execution from a previously executed statement. Once you have modified the location of the yellow arrow, go ahead and apply your correction and then click on the Step Into button to resume application execution and see if your change has fixed the error that was occurring.

DEVELOPING EXCEPTION HANDLERS

Run-time errors, also referred to as *exceptions*, can occur for many different reasons. Examples include collecting and processing user input that may not be valid and attempting to access local computer and network resources that may not be available. Obviously, it would be best if your applications were written in such a way that they could handle these unexpected exceptions without blowing up or confusing your users with cryptic error messages.

In order for your applications to be able to handle exceptions, you need to anticipate the locations within your applications where errors are most likely to occur and then develop code that handles the problem. For example, if an error could occur due to incorrect user input, then you should incorporate input validation checks into your applications. If your application needs to access local network hardware resources, you should add logic that notifies the user if the required resources are unavailable. There are numerous other ways of dealing with exceptions. For example, you might:

- Reword cryptic error messages
- Provide the user with additional instruction
- Apologize for the error and close down the application
- Request that the user report the error

Visual Basic 2008 Express allows programmers to add structured exception handlers to their applications to prevent exceptions from creating havoc with your applications, potentially causing them to crash.

A Run-time Exception Demonstration

To see first-hand just how Visual Basic handles exceptions, create a new Visual Basic application and modify its Load event procedure as shown here:

```
Public Class Form1

    Dim intX As Integer = 0
    Dim intY As Integer = 10
    Dim intZ As Integer

    Private Sub Form1_Load(ByVal sender As System.Object, _
        ByVal e As System.EventArgs) Handles MyBase.Load

        intZ = intY / intX

    End Sub

End Class
```

This application has been designed with a flaw in it that will produce an overflow error when it attempts to divide intY (10) by intX (0), because within Visual Basic, division by zero is impossible. Once you have everything keyed in, press F5 to test your application. Your application immediately runs into trouble and stops executing. Figure 11.9 shows the error message that is displayed.

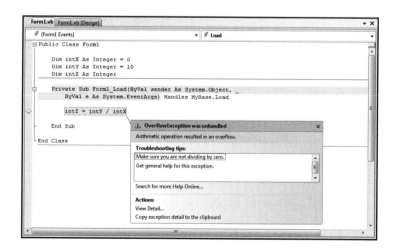

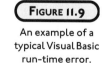

FIGURE 11.9

An example of a typical Visual Basic run-time error.

Create an executable version of your application by saving your application, clicking on the Build menu, and selecting the Build menu item. Locate and run the executable (Release) version of your new program. When you do, you will see the error shown in Figure 11.10 appear. Click on Quit to dismiss the error message and stop the execution of your application.

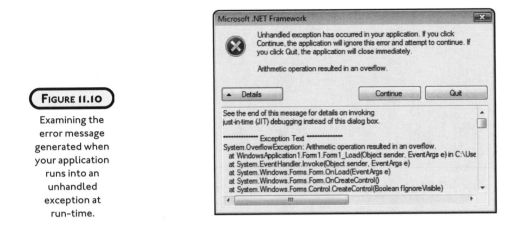

FIGURE 11.10

Examining the error message generated when your application runs into an unhandled exception at run-time.

Clearly, you don't want the users of your Visual Basic applications to see error messages like these. To avoid this, you will need to test your applications extensively to make them as bug-free as possible. In situations where you cannot eliminate the possibility of an error, you will need to develop effective exception handlers.

Structured Exception Handlers

Microsoft's recommended approach to developing exception handlers is the structured option, which uses the `Try…Catch…Finally` statement. Using the `Try…Catch…Finally` statement, you can block off program statements where errors are likely to occur and then attempt to handle them.

To use the `Try…Catch…Finally` statement, place the statements where exceptions may occur within the `Try` block and then place statements designed to handle the exception in the `Catch` block. If different exceptions are possible, you can insert additional `Catch` blocks, each designed to handle a different type of exception. Lastly, you can include an optional `Finally` block, which will always execute, regardless of whether an execution occurred at all or which `Catch` block executed. When included, the `Finally` block is always executed last and provides a place to store any program statements that will always have to be executed.

The following example demonstrates how to apply the `Try…Catch…Finally` statement to develop an exception handler for the previous example.

```
Public Class Form1

    Dim intX As Integer = 0
    Dim intY As Integer = 10
    Dim intZ As Integer
```

```
Private Sub Form1_Load(ByVal sender As System.Object, _
    ByVal e As System.EventArgs) Handles MyBase.Load

    Try
        intZ = intY / intX

    Catch ex As OverflowException
        MessageBox.Show("Error: The application has attempted " & _
            "to divide a number by 0.")

    Catch ex As Exception
        MessageBox.Show("Error: " & ex.Message)

    Finally

        MessageBox.Show("Please inform the developer if any " & _
            "errors occurred.")

    End Try

End Sub

End Class
```

TRICK The order in which Catch blocks occur is important. Visual Basic will execute the first Catch block that matches the specified criteria. When using multiple Catch blocks, always put the most specific Catch statements first, followed by the more general ones.

The statement that is likely to cause the error (a certainty in this example) is placed inside the Try block. Next, a Catch block is set up to handle the occurrence of an OverflowException. Note that a variable named ex has been declared. This variable will be used to access an Exception object that Visual Basic automatically generates when an exception occurs. By examining properties belonging to this object, you can get information about the exception.

A second Catch block is set up to handle all other types of exceptions not handled by previous Catch blocks. A Finally block is then specified that will execute every time the form's Load event procedure executes, even if an exception doesn't occur.

You can view a list of possible exceptions by typing Catch followed by a variable name and the keyword As when working with the code editor, as demonstrated in Figure 11.11.

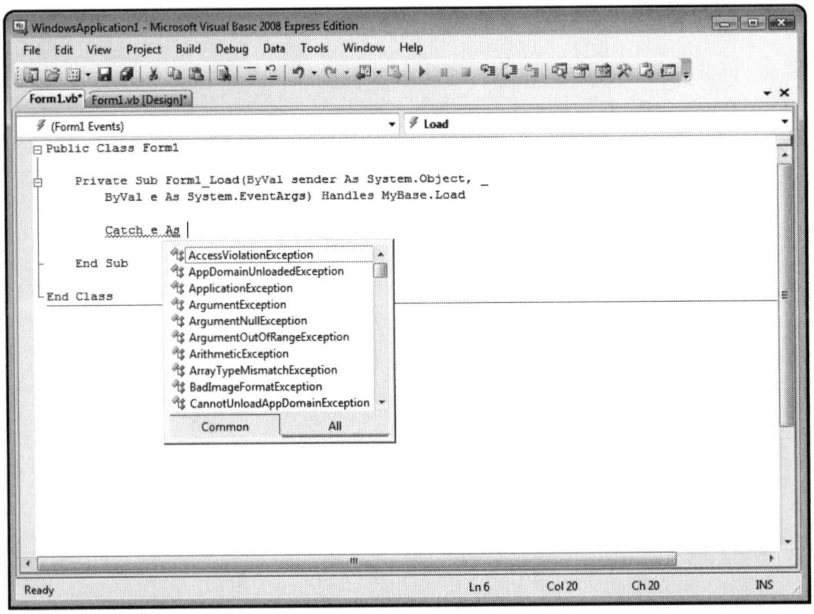

FIGURE 11.11

Using IntelliSense to examine exceptions.

Although the example that I have shown you here is relatively simple, it presents you with a template that you can copy and apply when you come across the need to handle run-time errors in your applications.

When deciding whether to create an exception handler to attempt to deal with a potential error in one of your applications, look at the likelihood of the exception occurring. If it is a pretty high possibility, then you should attempt to build a new procedure to your application that deals with the situation. However, if the possibility of an error occurring is unlikely (but still possible), then adding an exception handler may be the more appropriate option.

BACK TO THE TIC-TAC-TOE GAME

It is time to turn your attention to this book's final game project, the Tic-Tac-Toe game. You will create the Tic-Tac-Toe game by following the same five basic development steps that you have followed for all preceding game projects.

Designing the Game

The Tic-Tac-Toe game is played on a single window and is made up of one form and the 18 controls listed in Table 11.1.

TABLE 11.1	FORM CONTROLS FOR THE TIC-TAC-TOE GAME	
Control Type	**Control Name**	**Description**
Panel1	pnlLeft	Used to represent the left vertical bar on the game board
Panel2	pnlRight	Used to represent the right vertical bar on the game board
Panel3	pnlTop	Used to represent the top horizontal bar on the game board
Panel4	pnlBottom	Used to represent the bottom horizontal bar on the game board
PictureBox1	pbxA1	The left PictureBox control on the first row of the game board
PictureBox2	pbxA2	The middle PictureBox control on the first row of the game board
PictureBox3	pbxA3	The right PictureBox control on the first row of the game board
PictureBox4	pbxB1	The left PictureBox control on the second row of the game board
PictureBox5	pbxB2	The middle PictureBox control on the second row of the game board
PictureBox6	pbxb3	The right PictureBox control on the second row of the game board
PictureBox7	pbxC1	The left PictureBox control on the third row of the game board
PictureBox8	pbxC2	The middle PictureBox control on the third row of the game board
PictureBox9	pbxC3	The right PictureBox control on the third row of the game board
Button1	btnPlay	Used to initiate game play
Button2	btnExit	Used to terminate the game
Label1	lblOutput	Identifies the TextBox control that is used to display status messages
TextBox1	txtOutput	Used to display status messages
ImageList1	imlSquares	Stores an indexed collection of graphics used to represent player moves

Step 1: Creating a New Visual Basic Project

The first step in creating the Tic-Tac-Toe game is to open up Visual Basic and create a new project, as outlined here:

1. Start Visual Basic 2008 Express and then click on File and select New Project. The New Project dialog will appear.
2. Select the Windows Forms Application template.
3. Enter **TicTacToe** as the name of your new application and click on OK.

Step 2: Creating the User Interface

The first step in laying out the user interface is to add controls to the form and move and resize them to the appropriate locations. As you go through each step, make sure that you reference Figure 11.12 so that you'll know where each control needs to be placed and what size it needs to be.

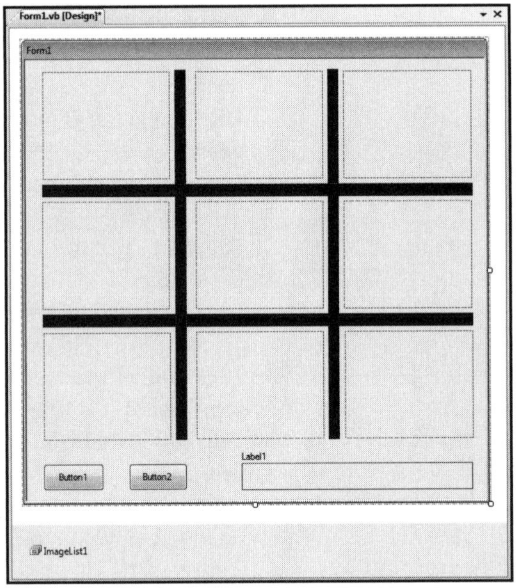

FIGURE 11.12

Completing the interface design for the Tic-Tac-Toe game.

1. Begin by setting the Size property of the form to 605, 591.
2. Next, create the grid lines that organize the game board by adding four Panel controls and resizing them as shown in Figure 11.12.
3. Add PictureBox controls inside each of the game board's nine cells and resize them until they take up almost all of the available space.
4. Add two Button controls to the bottom-left corner.

5. Add a TextBox control to the bottom-right side of the game board and resize it as shown in Figure 11.12.

6. Add a Label control and place it just over the upper-left corner of the TextBox control.

7. Finally, add an ImageList control.

Step 3: Customizing Form and Control Properties

Let's begin by making the required changes to properties belonging to the form object, as listed in Table 11.2.

TABLE 11.2 PROPERTY CHANGES FOR FORM1

Property	Value
Name	frmMain
ControlBox	False
Cursor	Hand
FormBorderStyle	Fixed3D
StartPosition	CenterScreen
Text	Tic-Tac-Toe

Make the property changes shown in Table 11.3 to the Panel controls.

TABLE 11.3 PROPERTY CHANGES FOR PANEL CONTROLS

Control	Property	Value
Panel1	Name	pnlLeft
	BackColor	Black
Panel2	Name	pnlRight
	BackColor	Black
Panel3	Name	pnlTop
	BackColor	Black
Panel4	Name	pnlBottom
	BackColor	Black

Make the property changes shown in Table 11.4 to the PictureBox controls.

TABLE 11.4   PROPERTY CHANGES FOR PICTUREBOX CONTROLS

Control	Property	Value
PictureBox1	Name	pbxA1
	Enabled	False
	Size	164, 134
	SizeMode	StretchImage
PictureBox2	Name	pbxA2
	Enabled	False
	Size	164, 134
	SizeMode	StretchImage
PictureBox3	Name	pbxA2
	Enabled	False
	Size	164, 134
	SizeMode	StretchImage
PictureBox4	Name	pbxB1
	Enabled	False
	Size	164, 134
	SizeMode	StretchImage
PictureBox5	Name	pbxB2
	Enabled	False
	Size	164, 134
	SizeMode	StretchImage
PictureBox6	Name	pbxB3
	Enabled	False
	Size	164, 134
	SizeMode	StretchImage
PictureBox7	Name	pbxC1
	Enabled	False
	Size	164, 134
	SizeMode	StretchImage
PictureBox8	Name	pbxC2
	Enabled	False
	Size	164, 134
	SizeMode	StretchImage
PictureBox9	Name	pbxC3
	Enabled	False
	Size	164, 134
	SizeMode	StretchImage

Make the property changes shown in Table 11.5 to the `Button` controls.

Control	Property	Value
TABLE 11.5	**PROPERTY CHANGES FOR BUTTON CONTROLS**	
Button1	Name	btnPlay
	Text	Play
Button2	Name	btnExit
	Text	Exit

Make the property changes shown in Table 11.6 to the `Label` control.

Control	Property	Value
TABLE 11.6	**PROPERTY CHANGES FOR LABEL CONTROL**	
Label1	Name	lblOutput
	Font.Bold	True
	Text	Status

Finally, make the property changes shown in Table 11.7 to the `TextBox` control.

Control	Property	Value
TABLE 11.7	**PROPERTY CHANGES FOR TEXTBOX CONTROL**	
TextBox1	Name	txtOutput
	Font.Bold	True
	ReadOnly	True
	TabStop	False

Step 4: Adding a Little Programming Logic

The first task in putting together the program code for the Tic-Tac-Toe game is to define class-level variables, as shown next. These variables represent values used by two or more procedures within the application.

```
Public Class frmMain

    Private strPlayer As String = ""  'Used to track whose turn it is

    'Declare variables representing game board cells
    Private strpbxA1 As String = "Open"
    Private strpbxA2 As String = "Open"
    Private strpbxA3 As String = "Open"
    Private strpbxB1 As String = "Open"
    Private strpbxB2 As String = "Open"
    Private strpbxB3 As String = "Open"
    Private strpbxC1 As String = "Open"
    Private strpbxC2 As String = "Open"
    Private strpbxC3 As String = "Open"

End Class
```

The first statement defines a variable named strPlayer, which is used to keep track of each player's turn. The remaining statements are used to keep track of when each of the game board cells have been selected by a player.

The form's Load event procedure, shown next, is responsible for preparing the game for initial play. This is accomplished by calling on two custom procedures.

```
'This procedure executes procedures required to set up the game
Private Sub frmMain_Load(ByVal sender As System.Object, _
   ByVal e As System.EventArgs) Handles MyBase.Load

    SetGameDefaults()  'Call procedure that sets default assignments
    ClearBoard()  'Call procedure that clears the game board

End Sub
```

The first procedure called by the form's Load event procedure is the SetGameDefaults procedure, shown next. When called, this procedure displays instructions in the TextBox control and sets Player X as the first player.

```
'This procedure sets default assignments
Private Sub SetGameDefaults()

    txtOutput.Text = "Click on Play to begin"  'Display opening message
    strPlayer = "Player X"  'Set Player X to go first

End Sub
```

The second procedure called by the form's Load event procedure is the ClearBoard procedure, shown next. This procedure is responsible for clearing off the game board by displaying blank squares in each of the game's PictureBox controls. The procedure also sets the values assigned to the variables used to track the status of each game board cell to Open.

```
'This procedure clears out the game board
Private Sub ClearBoard()

    'Load a blank image into each game board cell
    pbxA1.Image = imlSquares.Images(2)
    pbxA2.Image = imlSquares.Images(2)
    pbxA3.Image = imlSquares.Images(2)
    pbxB1.Image = imlSquares.Images(2)
    pbxB2.Image = imlSquares.Images(2)
    pbxB3.Image = imlSquares.Images(2)
    pbxC1.Image = imlSquares.Images(2)
    pbxC2.Image = imlSquares.Images(2)
    pbxC3.Image = imlSquares.Images(2)

    'Mark each game board cell as open and available for selection
    strpbxA1 = "Open"
    strpbxA2 = "Open"
    strpbxA3 = "Open"
    strpbxB1 = "Open"
    strpbxB2 = "Open"
    strpbxB3 = "Open"
    strpbxC1 = "Open"
    strpbxC2 = "Open"
```

```
      strpbxC3 = "Open"
```

End Sub

Game play cannot begin until the first player (Player X) clicks on the Button control labeled Play, at which time the btnPlay procedure, shown below, is executed. This procedure is responsible for executing two custom procedures. The first procedure that is called is the ClearBoard procedure, which we have already examined. The second procedure called is the PlayGame procedure.

```
'This procedure executes when the button labeled Play is clicked
Private Sub btnPlay_Click(ByVal sender As System.Object, _
   ByVal e As System.EventArgs) Handles btnPlay.Click

      ClearBoard()  'Call the procedure that clears out the game board
      PlayGame()   'Call the procedure that begins game play

End Sub
```

The PlayGame procedure, shown next, displays a text message in the game's TextBox control in order to identify whose turn it is. In addition, the procedure enables each of the PictureBox controls on the game board. This allows the first player to make the first move. Finally, this procedure disables the btnPlay Button control.

```
'This procedure begins game play
Private Sub PlayGame()

      'Post message that identifies whose turn it is
      txtOutput.Text = strPlayer & "'s turn."

      'Enable all game board cells
      pbxA1.Enabled = True
      pbxA2.Enabled = True
      pbxA3.Enabled = True
      pbxB1.Enabled = True
      pbxB2.Enabled = True
      pbxB3.Enabled = True
      pbxC1.Enabled = True
      pbxC2.Enabled = True
      pbxC3.Enabled = True
```

```
        btnPlay.Enabled = False 'Disable access to the button labeled Play
```

End Sub

Players can end the game at any time by clicking on the Button control labeled Exit, in which case the btnExit procedure, shown next, is executed.

```
'This procedure executes when the button labeled Exit is clicked
Private Sub btnExit_Click(ByVal sender As System.Object, _
  ByVal e As System.EventArgs) Handles btnExit.Click


      Application.Exit()
```

End Sub

Each cell on the game board is made up of a PictureBox control. The following statements make up the click event procedure for the game's first PictureBox control.

```
'This procedure executes when a player clicks on the first cell
'in the first row
Private Sub pbxA1_Click(ByVal sender As System.Object, _
  ByVal e As System.EventArgs) Handles pbxA1.Click

    Dim strGameOver As String = ""  'Used to track game status

    'Notify the player if the cell has already been selected
    If strpbxA1 <> "Open" Then
        txtOutput.Text = "The square has already been taken." & _
          ControlChars.CrLf & strPlayer & "'s turn."
        Return  'Leave the Sub procedure
    End If

    If strPlayer = "Player X" Then
        pbxA1.Image = imlSquares.Images(0)
        strpbxA1 = "Player X"
    Else
        pbxA1.Image = imlSquares.Images(1)
        strpbxA1 = "Player 0"
    End If
```

```
'Call the procedure that checks to see if the game has been won
strGameOver = CheckForWinner()

'Call the procedure that switched player turns or displays a
'message declaring a winner
DetermineGameStatus(strGameOver)

End Sub
```

This procedure declares a local variable named `strGameOver`. Next, an `If…Then` code block is used to check whether the cell has already been selected by examining the value assigned to the corresponding `strpbxA1` variable. If the cell is available, an `If…Then…Else` code block displays a graphic representing the current player in the cell. A call is then made to the `CheckForWinner` function procedure. If the game has been won, the `CheckForWinner` Function procedure will return a string of either `Player X` or `Player O`, which is then passed on to the `DetermineGameStatus` procedure.

The code for the second `PictureBox` control in the first row is shown next. As you can see, except for the changes in references that reflect the second cell instead of the first cell, the code is identical to that of the `pbxA1_Click` procedure.

```
'This procedure executes when a player clicks on the second cell
'in the first row
Private Sub pbxA2_Click(ByVal sender As System.Object, _
  ByVal e As System.EventArgs) Handles pbxA2.Click

    Dim strGameOver As String = ""   'Used to track game status

    'Notify the player if the cell has already been selected
    If strpbxA2 <> "Open" Then
        txtOutput.Text = "The square has already been taken." & _
          ControlChars.CrLf & strPlayer & "'s turn."
        Return   'Leave the Sub procedure
    End If

    If strPlayer = "Player X" Then
        pbxA2.Image = imlSquares.Images(0)
        strpbxA2 = "Player X"
    Else
        pbxA2.Image = imlSquares.Images(1)
```

```
          strpbxA2 = "Player O"
    End If


    'Call the procedure that checks to see if the game has been won
    strGameOver = CheckForWinner()


    'Call the procedure that switched player turns or displays a
    'message declaring a winner
    DetermineGameStatus(strGameOver)


End Sub
```

The code for the third `PictureBox` control on the first row is shown here:

```
'This procedure executes when a player clicks on the third cell
'in the first row
Private Sub pbxA3_Click(ByVal sender As System.Object, _
  ByVal e As System.EventArgs) Handles pbxA3.Click

    Dim strGameOver As String = ""  'Used to track game status

    'Notify the player if the cell has already been selected
    If strpbxA3 <> "Open" Then
        txtOutput.Text = "The square has already been taken." & _
          ControlChars.CrLf & strPlayer & "'s turn."
        Return  'Leave the Sub procedure
    End If

    If strPlayer = "Player X" Then
        pbxA3.Image = imlSquares.Images(0)
        strpbxA3 = "Player X"
    Else
        pbxA3.Image = imlSquares.Images(1)
        strpbxA3 = "Player O"
    End If

    'Call the procedure that checks to see if the game has been won
    strGameOver = CheckForWinner()
```

```
'Call the procedure that switched player turns or displays a
'message declaring a winner
DetermineGameStatus(strGameOver)

End Sub
```

The code for the first `PictureBox` control on the second row is shown here:

```
'This procedure executes when a player clicks on the first cell
'in the second row
Private Sub pbxB1_Click(ByVal sender As System.Object, _
  ByVal e As System.EventArgs) Handles pbxB1.Click

    Dim strGameOver As String = ""   'Used to track game status

    'Notify the player if the cell has already been selected
    If strpbxB1 <> "Open" Then
        txtOutput.Text = "The square has already been taken." & _
            ControlChars.CrLf & strPlayer & "'s turn."
        Return   'Leave the Sub procedure
    End If

    If strPlayer = "Player X" Then
        pbxB1.Image = imlSquares.Images(0)
        strpbxB1 = "Player X"
    Else
        pbxB1.Image = imlSquares.Images(1)
        strpbxB1 = "Player O"
    End If

    'Call the procedure that checks to see if the game has been won
    strGameOver = CheckForWinner()

    'Call the procedure that switched player turns or displays a
    'message declaring a winner
    DetermineGameStatus(strGameOver)

End Sub
```

The code for the second `PictureBox` control on the second row is shown here:

```
'This procedure executes when a player clicks on the second cell
'in the second row
Private Sub pbxB2_Click(ByVal sender As System.Object, _
  ByVal e As System.EventArgs) Handles pbxB2.Click

    Dim strGameOver As String = ""  'Used to track game status

    'Notify the player if the cell has already been selected
    If strpbxB2 <> "Open" Then
        txtOutput.Text = "The square has already been taken." & _
            ControlChars.CrLf & strPlayer & "'s turn."
        Return  'Leave the Sub procedure
    End If

    If strPlayer = "Player X" Then
        pbxB2.Image = imlSquares.Images(0)
        strpbxB2 = "Player X"
    Else
        pbxB2.Image = imlSquares.Images(1)
        strpbxB2 = "Player O"
    End If

    'Call the procedure that checks to see if the game has been won
    strGameOver = CheckForWinner()

    'Call the procedure that switched player turns or displays a
    'message declaring a winner
    DetermineGameStatus(strGameOver)

End Sub
```

The code for the third `PictureBox` control on the second row is shown here:

```
'This procedure executes when a player clicks on the third cell
'in the second row
Private Sub pbxB3_Click(ByVal sender As System.Object, _
  ByVal e As System.EventArgs) Handles pbxB3.Click
```

```
    Dim strGameOver As String = ""  'Used to track game status

    'Notify the player if the cell has already been selected
    If strpbxB3 <> "Open" Then
        txtOutput.Text = "The square has already been taken." & _
            ControlChars.CrLf & strPlayer & "'s turn."
        Return  'Leave the Sub procedure
    End If

    If strPlayer = "Player X" Then
        pbxB3.Image = imlSquares.Images(0)
        strpbxB3 = "Player X"
    Else
        pbxB3.Image = imlSquares.Images(1)
        strpbxB3 = "Player O"
    End If

    'Call the procedure that checks to see if the game has been won
    strGameOver = CheckForWinner()

    'Call the procedure that switched player turns or displays a
    'message declaring a winner
    DetermineGameStatus(strGameOver)

End Sub
```

The code for the first PictureBox control on the third row is shown here:

```
'This procedure executes when a player clicks on the first cell
'in the third row
Private Sub pbxC1_Click(ByVal sender As System.Object, _
  ByVal e As System.EventArgs) Handles pbxC1.Click

    Dim strGameOver As String = ""  'Used to track game status

    'Notify the player if the cell has already been selected
    If strpbxC1 <> "Open" Then
        txtOutput.Text = "The square has already been taken." & _
            ControlChars.CrLf & strPlayer & "'s turn."
```

```
            Return   'Leave the Sub procedure
        End If


        If strPlayer = "Player X" Then
            pbxC1.Image = imlSquares.Images(0)
            strpbxC1 = "Player X"
        Else
            pbxC1.Image = imlSquares.Images(1)
            strpbxC1 = "Player O"
        End If


        'Call the procedure that checks to see if the game has been won
        strGameOver = CheckForWinner()


        'Call the procedure that switched player turns or displays a
        'message declaring a winner
        DetermineGameStatus(strGameOver)


    End Sub
```

The code for the second `PictureBox` control on the third row is shown here:

```
'This procedure executes when a player clicks on the second cell
'in the third row
Private Sub pbxC2_Click(ByVal sender As System.Object, _
  ByVal e As System.EventArgs) Handles pbxC2.Click

    Dim strGameOver As String = ""   'Used to track game status

    'Notify the player if the cell has already been selected
    If strpbxC2 <> "Open" Then
        txtOutput.Text = "The square has already been taken." & _
            ControlChars.CrLf & strPlayer & "'s turn."
        Return   'Leave the Sub procedure
    End If


    If strPlayer = "Player X" Then
        pbxC2.Image = imlSquares.Images(0)
        strpbxC2 = "Player X"
```

```
      Else
          pbxC2.Image = imlSquares.Images(1)
          strpbxC2 = "Player O"
      End If


      'Call the procedure that checks to see if the game has been won
      strGameOver = CheckForWinner()


      'Call the procedure that switched player turns or displays a
      'message declaring a winner
      DetermineGameStatus(strGameOver)


End Sub
```

The code for the third PictureBox control on the third row is shown here:

```
'This procedure executes when a player clicks on the third cell
'in the third row
Private Sub pbxC3_Click(ByVal sender As System.Object, _
  ByVal e As System.EventArgs) Handles pbxC3.Click

    Dim strGameOver As String = ""   'Used to track game status

    'Notify the player if the cell has already been selected
    If strpbxC3 <> "Open" Then
        txtOutput.Text = "The square has already been taken." & _
           ControlChars.CrLf & strPlayer & "'s turn."
        Return   'Leave the Sub procedure
    End If


    If strPlayer = "Player X" Then
        pbxC3.Image = imlSquares.Images(0)
        strpbxC3 = "Player X"
    Else
        pbxC3.Image = imlSquares.Images(1)
        strpbxC3 = "Player O"
    End If


    'Call the procedure that checks to see if the game has been won
```

```
strGameOver = CheckForWinner()

'Call the procedure that switched player turns or displays a
'message declaring a winner
DetermineGameStatus(strGameOver)

End Sub
```

The CheckForWinner Function procedure, shown next, is responsible for executing a collection of If...Then statements to see if the current player has won the game. This procedure checks each row and column, as well as diagonally. In addition, the procedure checks to see if the two players have tied, which occurs when all nine cells have been selected without a winner being declared.

```
'This procedure determines whether the game has been won and by whom
Function CheckForWinner() As String

        'Check the first row for a winner
        If strpbxA1 = strPlayer Then
             If strpbxA2 = strPlayer Then
                  If strpbxA3 = strPlayer Then
                       Return strPlayer
                  End If
             End If
        End If

        'Check the second row for a winner
        If strpbxB1 = strPlayer Then
             If strpbxB2 = strPlayer Then
                  If strpbxB3 = strPlayer Then
                       Return strPlayer
                  End If
             End If
        End If

        'Check the third row for a winner
        If strpbxC1 = strPlayer Then
             If strpbxC2 = strPlayer Then
                  If strpbxC3 = strPlayer Then
```

```
                Return strPlayer
            End If
        End If
    End If
End If

'Check the first column for a winner
If strpbxA1 = strPlayer Then
    If strpbxB1 = strPlayer Then
        If strpbxC1 = strPlayer Then
            Return strPlayer
        End If
    End If
End If

'Check the second column for a winner
If strpbxA2 = strPlayer Then
    If strpbxB2 = strPlayer Then
        If strpbxC2 = strPlayer Then
            Return strPlayer
        End If
    End If
End If

'Check the third column for a winner
If strpbxA3 = strPlayer Then
    If strpbxB3 = strPlayer Then
        If strpbxC3 = strPlayer Then
            Return strPlayer
        End If
    End If
End If

'Check diagonally from top-left to bottom-right for a winner
If strpbxA1 = strPlayer Then
    If strpbxB2 = strPlayer Then
        If strpbxC3 = strPlayer Then
            Return strPlayer
        End If
```

```
            End If
    End If


    'Check diagonally from top-right to bottom-left for a winner
    If strpbxA3 = strPlayer Then
        If strpbxB2 = strPlayer Then
            If strpbxC1 = strPlayer Then
                Return strPlayer
            End If
        End If
    End If


    'Check to see if the game has resulted in a tie
    Select Case "Open"
        'Check each cell to see if it has been assigned to a player
        Case strpbxA1
        Case strpbxB1
        Case strpbxB1
        Case strpbxB1
        Case strpbxB2
        Case strpbxB3
        Case strpbxC1
        Case strpbxC2
        Case strpbxC3
        Case Else 'This option executes if all cells have been assigned
            Return "Tie"
    End Select


    Return ""


End Function
```

The DetermineGameStatus procedure, shown next, processes a single argument that identifies whether the game has been won, lost, or is still in progress. If the game is still in progress, the SwitchPlayers procedure is called in order to ready the game for the next player's turn. If the game has been won, the procedure enables the Button control labeled Play, calls the DisableSquares procedure, and displays a text message in the game's TextBox control identifying the winner of the game. Finally, if the game has ended in a tie, the btnPlay control is enabled, the `DisableSquares` procedure is called, and a text message is displayed in the game's `TextBox` control indicating that a tie has occurred.

```
'This procedure determines whether or not the game is over
Private Sub DetermineGameStatus(ByVal strGameOver As String)

    If strGameOver = "" Then   'The game is not over yet
        SwitchPlayers()  'Call procedure that switches player turns
        'Post message stating that it is time for players to switch turns
        txtOutput.Text = strPlayer & "'s turn."
    Else
        If strGameOver <> "Tie" Then   'There is a winner
            btnPlay.Enabled = True   'Enable the button labeled Play
            'Call procedure that disables game board cells
            DisableSquares()
            'Display game over message
            txtOutput.Text = "Game over. " & strGameOver & " has won."
        Else   'The game has resulted in a tie
            btnPlay.Enabled = True   'Enable the button labeled Play
            'Call procedure that disables game board cells
            DisableSquares()
            'Display game over message
            txtOutput.Text = "Game over. There was no winner."
        End If
    End If


End Sub
```

The `SwitchPlayers` procedure, shown next, is very straightforward. When called, it changes the value assigned to the `strPlayer` variable to reflect the next player.

```
'This procedure is responsible for toggling between player turns
Private Sub SwitchPlayers()

    If strPlayer = "Player X" Then
        strPlayer = "Player O"
    Else
        strPlayer = "Player X"
    End If
```

```
End Sub
```

The DisableSquares procedure, shown next, is the last procedure in the application. Its job is to disable each of the game board PictureBox controls in order to keep players from trying to take another turn once the game has ended.

```
'This procedure disables all game board cells
Private Sub DisableSquares()

    pbxA1.Enabled = False
    pbxA2.Enabled = False
    pbxA3.Enabled = False
    pbxB1.Enabled = False
    pbxB2.Enabled = False
    pbxB3.Enabled = False
    pbxC1.Enabled = False
    pbxC2.Enabled = False
    pbxC3.Enabled = False

End Sub
```

Step 5: Testing the Execution of the Tic-Tac-Toe Game
The Tic-Tac-Toe game is now ready to run. Go ahead and run the game by pressing F5 and make sure that everything works like it is supposed to. If you run into any problems, try using the troubleshooting tips presented in this chapter to track down any errors. Once things are in order, pass it around to a few of your friends and ask them what they think.

SUMMARY

In this chapter, you learned about syntax, logic, and run-time errors. You learned how to set breakpoints and then to step through program execution. You also learned to work with an assortment of debugging windows and to create exception-handling routines. On top of all this, you learned how to create the Tic-Tac-Toe game.

Don't look at the completion of the material in this book as the end of your Visual Basic programming education. Think of it as a launching point. Although this book has provided you with a solid foundation, there is still plenty more to learn. Before you run off and start tackling new and bigger programming projects, why not take just a little extra time and improve the Tic-Tac-Toe game by completing the following challenges.

CHALLENGES

1. Add sound effects to the game that indicate when the game has been won or tied.
2. Add logic to the game that keeps track of the number of games won, lost, and tied for each player.
3. Add logic to the game that identifies not only when a game has been won, but how it was won (diagonally, horizontally, or vertically).

INDEX